Ready for Advanced

coursebook with key

3rd Edition

Roy Norris
Amanda French

Updated in line with Cambridge English: Advanced (CAE) 2015 revisions

Contents map

Introduction

Welcome to *Ready for Advanced*, a course which is designed to help you prepare for the *Cambridge English: Advanced* examination, also known as *Certificate in Advanced English (CAE)*.

This book contains a wide range of activities aimed at improving your English and developing the language and skills which you will need to pass the examination. As well as providing relevant practice in reading, writing, listening and speaking, each unit of *Ready for Advanced* includes one or more Language focus sections, which analyse the main grammar areas at advanced level, together with Vocabulary slots, which give particular emphasis to collocation.

The course also includes a systematic approach to word formation, which appears as a task type in the Reading and Use of English paper. At regular intervals, you will find special sections which focus on the most important aspects of this task, ensuring that you are properly prepared to deal with it in the examination.

At the end of every unit, there is a two-page Review section, which enables you to revise and practise the new language you have encountered in the unit.

Throughout the book you will find the following boxes, which are designed to help you when performing the different tasks:

What to expect in the exam: these contain useful information on what you should be prepared to see, hear or do in a particular task in the examination.

How to go about it: these give advice and guidelines on how to deal with different task types and specific questions.

Don't forget!: these provide a reminder of important points to bear in mind when answering a particular question.

Useful language: these contain vocabulary and structures which can be used when doing a specific speaking or writing activity.

Further information and advice on each of the papers in the *Cambridge English: Advanced* exam is included in the five supplementary *'Ready for …'* units. These are situated at regular intervals in the book and can be used at appropriate moments during the course. The Ready for Writing unit contains model answers for each of the main task types, together with advice, useful language and further writing tasks for you to complete.

At the end of the book you will find an extensive Wordlist, which builds on the vocabulary areas seen in the units, as well as the Listening scripts and a Grammar reference. This contains detailed explanations of the grammar areas seen in the units.

Overview of the Examination

The *Cambridge English: Advanced* examination consists of four papers, as shown below and on page 5. The Writing, Listening and Speaking papers each carry 20% of the total marks; the Reading and Use of English paper carries 40% (20% for the Reading tasks and 20% for the Use of English tasks). A low mark in one paper does not necessarily mean a candidate will fail the examination; it is the overall mark which counts.

For more information and advice on each paper, see the appropriate *'Ready for …'* unit, as well as the relevant sections in the main units of the book.

Reading and Use of English 1 hour 30 minutes

There are eight parts to this paper: Parts 1 to 4 are grammar and vocabulary tasks; Parts 5 to 8 are reading tasks. For the Use of English tasks, each correct answer in Parts 1 to 3 receives one mark; each question in Part 4 carries up to two marks. For the reading tasks, each correct answer in Parts 5 to 7 receives two marks, and there is one mark for each question in Part 8.

Part	Task Type	Number of Questions	Task Format
1	Multiple-choice cloze	8	A text with 8 gaps; there is a choice of 4 answers for each gap.
2	Open cloze	8	A text with 8 gaps, each of which must be completed with one word.
3	Word formation	8	A text containing 8 gaps. The task is to complete each gap with the correct form of a given word.
4	Key word transformation	6	Gapped sentences which must be completed using a given word.
5	Multiple choice	6	A text followed by multiple-choice questions with four options.
6	Cross-text multiple matching	4	Four short texts followed by multiple-matching questions. These require candidates to compare opinions and attitudes expressed in the texts.
7	Gapped text	6	A text from which paragraphs have been removed. Candidates replace each of these in the appropriate part of the text.
8	Multiple matching	10	A text preceded by multiple-matching questions which require candidates to find specific information in a text or texts.

Writing 1 hour 30 minutes

There are two parts to this paper, each of which carries the same number of marks. Part 1 is compulsory, so must be answered by all candidates, whereas in Part 2 candidates choose one from three tasks. Candidates are required to write 220–260 words for each part.

Part	Task Type	Number of Tasks	Task Format
1	Essay	1 (compulsory)	Candidates write an essay based on two points from a choice of three. They explain which of the two points is more important, giving reasons for their opinions.
2		3 (candidates choose one)	A writing task with a clear context, purpose for writing and target reader. Candidates write one of the following: letter, proposal, report, review.

Listening about 40 minutes

This paper consists of four parts with a total of 30 questions, each of which carries one mark. Each part contains one or more recorded texts, and all recordings are heard twice. Candidates are tested on their ability to understand, for example, gist, main points, specific information, function, purpose, feelings, attitudes and opinions.

Part	Task Type	Number of Questions	Task Format
1	Multiple choice	6	Three short unrelated extracts from exchanges between interacting speakers. For each extract there are two multiple-choice questions, each with three options.
2	Sentence completion	8	A monologue lasting approximately 3 minutes. Candidates write a word or short phrase to complete sentences.
3	Multiple choice	6	A conversation between two or more speakers, lasting approximately 4 minutes. Multiple-choice questions have four options.
4	Multiple matching	10	Five short monologues on the same theme, each lasting approximately 30 seconds. There are two separate tasks. For each task you are required to select the correct option from a choice of eight.

Speaking 15 minutes

There are four parts to this paper. There are usually two candidates and two examiners. Candidates are required to demonstrate their spoken language skills in a range of contexts.

Part	Task Type	Time	Task Format
1	Social interaction	2 minutes	Candidates give personal information in response to questions from the interviewer.
2	Long turn	4 minutes	Each candidate talks about a set of pictures for about 1 minute, and comments on the other candidate's pictures for about 30 seconds.
3	Collaborative task	4 minutes	Candidates are given instructions with written prompts which they use for discussion (2 minutes) and then a decision-making task (1 minute). The giving of instructions takes about 1 minute.
4	Further discussion	5 minutes	The interviewer leads a discussion which is related to the topic of Part 3.

Roy Norris
Amanda French

1 Aiming high

Speaking
Part 2

Long turn

Look at these pictures. They show people facing different challenges.

Student A:
Compare **two** of the pictures, and say what challenges the people face, the kind of problems they might encounter, and how they might be feeling.

Student B:
When your partner has finished talking about the two pictures, say which of them represents the more difficult challenge.

How to go about it

- When comparing your pictures, talk about the similarities and differences between them.
  e.g. ***Both pictures show ..., but this one ..., whereas the other one ...***
- Speculate about the pictures as indicated in the instructions. You are not asked simply to describe what is happening.
  e.g. ***They might (well) have problems finishing.***
  She's likely to/She'll probably find it quite tough to begin with.
  I expect/imagine they're feeling a little lonely at the moment.
- Use a wide range of vocabulary. For example, when speculating about people's feelings, go beyond the use of simple words such as ***happy, sad*** or ***nervous.***

Before you do the task, complete the following exercise.

Useful language

Arrange the words and phrases in the box into three groups according to whether they can be used instead of:

very happy	sad or wanting to cry	nervous or worried
	tearful	

~~tearful~~ anxious delighted apprehensive miserable elated
close to tears thrilled tense weepy on edge overjoyed

Now change roles. Follow the instructions again using the remaining pictures.

Reading and Use of English
Part 5

Multiple choice

1 You are going to read an article about Parker Liautaud, a young man who has been on several polar expeditions. With your partner discuss your ideas on the following:

- the type of person who would take up such a challenge
- their reasons for doing so
- the preparation required
- the conditions or difficulties they experience in the Arctic and the Antarctic

2 Now read the article. For questions **1–6** on page 9, choose the answer (**A**, **B**, **C** or **D**) which you think fits best according to the text.

How to go about it

- Before you look at the questions, quickly read through the whole text to get an idea of the content.
  *Give yourself three minutes to read the text on page 8. Look for information on Parker Liautaud which is relevant to the points in exercise **1**. Compare your answers with a partner.*
- During both your quick read and your more detailed read, you will need to use context to help you guess the meaning of unknown vocabulary, as you may not take a dictionary into the exam.
  *Discuss with your partner the possible meanings of the words in **bold** in the first two paragraphs.*
- Read each question carefully and find the parts of the text which relate to each one. In Part 5 of the Reading and Use of English paper, the questions follow the same order as the information in the text.
  Don't choose your answers yet. In the margin, mark the general area of the text which is relevant to each question.
- For each question, eliminate the options which are clearly wrong and choose the best answer.
  Underline key phrases or sentences in the text which help you make your choice.
- Reread the questions. Do the options you have chosen accurately reflect the information you have underlined in the text?
  Justify your answers to your partner, explaining why other options are incorrect.

One cool guy

How Parker Liautaud aims to save the world, one polar expedition at a time

There are things that you expect to see **etched** into the face of every polar explorer: broken veins; the scars of a few battles with frostbite. On meeting Parker Liautaud at Venice Beach in sunny California, I see he has yet to gain a single one of these. Appearances can be deceptive, though. At 17, Parker has already taken part in three serious polar expeditions. It's also worth mentioning that he happens to have **impeccable** manners and that quiet sense of self-confidence common among the products of expensive boarding schools. Born in California, he and his four siblings spent their formative years in the UK, after their father, a successful businessman, decided that the family might benefit from spending some time in London.

Until 13, Parker was an ordinary kid. That changed after he met polar explorer Robert Swan. They began an email correspondence which **escalated** into a friendship that eventually saw the then 14-year-old invited to join a trip to the Antarctic. He said yes almost instantly. Friends and family, to whom he'd so far shown he had no particular interest in outdoor pursuits, particularly polar ones, were **perplexed** – to say the least. 'I was the second-choice goalkeeper for the third-lowest football team in school. So the prospect of me hauling a sled across miles of snow was kind of a **farce**, and I was really not taken seriously,' he recalls. He ate lots of chicken, spent a long time in the gym, and proved them wrong.

The following year, Liautaud cooked up a more ambitious plan: to become the youngest-ever person to trek to the North Pole. He found a new accomplice, the veteran explorer Doug Stoup, and through a mixture of charm and luck raised the roughly $150 000 cost of the record attempt. Then disaster struck. The early months of 2010, when the duo set out were among the warmest on record. The Pole, which is essentially a GPS location on a constantly-drifting collection of ice sheets, became virtually inaccessible, surrounded by patches of uncovered ocean. A trip which had intended to raise awareness of melting ice caps had been obstructed. By melting ice caps. 'We would get up, battle through these difficult conditions for 15 hours, then wake up the next morning and find that we were further away from the Pole than we'd started the previous morning,' he says. After 14 days' trying, and with rations running low, they admitted defeat.

Liautaud came home and decided to try again. He raised another six-figure sum and set off in spring 2011. Conditions were cold but perfect, and he and Stoup reached the Pole in no time. 'By complete coincidence, we arrived at the moment when a helicopter landed to drop off a group of tourists who'd paid to spend ten minutes there,' he recalls. 'Explorers call them "champagners". Anyway, it was all a little weird. It felt like I had just finished a cross-country ski race, or something.' Ignoring the onlookers, he promptly 'checked in' to the North Pole on the social media site, Foursquare. At the time, that was also a first.

While it might not have made him the youngest North-Poler, the success did give Liautaud a platform to continue advocacy against climate change, through both his campaigning website, *The Last Degree,* and work with pressure groups. His view is that it's his generation, rather than the one that today's world leaders belong to, that must push hardest for cuts in carbon emissions. They are the ones with the most at stake. Scientific opinion regarding the existence and scale of the problem is pretty much settled, he argues, adding that the portion of the public which still doubts the reality of man-made climate change – and remains hostile to legislation that might solve it – is largely ill-informed, although 'that isn't necessarily their fault'.

Liautaud's advocacy work has made him enemies. When Anthony Watts, a prominent climate change sceptic, wrote a scathing blog entry attacking one of his polar expeditions, Liautaud was referred to as a 'joke' by media figures. But Liautaud's high-profile polar trips are certainly shaping the climate-change debate. He has already contributed to research projects carried out by the International Atomic Energy Agency and will soon set up two stations to record weather data. It must be an exhausting life, fraught with hostility. But Liautaud seems to relish the fight. When you've hauled a sled across hundreds of miles of frozen tundra, lived off freeze-dried food for weeks, and learnt how to ward off a hostile polar bear, attempting to save Planet Earth is all in a day's work.

1 When the writer met Parker Liautaud at Venice Beach, he was

A impressed by his level of maturity.

B amused by his youthful appearance.

C concerned about his uninformed beliefs.

D prepared to find reasons to dislike him.

2 When Parker agreed to go to the Antarctic with Robert Swan, other people

A attempted to talk him out of it.

B advised him on aspects of preparation.

C were puzzled about his decision.

D were supportive of his plans.

3 Parker and Doug Stoup were prevented from reaching the North Pole by

A the movement of the ice.

B the failure of equipment.

C the severity of the weather.

D their own physical limits.

4 What is Parker emphasizing in the sentence 'It felt like I had just finished a cross-country ski race.'?

A his sense of relief on completing his trek

B the desire to celebrate a hard-won victory

C the fact that a crowd had witnessed his achievement

D the contrast between his previous attempt and this one

5 What does the writer suggest about Parker and his fight against climate change in the fifth paragraph?

A His arguments must be based on proven fact.

B He needs to adjust his approach if he wants a wider audience.

C He is yet to understand the complexity of politics.

D It is younger people that he wants to target.

6 What point does the writer make about the criticism directed at Parker?

A It is the reaction of a minority of people.

B Parker is quite capable of dealing with it.

C It has become increasingly unfair.

D It is not something that Parker pays attention to.

Reacting to the text

Is Parker Liautaud the sort of person you might admire? Why/Why not?

Parker has been able to fund his trips by getting large corporations and charities to sponsor him: why do you think these organizations were willing to help?

Talk about one of your own personal achievements. If possible, comment on what motivated you, your preparations and the feelings you experienced.

Language focus 1: Modal verbs 1: *Might, could, may* and *can*

1 Sentences **1–7** all contain the modal verb *might*. Match each of the sentences to the idea they express.

present possibility	future possibility	past possibility
past possibility which did not happen	annoyance	
concession	lack of enthusiasm	

1 You might at least help me!
2 I wish you'd drive more carefully. You might have had an accident back there.
3 I do hope they're OK. They might have had an accident or something.
4 I might be home a bit later tonight. I've got a meeting at five.
5 Put the telly on – there might be something good on.
6 There's nothing on telly, so we might as well go to bed.
7 He might be good-looking, but he can't sing very well.

With no change in meaning, *might* can be substituted by *could* in sentences **1–5** and *may* in sentences **3–7**.

2 Complete each of these sentences in an appropriate way. Compare your ideas with those of a partner.

1 I'm so angry with him. I do think he might have …
2 We've missed the beginning, so we may as well …
3 It was rather dangerous. Someone could have …
4 I can't find it anywhere. I think I may have …
5 She might have a university degree, but …
6 Cheer up! It might …

3 The following sentences **1–6** all contain the modal verb *can/can't*. Match each of the sentences to the idea they express.

request	deduction	criticism	inability
theoretical possibility	prohibition		

1 It can store up to 30 000 separate images.
2 You can be really irritating sometimes, you know.
3 Can you hold this for a second?
4 I can't do it – I'm not tall enough.
5 It can't be very healthy if it's got all that in it.
6 No, you can't! It's far too late.

4 With your partner, think of a context for each of the sentences in exercise **3**. Use modal verbs to express your ideas.

Example:

1 This could be somebody talking about a piece of software – a compact disc for example. It might be a shop assistant trying to sell it.

Read more about *might, could, may* and *can* in the Grammar reference on page 215.

Extension

1 In addition to using modal verbs, there are several alternative ways of expressing future possibility. In sentences **a** and **b** one of the four possibilities has a different meaning to the other three. Underline the odd one out.

a There's a *strong/distinct/faint/real* possibility that I could lose my job.
b There's *an outside/a slight/a fair/a remote* chance that Lara might be at the party tonight.

In sentences **c** and **d** underline the **incorrect** alternative.

c They have *every/good/little/no* chance of winning.
d You could *easily/well/conceivably/predictably* get there in under two hours.

What is the difference in meaning between sentences **e** and **f**?

e She'*s highly likely to* pass the exam.
f She'*s hardly likely to* pass the exam.

2 Complete the following sentences so that they express your true feelings about the future.

1 I think I stand a good chance of … (+ gerund).
2 To improve my chances of … (+ gerund), I need to …
3 In the world today we face the very real possibility that … will …
4 There's an outside chance that … will/might/could …
5 It seems highly unlikely that … will …

Comment on and discuss each other's views.

Vocabulary: Collocations

1 Complete each of the gaps with one of the nouns from the box.

challenge	success	motivation
ambition	failure	

a The film *Star Wars* **was an overnight** __________.
b I **have a burning** __________ **to** travel to Australia.
c When pupils tire of studying, a system of rewards can help **increase student** __________.
d Sadly, my attempts to learn Japanese **met with complete** __________.
e The government **faces the formidable** __________ **of** reducing unemployment.

2 In exercise **1**, the words in **bold** are 'collocates' of the nouns you wrote. This means that they are often used together with those nouns. Write a new sentence for each noun, using the collocates in **bold**. The sentences must be true.

3 Compare and discuss your sentences with another student.

4 In sentence **e** in exercise **1**, the verb *face* collocates with *challenge*. Which of the five nouns do each of the following pairs of verbs collocate with?

fulfil / realize a/an __________

end in / result in __________

achieve / enjoy __________

improve / lack __________

take up / rise to a/an __________

5 The adjective *formidable* also collocates with *challenge*. All three words in each of the groups below can be used in combination with one of the nouns from exercise **1**. Write an appropriate noun in each of the spaces.

a major/new/daunting __________
b secret/lifelong/main __________
c total/continued/dismal __________
d huge/great/resounding __________
e high/strong/poor __________

6 Study the collocations in this section for two minutes, then close your book and write down as many as you can remember. Compare your results with your partner's.

Listening
Part 1

Multiple choice 1.1–1.3

1 What awards, international and national, are well known in your country?

Have you ever won an award, prize or trophy for anything? If so, how did you feel about receiving it?

2 You will hear three different extracts. For questions **1–6**, choose the answer (**A**, **B** or **C**) which fits best according to what you hear. There are two questions for each extract.

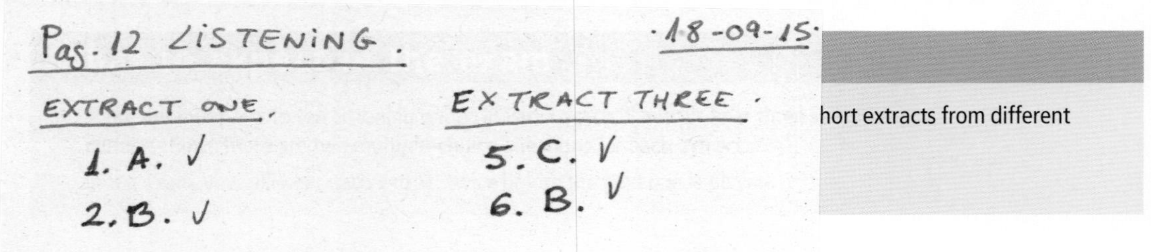

hort extracts from different

awards ceremony.

emony?

p

B will soon lose interest in their music.
C agree with their ideals and beliefs.

Extract Two

You hear part of a radio discussion in which two people are talking about sport.

3 The first man says that the home team lost because
A some team members were inexperienced.
B their training has not been effective.
C they were too confident of a win.

4 Both speakers dislike the way that two players
A react to media attention.
B are behaving in a disloyal way.
C have little to offer as role models.

Extract Three

You hear two university students talking about a fund-raising event called *40-hour Famine*.

5 According to the woman, the purpose of *40-hour Famine* is to
A encourage students to do some charity work abroad.
B persuade people to give money to charity regularly.
C help people understand the effects of famine on people's lives.

6 After taking part in last year's *40-hour Famine* event, the man says he was
A proud of what he had achieved.
B determined to do better in the future.
C disappointed he had not fulfilled his aim.

3 Do you know of any cases where someone has turned down an award? Why did they reject it?

Talk about something you failed to achieve. How disappointed were you?

Word formation: Nouns

1 Which suffixes are added to the following verbs to create nouns?

achieve motivate fail

2 Complete each gap with an appropriate noun form of the word in capitals at the end of the line. Use each suffix in the box once only and make any further spelling changes necessary. The noun you require may also need a plural ending or a negative prefix (*un-*, *in-*, *im-*, *dis-*,etc). There is an example at the beginning (**0**).

-hood -ship -ure -al -ness ~~-ation~~
-ance -ence -iety -ity -ment -age -cy

0 His **latest** *publication* is **a book** of verse on the theme of relationships. **PUBLISH**
1 **Light** ____________ **will be served** from 3.30pm in the main hall. **REFRESH**
2 Union members **expressed their** ____________ **of** the management's offer by walking out of the meeting. **APPROVE**
3 **In her** ____________ **to** answer the phone, she almost fell down the stairs. **EAGER**
4 In the interests of safety, a number of **standard** ____________ need to be **followed**. **PROCEED**
5 Her 5000-metre run **paled into** ____________ when compared with the marathon her grandfather completed the following week. **SIGNIFY**
6 The ____________ of the device is what has made it so popular. **SIMPLE**
7 I cannot comment; I have been **sworn to** ____________ on the matter. **SECRET**
8 **The cost of** ____________ has increased by 10% this year. **MEMBER**
9 Customers will be required to **pay for any** ____________ . **BREAK**
10 **There is every** ____________ **that** prices will continue to rise next year. **LIKELY**
11 He **valued his** ____________ too much to ever want to get married. **DEPEND**
12 It's quite natural to **experience a certain amount of** ____________ on your first day at work. **ANXIOUS**

3 Using the same suffixes as in exercise **2**, write noun forms for the following words. The same suffix is needed for all three words. Some words require further spelling changes. The exercise begins with an example (**0**).

0	notorious	*notoriety*	various	*variety*	sober	*sobriety*
1	please	____	expose	____	close	____
2	appear	____	annoy	____	rely	____
3	store	____	short	____	pack	____
4	rehearse	____	renew	____	propose	____
5	efficient	____	intimate	____	vacant	____
6	enjoy	____	require	____	commit	____
7	prosperous	____	original	____	familiar	____
8	leader	____	companion	____	partner	____
9	neighbour	____	father	____	adult	____
10	absent	____	persistent	____	evident	____
11	selfish	____	tired	____	careless	____
12	explain	____	interpret	____	apply	____

4 Look back at the reading text on page 8 and underline those nouns which have been formed by the addition of a suffix to a verb, adjective or another noun. Add them to the list in exercise **3**.

Language focus 2: Spelling

1 Look at these two extracts from the reading text on page 8.

After 14 days' trying, ... they ***admitted*** *defeat.*

Liautaud was ***referred*** *to as a 'joke' by media figures.*

The final consonant of the verbs *admit* and *refer* is doubled to form the past tense. Similarly, the consonant is doubled in *drumming* and *beginning*, but not in *claiming* or *opening*. Why is this?

2 What is the *-ing* form of the following verbs?

fulfil	limit	set	upset	target
forbid	write	wait	travel	panic

3 For each of the following groups of four words, find the incorrectly spelt word and correct it. The exercise begins with an example (**0**).

0	importance	~~insistance~~ *insistence*	appearance	tolerance
1	apparent	pleasent	different	independent
2	occasion	accountant	neccessary	accident
3	publically	optimistically	scientifically	dramatically
4	separate	desperate	immediate	definate
5	unreasonable	irresponsable	irritable	indispensable
6	chefs	roofs	safes	leafs
7	exceeding	succeeding	proceeding	preceeding
8	embarrassment	accommodation	bussiness	committee
9	unnatural	unknown	dissappointed	dissatisfied
10	believe	recieve	seize	weird
11	financial	influencial	commercial	beneficial
12	cemetery	factery	bakery	surgery

4 Work with a partner. You are going to dictate ten two-word items of vocabulary to each other. Student A should turn to page 204 and Student B to page 207.

Writing
Part 2

Formal letter

What to expect in the exam

In Part 2 of the Writing paper, you might have the opportunity to write a letter or an email. You may be required to use a formal or less formal style, depending on your reason for writing, and on the target reader. You will not need to include addresses, but you should know how to begin your letter/email appropriately (e.g. To the Editor, Dear Sir/Madam, Dear Simon Smith, To whom it may concern, To all staff members, Hi Rose) and finish it (e.g. Yours sincerely, Regards, Thank you for your attention, See you soon).

1 Read the following Part 2 task and the model answer.

Does the answer address all aspects of the task?

Would it have a positive effect on the manager reading it?

> You are planning an event to raise public awareness about a project that is important to you. You decide to write a letter to the manager of a large organization to ask for money to help finance the event.
>
> Your letter should explain
>
> - what the project is.
> - what the event will involve.
> - how the money will be used.
>
> Write your **letter** in **220–260** words.

Dear Ann Robertson

I am writing on behalf of Devonport Community Centre, where I am Social Secretary. As you may know, the community centre runs many evening classes for adults and provides a variety of sports programmes for teenagers. We also offer after-school care and activities for many local children whose parents are at work. Unfortunately, our kitchen facilities are in urgent need of an upgrade, and as a non-profit organization, we need assistance to raise the necessary funds.

We are planning to hold a fair in March to help finance our project. There will be demonstrations by our tae kwon do group, entertainment from our musicians, food stalls set up by parents and many activities for young children to enjoy. We hope that the event will not only help us to buy new equipment for the kitchen, but will also encourage local builders, plumbers and other craftsmen to volunteer some of their time.

In order to attract people to our fair, we would also like to set up a rock climbing wall and inflatable castle. We are therefore hoping that you might be able to help us by paying for the hire of this equipment. Naturally, we would be very happy to promote you as our key sponsor.

If sponsorship from Fresh World were possible, I would be happy to arrange a meeting at any time that was convenient to you.

Thank you for your attention.

Yours sincerely

Jason Norwood

2 Appropriate paragraphing and good use of a range of linking devices are essential features of all writing tasks in the *Cambridge English: Advanced* exam.

- What information is contained in each paragraph of the model answer above?
- Underline examples of words or phrases that link ideas or sentences.

3 For most *Advanced* writing tasks, you will need to persuade the target reader that something is a good idea or the right course of action to take.

How might the following elements of the model answer have a positive effect on the manager?

- the way the writer describes the community centre and the event
- the point at which the writer asks for money
- the verbs and tenses used by the writer in the third and fourth paragraphs

4 To obtain a high mark in the *Advanced* examination you need to use a wide range of relevant vocabulary and structures.

Circle language the writer uses to refer to the issue of 'money' without using the word, e.g. *non-profit organization*.

5 Write your own **letter** for the question in exercise **1** in **220–260** words.

How to go about it

- Plan carefully what you will say for each part of the question. Organize your ideas into logical paragraphs.
  For this question you could devote one paragraph to each of the three bullet points, as in the model answer.
- Be persuasive, but not aggressive. Write your answer in an appropriate register.
  A formal register would help ensure that your request for money is taken seriously by the manager.
- Use a range of relevant vocabulary, grammatical structures and linking devices.
- Begin and end your letter in a suitable way.

1 Review

Modal verbs

Complete each gap with one word.

1 Sometimes you _______ be so uncaring – I do think you might _______ come to see me in hospital after I'd had my operation!

2 She _______ be just a six-month-old baby, but she's already showing signs of being intelligent.

3 The next bus isn't likely _______ come for an hour or so, so we may as _______ walk.

4 It seems highly _______ that it will rain today, but we _______ well have a few showers tomorrow.

5 You could _______ least have made the effort to do some revision. Now you have absolutely _______ chance of passing the exam.

6 The ruling party succeeded _______ being re-elected, but didn't manage _______ retain their overall majority in parliament.

Spelling

Each numbered line in the following text contains a spelling mistake. Find the mistakes and correct them.

1 Clearly, student motivation is an importent influence on learning. It is also believed,
2 though, that students' perceptions of their learning experiences generaly influence
3 their motivation more than the actual, objetive reality of those experiences. The
4 Attribution Theory of Motivation identifys two types of student. The first type credit
5 their success to their own ability and effort. If they are successfull in an exam, they
6 attribute their achievement to themselfs, feel proud and are keen to take on further
7 tasks off this nature. They work hard because they see a clear relationship between
8 the effort made and the results obtained. If they fail, they put this failure down too
9 their own lack of effort and are confidant that if they try harder in the future, they
10 will have more success. The second type attribute success to external facters. If they
11 perform well in an exam, they consider that it was easy and they where lucky. They
12 feel little pride in their achievements and show little intrest in taking on further
13 tasks. If they fail, they attribute there poor performance to their own lack of ability
14 and are unlikely to see any reason to hope for an improvment in the future. They
15 do not percieve the link between effort and results, and lack the motivation to keep trying.

Word formation

For questions **1–8**, read the text below. Use the word given in capitals at the end of some of the lines to form a word that fits in the gap **in the same line**. There is an example at the beginning (**0**). Write your answers **IN CAPITAL LETTERS**.

Don't forget!

You may need to write the negative or plural form of a word.

REWARDING CHILDREN

Cash rewards are a common form of **(0)** MOTIVATION used by parents	**MOTIVATE**
with high **(1)** .... to encourage their children to work hard at exam	**EXPECT**
time. Some youngsters receive **(2)** .... of as much as £100 for	**PAY**
each A grade they obtain. But should such 'bribes' be based on exam	
(3) .... or should they, as many parents and teachers feel, be	**PERFORM**
offered in **(4)** .... of a child's effort, regardless of results? The	**RECOGNIZE**
latter approach would solve the problem of how parents reward children	
with different levels of **(5)** .... ; imagine, for example, a family	**ABLE**
with one child who is academically gifted and another who has learning	
(6) .... The dangers of result-related incentives for the second child	**DIFFICULT**
are clear; with little hope of obtaining the higher grades, the withholding	
of promised financial rewards would only compound the child's feeling	
of **(7)** .... However, some leading educational psychologists believe	**FAIL**
that parents should rely on their own **(8)** .... in such matters. They	**JUDGE**
maintain that if parents know that money will motivate their child, then	
they should not be condemned for operating a system of cash payouts.	

Word combinations

For sentences **1–10** underline the correct alternative.

1 There's a *heavy/hard/strong/tough* possibility I'll get a pay rise in January.
2 He hasn't got the *fairest/slightest/longest/thinnest* chance of winning the election. He's far too unpopular.
3 There is *every/each/all/very* likelihood that the government will introduce the measures this year.
4 There were far more of them than us. We didn't *stand/face/hold/keep* a chance against them.
5 She was clearly rather worried and seemed close to *edge/nerves/tension/tears*.
6 I'm *elated/delighted/pleasant/anxious* to meet you at last, Mr Wood. Let me take your bag.
7 The young singer *fulfilled/enjoyed/was/became* overnight success last year when her debut single *Burning Ambition* reached number 1.
8 He had never acted before, but he *rose/arose/aroused/raised* to the challenge and gave a very convincing performance.
9 At 85 she says she's unlikely to realize her *resounding/longing/lifelong/overall* ambition of learning to fly.
10 Snacks and *easy/loose/light/full* refreshments are available in the lounge area.

2 Times change

Listening 1
Part 2

Sentence completion 1.4

1 These photographs were all taken over 50 years ago.

How has life changed since then? If the same photographs were taken now, which features would be the same and which would be different?

2 You will hear a student called Simon Todd, giving a presentation about a visit he made to a national museum. What different aspects of history and human development do museums show?

What to expect in the exam

- There is always a pause before you hear the listening. Use this to read through the questions and predict the type of answer required; for example, a place name, an area of study, a type of job, an object or a process.
- You should write the actual words you hear in the recording.
- Answers are usually single words or short noun phrases of no more than three words.
- For some of the questions you will hear distractors: words which might at first seem relevant, but which do not complete the answer correctly. For question 1, for example, you will hear Simon mention two fields of research, but only one of these is related to the curator's museum job.
- Check your answers; incorrect spelling and grammar may lose marks.
- Part 2 is always a monologue. As with all recordings in the Listening paper, it is played twice.

3 Before you do the task, read all the questions and try to predict the type of information you might hear for each one.

4 For questions **1–8**, complete the sentences with a word or short phrase.

Working at the National Museum

The curator had chosen **(1)** .... as her specialization in the museum.

The curator said that good **(2)** .... were vital for anyone working at the museum.

The curator explained that the **(3)** .... of an item often requires collaboration.

Simon says that keeping **(4)** .... would be his weak point if he were a curator.

As well as working with other professionals, the curator deals with questions from the **(5)** ....

Simon recommends looking at the old **(6)** .... on the walls.

Simon says that the museum often has to turn down **(7)** .... that people want to donate.

The curator told Simon that finding ways to save **(8)** .... was the museum's greatest challenge.

Speaking
Part 3

Collaborative task 

Read tasks **1** and **2** below. Then, before you do the tasks, read the information in the boxes at the bottom of the page.

1 Here are some items which might represent our lives today in a new museum exhibition.

Talk with your partner about how well these items represent our lives today.

How representative might these items be of our lives today?

- clothes by a popular fashion brand
- a popular internet clip
- a fast food menu
- a newspaper
- examples of currency

2 Now decide which item would be of most interest to future generations visiting the museum.

How to go about it

- Part 3 is an interactive task. As well as giving your own opinions, ask your partner what they think and respond to their comments. Always give reasons for your opinions.
- In task **1**, you can talk about the areas in any order you choose. Say as much as you can about each one.
- Do not start to make your decisions for task **2** while you are doing task **1**. They are two separate tasks.
- In task **2**, you do not have to agree with your partner when making your final decision.
- In both tasks, aim to demonstrate your linguistic ability by using a wide range of vocabulary and structures.

Useful language

Complete each of the gaps with one of the phrases in the box. There is an example at the beginning **(0)**.

are unlikely to be using
be intrigued to see
would not be complete without
~~is a distinct possibility that~~
might conceivably be obsolete
would demonstrate very clearly
is a part of everyday life

0 There *is a distinct possibility that* people in the future won't ever have seen coins or cash.
1 The exhibition ______________________ one or two items of fashion clothing.
2 Fast food ______________________, so something representing that would be of interest.
3 Future generations would ______________________ the various means of payment we use today.
4 This kind of video ______________________ what many people today enjoy watching on the Internet.
5 Newspapers ______________________ within the next ten years.
6 People ______________________ newspapers as a source of information in 100 years' time.

Reading and Use of English 1
Part 2

Open cloze

What to expect in the exam

- The open cloze is a short text with eight gaps, each of which has to be filled with one word.
- The main focus is on grammatical words, e.g. prepositions, auxiliary verbs, articles, relative pronouns and conjunctions.

1 Read the following text, ignoring the gaps for the moment. Which famous toy is being described?

THE IMPOSSIBLY CURVY DOLL

More than one billion have been sold **(0)** SINCE her first appearance at the New York Toy Fair in 1959. Originally known **(1)** .... the 'Teenage Fashion Model', she was a perky blue-eyed blonde with a ponytail in a swimsuit.

It was while she was watching her daughter Barbara playing with cut-outs of adult women **(2)** .... creator Ruth Handler first came up **(3)** .... the idea. At the time, dolls in America always took the form of babies so when she first proposed a prototype to executives at the toy company, Mattel, she **(4)** .... turned down.

But eventually Handler won over the all-male management, and the first toy doll in the USA with breasts went **(5)** .... production. Fame was not long in coming, and as her world expanded, so too **(6)** .... the profits for Mattel. She took on numerous different identities, **(7)** .... as astronaut, vet or surgeon and she acquired many friends, notably Ken, **(8)** .... name came from Handler's son.

2 Read the text again and think of the word which best fits each gap. Use only **one** word in each gap. There is an example at the beginning (**0**). Write your answers **IN CAPITAL LETTERS**. Make sure you read the example.

When you have finished, justify your answers to your partner, with particular reference to words and sentences before and after the gaps.

3 Here is the final paragraph of the text above. Read it and discuss the following question: Do you agree more with Handler or the feminists?

She was not without her critics. Her shapely figure was essentially unattainable and feminists attacked Handler for presenting young girls with an image of adult beauty they could never achieve. Handler was not bothered by this. 'My whole philosophy was that through the doll, the little girl could be anything she wanted to become,' she later wrote.

Language focus 1: Talking about the past

A Review

Complete each of the spaces with an appropriate form of the verb in brackets. Choose from the past, past perfect or present perfect, in either the simple or continuous form. There may be more than one possible answer. If so, explain any differences in meaning.

1 I ____________ (never/kiss) anyone until I ____________ (meet) you.
2 That's the third time I ____________ (have) to tell you to stop shouting!
3 It looks as if he ____________ (cry) again. His eyes are all red and puffy.
4 I used to get so annoyed with him. He ____________ (always/lose) things.
5 She ____________ (eat) a particularly large meal and she suddenly started to feel sick.
6 Marjorie ____________ (leave) when Paul ____________ (arrive).
7 You know that book you ____________ (tell) me about last week? Well, I ____________ (buy) it. Look.
8 I hated that school. If I ____________ (not do) my homework, they used to punish me. If I ____________ (do) it, they'd tell me to do it again.

B Further ways of talking about the past

1 Underline the correct alternatives in the following sentences. Either one, two or all three alternatives may be possible.

1. **When I was a teenager** I *used to know/would know/ knew* the words to all *The Beatles* songs.
2. **It's years since** *I've ridden/I haven't ridden/I rode* a bike. I'm not sure if I could do it now.
3. **I'd** *like to have travelled/have liked to travel/have liked to have travelled* **more when I was younger**.
4. **I remember** that concert. **It was the first time** *I've seen/ I'd seen/I was seeing* the band play live.
5. **I'd rather my parents** *didn't make/wouldn't have made/hadn't made* me go to piano lessons **when I was little**.
6. She was *going to work/thinking to work/to have worked* in her mother's business, but decided instead to continue her studies.
7. *After he'd done/Having done/Being done* it once, he was happy to give another presentation.
8. It has not rained since *he's been here/he got here/ his arrival*.

Check your answers by reading the Grammar reference on pages 215 and 216.

2 Rewrite sentences **1–5** so that they are true for you. Use the words in **bold** together with an appropriate verb in the correct form. Compare your sentences with those of your partner.

Reading and Use of English 2 Part 8

Multiple matching

1 What period of time do you think each of these images is from?

These images appear in four different books dealing with a particular historical subject. What do you think the subjects might be?

2 You are going to read a review of history books. For questions **1–10**, choose from the sections (**A–D**). The sections may be chosen more than once.

How to go about it

- Skim through all four sections quickly to get an idea of their content.
- Read all the questions to see the kind of information you are looking for.
- Read section **A**, then look again at the questions, answering any that you can.
- Do the same for the other three sections.
- If there are any questions you have not answered, scan the sections again, looking for the specific information you need.
- To help you, parts of section **A** have been underlined. Match these parts to the appropriate questions. As you answer the other questions, underline the relevant parts of sections **B–D** in the same way.

In which section are the following mentioned?

personal stories being expressed in an amusing way	1
the idea of enjoyment coming from a sense of nostalgia	2
the possibility that people will not be reading page by page	3
the fact that certain people have been looking forward to a book's publication	4
an element that makes the book superior to others on the same topic	5
the effective way the book has been compiled from different kinds of text	6
the reviewer's disapproval of the insufficient depth of investigation	7
the view that this book will alter the way you feel about the subject matter	8
an autobiographical element explaining the author's motivation	9
the possibility of disapproval of the author's handling of a particular issue	10

This month's history books

Eric Moore reviews a selection of history publications

Britain under the reign of Queen Victoria (1837–1901) witnessed a great leap forward in technological terms, propelled by the Industrial Revolution. Social reform, however, took longer to gain momentum. In *The Unseen*, Amelia Drew skilfully intersperses extracts from Victorian household management manuals describing the duties of young servants with contemporary pamphlets calling for improvements in working conditions. The diary entries of Drew's great-grandmother also appear, allowing us a glimpse into the gruelling and monotonous life of a housemaid. Drew does not shy away from providing meticulous descriptions of the foul tasks that servants were charged with and the kind of horrific injury that befell very young factory workers, and in doing so, dispels any lingering romantic notions of this era. This is a compelling book, but I suspect one that will be dipped into rather than read in its entirety.

In January 1918, the first cases of a new strain of influenza were observed in Kansas, USA. The ensuing pandemic lasted to December 1920, spreading across Europe, and even to the Arctic, claiming an estimated 20–50 million lives. With little understanding of how the 'Spanish flu' virus spread, many people were forced to rely on folk remedies such as eating onions or wearing goose fat poultices. In *Contagion*, Dirk Smithey takes a comprehensive look at over 2000 years of disease and treatment. He is not the first to attempt this, but he writes with unusual compassion, and in doing so, elevates his work above the rest. Interestingly, once we arrive in the 21st century, Smithey makes reference to the anti-immunization trend, but does not enter the debate, a decision I suspect may irritate those working towards the elimination of needless childhood disease. All in all, an alarming yet fascinating read.

Since walking out of the continent now known as Africa, modern man has regularly packed his bags and moved on. Such journeys into the unknown often require a leap of faith. This is the case for many of the subjects interviewed in Aisha Dunbar's *Worlds Apart*, a group of people who underwent the immigrant experience in the 1970s. As they recall the cultural and language barriers they once had to face, they all speak of the need to believe that life will get better. In the first chapter, Dunbar herself provides a first-hand account of being on the receiving end of racism and the strategies she employed to deal with those who abused her, and cites this as her incentive for assembling this collection of other voices. *Worlds Apart* is, admittedly, a slightly sentimental book, particularly in the narrative thread that connects each person's story, but the anecdotes they tell are often genuinely humorous and uplifting.

Fans of Neil Gough's *The Right Man*, a look at political campaigning in the 21st century, have eagerly anticipated a follow-up, but whether his latest volume, *In Retrospect*, rises to the challenge is arguable. This book poses the question 'does advertising merely reinforce stereotypes or create them?' It is bursting with commercial artwork and slogans from the 1950s onwards, and some may appreciate the trip down memory lane to a time when 'real men' smoked pipes and wore fedora hats, and when slogans such as '*Christmas morning she'll be happier with a Hoover*' and '*Don't worry darling, you didn't burn the beer*' were perfectly acceptable. Where *In Retrospect* falls down is its lighter emphasis on the analysis side of things, and thus it feels a superficial read at times. Nevertheless, a treasure worth buying or giving.

Reacting to the text

Which of these books would you be interested to read? Why?

Describe a book, film or TV programme that provides an insight into the way people once lived. Which period of time does it deal with? Is it historically accurate?

Language focus 2: Nouns in formal English

1 Look at the following pairs of sentences. In each case the second sentence is an alternative way of expressing the first sentence, which appeared in the reading text above. What differences do you notice between each pair of sentences? Comment on the use of nouns and verbs.

1 a Smithey makes reference to the anti-immunization trend.
b *Smithey mentions indirectly the fact that they were generally against immunizing people.*

2 a Such journeys into the unknown often require a leap of faith.
b *When you set off like this and put yourself into new situations, you often have to believe that things will get better, even though you can't be sure of this.*

2 Nouns help to convey information clearly and concisely, and are far more frequent in formal written English than in conversation. For questions **1–4**, use the information in **a**, which is more conversational, to complete the gaps in **b**, which is more formal.

Example:
a *I thought the painting was very simple and different to anything else I'd seen before. I was very impressed.*
b *I was most impressed by the simplicity and originality of the painting.*

1 a He applied for the job and he was clearly a bit disappointed when he heard they'd turned him down.
b He was unable to hide his ____________ at their rejection of his ____________ .

2 a The employees said they thought it would be a good idea if the company reduced the working day by just a little, but management said they didn't approve of the idea at all.
b Management voiced their strong ____________ of the employees' ____________ for a slight ____________ in the working day.

3 a I have to tell you that I'm not satisfied with the service you offer. I often have to wait a long time for things to get here, even though you say that you send them sooner than 24 hours after you receive an order.
b I must express my ____________ with the standard of your service. Delivery of goods is often subject to ____________ , despite your ____________ that orders are dispatched within 24 hours.

4 a People fail to understand how important it is to recycle waste, and I think it's because they don't know anything about the environment and they don't get taught enough about it at school.
b People's ____________ to understand the ____________ of recycling waste is the ____________ of a lack of environmental ____________ and insufficient ____________ on the subject.

3 In **1–4** in exercise **2**, there are more verbs in **a** than in **b**, and more nouns in **b** than in **a**. What other differences do you notice between the language used in informal and formal registers?

Review

1 Which of these films (1–5) would you be most likely to watch? Why?

1

2

3

2 Read the following Part 2 task and the model answer.
Which film shown in the five posters do you think the review is describing?

You see the announcement below on a film review website called *FilmScape*.

The Past is Back

The film industry has often turned to history as a source of inspiration, but some of its attempts to bring the past to life have been better than others. Next month we'll be bringing you our top ten recommendations for historical films, and we welcome your suggestions.

So, send in a review which describes a historical film, explaining why it is worth watching, and in what ways it could have been better.

Write your **review** in **220–260** words.

____________________________ is a spectacular dramatization of the events that took place in the early 17th century when English settlers first made contact with Native Americans. The legendary story of Pocahontas, a powerful chief's daughter, and how she saved the life of John Smith, has been told many times in literature, song and film, but in this period piece, director Terrence Malick takes a more honest approach.

Smith, played by Colin Farrell, is portrayed as a fantasist; a man who ignores the brutality of the 'noble savages' and at the same time alienates his fellow Britons who are struggling to survive the harsh winter. As for Pocahontas (actress Q'Orianka Kilcher), the movie quite rightly implies that it is not love that makes her save Smith, but curiosity and empathy for the hardship this strange man faces. Indeed, the element of 'strangeness' is what really makes the film stand out. The Algonquin people and the Britons are shown regarding each other in complete wonder. There is a moving scene in which Smith and Pocahontas teach each other simple words; this sort of scenario often feels rather contrived, but here there is a genuine feeling of discovery.

This is a visually stunning epic, and skilfully avoids the usual stereotyping of Native Americans. However, if historical accuracy is what you are after, you may feel let down. Pocahontas is shown as a young woman, whereas in reality, she is said to have been ten years old when she first met Smith. Her later life in London also seems slightly idealized. All in all, a masterful film.

4

5

3 What is the purpose of each paragraph?

4 In your own words, say why the writer thinks the film is 'worth watching' and how it 'could have been better'.

5 Some sentences in the review use past forms of a verb and others use present forms. Underline four examples of each. Then decide why a present or past form is used.

6 Make a note of those adjectives used by the writer to express an opinion. Include any accompanying adverbs or nouns.

Example: *spectacular dramatization*

Divide the adjectives in section **B** on page 211 into two groups, positive and negative.

7 Complete each of the spaces with one of the nouns from the box.

objection	development	fact	adaptation	performances	clichés	eyes

1. Both lead actors give remarkable ____________ which won them each an Oscar®.
2. Told through the ____________ of a young soldier named Jamie, it opens on a sweet note and quickly turns tragic.
3. This is a clever ____________ of the original story, and goes on to explore the motives of the hero.
4. Unfortunately, the film relies too heavily on special effects rather than character ____________ .
5. It was let down by the usual ____________ of most action movies; the big speech just before the battle, for example.
6. My one ____________ to the movie is that the accents of the supporting cast are often unconvincing.
7. The end of the film is hardly based on ____________ . Indeed, no survivors were ever found.

8 Now write your own answer to the task in **220–260** words.

Don't forget!

- Aim to grab the reader's interest from the beginning.
- Express your opinions throughout your answer.

Listening 2
Part 4

Multiple matching 1.5–1.9

1 You will hear five short extracts in which people are talking about changes in their lives.

2 To make your first Part 4 Listening easier, there are only six options, not eight, to choose from in each task.

What to expect in the exam

- Part 4 consists of a multiple-matching format in which there are five short monologues on the same theme.
- There are two connected tasks. For each task, you must choose five correct answers from a list of eight options.
- In the exam, you will have 45 seconds to read through the tasks.
- You hear all the extracts once, then the whole sequence is played again.

TASK ONE
For questions 1–5, choose from the list (A–F) what led to the change in the life of the speaker.

TASK TWO
For questions 6–10, choose from the list (A–F) how the speaker feels about this change.

While you listen you must complete both tasks.

	Task One				Task Two		
A	the desire to avoid unwanted attention	Speaker 1	1	**A**	excited	Speaker 1	6
B	the desire to travel	Speaker 2	2	**B**	regretful	Speaker 2	7
C	the desire to maintain a positive relationship	Speaker 3	3	**C**	ashamed	Speaker 3	8
D	the desire to be challenged	Speaker 4	4	**D**	scared	Speaker 4	9
E	the desire to show other people were wrong	Speaker 5	5	**E**	grateful	Speaker 5	10
F	the desire to fulfil an ambition			**F**	proud		

3 Talk to your partner about a time in your life when something changed. Mention the following in relation to the change:

- the reasons for it
- how easy or difficult it was
- your feelings before and afterwards
- other people's attitudes
- the consequences of the change

Vocabulary: Changes

A Verb + noun collocations

When or why might you change each of the items in the box?

Example:
You might change your doctor if you moved house or if you weren't happy with the treatment you were receiving.

your doctor	your name	your mind	your tune		
gear	the subject	sides	places	a tyre	your ways

B Adjective + noun collocations

1 The following adjectives can all be used with the noun *change*.

Complete each of the sentences **1–4** with a suitable group of adjectives **a–d**. All of the adjectives in each group must be appropriate for the sentence you choose.

a economic/political/social
b dramatic/sudden/considerable
c pleasant/refreshing/welcome
d far-reaching/significant/sweeping

1 It **made a/an** ________________ **change to** see Alex in a suit. He looked very smart for once.
2 The government has announced plans **to make** ________________ **changes** to the tax system next year.
3 The **pace of** ________________ **change** has been rather slow in this country recently.
4 The lottery win **brought about a/an** ________________ **change** in her circumstances, which she is finding it difficult to cope with.

2 Rewrite sentences **1–4** so that they are true for you/your country/the world in general. Use the words in **bold**, together with an appropriate adjective. Compare your sentences with those of other students in your class.

C Other verbs of change

For questions **1–5** decide which word, **A**, **B**, **C** or **D** best fits each space. The verb you choose must be appropriate for the gaps in both sentences. The words in **bold** are typical collocates of the verb.

1 a It took him a while to ___________ **to being a parent**.
b You can ___________ **the height of the chair** by pulling this lever here.
A switch **B** alter **C** vary **D** adjust

2 a The old windmill has been ___________ **into a small** guest house.
b Graham Greene ___________ **to Catholicism** at the age of 21.
A transferred **B** transformed **C** converted **D** adapted

3 a **Prices** ___________ **according to** the time of year you decide to travel.
b We were advised to ___________ **the children's diet** as much as possible.
A adapt **B** shift **C** vary **D** modify

4 a Members of the rock group were asked to ___________ **their behaviour** or else leave the hotel.
b We had to ___________ **the design** of the car to take account of the rough terrain.
A modify **B** amend **C** transfer **D** convert

5 a Twelve European countries ___________ **over to the euro** on 1 January 2002.
b I ___________ **shifts with** Brian so I could go to my sister's wedding.
A shifted **B** switched **C** transformed **D** altered

2 Review

Language focus: Talking about the past

In **1–8**, write one of the auxiliary verbs from the box in the first space and an appropriate verb in the correct form in the second space. Use each auxiliary verb once only. There is an example at the beginning (**0**).

have	been	having	had	would
was	~~were~~	has	did	

0 The phone rang just as we *were* *leaving* the house.

1 It was the first time I ____________ ____________ abroad.

2 ____________ ____________ his ambition, he promised to spend more time with his family.

3 Since I've known him he ____________ ____________ that suit twice.

4 He was to ____________ ____________ in the final, but he was injured in a league match.

5 It's years since I ____________ ____________ out to dinner by my partner.

6 When we were little, my dad ____________ often ____________ us a story at bedtime.

7 I'd have liked to have ____________ ____________ a second chance, but it wasn't possible.

8 I wasn't allowed to see the film, but they ____________ ____________ me read the book.

Vocabulary: Changes

1 For **1–8**, decide whether the meaning of the two items of vocabulary is more or less the same or different. Explain any differences in meaning.

Example:

0 transfer money/convert money
Different. When you transfer money, you move it from one place to another, e.g. from one account to another. When you convert money, you change it from one currency to another.

1 adjust to university life/adapt to university life
2 adjust a piece of clothing/alter a piece of clothing
3 convert a farm into a hotel/transform a farm into a hotel
4 change your ways/modify your behaviour
5 change your ways/change your tune
6 vary the menu/adapt the menu
7 change sides/switch sides
8 switch to the euro/convert into euros

2 Match each of the verbs in the box with the group of words which collocate with it. The first one has been done for you.

adjust	convert	modify	switch	~~vary~~

1 *vary* the menu/your routine/in size
2 ____________ to Islam/dollars into euros/the loft into a bedroom
3 ____________ your belt/the straps on a bag/the brakes on a car
4 ____________ TV channels/university courses/from dictatorship to democracy
5 ____________ your language/your views/a piece of equipment

Multiple-choice cloze

1 Read the following text quickly, ignoring the gaps for the moment. Is the writer of the text generally positive or negative about the experience of the first immigrant workers in Britain?

2 For questions **1–8**, read the text again and decide which answer (**A**, **B**, **C** or **D**) best fits each gap. There is an example at the beginning (**0**).

CHANGING COUNTRIES

(0) .... a new life and hoping for a significant **(1)** .... in their standard of living, foreign workers began flocking into Western Europe during the 1950s. In Britain, some of the first immigrants arriving from the West Indies and the Indian subcontinent were welcomed by brass bands, but the dream of a new life soon **(2)** .... sour for many.

Attracted by the promise to earn good money and learn new skills, the reality they found was often one of low wages and, in many **(3)** .... , unemployment. There were times when the newcomers encountered open hostility; in 1958, riots **(4)** .... out in Notting Hill, west London, when gangs of white youths began taunting immigrants.

Yet despite the **(5)** .... difficulties they encountered, many foreign workers did manage to **(6)** .... to their new conditions, settling in their new adopted country and prospering. Their contribution had the effect not only of speeding up the **(7)** .... of economic change in the post-war period, it also **(8)** .... Western Europe into a multiracial society.

	A	B	C	D
0	Searching	Wishing	<u>Seeking</u>	Leading
1	switch	change	modification	variation
2	turned	converted	switched	moved
3	occasions	examples	ways	cases
4	broke	carried	came	started
5	several	high	numerous	heavy
6	fit	adjust	match	suit
7	growth	motion	pace	step
8	transformed	transferred	modified	shifted

3 Gathering information

Speaking
Part 2

Long turn

Look at these pictures. They show people who are trying to obtain information in different ways.

Student A:
Compare **two** of the pictures, and say what kind of information they might want to obtain, and why they might have chosen this way to obtain it.

Student B:
When your partner has finished talking, say which of these ways might provide the more reliable information.

- What kind of information might these people want to obtain?
- Why might they have chosen this way to obtain the information?

Now change roles. Follow the instructions again using the remaining pictures.

Don't forget!

- Talk about the similarities and differences between the two pictures.
- Do not simply describe the pictures. Speculate about them as indicated in the instruction.
- Use a wide range of vocabulary including some of the verbs and adjectives in the Useful language section.

What to expect in the exam

- Each candidate is given **three** pictures and asked to compare **two** of them.
- Candidate A's instructions appear as written questions above the pictures.

Useful language

In **1** and **2** below, the adjectives and verbs in the boxes can all be used in the corresponding sentence. Mark each adjective P or N, according to whether it has a positive or negative meaning.

	Adjective		**Verb**	
1 It is(n't) a very	efficient costly convenient unreliable frustrating cost-effective handy time-saving inexpensive rapid	method/way of	getting obtaining accessing finding gathering collecting	information.

	Verb		**Adjective**
2 The information	gathered compiled obtained accessed collected	would/could/might be	(ir)relevant. (un)reliable. (in)accurate. (un)clear. (un)ambiguous. useful/useless. comprehensive. limited. up-to-date. misleading. vague.

Listening 1
Part 1

Multiple choice 1.10–1.12

1 You will hear three different extracts. For questions **1–6**, choose the answer (**A**, **B** or **C**) which fits best according to what you hear. There are two questions for each extract.

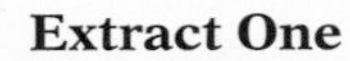

Extract One

You hear part of a radio discussion in which two writers are talking about their books.

1 How does the man feel about the last book he wrote?

A relieved that it has now been completed
B sorry that its scope could not be wider
C uncertain that it will have wide appeal

2 The woman says that using the Internet for research purposes

A has generally made things easier for writers.
B is a rather unreliable way of obtaining information.
C will not replace traditional methods of investigation.

Extract Two

You overhear two university students talking about choices they have made.

3 The man has decided to go to Greece in order to

A take some time to reflect on his career choices.
B carry out some research for his university course.
C take part in a project that needs volunteers.

4 What does the woman regret doing?

A starting a job as soon as her studies were over
B choosing a career that was not fulfilling
C failing to take her studies seriously enough

Extract Three

You hear two game designers talking about their work.

5 When beginning work on a new game, the first designer

A confers with others in the field.
B focuses mainly on character development.
C decides on an overall objective first.

6 Both speakers say that the best game designers

A have a wide range of interests beyond gaming.
B work with their fan base constantly in mind.
C experiment with multiple genres within the industry.

2 Is there still a need for traditional libraries in the modern world?

Is there an ideal time of life to attend university?

What makes some video games better than others?

Language focus 1: Hypothetical past situations

A *Wish*/*If only* and alternatives

1 Look at the following utterance from the first conversation in Listening 1.

If only we'd had (the Internet) when I was first starting out.

If only is used to add emphasis to hypothetical situations. With past events it can also be used to express regret and/or criticism. Look at the following alternative ways of saying the same thing.

1 If only ...	
2 I wish ...	she hadn't told him.
3 I'd rather/sooner ...	

In each case:

a Did she tell him?
b How does the speaker feel about this?

2 If the subject is the same in both parts of a sentence introduced by *would rather, would sooner, would prefer to* or *would like to*, a perfect infinitive is used when referring to the past, e.g.

I'd rather/sooner have seen it with subtitles. Wouldn't you?
She'd prefer to have travelled on her own.
He'd like to have come, but he's very busy these days.

How does the meaning change if the present infinitive, *see, travel* and *come*, is used in these sentences?

Practice

For **1–6**, complete the second sentence so that it has a similar meaning to the first sentence.

1 If only I'd gone to France instead.
I'd sooner ______________________________ .
2 I do think you might have phoned earlier.
I wish ______________________________ .
3 We don't think you should have done that.
We'd rather ______________________________ .
4 Don't you regret not going to university?
Don't you wish ______________________________ ?
5 If only you'd mentioned it before!
You should ______________________________ !
6 Do you wish you had stayed longer?
Would you like ______________________________ ?

B Past conditionals

1 Third conditional sentences can be used to talk about imaginary situations in the past, as in this example:

If the police had received this information earlier, they might have had more success in solving the crime.

Here is a more formal way of expressing the underlined part of the sentence:

Had the police received this information earlier, they might have had ...

2 Match each sentence beginning **1–6** with an appropriate ending, **a–f**.

***Example:** 1 c*

1 If she hadn't found his name on the Internet,
2 Had I known it was going to rain so heavily,
3 If it hadn't been for her quick thinking,
4 If I didn't have three kids and a mortgage,
5 If they hadn't lost their last three matches,
6 If I got into trouble at school,

a she could have had a serious accident.
b they'd be top of the league now.
c they might never have seen each other again.
d my parents used to stop my pocket money.
e I'd have given up this job a long time ago.
f I would have taken my waterproofs.

3 Look at the sentences in exercise **2** and answer these questions.

1 Which sentences are third conditionals?
2 Which sentences include a combination of past and present time reference (mixed conditionals)?
3 Which sentence uses the past simple to refer to past time?

Read more about the points in sections **A** and **B** opposite in Part A of the Grammar reference on pages 216 and 217.

Practice

1 Rewrite the ideas expressed in the following sentences using the structures studied in **A** and **B** opposite. Write one sentence for each situation, using a different structure each time.

Example:
We didn't get back in time to see him. It was a real shame.
If only we'd got back in time to see him.

1 He didn't revise for his exams. He regrets this now.
2 I didn't take any books with me on holiday. I got really bored.
3 It's a good job Steve was there. Thanks to him we were able to get the car started.
4 My parents bought me an iPod. An iPad would have been better.
5 I couldn't see the film on telly last night. That was a pity – I really wanted to.
6 My French isn't very good. That's probably why I didn't get the job.
7 They showed us all their holiday snaps. I was hoping to watch the football.

2 With a partner write a six-line dialogue. The first or last line of the dialogue must be one of these sentences.

I wish you'd told the truth.
I'd rather you hadn't lent it to him.
If only you'd been there – it was so funny.
I'd love to have seen his face when he found out.
If it hadn't been for your stupidity, we wouldn't be in this mess.

3 Read your dialogue to another pair of students, but do not read out the sentence from exercise **2**. Can the other students guess which sentence you chose?

Word formation: Adjectives and adverbs

1 In the first and third conversations in Listening 1, which suffix was added to all of the following nouns to create adjectives?

count________ limit________ point________

2 Using the suffixes in the box, write the corresponding adjective for each of the words below. The same suffix is needed for all three words in each group, though spelling changes may be required in some of them. The exercise begins with an example (**0**).

-ory	-less	-able	-ent	-ative	-ial	~~-ic~~	-ous	-y

0	allergy	*allergic*	science	*scientific*	drama	*dramatic*
1	approach	________	apply	________	believe	________
2	argument	________	administer	________	provoke	________
3	introduce	________	contradict	________	prepare	________
4	chat	________	mud	________	rock	________
5	luxury	________	mystery	________	monster	________
6	end	________	price	________	sleep	________
7	persist	________	appear	________	obey	________
8	manager	________	secretary	________	territory	________

3 Complete each gap with the appropriate form of the word in capitals at the end of the line. The word you need may be an adjective or an adverb. A negative affix may also be needed. The exercise begins with an example (**0**).

0 I don't understand how he got the job. He's far too *incompetent* to be put in charge of a school. **COMPETENCE**

1 Her work has been acclaimed for its sensitivity of style and ________________ use of imagery. **IMAGINE**

2 Her performance at work was considered ________________ and her contract was not renewed. **SATISFY**

3 It is becoming ________________ difficult for artists to obtain public funding for their work. **INCREASE**

4 The assistants in Gamidges are unhelpful and ________________ . I shall shop elsewhere in future! **COURTESY**

5 My grandfather was extremely ________________ about astronomy; the planets were his great passion. **KNOWLEDGE**

6 We strayed from the path at some point and got ________________ lost. **HOPE**

7 Although several companies made ________________ losses, the market as a whole was buoyant. **SUBSTANCE**

8 The bookcase was placed ________________ near the door to hide a huge crack in the wall. **STRATEGY**

Writing
Part 2

Report

1 Read the following Part 2 task, then look at the two sample answers on page 35 and decide which is better.

You have been asked to **write a report** for an international research company about the nature and quality of advertising in your country.

Your report should
- describe some of the positive and negative aspects of **two** different forms of advertising in your country.
- say how effective these advertising methods are.
- suggest one or two changes which could be introduced to counter the negative aspects.

Write your **report** in **220–260** words.

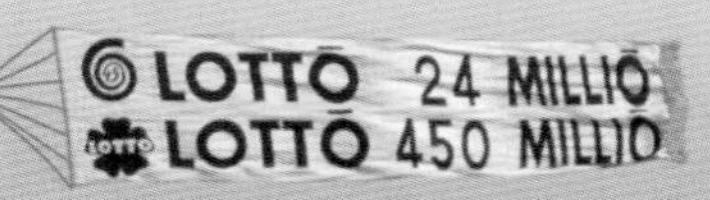

A

Introduction

The aim of this report is to outline the positive and negative features of two different forms of advertising in my country, namely roadside hoardings and banners trailed by light aircraft. It will also consider the effectiveness of these methods and make recommendations for improvements.

Advertising hoardings

These add a touch of colour and sometimes humour to our otherwise drab urban landscapes. Moreover, the size of the posters and the pithiness of the accompanying slogans attract the attention of passers-by and help make the advertisements memorable.

Unfortunately, however, hoardings are also to be found in rural areas, where they appear unsightly and are clearly out of place. In addition, the advertisements can lead drivers to lose their concentration momentarily and are a relatively common cause of accidents.

Aeroplane advertising

Equally distracting are banners attached to light aircraft, which fly for extended periods over our built-up areas and popular coastal resorts. Furthermore, the noise is a considerable source of irritation to local residents and the consumption of large quantities of air fuel can only be harmful to the environment.

On the other hand, aeroplane banners are currently enjoying great success here as an advertising medium. This is largely due to the originality of the approach and its difference from mainstream alternatives.

Recommendations

To discourage noise, air and visual pollution, I would recommend restricting the location of hoardings to towns and cities and limiting the amount of flying time for advertising aircraft. Additionally, smaller hoardings might reduce the risk of accidents caused by distracted drivers.

B

In this report I'm going to describe some of the positive and negative aspects of two different forms of advertising, say how effective these advertising methods are and suggest one or two changes which could be introduced to counter the negative aspects.

Advertising hoardings are very colourful and sometimes very funny, and they look good in our sad, grey cities. And they're very big, too, with interesting slogans and that makes people look at them and remember them.

But you get them in the countryside, too. They look ugly and I don't think they should be there. They also cause accidents because people look at them when they're driving.

Banners pulled by small aeroplanes also cause accidents. The aeroplanes fly for a long time over the cities and beaches. They're noisy too and that irritates people and they use up a lot of petrol. That's bad for the environment.

But banners like this are very successful here because they're original and different from the typical advertising techniques.

I think they should make it illegal to have hoardings in the countryside and not let aeroplanes with banners fly for very long.

That would stop all the noise, the pollution and the ugly views. And hoardings should be smaller because then they might not distract drivers and cause accidents.

2 The content of the two answers is roughly the same, but the type of language used is very different. Work with your partner.

Comment on the following features in each answer:

- linking devices
- number of nouns
- types of adjective

What other differences do you notice?

Find examples in **A** of how the writer makes reference to his/her country.

3 Now write your own answer to the task on page 34.

How to go about it

- Decide on the two forms of advertising. Choose from TV, radio, the Internet, mailshots, telephone, newspapers and magazines, fliers, transport, sports events or any other medium used in your country.
- For each method, note down your ideas in four separate columns: *Positive aspects, Negative aspects, Effectiveness, Recommendations.*
- Look at the adjectives in section **C** on page 209 and decide which, if any, will be relevant to your answer.
- Decide how you will organize your ideas into paragraphs. The paragraph structure in the two sample answers is one possibility. How else could you structure your report?
- Write your report using a consistently formal style. Aim to use a wide range of vocabulary and a greater number of nouns than verbs.

Listening 2
Part 3

Multiple choice 1.13

1 Do you know where the following languages are spoken?

Sami Breton Ladin Provençal Frisian Galego

2 You will hear a woman called Helena Drysdale being interviewed about her research for a book on minority languages. For questions **1–6**, choose the answer (**A**, **B**, **C** or **D**) which fits best according to what you hear.

What to expect in the exam

Part 3 of the Listening paper always contains six multiple-choice questions about a conversation or interview between two or more speakers. The recording lasts approximately four minutes.

1 The main purpose of Helena's journey was to
- **A** establish precisely where Europe's minority languages are spoken.
- **B** investigate the effects of climate and location on language.
- **C** calculate the exact number of minority languages in Europe.
- **D** assess the current condition of Europe's minority languages.

2 One problem of living in the mobile home was that
- **A** there wasn't much space.
- **B** the children had nowhere to play.
- **C** it became very hot.
- **D** they all got bored with each other.

3 What does Helena say about the people she met?
- **A** Not all of them spoke a minority language.
- **B** Some were more willing than others to express their views.
- **C** Intellectuals gave more biased information than other people.
- **D** Older people had a rather unbalanced view of the situation.

4 We learn that people who were punished for speaking Provençal
- **A** did not take their punishment seriously.
- **B** felt they were treated unfairly.
- **C** were made to feel embarrassed.
- **D** regretted what they had done.

5 What point does Helena make about some local people in a tourist area?
- **A** They are not interested in preserving their culture.
- **B** They complain too much about tourists.
- **C** They sell their land in order to make large profits.
- **D** Their actions are not consistent with their opinions.

6 According to Helena, language
- **A** enables people to express their emotions.
- **B** is an expression of one's identity.
- **C** is the key to integration.
- **D** makes everyone different.

3 Are any minority languages spoken in your country? Is anything done to ensure their survival? Do you think more could or should be done?

Helena says: *If you spoke a different language, you'd be a different person.* Do you agree with her? Why/Why not?

Language focus 2: Present and future conditionals

1 Match each of the conditional sentences from the listening with one of the explantions **a–c**.

Zero conditional: *If you cut (a tree back), it grows much stronger.*
First conditional: *If no positive action is taken, they'll simply die out.*
Second conditional: *If you spoke a different language, you'd be a different person.*

a an imaginary situation in the present or future
b a possible future situation and its probable result
c a situation which is always true

2 Look at the following alternative structures to those used in two of the above examples from the listening.

First conditional

If + happen to/should makes an event seem more unlikely, or more of a chance possibility.

If I happen to ... *see anything I think she might like for her birthday, I'll buy it.*
If I should (happen to) ...

In more formal contexts, the following inversion is possible:

Should you require any further information, please do not hesitate to contact us.

Second conditional

A *If + were to* + verb also makes an event seem more unlikely.

If I were to tell the boss what you've just said, he'd probably sack you.
Again, an inversion is possible in formal contexts:
Were you to accept our proposal, some funding would be made available to you.

B Compare the following two structures. Which refers to the present and which to the past?

If it weren't for my dog, I'd probably go away more.
If it hadn't been for his time in prison, he might have got the job.

C *Supposing/Suppose/Imagine* can all be used instead of *if*, especially in everyday speech.
Imagine you lost your job. What would you do?

3 For **1–6** opposite, find one unnecessary word in each sentence or pair of sentences. The word is either grammatically incorrect or does not fit in with the sense of the sentence(s).

Example:
If you ~~would~~ have enough time, will you help me to clean the garage out?

1 If it weren't broken for my leg, I'd definitely run in the London Marathon next month.
2 It's very unlikely you'll see her at the concert, but if you should happen bump into her, give her my regards, won't you?
3 She's always moaning about him – I wouldn't be in the least bit surprised if she would split up with him soon.
4 I know you don't think there's much chance of it happening, but just if suppose you did win first prize. How do you think you'd spend all that money?
5 Imagine that you came face to face with a bull: what might be the sensible thing to do? Would you have run away, for example?
6 We'd have to come to some sort of decision ourselves if the meeting were to put off for any reason.

If + will/would/going to

1 In some situations *if* can be followed by *will, would* or *going to* in the same clause. Match each of the functions in the box with one of the sentences **1–5**, according to the idea expressed in the *if* clause. The exercise begins with an example (**0**).

Willingness	Refusal	~~Request~~
Intention	Insistence	Result

0 If you'll come this way, Ms Taylor will see you now.
Request

1 If you will keep eating chocolate, it's no wonder you're putting on weight.
2 If you won't turn your music down, we'll just have to call the police.
3 If it'll help you relax, I'll get you a drink or something.
4 If we're going to go for a walk, I think we should leave now.
5 If you would just let me explain, I'm sure you'd change your mind.

2 Choose three of the sentences in exercise **1** and for each one rewrite the second clause (the part after the comma). Ask your partner to match each of the new sentence halves to an appropriate *if* clause in exercise **1**.

Example:
0 ... I'll show you where the lift is.

Read more about present and future conditionals in Part B of the Grammar reference on page 217.

Reading and Use of English Part 7

Gapped text

1 In what ways is smell an important source of information?

Think of three smells which are in some way important to you, and tell your partner about them. Do you like the smells? Do they bring back any memories?

What precautions would you need to take if you had no sense of smell?

2 You are going to read an extract from a newspaper article. Six paragraphs have been removed from the extract. Choose from the paragraphs **A–G** the one which fits each gap (**1–6**). There is one extra paragraph which you do not need to use.

How to go about it

- Before you start to make any choices, read through the base text (the main text with the gaps) and answer the following question:
  How can people's lives be affected by having no sense of smell?
- Read all the missing paragraphs and then try to decide where each one should go. (Remember, there is one extra paragraph.) Some parts of the article have been underlined to help you.
  When making your choices, be sure to look at the information both before and after the gap. Underline those parts of the missing paragraphs which help you reach your decision.
- Finally, check your answers by reading the whole article again to ensure that it makes sense. Check that the extra paragraph does not fit into any of the gaps.

SCENTS AND SENSITIVITY

She has never known the fragrance of a beautiful flower – or been able to tell by sniffing whether food is safe to eat. Lucy Mangan on being born with no sense of smell

I am not a fully sentient being. I am referring to the fact that 5 I am congenitally anosmic; or, as I more helpfully put it when people thrust perfumed articles under my nose and invite an opinion on the aroma, I was born without a sense of smell.

1 ______

That experience, however, does not compare to the time I was persuaded by school friends that as I couldn't smell Emma 10 Webster's perfume, I should drink it. This was, I recall, on the grounds that taste and smell are so closely linked that it would give me at least some idea of the delicious scent I was missing. Alas, all it taught me was that perfume is not a beverage, and I was left feeling sick for days.

2 ______

15 I had enough sense to buy a smoke alarm, but it wasn't until my sister called round and nearly collapsed from the smell of a hob burner I had accidentally switched on that I realized I needed a detector that would alert me aurally to gas leaks before I blew up the street. A few bouts of food poisoning 20 alerted me to the fact that I can eat food which would cause those with functioning nasal passages to call in the public health authorities. I now check best-before dates assiduously and treat three-day-old milk with the respect it deserves.

3 ______

I subscribe to the 'what you've never had, you never miss' 25 school of thought, but for those who lose their sense of smell, the effect on their quality of life can be enormous. Professor Tim Jacob at Cardiff University, who researches olfaction, explains 'Anosmics will have found other ways of adapting, using texture and consistency to get information about food. 30 But people who once relied on their sense of smell do not know how to cope without it.'

4 ______

And those are just the obvious things. As Jacob also notes: 'You lose lots of subliminal information and links with the emotional centres of the brain. Smells are inextricably linked 35 with memories and form the backdrop to your sensory experience. The smell of your first girlfriend's perfume or boyfriend's aftershave, anything associated with strong emotion, will always trigger a rush of memory.'

5 ______

Alarmed at the thought of producing sickly babies, I enquire 40 about treatment. For those who have lost their sense of smell through infection or damage, the news is relatively good. 'They usually regain some ability because the olfactory nerve is capable of regeneration,' says David Roberts, ear, nose and throat consultant at Guy's & St Thomas's Hospital 45 in London.

6 ______

I will have to soldier on, and draw what comfort I can from a recent exchange with an ex-boyfriend who, as we reminisced about our relationship said wistfully, 'You were the best 50 girlfriend in the world. You let me eat all the garlic I wanted and it didn't bother you.' I'm putting it in my next personal ad.

A Naturally, the problems of being olfactorily-challenged don't compare to those which attend blindness or deafness. Nevertheless, certain things do have to be taken into account, and certain precautions taken, which you only fully appreciate when you start living alone.

B 'The tongue can only distinguish the four basic tastes: bitter, sweet, salty, sour. Smell detects flavour and nuance, so they lose all significant sense of taste. About 17% become clinically depressed. Some become oversensitive about having body odour and are frightened of going out.'

C Steroid-based drug treatments can help further. Nasal polyps causing blockages to olfactory passageways can be treated medically and surgically. But, as one might expect, less can be done to rectify causes one is born with.

D 'It's a very emotive sense,' he explains. 'The nerves stimulated by smell send messages to one of the oldest, most primitive parts of our brain, which is why it's so integral to our lives and why people feel they cannot do without it.'

E It took until I was seven to convince my mother of this. She reluctantly acknowledged the truth of my claim after making me sniff the fumes from her bottle of nail varnish remover until I looked up hopefully and said 'My eyes are burning – is that what you mean?'

F I am beginning to feel quite intrigued by this unknown world of smells taking you back in time, but this quickly deepens into concern about what else I am missing. 'And, of course, you are attracted to people who smell different from you, because it suggests they have a different immunotype,' says Jacob. 'It's the evolutionary system trying to get you to pass on two sets of immunity advantages to your offspring.'

G I have also learnt to stock my shelves with visitors as well as myself in mind. So I have fruit teas in the house even though they appear to be nothing more than an expensive way of colouring a mugful of hot water, and herbs, even though they are a matter of supreme indifference to me. When I cook for other people and a recipe says 'season to taste', I have to hope for the best.

Vocabulary: Smell

Adjective + noun collocations

1 **a** Complete each gap with a word from the box.

bodies	bread	coffee	fruit
fumes	milk	rubber	spices

1 The **stale smell** of sweaty _________ .
2 The **acrid odour** of burning _________ and petrol _________ .
3 The **mouth-watering aroma** of freshly brewed _________ and baked _________ .
4 The **rancid smell** of sour _________ and butter that has long since passed its sell-by date.
5 The **pungent aroma** of herbs and _________ and ripe tropical _________ .

b Where might you find the above smells?

Example:

1 You might notice this smell in a gym changing room or on a crowded bus.

2 Arrange the adjectives in **bold** in exercise **1** into the columns below, according to their meaning. The first one has been done for you.

Positive	**Negative**	**Neutral**
	stale	

3 Add the following adjectives to the columns in exercise **2**.

fresh	faint	strong	musty	sweet
unmistakable	overpowering	sickly		

4 Do the speaking activity on page 204.

3 Review

Reading and Use of English
Part 3

Word formation

For questions **1–8**, read the text below. Use the word given in capitals at the end of some of the lines to form a word that fits in the gap **in the same line**. There is an example at the beginning (**0**). Write your answers **IN CAPITAL LETTERS**.

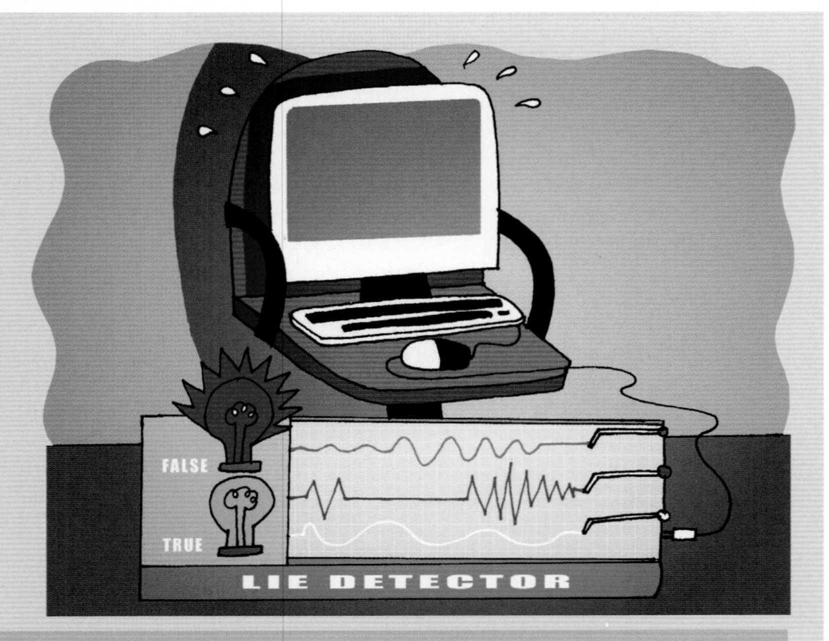

Don't forget!

- You may need to write the negative or plural form of a word.
- Check the spelling of your answers. No marks are given for a word which is misspelt.

CAN YOU TRUST THE INTERNET?

There is a general **(0)** AWARENESS amongst internet users that	**AWARE**
online articles which seem to be based on thorough research	
and academic study, are not always as **(1)** .... as they	**FACT**
claim. Online, a writer has the kind of **(2)** .... powers	**EDIT**
that no ordinary journalist or author would ever have, and the	
reader is forced to distinguish between what is **(3)**	**OBJECT**
and what is mere opinion. And even sites which were once thought	
to be **(4)** .... now suffer from attacks carried out by	**RELY**
internet vandals intending to cause deliberate **(5)**	**ACCURATE**
with statistics. Another **(6)** .... issue is that of writers	**CONTROVERSY**
claiming to have academic backgrounds or **(7)**	**EXPERT**
in an area when they do not. Online encyclopaedia Wikipedia	
once admitted that one of their editors, a professor of	
religious studies who other editors believed to be entirely	
(8) .... , was actually a 24-year-old student	**TRUST**
called Ryan Jordan. Before he was unmasked, Jordan had made	
over 20 000 alterations to the entries people had posted on	
the encyclopaedia.	

Open cloze

For questions **1–8**, read the text below and think of the word which best fits each gap. Use only **one** word in each gap. There is an example at the beginning (**0**). Write your answers **IN CAPITAL LETTERS**.

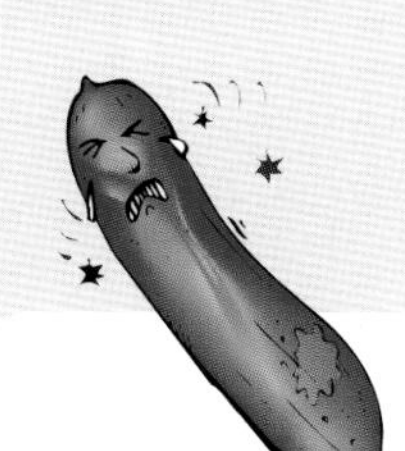

Don't forget!

- Always read the text through once before you start to complete the gaps.
- Look carefully at the words and sentences both before and after a gap.

LISTENING TO VEGETABLES

Scientists have developed a method of listening to sounds from plants normally inaudible **(0)** ...TO... the human ear. When a leaf or stem is sliced, the plant signals distress **(1)** .... releasing the gas ethylene over its surface. The gas molecules are collected in a bell jar and bombarded with laser beams, **(2)** .... makes them vibrate. The resultant sound waves are detected with a sensitive microphone. The scientists have discovered that the **(3)** .... a plant is subjected to stress, the louder the signal.

One surprising result came from an apparently healthy cucumber that was virtually shouting **(4)** .... agony. A closer study showed it **(5)** .... developed a harmful fungus. Listening to plants in this **(6)** .... could be of great benefit to farmers in detecting pests and disease, and as an aid to efficient storing and transporting. Apples, for instance, give **(7)** .... high levels of ethylene, increasing with ripeness and causing neighbouring fruit to rot. Invisible differences of ripeness could be detected acoustically, enabling fruit to be separated so **(8)** .... to prolong its freshness.

Key word transformation

For questions **1–6**, complete the second sentence so that it has a similar meaning to the first sentence, using the word given. **Do not change the word given.** You must use between **three** and **six** words, including the word given. Here is an example (**0**). Write your answers **IN CAPITAL LETTERS**.

0 If the bank refuses to lend us money, we might have to ask your parents instead.
REQUEST
If the bank turns ...DOWN OUR REQUEST FOR... a loan, we might have to ask your parents instead.

1 Having a holiday together was a mistake because we argued all the time.
NEVER
I wish .... on holiday together because we argued all the time.

2 You were not supposed to tell anyone about my news!
SECRET
I'd rather .... instead of telling everyone!

3 Although I wanted to quit smoking gradually, my doctor told me to stop immediately.
PREFER
I .... up smoking gradually, but my doctor told me to stop immediately.

4 I would find Andy more attractive if he didn't laugh at strange things.
SENSE
If it were .... humour, I would find Andy quite attractive.

5 If you should ever come to France, please feel free to visit us.
HAPPEN
Please feel free to visit us .... to France.

6 The most likely reason for the scientists getting the conclusion wrong is that they were not thorough enough with their research.
PROBABLY
If their research had been more thorough, the scientists .... to the wrong conclusion.

Ready for Use of English

Introduction

In the **Reading and Use of English** paper, you have 90 minutes to complete eight different tasks. In this unit, we will look at three of the four Use of English tasks:

Part 1 Multiple-choice cloze

Part 3 Word formation

Part 4 Key word transformation

We will look at the four Reading tasks, Parts 5–8, on pages 82–89.

Part 1: Multiple-choice cloze

1 **a** What effects do you think noise might have on the behaviour of birds that live in towns and cities?

b Read the text below, ignoring the gaps, and compare your ideas.

2 For questions **1–8**, read the text below and decide which answer (**A**, **B**, **C** or **D**) best fits each gap. There is an example at the beginning (**0**).

Twitter in the city

While cities and urban areas are attractive, food-rich environments for birds, there is a **(0)** .... to be paid. And the **(1)** .... of living in a noisy environment can be significant for birds that use acoustic signals to attract mates, defend territories, **(2)** .... of dangers and deter competitors. Many human beings find urban noise uncomfortable, but for birds, having vital communications drowned or muffled **(3)** .... their breeding and survival.

Research indicates that birds are **(4)** .... to the challenge by adapting their acoustic signals so they can be heard above the urban din. Their songs are becoming shorter, louder and with longer pauses. They are also increasingly singing at night, when noise **(5)** .... are lower. And there's **(6)** .... of an ability to adjust songs by leaving out lower pitch notes which would be drowned by traffic noise.

Some researchers believe that these changes will **(7)** .... to urban and rural birds of the same species becoming reproductively isolated. It's also been suggested that birds and species which **(8)** .... to adapt will abandon city life, reducing urban biodiversity.

	A	B	C	D
0	**A** charge	**B** price	**C** value	**D** fee
1	**A** downturn	**B** downfall	**C** downside	**D** downgrade
2	**A** warn	**B** notice	**C** announce	**D** declare
3	**A** risks	**B** suffers	**C** intimidates	**D** threatens
4	**A** lifting	**B** emerging	**C** elevating	**D** rising
5	**A** levels	**B** heights	**C** amounts	**D** degrees
6	**A** basis	**B** support	**C** evidence	**D** mark
7	**A** result	**B** lead	**C** bring	**D** end
8	**A** omit	**B** decline	**C** wait	**D** fail

Don't forget!

Read through the whole text before you start making your choices.

3 In the Part 1 Multiple-choice cloze task, an option may be correct for one or more of the following reasons:

a It is part of a collocation or set phrase, e.g. ***0*** *(there is a) price (to be paid)*

b It fits the meaning of the sentence, e.g. ***1*** *downside*

c It fits the surrounding grammar, e.g. ***2*** *warn (**of** dangers)*

For answers **3–8** in exercise **2** on page 42, say which factors, **a–c**, are important when choosing the correct answer.

4 For questions **1–8**, read the text below and decide which answer (**A**, **B**, **C** or **D**) best fits each gap. There is an example at the beginning (**0**).

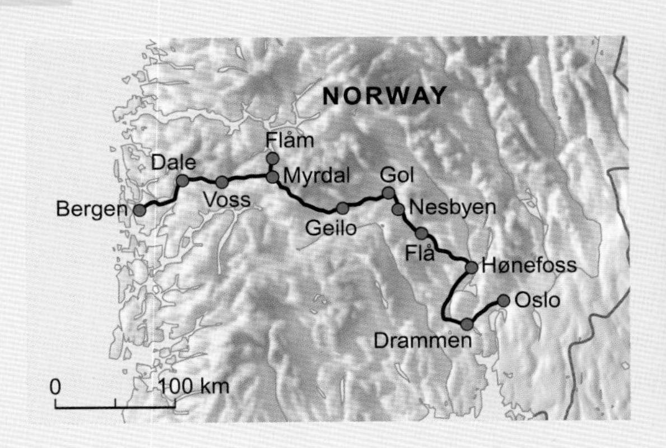

The Bergen Line

Few European railways **(0)** .... such desolate mountain terrain as the 310-mile line **(1)** .... Norway's capital with its principal port and second city, Bergen. It is the highest mainline railway in northern Europe, **(2)** .... the Hardangervidda plateau at 4060ft, and for nearly 60 miles it is above the tree line, in terrain with few **(3)** .... of human life.

It was also one of the most difficult railways to build. There were few roads for supplies; deep snow and freezing temperatures for months on **(4)** .... reduced productive days; and 11¼ miles of tunnel had to be bored, mostly through solid gneiss. The line opened in **(5)** .... from 1883, one of the opening trains becoming **(6)** .... in snow, but the first scheduled train for Bergen did not leave Oslo until 1908.

It has become a popular journey for tourists, not only for the main line itself but also as a way to **(7)** .... access to the branch line and the fjord village of Flåm. Snow is a **(8)** .... almost throughout the year, because the average snow-line in Norway is at about 3000ft, compared with 7000ft in Switzerland.

0	**A** travel	**B** transcend	**C** <u>traverse</u>	**D** transfer
1	**A** relating	**B** bonding	**C** linking	**D** combining
2	**A** reaching	**B** acquiring	**C** scanning	**D** ranging
3	**A** marks	**B** proofs	**C** factors	**D** signs
4	**A** end	**B** time	**C** row	**D** line
5	**A** pieces	**B** sections	**C** portions	**D** segments
6	**A** surrounded	**B** loaded	**C** buried	**D** fallen
7	**A** hold	**B** gain	**C** make	**D** bring
8	**A** feature	**B** vision	**C** part	**D** deal

Part 3: Word formation

What to expect in the exam

Part 3 contains a text with eight gaps, each of which has to be filled with the correct form of a word given in capital letters. In the example below, the infinitive form of the verb is needed after the modal *can*. The missing words are usually nouns, adjectives, adverbs and occasionally verbs. Sometimes the words you write will need to be in the plural, and sometimes a negative form is required. The meaning of the text surrounding the gaps will help you to decide.

1 For questions **1–8**, read the text below. Use the word given in capitals at the end of some of the lines to form a word that fits in the gap **in the same line**. Use the words in **bold** to help you to decide on the correct form of your answer. There is an example at the beginning (**0**). Write your answers **IN CAPITAL LETTERS**.

What a pain!

We've all felt pain at some time or other, but what is its function	
and **how can we (0)** ..*MINIMIZE*.. **it** in our lives?	**MINIMUM**
According to the International Association for the Study of Pain,	
the (1) .... **of pain** is as follows: 'an unpleasant **sensory**	**DEFINE**
and (2) .... **experience** associated with actual or	**EMOTION**
potential tissue damage.'	
Our understanding of pain is influenced by **a (3)** .... **of**	**VARY**
factors including **our (4)** .... **state**, memories of past	**PSYCHOLOGY**
pains, and how our **cultural (5)** .... **affect** our lives. Some	**BELIEVE**
people believe that women **should (6)** .... **have** a much	**THEORY**
greater (7) .... **for** pain than men, since they are capable	**TOLERATE**
of giving birth, which can be intensely painful. **However**, one study	
conducted at the University of Bath in the UK involving men and	
women submerging their arms in iced water, actually discovered	
that the women found the pain **more (8)** .... **than** the	**BEAR**
men did.	

Don't forget!

Check the spelling of the words you write. No marks will be awarded for a misspelt word.

2 Describe each answer in exercise **1** using the words in the box below.

noun	adjective	adverb	verb
negative	plural	prefix	spelling

Example:

(0) 'Minimize' is a verb. It requires a spelling change to form the ending 'ize'.

3 You are going to read a short text entitled *Moths count!* What do you think the text will be about?

4 Turn to page 205. Read through the text quite quickly, ignoring the gaps, and check your predictions.

Then read the text again and for questions **1–8**, use the word given in capitals at the end of some of the lines to form a word that fits in the gap **in the same line**.

Part 4: Key word transformation

For questions **1–6**, complete the second sentence so that it has a similar meaning to the first sentence, using the word given. **Do not change the word given.** You must use between **three** and **six** words, including the word given. Write your answers **IN CAPITAL LETTERS**.

What to expect in the exam

- Part 4 requires you to use a range of structures to express ideas in different ways. You are tested on your knowledge of both lexis and grammar.
- The key word might be part of a collocation, a phrasal verb or a set phrase. It might relate to a particular grammar point or it could be a synonym or antonym of a word in the first sentence.
- When you complete each gap, pay attention to the correct use of verb patterns, prepositions, negatives, conjunctions and so on.
- Answer the questions in *italics* after each pair of sentences before you complete the task. Questions like these will not appear in the exam.

1 Karen's shyness means that she tries not to speak about anything personal in front of other people.
HERSELF
Karen prefers to avoid .... public, as she is terribly shy.
Which key verb in the first question is missing from the second?
Is 'avoid' followed by a gerund or infinitive?
What preposition goes before 'public' so that it means 'in front of other people'?

2 It would be a good idea if you could lose a couple of kilos.
WEIGHT
I don't think that .... you any harm.
To form the subject of the clause after 'I don't think that', do we use the gerund or infinitive?
What common verb begins the expression '... you any harm'?

3 I think this report needed to be written more carefully.
CARE
You should .... writing this report.
Is the speaker referring to past, present or future?
What verb often collocates with 'care'?

4 Since the director could not speak at the awards ceremony himself, one of the actors took his place.
BEHALF
One of the actors made .... the director at the awards ceremony.
What noun is formed from the verb 'speak'?
What two prepositions go on either side of 'behalf'?

5 After the noise from the machine has stopped, you can open the lid.
UNTIL
Do not open the lid of the machine .... that noise.
Which of the following structures means that the verb/activity no longer happens:
stop + gerund or stop + infinitive
What verb often collocates with 'noise'?

6 I regret not concentrating more on what the teacher said during my French lessons.
ATTENTION
I now wish .... the teacher during my French lessons.
What structure comes after 'wish' to refer to a past regret? (See Unit 3)
Which verb often collocates with 'attention'?
What preposition follows 'attention'?

4 Work time

Language focus 1: Punctuation

1 Read the following quotations on the theme of work. Comment on each one with your partner, saying whether you like or dislike it, agree or disagree with it. Give reasons for your opinions.

1 'Work is a necessary evil to be avoided.

Mark Twain

2 'Hard work never killed anybody, but why take a chance.'

Charlie McCarthy

3 'People, who work sitting down get paid more than people who work standing up.'

Ogden Nash

4 'I like work; it fascinates me I can sit and look at it for hours.'

Jerome K. Jerome

5 'A lot of fellows nowadays have a BA, MD or PhD. Unfortunately, they dont have a JOB.'

Fats Domino

6 'Its not the hours you put in your work that counts, it's the work you put in the hours.'

Sam Ewing

7 'Far and away the best prize that life offer's is the chance to work hard at work worth doing.'

Theodore Roosevelt

2 Each of the quotations above contains one punctuation mistake. Find the mistakes and correct them.

Read more about punctuation in the Grammar reference on page 217.

3 Punctuate the following newspaper article on working trends in Britain. Add capital letters where necessary.

HOME-WORKING

if you had the choice would you prefer to work from home or in an office British workers seem to be in no doubt one in four of them has given up commuting to the office in favour of a more domestic working environment and the figure is growing

the number of home-workers is likely to increase by more than 50% over the next five years claimed a spokesperson for Datamonitor the London-based market research company as a result of this trend consumers will spend a great deal less on certain goods and services transport petrol eating out and drinks moreover because home-workers usually take fewer showers the sale of personal care products such as deodorants and soap will also be affected

the study which shows that home-workers tend to be the more highly qualified professionals in a company says that firms are in danger of losing their best employees if they do not allow home-working unfortunately however there are some who abuse the trust which has been placed in them Datamonitor discovered that many like to watch television listen to the radio and browse social networking sites while they work

4 Check your answer with the suggested version.

5 What are the advantages and disadvantages of home-working?

Would you prefer to work from home?

Listening 1
Part 4

Multiple matching 1.14–1.18

1 What advice would you give to someone going for a job interview?

Example: *Dress smartly.*

2 You will hear five short extracts in which people are talking about interviews they attended.

How to go about it

- Read through both tasks carefully before you start to listen. Note that in Task One, you are listening for the advice the person received, not what they actually did.
- Try to predict the language you might hear for each prompt.

  Example:

  A mind your body language – the way you sit or stand; what you do with your arms, hands and legs.
- Concentrate mainly, but not exclusively, on Task One the first time you listen. The second time you listen, give more attention to Task Two.
- Don't leave any questions unanswered.

TASK ONE

For questions **1–5**, choose from the list **(A–H)** the advice each speaker received.

TASK TWO

For questions **6–10**, choose from the list **(A–H)** the problem each speaker encountered.

While you listen you must complete both tasks.

Task One:

A mind your body language
B arrive early for the interview
C wear the right clothes
D show interest in the prospective employer
E hide your enthusiasm for the job
F practise the interview beforehand
G think of an unusual situation
H control your nerves

	1
	2
	3
	4
	5

Task Two:

A feeling unwell
B having the wrong information
C not having the right personality
D arriving late for the interview
E having a slight accident
F not having the right qualifications
G being unable to answer questions
H being unhappy about the pay

	6
	7
	8
	9
	10

Don't forget!

- There are two questions for each speaker; one in Task One and one in Task Two. Questions 1 and 6 correspond to the first speaker; questions 2 and 7 to the second speaker, and so on.
- Three of the prompts in each task are not used.

3 If you have had an interview or an oral examination, tell your partner about how you prepared for it, what you remember about the interview and what the outcome was.

If you have never had an interview, tell your partner what you would fear most about going for an interview and what you would do to overcome this fear.

Language focus 2: Gerunds and infinitives

A Review

The following sentences are all from the listening. Discuss with your partner the reasons why the words underlined are in the gerund or the infinitive.

Example:
1 The noun 'way' is often followed by the infinitive. 'Going' is in the gerund because it follows the preposition 'by'; all prepositions take the -ing form of a verb.

1 The best way to prepare for an interview is by going to the company's website.
2 They can see you've done your homework.
3 You're not to get all uptight and on edge.
4 Projecting self-confidence at an interview is vital for success.
5 I put on my best suit to give me that confidence.
6 I think I managed to hide it.
7 It's advisable to lean forward.
8 They recommended imagining the interviewer in the bath.

B Common problems

1 In **1–8** below, there is a mistake in one of the two sentences. Find the mistake and correct it.

Example: *feeling*
a You can't help ~~to feel~~ sorry for John, losing his job like that.
b The company says it'll help him to find another, but it's not the same.

1 a I have been made to feel very welcome in my new job.
b They even let me to leave early so I can pick up my son from school.
2 a It's taken me time to adjust to working in an open-plan office.
b I still can't get used to share the same working space with the boss.
3 a It's not worth to make an effort in my job – the pay is so low.
b And there's certainly no point taking work home at weekends.
4 a We appreciate your agreeing to give a talk at the conference.
b We would like that you are our guest for dinner after your talk.
5 a As soon as I get to work all the phones start ringing.
b They don't stop to ring all day.
6 a I don't mind to go to the office meal tonight, …
b … but I really don't feel like having a cocktail with the boss beforehand.
7 a I advised him to buy a new suit for his interview.
b I also recommended to have a haircut.
8 a We were to have received a pay rise this year.
b Management have admitted to have broken their promise to increase salaries.

Check your ideas in the Grammar reference on page 218.

2 Work with a partner. Talk to each other about something

- you would miss being able to do if you lived abroad.
- you would refuse to do under any circumstances.
- you remember doing when you were a very small child.
- you are planning to do in the next few months.
- you regret doing.
- your parents didn't let you do as a child.
- you always have difficulty doing.
- you often forget to do.

C Nouns followed by the infinitive

Each of the nouns in the box can be followed by the infinitive with *to*. For each question **1–5**, use the information in the informal sentence **a** to complete the gaps in the formal sentence **b**, using the words in the box. You should use each word once only.

effort	attempts	willingness	opportunity
capacity	ability	decision	
determination	tendency	refusal	

1 a It's very obvious that he really wants to get on in the company and he's done a lot to get over his shyness.
b He has shown a clear ________________ to make progress in the company and he has made a great ________________ to overcome his shyness.
2 a She usually thinks it's her fault if work doesn't get done on time, even though I've tried to tell her several times it's not true.
b She has a/an ________________ to blame herself if deadlines are not met, despite my various ________________ to persuade her otherwise.
3 a He never misses a chance to become a better salesman and what I admire most is the fact that he doesn't get fed up if things aren't going well.
b He takes advantage of every ________________ to develop as a salesman, and his ________________ to become despondent in the face of difficulties is his most admirable quality.
4 a He also doesn't seem very capable of controlling his pupils and I think he's right to want to get out of teaching.
b Furthermore, he seems to lack the ________________ to maintain classroom discipline, and I can only support his ________________ to leave the teaching profession.
5 a The best things about her are that she's prepared to take on new challenges and she can handle stressful situations.
b Her greatest strengths are her ________________ to accept new challenges and her ________________ to cope with pressure.

Speaking 1
Part 3

Collaborative task

1 Here are some things that school students can do to help them prepare for their working lives.

Talk to each other about how useful these experiences might be in preparing school students for their working lives.

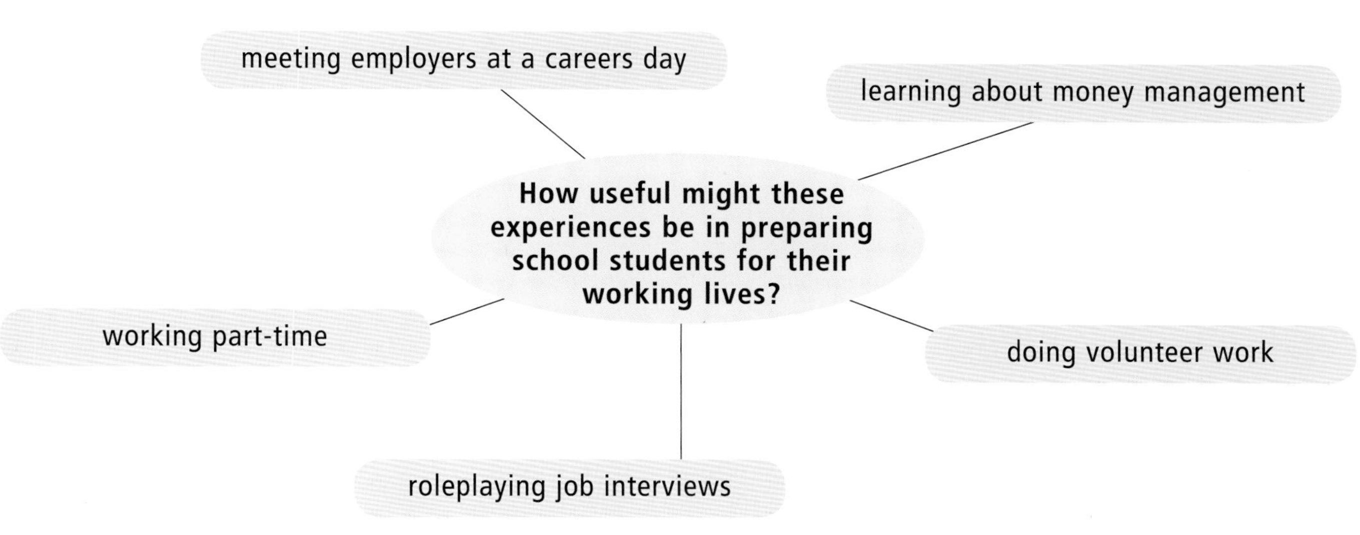

2 Now decide which experience would have the greatest effect on a student's self-confidence.

Writing
Part 1

Essay

What to expect in the exam

In Part 1 of the Writing paper, you are asked to write an essay in response to a proposition and an accompanying input text. The input text will take the form of notes made during a seminar, lecture, panel discussion or documentary. Your essay should be written in a formal and persuasive style. You will be asked to write between 220–260 words.

1 Read the following Essay task and answer the questions below:

a Who is your target reader?

b How many of the listed methods do you need to write about?

c What else do you have to do in your essay?

d Whose opinions are quoted?

e What is the connection between the listed methods and the three opinions?

f Is it necessary to refer to the three opinions?

g What do you need to persuade the target reader about?

Your class has recently watched a TV documentary on what methods governments should use to encourage young people to pursue further education. You have made the notes below:

Methods governments should use to encourage young people to pursue further education

- e-learning
- work placements
- cheaper fees

Some opinions expressed in the TV documentary:

'Nowadays, people should be able to study from home.'

'There should be some guarantee of a job at the end of the course.'

'Maybe young people would go to college if they could afford it.'

Write an essay for your tutor discussing **two** of the methods in your notes. You should **explain which method you think is more important** for governments to consider, **giving reasons** in support of your answer.

You may, if you wish, make use of the opinions expressed in the TV documentary, but you should use your own words as far as possible.

2 Read the model answer and answer the following question.

Which of the listed methods does the writer suggest is more important?

Encouraging school-leavers to take college courses

Over the last ten years there has been a rise in the number of teens finishing their studies at age 16 or 17. Statistics indicate that they are opting to leave school as early as possible, either because they are unable or unwilling to take their education further. It is clear that this could have a long-term impact on the skills, knowledge and qualifications of the general workforce. It is therefore essential that governments find ways to reverse this trend.

We need to begin by asking why young people do not see college as a good option. A major factor is certainly the cost. For many low-income families, course fees, materials and equipment are simply unaffordable. Reducing fees would therefore enable many more students to attend college. However, for the government to do this, it would need to use a very large part of its total budget for education, year after year.

It might be a more practical solution to offer young people more flexibility in *when* and *how* they study. If governments supported colleges in developing online courses and blended learning programmes, more young people could study at a time and place that was convenient to them. Students with daytime jobs, for instance, could choose to do their coursework and view workshops or online webinars in the evening or weekends.

Setting up these kinds of programme would be expensive at first, but once the courses were established, it would be a cost-effective approach. Now we have the technology, we should use it to maximize educational opportunities for the young generation.

3 Which of the three possible paragraph plans, **A**, **B** or **C**, does the essay follow?

A

Introduction:

Explain reasons for young people not pursuing further education.

Central paragraphs:

Explain the advantages and disadvantages of two proposed methods.

State my own opinion about which method is better.

Conclusion:

Summarizing statement

B

Introduction:

Describe effect of young people not pursuing further education and outline methods to be discussed.

Central paragraphs:

Describe one method and give reasons why government should consider it.

Describe second method and say why it might also be considered.

Conclusion:

Weigh up arguments given and state opinion. Give reason(s).

C

Introduction:

Provide general information about the current trend regarding young people and further education. Indicate purpose of essay.

Central paragraphs:

Discuss one proposed method and suggest why it may not be effective.

Discuss second method and give reasons why the government should consider it.

Conclusion:

Reaffirm why one method is preferable to the other.

4 **a** The following structures from the model in exercise **2** could be used in other essays you write:

Over the last ... years there has been ...

Statistics indicate that ...

Underline more structures in the model which could be used in other essays.

b Four different modal verbs are used in the model. Which are they?

5 Read the Part 1 task below and write your essay.

Your class has recently attended a panel discussion on what methods governments should use to prepare young people for working life. You have made the notes below:

Methods governments should use to prepare young people for working life
- apprentice schemes
- work-related subjects at school
- visits from employers

Some opinions expressed in the panel discussion:

'Young people should balance their academic studies with practical experience in a job.'

'Schools must teach things like money management and interview techniques.'

'Maybe kids would choose the right job if they really knew what it was about.'

Write an **essay** for your tutor in **220–260** words discussing **two** of the methods in your notes. You should **explain which method you think is more practical** for governments to propose, **giving reasons** in support of your answer.

You may, if you wish, make use of the opinions expressed in the discussion, but you should use your own words as far as possible.

How to go about it

- There are always three points to choose from in Part 1 writing tasks. Decide which two you want to discuss.
- Decide what ideas relating to these two general points you want to explore.
  Here are some possible ideas for the three methods proposed in this question:
  - ***apprentice schemes:*** *school students go to work for one day during the week, the job should be related to their studies, etc.*
  - ***work-related subjects at school:*** *filling in forms, practising interview techniques, learning about money management, etc.*
  - ***visits from employers:*** *presentations, question-and-answer sessions, opportunities to visit the employer's company, etc.*
- Organize your ideas into logical paragraphs.
  *For this question, follow paragraph plan C in exercise **3**. Note that you could put the more important method in either paragraph two or three, and the same applies for the method which is not so practical.*
- Write your essay using a range of vocabulary and structures.
  Use some of the language you have seen in this writing section.
- Make sure you support your opinions with reasons.

Cross-text multiple matching

1 What 'office politics' situations do the pictures below show?
Have you ever been involved in similar situations at school or work?
What other 'office politics' situations might exist in some companies?
What do you think might be the best way to deal with them?

2 You are going to read four extracts from articles about office politics. For questions **1–4**, choose from the extracts **A–D**. The extracts may be chosen more than once.

How to go about it

- Read the rubric, the title and the subtitle carefully.
  What is the central theme of the four texts?
- Read the four questions and identify the key information to focus on.
  Underline relevant words in the questions. The first one has been done for you.
- Quickly read each of the four texts to get an idea of what each one is about.
- Read each text more carefully to locate a reference to each of the four questions.
  For question 1, the references to the role of managers in text A have been underlined. Now do the same for texts B, C and D.
- Identify the opinion that each writer has on each question and compare it to that of the other writers.
  Which writer has a different opinion from the others on the appropriate role of managers in dealing with office politics? (This will be the answer to question 1.)

Office Politics

Four writers talk about problems at work and how they should be resolved

A

At surface level, the subject of office politics may appear to be a trivial one; images arise of gossiping staff at the photocopier, intra-department emails taking exception to a colleague's time off for childcare commitments, the new assistant manager being given the cold shoulder
5 because of his new dress code policy. Yet all these situations may have a profound impact on the workplace dynamics of any business or industry. Unfortunately, office politics is an area that a number of department heads admit to ignoring, in the vain hope that problems will resolve themselves. Although it is not advisable for them to intervene directly,
10 they do need to get Human Resources involved immediately.

B

It is because office politics has such an impact on company morale and productivity that business leaders must keep their ear to the ground and be alert to potential problems. I should, at this point, set out what I mean by office politics. We are not talking here about minor concerns such as
15 arguments over the timekeeping of workmates, but rather how people will spread blame and employ deception to advance their own interests. By no means is this kind of behaviour common to all workplaces, although it appears to be endemic in television production, banking and advertising. Once they *are* alert, on no account should a department head or other
20 person in authority approach the individuals concerned in a particular 'office politics' situation. Instead, the matter should be dealt with, at least as a first step, by Human Resources, who must be equipped with clear policies.

C

Despite the fact that office politics occurs in all kinds of business, owners and department heads are often irritated whenever the
25 suspicion arises that there are conflicts between staff members. Research suggests that in many cases, they will just turn a blind eye to such situations. This may not matter so much when it comes to petty gossip about the social lives of colleagues outside of work, for example, and besides, this sort of problem does not really fit
30 within the category of office politics. However, when employees are dishonest, taking credit for the work of others or pointing the finger when a mistake is their own, we are dealing with the kind of situation that needs a strong response, which, in the first instance, must be from Human Resources or an intermediary. If senior managers step in before proper
35 procedures have been followed, they risk being accused of favouritism.

D

Over the last decade, my research team and I have studied a range of workplaces with office politics issues, from small family-run enterprises to vast corporations. We have found indisputable evidence that swift and direct intervention by immediate superiors is the most effective way to stop
40 minor issues amongst juniors from getting out of hand and escalating into major crises. Indeed, many of the staff we surveyed said that this approach to dealing with conflict played a large role in maintaining their overall job satisfaction. Essentially, it appears that staff are less likely to bear a grudge against fellow employees or managers when they perceive that a problem
45 has been dealt with in an open and frank manner. Conversely, when they perceive that others have been talking about them behind their backs, resentment is likely to remain. Interestingly enough, these attitudes were held by both long-term employees and more recently-appointed ones.

Which writer

has a different opinion from the others on the appropriate role of managers in dealing with office politics? 1 ___

shares writer B's view regarding the definition of office politics? 2 ___

expresses a different view from the others regarding the extent to which office politics exists in companies? 3 ___

takes a similar view to writer C on the attitudes of some managers towards office politics? 4 ___

Reacting to the text

Some of the writers suggest that people in authority should intervene when there is a dispute or bad feeling between colleagues or people within the same peer group. Do you think this is the right approach? What might it depend upon?

Vocabulary 1: Body idioms

1 a Complete each of the idioms with a part of the body. You may need to use a plural form.

1 ... the new assistant manager **being given the cold** _________ because of his new dress code policy. (A)

2 ... business leaders must **keep their** _________ **to the ground** and be alert to potential problems. (B)

3 Research suggests that in many cases, they will just **turn a blind** _________ **to** such situations. (C)

4 ... when employees are dishonest, taking credit for the work of others or **pointing the** _________ when a mistake is their own ... (C)

5 ... direct intervention by immediate superiors is the most effective way to stop minor issues amongst juniors from **getting out of** _________ and escalating into major crises. (D)

6 ... when they perceive that others have been **talking about them behind their** _________ , resentment is likely to remain. (D)

b Check your answers in the reading text on pages 52 and 53. The letters in brackets refer to the sections in which the idioms can be found.

2 Use the context to work out the meanings of the idioms in exercise **1**.

Speaking 2
Part 2

Long turn

1 Look at these pictures. They show people working in stressful situations.

Student A:
Compare **two** of the pictures, and say what might be causing the stress, and what action the people might take as a result.

Student B:
When your partner has finished talking, say which situation in the two pictures looks more difficult to resolve.

2 Now change roles. Follow the instructions again using the remaining pictures.

Listening 2
Part 2

Sentence completion 1.19

1 'Too much to do and not enough time to do it.' To what extent does this apply to you? How well do you organize your time?

2 You will hear part of a talk by time management expert David Markham. For questions **1–8**, complete the sentences with a word or short phrase.

Don't forget!

Read through all the questions and predict the type of information required.

David says that the key to good time management is **(1)** ....

It's important to have **(2)** .... expectations of what we can achieve.

David warns that **(3)** .... can prevent us achieving what we set out to do.

He recommends giving priority to **(4)** .... if we feel overwhelmed.

David advises against always trying to achieve **(5)** .... in our work.

Housework requires the same **(6)** .... that we need to exercise at work.

David suggests we should reserve time for those pursuits we find **(7)** ....

He says it is a mistake to think of the **(8)** .... as a form of relaxation.

3 Do you manage 'to achieve the right balance between work and relaxation'?

Vocabulary 2: Time

1 Complete each gap in these extracts from the listening with a word from the box.

against	aside	for	for	in	off	up

1 … what you hope to accomplish _____ **the time available** …
2 … you have to phone in sick and **take time** _____ **work**.
3 … if **time is** _____ **you**, if you're **pressed** _____ **time**, … don't worry if what you produce is less than wonderful.
4 … what we all work for is to **make time** _____ **ourselves**, to **free** _____ **time for** the things we really want to do …
5 It's essential to **set** _____ **enough time** to pursue your interests …

2 The following words can all be used before the noun ***time***. Add a word from the box to the appropriate group **a–f**, then discuss the possible context in which you might expect to use or hear the collocations.

half	flying	harvest	prime	record-breaking	sale	~~spare~~

Example:
free leisure _spare_

You could use free time, leisure time and spare time when talking about what you do when you're not studying or working.

a kick-off injury __________
b qualifying winning __________
c arrival departure __________
d peak viewing off-peak viewing __________
e opening closing __________
f sowing milking __________

3 Choose three of the collocations from exercise **2** and write a sentence for each, leaving a gap where the collocate of *time* should be. Then show your sentences to your partner who will try to guess the missing word(s).

Example:
United scored the winning goal in the last minute of __________ *time.*
[Answer: *injury*]

4 Review

Word combinations

For sentences **1–10**, underline the correct alternative.

1 We need to take action now, before the situation gets out of *head/hold/hand/help*.

2 When considering the reasons for the fall in productivity, management was rather too quick to *aim/point/show/target* the finger at workers.

3 I'm sorry, I can't deal with it now – I'm a little *delayed/pressed/late/short* for time.

4 None of the TV stations here put educational programmes on at peak *showing/sighting/seeing/viewing* times.

5 You should *give/find/set/keep* aside at least half an hour a week to read an English newspaper or magazine.

6 Write on the other side of the paper if you can't fit everything into the space *free/spare/available/providing*.

7 I was most impressed by his *way/tendency/ability/capacity* of thinking and expressing himself.

8 I *hate/avoid/admit/can't help* to say it, but I thought it was a terrible film.

9 Sarah has made *combined/predetermined/great/wide* efforts to catch up with the work she missed during her long absence.

10 We offer excellent promotion prospects and you will be given *every/much/great/all* opportunity to progress in your career.

Gerunds and infinitives

For **1–8**, complete each of the gaps with the correct form of the verb in brackets.

1 I really don't feel at all like ______________ (go) out tonight, so it's no use ______________ (try) ______________ (get) me ______________ (go) clubbing with you.

2 As soon as I stopped ______________ (smoke), I started ______________ (eat) more.

3 I couldn't help ______________ (notice) you were wearing Gucci® shoes. I hope you don't mind me ______________ (ask), but how much were they?

4 I'll try ______________ (not keep) you for too long. I wouldn't like you ______________ (think) I was wasting your time.

5 We really do appreciate you ______________ (give) up your valuable time __________ (come) and ______________ (talk) to us today, Mr Wilson.

6 I distinctly remember Steve ______________ (agree) ______________ (help) us with the move today. He either forgot ______________ (set) his alarm, or he's found something better ______________ (do).

7 The police made several unsuccessful attempts ______________ (enter) the building, and even firefighters had difficulty ______________ (cut) through the thick metal door.

8 He recommended me ______________ (claim) compensation for unfair dismissal, but he suggested ______________ (seek) legal advice first.

Key word transformation

For questions **1–6**, complete the second sentence so that it has a similar meaning to the first sentence, using the word given. **Do not change the word given.** You must use between **three** and **six** words, including the word given. Here is an example (**0**). Write your answers **IN CAPITAL LETTERS**.

0 The man is armed and you should not approach him under any circumstances.
ACCOUNT
The man is armed and ON NO ACCOUNT SHOULD you approach him.

In this exercise, all of the target language can be found in the article *Office Politics*.

How to go about it

- Match the key information in the lead-in sentence with the information in the second sentence. Then decide what information is still missing from the second sentence – and how the key word can supply this.
- It is important to be accurate. For example, if the key word is a verb, you need to remember if it takes a preposition, and whether it is followed by the gerund or infinitive. If the key word is a noun, you may need to think of the verb that collocates with it.

Don't forget!

- Do not change the word given in capital letters.
- Write between three and six words.

1 It's mostly thanks to John that the project succeeded.
CREDIT
It's John who should .... of the project.

2 If you don't acknowledge your sources, there's a danger people will accuse you of plagiarism.
RISK
If you don't acknowledge your sources, you .... plagiarism.

3 The crisis has affected business so much that we may have to close down the company.
IMPACT
The crisis .... business that we may have to close down the company.

4 He's not a good guitarist, but there is no better singer than him.
COMES
He's not a good guitarist, but .... singing, he is the best.

5 The party leader admitted she had pretended not to notice the corruption amongst her own politicians.
EYE
The party leader admitted to .... the corruption amongst her own politicians.

6 It is the line manager who should deal with this matter.
BE
It is advisable for .... by the line manager.

5 Getting on

Speaking 1 Part 2 Long turn

- What might the people be talking about?
- How well do you think they get on with each other?

1 The pictures above show people in conversation with one another.

Student A:
Compare **two** of the pictures and say what the people might be talking about and how well you think they get on with each other.

Student B:
When your partner has finished talking, say which people in the two pictures you think argue more.

What to expect in the exam

Student A's instructions also appear as written questions above the pictures.

Don't forget!

Use a wide range of vocabulary. *Look at the list of adjectives in section **A** on page 210 and note down those which might be useful when talking about your two pictures.*

2 Now change roles. Follow the instructions again using the remaining pictures.

Listening 1
Part 3

Multiple choice 1.20

1 You will hear an interview with a sociologist and former counsellor called Adrian Mitchell, who has just published a book on family relationships. For questions **1–6**, choose the answer (**A**, **B**, **C** or **D**) which fits best according to what you hear.

1 Why did Adrian decide to write a book on family relationships?

A He was persuaded by others in his field.

B He was encouraged by the success of his previous publication.

C He felt it was a natural outcome of his work in sociology.

D He believed it was probably expected of him.

2 Adrian says that he gave up his role as a counsellor because

A he was unable to remain objective.

B he felt overloaded with responsibility.

C it no longer provided sufficient challenge.

D he resented its impact on his own physical health.

3 Adrian says that the average 21st-century husband

A may be suffering a form of identity crisis.

B is still reluctant to participate in housework.

C secretly wishes to earn more than his wife.

D is happy to have been relieved of certain duties.

4 Adrian explains that his children did not feature in his book because

A academic publications should have an impersonal tone.

B they were unwilling to be exposed in such a way.

C he was reluctant to take advantage of their willingness to please.

D descriptions of family experiences were becoming formulaic.

5 Adrian criticizes certain media reports on social issues for

A their misleading use of statistics.

B the sensational style they are written in.

C the way they overlook areas of progress.

D their focus on superficial subjects.

6 What does Adrian say about the institution of marriage?

A It will continue to decline in popularity.

B It is undervalued in modern society.

C Its purpose is not the same for everyone.

D It requires more compromise than many people realize.

2 Do you agree with Adrian that newspapers tend to focus on the negative when they are discussing new trends in society?

To what extent can we believe the information presented in printed and online newspapers?

Reading and Use of English
Part 7

Gapped text

1 When you are upset or have a problem, who do you turn to first for help and advice? Why?

Has this always been the case?

2 You are going to read a magazine article about the relationship between mothers and their sons. Six paragraphs have been removed from the extract. Choose from the paragraphs **A–G** the one which fits each gap (**1–6**). There is one extra paragraph which you do not need to use.

Don't forget!

- Read the whole of the base text and all the paragraphs before you start to make any choices.
- Underline words or phrases which show links between base text and missing paragraphs.

  Some parts of this base text have already been underlined to help you. As you do the task, underline any relevant parts of the paragraphs A–G.
- Check your answers by reading the whole article through again to ensure that it makes sense. Check that the extra paragraph does not fit into any of the gaps.

MOTHERHOOD'S BEST-KEPT SECRET

One night, not so long ago, just as I was drifting off in bed, the phone rang. It was my 19-year-old son, who is at university in Edinburgh, calling to say that he had broken up with his girlfriend and had been wandering around the city ever since, not knowing what to do. I told him to catch the first train home. He arrived looking a wreck, but after a good sleep and some home cooking, he began to feel his old self again.

1 ______

Girls I knew then were reasonably open with their mothers, but that was a mother-daughter thing. No male contemporary would ever have admitted asking his mother for advice. Despite all our talk about how important it was for men to let down their defences and learn how to express their feelings, most of us still secretly subscribed to the idea that any man who depended on his mother too much was a bit of a mummy's boy.

2 ______

But things don't work that way anymore. In a world of short-term contracts, downsizing and redundancy, even the most promising of our children experience lows early on in their careers; and whenever they hit those depths, many of them will return to the nest. Indeed, a typical son will continue to be at least partly dependent on his mother well into his twenties.

3 ______

They're also better able to see through the mask of apparent self-confidence. When my boy was growing up, he always maintained a fairly invincible front. His early imaginary play involved sieges, ambushes and surprise attacks. His starting point, though, was always a danger against which he needed to defend himself. He used the games he played as a child to convince himself that he could prevail.

4 ______

In his teens, he used many of these same tricks to keep me at bay. If I drove him anywhere to meet his friends, he insisted I drop him off out of sight of where they were waiting. There were girlfriends I never met and phone conversations which were all in code. But occasionally, a confidential mood would come over him and he would air whatever happened to be on his mind.

5 ______

'And there's another important change,' she adds. 'Most of us took pains to reassure our sons that it was OK for them to show physical affection or cry. If our boys are not so anxious now about showing their emotions, our efforts in this area have not been in vain.' This seems to be backed up by research, which shows that boys call their mothers on their mobile phones more than anyone else.

6 ______

What I didn't anticipate was for the same thing to happen with my son. I assumed I would lose him, just like all the experts said. It may be that they were wrong all along – that sons have always confided in their mothers – and just made sure that no one else knew. Have I stumbled on motherhood's best-kept secret? Even if I have, it doesn't diminish my sense of wonder. It's still like getting a present you never expected.

A These days, however, mothers can expect to be relied on almost indefinitely for the type of advice that calls on our experience of the outside world. A generation ago, it was accepted that sons would eventually leave their mothers to join the world of men and work. Mothers put their 18 years in and then opened the door to allow their sons to move into jobs for life.

B Other mothers told me that they, too, were getting the same volume of confidences. According to my psychotherapist friend, this is normal behaviour for today's boys. Our sons will tell us more than their fathers told their mothers, because we have brought them up to do so. Our norm has been to empathize with children when they talk about their feelings, whereas the previous generation tended to be shocked.

C They are not in any doubt about how to respond to the situation. As one friend said of her rather reticent son: 'My job is to give my son courage.' And whilst we might welcome the chance to see more of our children, one does have the feeling that there is something anti-natural in all this.

D Many mothers I know are surprised at this reluctance to break away. One of my friends, however, who happens to be a psychotherapist, assures me that the mother-son intimacy is nothing new. 'Mums have always been easier to talk to,' she points out. 'They're more cuddly than their fathers, and sons realize early on that their mothers are more accepting of human frailty.'

E But don't assume that girls are any tougher than boys. 'Daughters need their mothers, too,' she says. Certainly, I know how much my own daughters need me. But this continuing mother-daughter bond is something I expected.

F Some of the details began to emerge on the following day. Then he told me more. And more. And even more. A moment arrived when I couldn't help asking myself, should I be hearing all of this? It wasn't that I was shocked. He reminded me of myself in my own student years, but with one important difference – I would never have confided in my parents this way.

G As he got older and had to ride to school on a bus with other children, all too often there were situations in which he did not. I had to teach him how to put up new defences so that his rougher classmates would not see his weaknesses.

Reacting to the text

To what extent have parent-children relationships changed in recent decades in your own country? Is the relationship very different for sons and daughters?

Vocabulary 1: Verb + noun collocations

1 Find and circle the following nouns in the base text on page 60. Write them in your vocabulary notebook, together with the verb which is used with each one. Record any adjectives which are used as well.

Example: *maintain a fairly invincible front*

front feelings pains
affection emotions

2 Find and circle the following phrasal verbs in the base text and paragraph D and with your partner, discuss their meaning in context.

drift off break away see through
back up stumble on let down

Record the verbs in your notebook, together with the noun which follows each one.

Language focus 1: Reference and ellipsis

A Reference

1 Find the following sentences in the reading text on pages 60 and 61 and decide what the words in **bold** refer to. Sentences **a–d** can be found in the paragraph of the base text immediately after the number given in brackets.

- **a** Girls I knew **then** were reasonably open with their mothers. (1)
- **b** But things don't work **that way** anymore. (2)
- **c** In his teens, he used many of **these same tricks** to keep me at bay. (4)
- **d** … our efforts in **this area** have not been in vain. (5)
- **e** According to my psychotherapist friend, **this** is normal behaviour for today's boys. (paragraph B)
- **f** Our sons will tell us more than their fathers told their mothers, because we have brought them up to **do so**. (paragraph B)

2 Words such as **do so** in **f** above are often called 'substitute words'; they substitute and avoid repetition of words and phrases which have already been used.
In **1–6** below, underline the correct substitute word. There is an example at the beginning (**0**).

0 She can't sing and *so/not/nor/never* can I.

1 **A** Do you think the weather will clear up by tomorrow?
B I certainly hope *it/this/so/will*.

2 Can you lend me your helmet? If *yes/so/not/no*, don't worry – I'll borrow Mike's.

3 **A** Elaine wants to go to the beach.
B I *want/go/am/do*, too.

4 Last Christmas it was orange trousers; this year she gave me these yellow *pair/ones/types/colour*!

5 Students passing the exam will automatically go into the next level. All *those/these/them/ones* that fail will have to repeat this *same/such/one/also*.

6 Suddenly, Brenda appeared. *Such/Then/When/This* was the moment he had been waiting for.

B Ellipsis

1 Sometimes, to avoid repetition, it is enough to simply omit a word or words. This is called ellipsis. Find the following sentences in the text and decide which word or words have been omitted.

- **a** … and had been wandering around the city ever since ______________ . (introductory paragraph)
- **b** Even if I have ______________ , it doesn't diminish my sense of wonder. (6)
- **c** As he got older and ______________ had to ride to school on a bus with other children, all too often there were situations in which he did not ______________ . (paragraph G)

2 In **1–6** below, decide which words could be omitted to avoid repetition. There is an example at the beginning (**0**).

0 My brother was afraid of the dark, but I wasn't ~~afraid of the dark~~.

1 **A** Do you think you'll be home before midnight?
B I should be home before midnight.

2 I asked him to play a tune on the piano and he said he didn't want to play a tune on the piano.

3 She always comes to class on Tuesdays, but she hardly ever comes to class on Thursdays.

4 He left without saying goodbye. I have no idea why he left without saying goodbye.

5 **A** I have a feeling he was sacked from his last job.
B Yes, he might well have been sacked from his last job.

6 He told me to apologize to her, but I'd already apologized to her.

Read more about reference and ellipsis in the Grammar reference on pages 218 and 219.

3 Use substitute words and ellipsis to reduce the amount of repetition in the following text. There is an example at the beginning.

A family of teachers

For most of ~~my mother's~~ *her* working life my mother taught chemistry in a secondary school. She always said the reason she had entered the teaching profession was because her father had virtually forced her to enter the teaching profession. Her father was a teacher and her mother was a teacher as well, though she herself had no intention of becoming a teacher. However, whereas my grandmother felt that my mother should only follow in their footsteps if my mother wanted to follow in their footsteps, my grandfather was determined that she should teach for a living – so she taught for a living.

She'd actually like to have become a pharmacist and run her own business, but she wasn't sufficiently qualified to become a pharmacist and have her own business. Apart from the fact that she wasn't sufficiently well qualified, she might well have had problems raising the necessary capital, and if she'd asked her father to lend her the necessary capital he probably wouldn't have lent her the necessary capital. I think my mother resented my grandfather for the pressure my grandfather had put on her, and my mother always encouraged me to make my own decisions. I made my own decisions – and now I work as a teacher, and my son works as a teacher, too!

Vocabulary 2: Relationships

1 Complete each gap with the appropriate form of one of the verbs from the box. In each section **1–7**, the verb required for both spaces, **a** and **b**, is the same.

have	look	take	get	put	turn	keep

1 a Sally and my father ________ **on like a house on fire**; she loves going to see him.

b The noise from the neighbours is beginning to ________ **on my nerves**. I'm going to complain if it doesn't stop soon.

2 a His gambling problem has ________ **a great strain on** our relationship. I'm seriously thinking of leaving him.

b It was just a joke – I wasn't trying to ________ **you down**. I'd never deliberately set out to make anyone feel stupid.

3 a The maths teacher ________ **it in for me**; she was always giving me extra homework or keeping me behind after school.

b They ________ **a** fairly **rocky relationship** at first, but they're talking of getting married now.

4 a They set up in partnership in 2005, but **the relationship** ________ **sour** when Jim's risky investments seriously jeopardized the business.

b When her father returned after nine years' absence, Sue did not have the heart to ________ **her back on him**.

5 a She'd always approved of his girlfriends before, but she never really ________ **to** Sandra.

b Sandra ________ **an instant dislike to** his mother, but she did her best to hide it.

6 a He's well liked, and a lot of the younger members of staff ________ **up to him** as a role model.

b I used to ________ **down on** art students at university, but now they're probably all earning far more than me.

7 a He ________ **himself to himself** on the holiday, eating alone and opting out of the organized excursions.

b I left over ten years ago, but I've managed to ________ **in touch with** some of my former colleagues.

2 Look at the expressions in **bold** in exercise **1** and decide whether each one has a negative or a positive meaning.

3 Choose three of the expressions from exercise **1** and use them to talk about your own relationships, past or present.

Example:
*My cousin used to really **get on my nerves**. He was always phoning me up or coming to see me. He never gave me a moment's peace. Things are fine now – he went abroad to live so I just get the occasional letter.*

Speaking 2
Part 3

Collaborative task

1 Here are some things that can affect a couple's relationship.

Talk to each other about what effect these things might have on a couple's relationship.

income

shared interests

What effect might these things have on a couple's relationship?

communication skills

cultural background

parental approval

2 Now decide which of these things is the most vital for achieving success in a relationship.

Speaking 3
Part 4

Further discussion

Discuss the following questions:

- How important is it for a couple to have the same goals in life?
- Some people find it difficult to choose a suitable partner. Why do you think this is?
- Do you think it is important for couples to share responsibility for looking after the house and the children?
- What do you think are the greatest challenges for people who decide to settle down together?
- Some people say that men benefit from marriage more than women do. What do you think?

How to go about it

- Give full answers to the questions, justifying your opinions. Remember, it is your language which is being assessed and not your ideas.
- Respond to what your partner says, as in Part 3 above, and develop the discussion.

Listening 2
Part 1

Multiple choice 1.21–1.23

You will hear three different extracts. For questions **1–6**, choose the answer (**A**, **B** or **C**) which fits best according to what you hear. There are two questions for each extract.

What to expect in the exam

In Part 1 of the Listening paper, the three extracts are all on different themes. However, for the task you are about to do, the extracts are all on the same theme of relationships.

Extract One

You hear part of an interview with an actress called Miriam Landers talking about a director she has worked with.

1 How does Miriam feel about acting in her new play?
A She is nervous about the first night of the production.
B She feels certain her performance will be convincing.
C She is concerned that it will leave her feeling very tired.

2 What does Miriam say about her relationship with her director, Malcolm Rush?
A He makes all the important decisions.
B He always finds something to criticize.
C He is prepared to listen to her suggestions.

Extract Two

You hear two university students talking about their experience of groupwork.

3 What do both speakers say about working within a group?
A It was very productive.
B It resulted in conflict.
C It took up too much time.

4 What did the woman find most challenging about her project?
A stating her opinion
B meeting the deadline
C finding source material

Extract Three

You hear part of an interview with a professional rally driver.

5 What is worrying the driver about his next race?
A the fact that he has a new co-driver
B the possibility that he may lose control of the car
C the risk of the car having engine failure

6 What does he say about the role of the co-driver?
A A co-driver is supposed to keep the driver calm.
B Many people do not appreciate what the co-driver does.
C It is always the co-driver's fault when accidents occur.

Language focus 2: Relative clauses

1 Read sentences **a–f** from the listening. Then answer questions **1–4** below.

a It's Scott **who** has the map and the notes.
b Are you at all anxious or is opening night an occasion **which** no longer bothers you?
c You don't just learn the part – you live it, **which** takes away any fears you might have of not being able to persuade an audience you're real.
d Actors I've worked with, some of **whom** have been rather new to the stage, know that he's going to be tough with you.
e ... your new play, **which** opens next week, is described as a black comedy.
f Our discussions generated ideas I hadn't even thought of.

1 What or who do each of the relative pronouns in **a–e** refer to?
2 Why are commas used before the relative pronoun in **c**, **d** and **e** but not in **a** or **b**?
3 Which of the relative pronouns could be replaced by **that**?
4 Which relative pronoun has been omitted from **f**? Why is it possible to leave it out of this sentence but not the others?

G Check your ideas in the Grammar reference on page 219.

2 Complete each of the spaces with one of the words from the box. Each of the words can be used more than once. Then decide whether:

a commas are required or not
b **that** can be used instead of the word you have chosen
c the word can be omitted

who	which	whose	who's
where	why	what	

1 I went walking with my husband at the weekend ________ is something ________ we haven't done for a long time.
2 The novel is set in Kaunas ________ at that time was the capital of Lithuania. The initial chapters focus on Vitas's father ________ fiery temperament had a lasting effect on the boy.
3 ________ I'd like to know is what happened to that boxer ________ she was seeing. Are they still going out together?
4 He left all his money to a woman ________ had never shown him any affection. The reason ________ he did this has never been fully understood.
5 Her mother ________ hated city life longed to return to the village ________ she grew up in and ________ she still owned a small plot of land.
6 Is there anyone ________ got a car or ________ mum or dad could give us a lift?

Writing
Part 2

Proposal

What to expect in the exam

In Part 2 of the Writing paper, you might have the opportunity to write a proposal. You may be asked to suggest ways to improve morale at work, amenities in your local town, self-study facilities for students at your college and so on. To do this task well, you need to think about your target reader: either the person/people who asked you to write the proposal, or the group assessing your proposal. You will need to write in a way that persuades your target reader that your ideas and suggestions are worth considering.

1 Read the following Part 2 task and the model answer. Does the answer address both aspects of the task?

Your company has problems with some employees not working well with each other and needs to improve relations between them. You have been asked by your manager to propose ways in which relations can be improved.

Your proposal should

- outline reasons for the problems.
- suggest ways to improve relations.

Write your **proposal** in **220–260** words.

Proposal: Improving staff relations at I-tech

Introduction

Over the last few months there has been tension between members of staff in the company. This has had a negative effect on productivity.

New staff

Four employees have recently transferred to our branch from the city branch. However, some long-term employees at this branch have complained that their new colleagues have not been doing their job properly and ill feeling has resulted from this. I have carried out some informal interviews and I suspect that they are simply not familiar with our particular systems.

I suggest that we have a training day for all the new staff, preferably as soon as possible. I recommend this be led by Daniel Billep as he has organized training sessions before and has good rapport with the new group.

Staff with family commitments

We have a number of employees with young families. This sometimes means that an employee needs to leave work early if their child is sick. However, some staff members without children are unhappy with this situation.

I propose that we create a clearer policy about taking time off for family commitments. We should indicate how staff can make up any hours they have lost; for instance, by working from home or extending their hours on another day. In this way, other employees will know that the company is not discriminating against anyone.

Conclusion

I feel that the current problems we are experiencing with staff relations can be resolved, providing new staff receive the necessary training, and that all staff perceive that their workmates are fulfilling the terms of their contract.

2 Clear organization and appropriate paragraphing are essential features of all *Advanced* writing task types. For proposals, as with reports, a relevant title and paragraph headings are also useful.

Which of these two possible plans does the proposal follow?

	A	**B**
First paragraph	Introduction: general background	Introduction: general background
Central paragraphs	• reason for one problem	• reason for one problem
	• reason for second problem	• suggestion
	• suggestion	• reason for second problem
	• suggestion	• suggestion
Final paragraph	concluding positive comment	concluding positive comment

3 To obtain a high mark in the *Advanced* examination, you need to use a wide range of relevant vocabulary and structures.

Copy the following table into your notebook and complete it with language from the model answer which is relevant to a work situation.

Activities/verbs	People	Other
transfer (to/from a branch)	*members of staff*	*productivity*

4 The model answer above is written for someone in a senior position, so a formal style is appropriate and will have a positive effect on the target reader.

a Which formal language is used to make suggestions in the model?

Example: *I suggest that we have …*

b Which structures are used to talk about consequences?

Example: *This has had a negative effect on …*

5 Either **a** write your own answer to the question in exercise **1**.
or **b** answer the question on page 206.

For both questions, read the How to go about it box on page 206 before you write your answer.

5 Review

Vocabulary

Complete each of the gaps with one of the words from the box. Some of the words will be required more than once.

up	down	in	on	to	for

1 I'm not surprised she feels humiliated – he's always putting her ______ in public like that.

2 You can't turn your back ______ me now, not after all I've done for you in the past!

3 The mortgage is putting a real strain ______ our finances.

4 The Brazilian striker never really took ______ his new coach and by the end of his first season he was asking for a transfer.

5 He really gets ______ my nerves. He never stops complaining.

6 My boss has always had it ______ ______ me; nothing I do is good enough for him.

7 Greta Garbo took such a strong dislike ______ her co-star Fredric March that she used to eat garlic before filming their love scenes.

8 My brother has done very well for himself, but he does tend to look ______ ______ me. Or is it my inferiority complex?

9 I asked Lucy to tell my parents I was with her last night and not at Steve's party, but she refused to back me ______ .

10 Mike's not what you'd call a social animal; he tends to keep himself ______ himself.

Reference and ellipsis

In each of the following sentences or dialogues there is one mistake. Find each mistake and correct it.

1 We're going to buy a new washing machine – our old keeps breaking down.

2 **A** Do you think it'll rain?
B I hope no – I haven't brought my umbrella.

3 **A** Haven't you been to see the Kandinsky exhibition?
B No, I'm not interested in abstract art, and so isn't my wife.

4 Harry doesn't think they'll win at the next elections, but I do so.

5 Are you coming? Whether so, can you hurry up? We're already late.

6 **A** Do you think this milk is OK to drink?
B It should – I only bought it two days ago.

7 **A** Put some salt in the potatoes, will you?
B I've already!

8 It's a shame I can't go with you on Saturday – I'd really love.

9 We weren't consulted on this matter, and I think we should have.

10 He said he'd phone me today, but he hadn't. I'll give him a ring tomorrow.

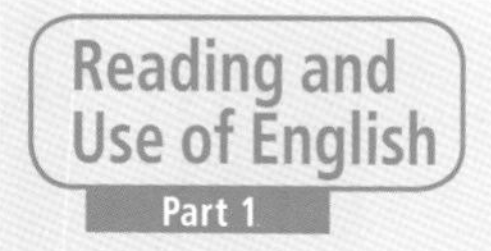

Multiple-choice cloze

For questions **1–8**, read the text below and decide which answer (**A**, **B**, **C** or **D**) best fits each gap. There is an example at the beginning (**0**).

Why marriage leads to a long life

An analysis of the benefits of relationships has confirmed a truth that many have long **(0)** .... to be self-evident: marriage is good for you. Not only does it **(1)** .... physical health in men and mental well-being in women, but the longer it lasts, the greater the benefits all round, **(2)** .... in a longer and more satisfying life. A study **(3)** .... millions of people over many years across seven European countries, has **(4)** .... that married couples had mortality rates 10–15 per cent below the population as a **(5)** .... This figure rises with the longevity of a marriage.

The selection hypothesis argues that well-adjusted individuals are more likely to **(6)** .... long-term relationships, suggesting that the determining **(7)** .... might not be marriage itself, but more the kind of people who are likely to wed and stay wed. The authors of the study argue that commitment is also **(8)** .... to higher living standards, with the associated network of supportive families, shared friends and healthy lifestyles bringing a range of benefits.

	A	B	C	D
0	**A** insured	**B** meant	**C** <u>held</u>	**D** proved
1	**A** enhance	**B** enchant	**C** enjoy	**D** endure
2	**A** leading	**B** finalizing	**C** improving	**D** resulting
3	**A** consisting	**B** involving	**C** implying	**D** composing
4	**A** manifested	**B** exposed	**C** revealed	**D** considered
5	**A** whole	**B** set	**C** total	**D** group
6	**A** launch	**B** found	**C** base	**D** establish
7	**A** part	**B** moment	**C** factor	**D** event
8	**A** combined	**B** linked	**C** blended	**D** joined

Open cloze

For questions **1–8**, read the first part of the following article and think of the word which best fits each gap. Use only **one** word in each gap. There is an example at the beginning (**0**). Write your answers **IN CAPITAL LETTERS**.

GRANDPARENTS: THE NEW GENERATION

Always **(0)** ....A.... sure source of affection, my grandparents **(1)** .... hugely important figures in my life. They **(2)** .... shower my sisters and me with sweets, indulgences and stories, and tell tales about my parents as naughty children. Finally, when the last of **(3)** .... died, we all wondered who would hold the family together.

People have relied on grandparents in Britain **(4)** .... the Industrial Revolution, when whole families moved into cities from the country **(5)** .... get work in the new factories, taking grandmother along to look after the children. **(6)** .... the fact that more grandmothers are working now, grandparents are still the backbone of childcare in Britain. They provide 44 per cent of full-time care for pre-school children, **(7)** .... makes you wonder how the country would manage **(8)** .... them.

6 All in the mind?

Claude Monet

J. K. Rowling

Speaking and reading

1 Rank the people above according to how intelligent you think each one is or was: 1 = most intelligent, 7 = least intelligent.

Compare your list with your partner's, giving reasons for your decisions.

2 Read the following extract from an article on Howard Gardner's theory of multiple intelligences. How would he rank the people shown in the photos?

Charles Darwin

Meryl Streep

Marie Curie

Albert Einstein

Cristiano Ronaldo

MULTIPLE INTELLIGENCES

Albert Einstein was one of the greatest thinkers the world has ever known. He formulated theories of relativity, successfully described the nature of the universe and came up with the most famous 5 equation in the world. David Beckham was a footballer whose skill and precision made him one of the most gifted sportsmen of his generation. Who is the more intelligent?

Howard Gardner's theory of multiple intelligences 10 (MI) dares us to put these two men on neighbouring pedestals. Instead of regarding intelligence as a single quantity (g) measurable by pen-and-paper tests, Gardner, an education professor at Harvard University, divides human intelligence into no fewer than eight 15 separate categories ranging from mathematical to musical competence. His ideas have provoked vigorous debate about how one defines intelligence, about how children should be educated and how society treats those who do not sit at the top of the academic heap. 20 They have certainly divided parents – Celebration, the American town created by the Disney Corporation®, based its school around Gardner's fundamental ideas. Several parents subsequently complained that their children were not being taught satisfactorily, and 25 withdrew them. Gardner's point is that g measures only one capacity, the sort of mental agility that is valued in academic achievement, and that this single number does not do justice to human potential. So he has created his own spheres of achievement. 30 Some categories are easily reconcilable with general perceptions about IQ. For example, 'linguistic' intelligence confers a mastery of language, and is the preserve of such people as poets, writers and linguists. 'Logical mathematical' intelligence marks out people 35 who take a reasoning approach to physical things, and seek underlying principles. Einstein is the standard-bearer for this group, which also includes philosophers. These two categories are the main components of what we generally think of as 'intelligence'.

40 'Musical' intelligence characterizes musicians, composers and conductors. 'Spatial' intelligence is about being able to picture perspective, to visualize a world in one's head with great accuracy. Chess players, artists and architects would rate highly in this category. 45 Dancers, athletes and actors are lumped under the 'bodily-kinesthetic' heading; these individuals, like Beckham, are able to control their bodies and movements very carefully.

Then come two types of 'personal' intelligence – 50 intrapersonal, the ability to gauge one's own mood, feelings and mental states, and interpersonal, being able to gauge it in others and use the information. These two categories could be interpreted as emotional intelligence. Psychiatrists are particularly adept at the 55 former, while religious leaders and politicians are seen as people who can exploit the latter.

Charles Darwin is perhaps the perfect embodiment of the eighth intelligence – 'naturalist'. This label describes people with a deep understanding of the 60 natural world and its objects. Zoologists and botanists can count themselves among this group. Gardner has tentatively named a ninth, 'existential' intelligence, which characterizes those who ask fundamental questions about the universe. The Dalai Lama and Jean-65 Paul Sartre would reside in this classification. This ninth addition, however, has yet to be confirmed to Gardner's satisfaction.

These eight (or nine) categories certainly reflect the fact that, in these areas, there is a spectrum of human ability 70 ranging from the hopeless to the brilliant. But are these really intelligences, or could these competences be more accurately described as gifts or talents?

Reacting to the text

1 How would you answer the question in the final paragraph?

2 In which of the nine categories do you perform the best? What encouragement or help have you received in realizing your potential in this field?

3 Do you think children should be educated differently in the light of this theory?

Should schools focus less on traditional notions of intelligence and take more account of each individual's specific strengths?

Listening 1
Part 4

Multiple matching 1.24–1.28

1 You will hear five short extracts in which people are talking about education and learning.

TASK ONE
For questions **1–5**, choose from the list **(A–H)** the person who is speaking.

TASK TWO
For questions **6–10**, choose from the list **(A–H)** the attitude that each person has towards education.

While you listen you must complete both tasks.

A a researcher
B a novelist
C a teacher
D a musician
E an examiner
F a politician
G a scientist
H a parent

	1
	2
	3
	4
	5

A It should offer a wide range of subjects.
B It should allow students to learn at their own pace.
C It should teach students practical work-related skills.
D It should encourage a sense of responsibility.
E It should enable students to perform to their full potential.
F It should improve communication skills.
G It should encourage creativity.
H It should encourage students to join in.

	6
	7
	8
	9
	10

2 Discuss each of the views expressed in the recording, saying how much you agree or disagree with them.

How would you complete the sentence beginning '*Education should …*'?

Language focus 1: Passives 1

1 Match each of the following extracts to one of the photos on page 70. Ignore any mistakes you find for the moment.

a She is, of course, famous for being written a series of books about a young wizard and his adventures at wizard school. The stories, which have being translated into more than 50 different languages, are read by children and adults of all ages all over the world.

b And now we come to a series of pictures of Rouen Cathedral. These masterpieces of Impressionism have all been painted at the end of the 19th century by the man who has generally regarded as the leader of the movement.

c In 1894 she met Pierre, the man with whom she would change the course of science. He was introduce to her by a Polish acquaintance, who thought Pierre might be able to find room in his lab for her to carry out the study she had been commissioning to do by the Society for the Encouragement of National Industry.

d The Port of Salvador, Brazil, was arrived by him aboard the *HMS Beagle* on 28 February 1832 and so began his five-year study of the flora and fauna of South America. During his travels there he contracted Chagas Disease and he was being plagued by fatigue and intestinal sickness for the rest of his life.

e She thoroughly deserved the Best Actress award for her performance as Margaret Thatcher in *The Iron Lady* (2011). Perhaps less of the film should had been devoted to showing Thatcher in her old age, but it was fascinating to see the former British Prime Minister being played for this talented and versatile American.

2 In each extract there are two mistakes related to the passive. Find the mistakes and correct them.

3 The agent, the person or thing that performs an action, is often not mentioned in passive constructions. Match the reasons **a–d** to the examples **1–4**.

Reasons why the agent is not mentioned
a to avoid the use of 'you' in official notices
b the agent is unknown or unimportant
c it is obvious who the agent is
d the agent is 'people in general'

Examples:
1 *Several parents subsequently complained that their children were not being taught satisfactorily, and withdrew them.*
2 *But are these really intelligences, or could these competences be more accurately described as gifts or talents?*
3 *The stories have been translated into over 50 different languages.*
4 *All library books must be returned before the end of term.*

4 a The use of either the active or passive is often determined by context. In English 'given', or previously mentioned information tends to come at the beginning of a clause or sentence, and new information towards the end. This is illustrated in the second sentences of each extract in exercise **1** above.

Example: *a*
The stories is 'given' information: they are mentioned in the previous sentence.
are read by children and adults of all ages all over the world is new information: this fact has not yet been mentioned.

Because the 'given' information, 'The stories', is not the agent of the verb 'read', then the passive form is required.

b Circle the given information at the beginning of the second sentences in extracts **b–e**. Are the subsequent verbs in the active or the passive?

5 a There is also a tendency in English to place long phrases towards the end of a clause. Consequently, if the agent is a long phrase, then this appears at the end of the clause and the passive form of the verb is required.

Example: *a*
... by children and adults of all ages all over the world.

b Underline the agent in each of the second sentences in **b–e** in exercise **1**.

Read more about passives in Parts A–C of the Grammar reference on page 219.

Practice

The extracts **1–5** below and on page 73 have been taken from students' written work. For each extract, consider the whole context and rewrite the second sentence if you think it would sound more natural in the passive. If you change a sentence, decide whether the agent needs to be mentioned.

1

I am writing with regard to an article which recently appeared in your newspaper on the subject of this year's Charity Fun Run. Steven Ward, former Olympic® athlete and manager of the Hythe sports centre, which sponsored the event, wrote the item.

2

Many young people are now turning their backs on hamburgers in favour of their own national dishes. This development, together with the recent beef scare, has obviously caused problems for the American fast food chains here.

3

However, we feel it would be more appropriate to celebrate the school's anniversary by organizing a concert, possibly during the last week of the academic year. The 2000-seater Mulberry Hall Function Room in Scarcroft Road is where the school could hold the event.

The aim of this report is to present the findings of a survey into local shopping habits and to make recommendations for improvements in facilities and services. First-year students at Holmbush Business College, who designed their own questionnaire as part of their coursework, carried out the survey during the busy pre-Christmas shopping period.

For the past eight years I have been working at the Birmingham-based engineering firm, Holwill & Deaks plc. The management of the company has recently promoted me to the post of Chief Accounts Clerk, in charge of a staff of five.

Vocabulary 1: Intelligence and ability

1 In **a–e** underline the informal word or expression in each group.

a a bright child/a child prodigy/a whizzkid
b a brilliant/brainy/gifted student
c I have a flair for languages/I have a gift for music/I'm a dab hand at painting.
d I'm (an) ace at tennis/I'm a skilful card player/I'm a strong swimmer.
e I'm weak at maths/I'm hopeless at cooking/I have a poor memory.

2 Tell your partner which of the words and expressions in exercise **1** could apply to you. Explain why.

3 Tell your partner about anyone you know who is

a a competent skier.
b a proficient typist.
c a skilled craftsman or woman.
d an expert cook.
e a computer expert.
f an accomplished musician.

4 One of the adverbs in each group does not normally collocate with the adjective in capital letters. Underline the adverb which does not fit.

a	highly	naturally	academically	practically	musically	GIFTED
b	highly	exceptionally	enormously	hugely	largely	TALENTED
c	highly	extremely	absolutely	very	quite	PROMISING

5 In the reading text we were told that David Beckham was 'one of the most gifted sportsmen of his generation'. Think of one famous person for each of the following descriptions and tell your partner about him or her.

a a highly talented young actor
b an exceptionally gifted musician
c a very promising young (tennis, football, etc) player or athlete

Writing
Part 2

Review

1 What do you think is the connection between the people in the photographs?

2 Read the following Part 2 task and the model answer. Given the information in the answer, which of the two films would you prefer to see?

An international magazine has asked its readers to send in a review for its regular arts section. Write a **review** for the magazine comparing and contrasting two books, films or music albums. Comment on their similarities and differences, and say which of the two books, films or music albums you would recommend and why. Write between **220** and **260** words.

All in the mind

The real-life struggle of brilliant minds with paranoid schizophrenia and Alzheimer's disease may not sound like the ingredients of an entertaining afternoon's viewing. But Russell Crowe's stunning performance as mathematical genius John Nash in 'A Beautiful Mind' and Judi Dench's moving portrayal of philosopher and novelist Iris Murdoch in 'Iris', will have you rushing out to buy the books on which these two Oscar®-winning films are based.

It is in their thematic content that the two films resemble each other most. Both focus on the withdrawal of the protagonists into their own inner world and the effect this has on their long-suffering but devoted marital partners. Also common to both films is the fact that we witness the two academics in their youth and old age. Hats off here to Crowe's make-up team – he is remarkably convincing as the 66-year-old Nash receiving his Nobel Prize in 1994.

'Iris' differs from 'A Beautiful Mind' in this respect, relying instead on other actors to play the vivacious young Iris – a very credible Kate Winslet – and her stuttering companion, John Bayley. In addition, unlike the more linear American film, flashbacks are used to good effect to switch backwards and forwards between the two contrasting stages of Murdoch's life.

The strength of 'Iris' lies in its powerful acting and mundane realism, with the novelist seen doing the shopping, or watching children's TV in her cluttered Oxford house. However, if, as I do, you favour something more visually appealing, but no less plausible, then 'A Beautiful Mind' is a definite must-see.

3 What information is contained in each paragraph? How many paragraphs include the writer's opinion?

Don't forget!

- Aim to grab the reader's interest from the beginning.
- Express your opinions throughout your answer.

4 Make a note of those adjectives used by the writer to express an opinion on the film or the acting. Include any accompanying adverbs or nouns.

Example: *stunning performance*

5 Which words and expressions are used in the model to compare and contrast the two films? Make a note of them together with any other relevant words.

Example: *the two films resemble each other*

6 Do the vocabulary exercise on page 204.

7 Now write your own answer to the task in exercise **2**. Use some of the vocabulary from sections **B** and **C** of the Wordlist on page 211.

Reading and Use of English Part 5 — Multiple choice

1 Look at the paintings and discuss these questions:

Which of these pictures

- is an example of Impressionist art?
- can be described as 'abstract'?
- was most likely created by an animal?

2 **a** The title of the article on page 76 is a shortened version of the saying 'Beauty is in the eye of the beholder'. Read the dictionary definition of 'behold' and discuss the possible meaning of the saying.

> **behold** verb [T] *literary* to see something

b The article refers to a field of study called 'neuroaesthetics'. What does the prefix 'neuro' always refer to?

What are aesthetics?

3 Read the first two paragraphs of the article on page 76. Choose a suitable subheading.

A What could explain the way we are drawn to abstract art?
B What is different about the minds of artists who produce abstract work?
C Which forms of art are likely to provoke the strongest reaction?

4 Read the article. For questions **1–6** on page 77, choose the answer (**A**, **B**, **C** or **D**) which you think fits best according to the text.

In the eye of the beholder

Standing in front of Jackson Pollock's *Summertime: Number 9A* last June, I was struck by an unfamiliar feeling. What I once considered an ugly collection of random paint splatters now spoke to me as a joyous celebration of movement and energy. It was the first time a piece of abstract art had stirred my emotions. Like many people, I used to dismiss these works as a waste of time and energy. Since then, I have come to appreciate the work of many more modern artists, who express varying degrees of abstraction in their work. Even so, when I tried to explain my taste, I found myself lost for words. Why are we attracted to paintings that seem to bear no relation to the physical world?

Little did I know that researchers have already started to address this question. By studying the brain's responses to different paintings, they have been examining the way the mind perceives art. Although their work cannot yet explain the nuances of our tastes, it has highlighted some of the unique ways in which these masterpieces hijack the brain's visual system. The studies are part of an emerging discipline called neuroaesthetics, which aims to bring scientific objectivity to the study of art, in an attempt to find neurological bases for the techniques that artists have perfected over the years. It has already offered insights into many masterpieces. The blurred imagery of Impressionist paintings seems to cause activity in the brain's amygdala, for instance, and since this plays a crucial role in our emotions, that finding might explain why many people find these pieces moving. Could the same approach tell us anything about the abstract pieces characteristic of modern art?

Although abstract artworks often sell for immense sums of money, (Pollock's *No. 5* fetched $140 million in 2006) they have attracted many sceptics, who claim that modern artists lack the competence of the masters before them. Instead, they believe that people might claim to like them simply because they are in vogue. In the scathing words of the American satirist Al Capp, they are the 'product of the untalented, sold by the unprincipled to the utterly bewildered'.

When an experiment requires people to make simple perceptual decisions such as matching up a shape with its rotated image, for instance, the average person will often choose a definitively wrong answer if they see others doing the same. It is easy to imagine that this phenomenon would have an even greater impact on a fuzzy concept like art appreciation, where there is no right or wrong answer, only subjective ones.

Angelina Hawley-Dolan of Boston College, Massachusetts, responded to this debate by designing an experiment that played with her volunteer's expectations of the pieces they were seeing. They viewed pairs of paintings – either the creations of famous abstract artists or the doodles of amateurs, infants, chimps and elephants – and then judged what they preferred. A third of the paintings were given no captions, while the rest were labelled. The twist was that sometimes labels were mixed up, so that the volunteers might think they were viewing a chimp's messy brushstrokes when they were actually seeing an expressionist piece by Mark Rothko. Some sceptics might argue that it is impossible to tell the difference, but in each set of trials, the volunteers generally preferred the work of the well-accepted human artists, even when they believed it was by an animal or child. Somehow, it is evident that the viewer can sense the artist's vision in these paintings, even when they can't explain why.

But why do such paintings hold our attention? Alex Forsythe, a psychologist at the University of Liverpool, has found that many abstract pieces show signs of fractal patterns – repeating motifs that re-occur at different scales. Fractals are common throughout nature – you can see them in the jagged peaks of a mountain or the unfurling fronds of the fern. It is possible that our visual system, which evolved in the natural environment, finds it easier to process these kinds of scenes. The case for this hypothesis is not watertight, though, since the fractal content in the paintings she analysed was considerably higher than you would normally find in natural scenes – to the point that, in other circumstances, it would be considered too busy to be pleasant. Forsythe thinks that artists may choose their colours to 'soothe a negative experience we would normally have when encountering too high a fractal content'. It's still early days for the field of neuroaesthetics and this kind of study is probably only a taste of what is to come.

Don't forget!

- First, find the parts of the text which relate to each question. The questions follow the same order as the information in the text.
- Eliminate the options which are clearly wrong and choose the best answer, underlining key phrases or sentences in the text.
- Reread the questions and check that the options you have chosen accurately reflect the information you have underlined in the text.

1 When the writer viewed the Jackson Pollock painting in June, she was

A not in the right mood to appreciate it.

B taken aback by her own response.

C reluctant to admit her opinion to others.

D puzzled by the reaction of other people.

2 We are told that researchers in the field of neuroaesthetics

A intended to locate the areas of the brain associated with artistic ability.

B have shown which artistic styles are likely to enjoy popular appeal.

C wanted to see how brain processes influence people's response to art.

D have identified the kind of person who would respond to abstract art.

3 In the third paragraph, the writer is

A outlining criticisms levelled against modern art.

B contrasting the views of opponents and supporters of modern art.

C expressing a degree of cynicism towards the sums paid for artworks.

D implying that paintings are viewed as commodities rather than art.

4 In the fourth paragraph, the writer is casting doubt upon

A the belief that people can learn to recognize good art.

B the ability of people to have independent thought.

C the assumption that art can be fairly evaluated.

D the validity of a particular kind of experiment.

5 When referring to Hawley-Dolan's experiment, the writer puts forward the view that

A people instinctively recognize the work of a good artist.

B there were flaws in the way the research was conducted.

C the preference for human art was largely predictable.

D the art of non-human species can be unexpectedly skilful.

6 What does the writer suggest about Alex Forsythe?

A She has inspired others to take up the discipline of neuroaesthetics.

B She needs to take a less emotive approach to her research.

C The scope of her research has been impressively wide.

D Her theory is not entirely convincing.

Reacting to the text

Do you agree that abstract artworks are the 'product of the untalented, sold by the unprincipled to the utterly bewildered'?

Do you think that artistic ability is something we are born with or can it be learnt?

Listening 2
Part 2

Sentence completion 1.29

Don't forget!

You can normally write the actual words you hear in the recording.

1 Have you ever suffered from any sleep disorders such as insomnia or sleepwalking?

2 What causes people to have difficulty sleeping?

3 Do you think it would be worse to suffer from insomnia or narcolepsy – a sleep disorder which means that you can fall asleep suddenly at any time?

4 You will hear part of a medical lecture on the topic of narcolepsy, a sleep disorder which causes people to suddenly fall asleep. For questions **1–8**, complete the sentences with a word or short phrase.

Narcolepsy – an incurable sleep disorder

For many people suffering narcolepsy, an accurate **(1)** .... takes a long time.

It is possible that the lack of a specific **(2)** .... is the cause of narcolepsy.

Strong **(3)** .... can also bring on a loss of muscle control.

Other common symptoms are sleep paralysis at night and **(4)** .... in the day.

The **(5)** .... of narcoleptics is often greatly reduced.

The prejudice of others means that some narcoleptics cannot get a first **(6)** ....

Narcoleptics are unlikely to be allowed to use **(7)** .... at work.

The need to keep calm can mean narcoleptics have to alter their **(8)** ....

Vocabulary 2: Sleep

1 Look at the underlined words in the first half of the listening script for Listening 2 on page 230 and find

a a verb which means 'to sleep for a short time, especially during the day'.
b three verbs which mean 'to go to sleep, usually without intending to'.

2 Complete the spaces with one of the adjectives or adverbs from the box.

A

good	deep	fast	soundly

1 The kids are staying over at their cousins' so we should **get a** ________ **night's sleep**.
2 The passengers **slept** ________ in their cabins, unaware of the coming storm.
3 The doctor gave him a sedative and he **fell into a** ________ **sleep**.
4 Don't worry, you won't wake her up – she's ________ **asleep**.

B

wide	light	sleepless	rough

1 Over 2000 homeless people are forced to **sleep** ________ in this city.
2 It's midnight and I feel ________ **awake**. I shouldn't have had that coffee.
3 My baby daughter's teething, so we've **had** a few ________ **nights** recently.
4 I've always been **a** ________ **sleeper**; I wake up at the slightest sound.

3 Discuss the following questions with your partner.

1 How long does it usually take you to **get to sleep** once you've gone to bed?
2 Do you ever **lie awake** in bed worrying about things? Does anything else **keep you awake** at night?
3 What advice would you give to someone **suffering from insomnia**? Do you know of any remedies?
4 Certain types of music or a film after lunch **send some people to sleep**. Does anything have this effect on you?

Language focus 2: Passives 2

A Reporting verbs

1 The following structure can be used with certain verbs to give generalized opinions or facts.

Narcolepsy **is known to affect** at least 2500 people in the UK.
It**'s** widely **believed to be** the result of a genetic mutation.
(= Many people believe it is the result of a genetic mutation.)
Sufferers **are** often mistakenly **considered to be** inebriated or lazy.

With past reference, the perfect infinitive is used.

Jenkins **is said to have had** financial problems.
(= People say that Jenkins had financial problems.)
She **was thought to have fled** the country.
(= The police thought she had fled the country.)

2 Rewrite **a–e** below. Start the beginning of each new sentence with the underlined word or words.

a People expect that the Prime Minister will announce his resignation later today.
b They understand that the 22-year-old striker is considering a move to a Spanish club.
c There's a rumour going round that the band have sacked their lead guitarist.
d The police alleged that he had been selling stolen goods.
e One report says that she was paid over £2 million for her part in the film.

B *Have/Get something done*

1 What is the difference between the following sentences?

a We're painting the house at the weekend.
b We're having the house painted at the weekend.
c We're getting the house painted at the weekend.

2 What is the difference in the use of *have* in the following two sentences?

a I had my watch repaired last week.
b I had my watch stolen last week.

C Other passives with *get*

Get can also be used as an informal alternative to *be* in passive sentences.

Example:
I've applied for loads of jobs but keep getting turned down.

Get meaning 'become' is also common with the following past participles, sometimes with an object.

get stuck get caught get burnt get left
get lost get dressed get involved get hurt

Examples:
The postman got stuck in the lift this morning.
She got her head stuck in the back of the chair.

Read more about the points in sections **A**, **B** and **C** in Part D of the Grammar reference on page 220.

Practice

1 Complete each gap with a suitable phrase with *have* or *get*. The first two have been done for you.

a Hurry up or you'll *get left* behind!
b I go to a reflexologist every month *to have my feet* massaged.
c This is the first time I ______________ cleaned since I bought it for our wedding.
d They've got a map and a compass so they're hardly likely ______________ .
e I do wish you ______________ tested – I really think you need glasses, you know.
f I'm seriously thinking ______________ pierced.
g He ______________ writing graffiti on the bus and they fined him £50.
h We ought ______________ serviced – the engine's making all sorts of funny noises.
i We ______________ broken into at the weekend. They took the computer, TV, DVD player – everything.
j I think you ______________ cut before your interview.

2 Tell your partner about

- something you've had done recently.
- something you'd pay to have done if you had the money.
- something you'd never have done, ever.
- an occasion when you got lost.
- a time when you got caught doing something you shouldn't have been.

6 Review

Word formation

For questions **1–8**, read the text below. Use the word given in capitals at the end of some of the lines to form a word that fits in the gap **in the same line**. There is an example at the beginning (**0**). Write your answers **IN CAPITAL LETTERS**.

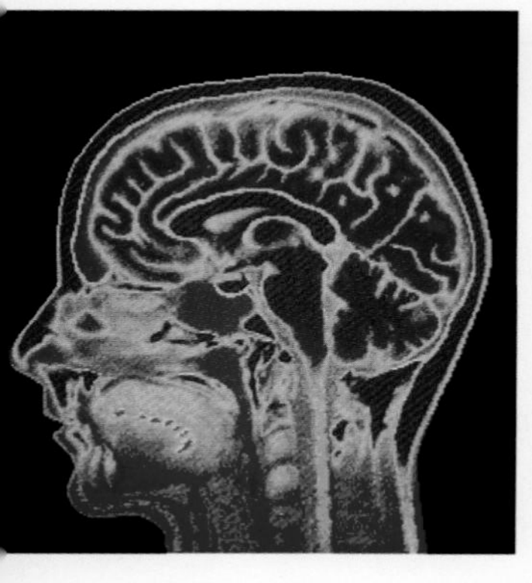

Amnesiacs struggle to imagine future events

People with amnesia have difficulty imagining future events with
any **(0)** ...*RICHNESS*... of detail and emotion, according to **RICH**
Eleanor Maguire at the Wellcome Trust Centre for Neuroimaging
in London. The five amnesiacs she studied had all suffered
(1) .... that had damaged a brain region called **INFECT**
the hippocampus. The damage left the subjects with no recollection
of past events. Researchers asked the **(2)** .... – and a **PARTICIPATE**
control group without amnesia – to imagine several future scenarios,
such as visiting a beach, and to describe what the experience would be
like. They then carried out a lengthy **(3)** .... of the subjects' **ANALYSE**
descriptions, scoring each statement based on whether it involved
references to **(4)** .... relationships, emotions or specific **SPACE**
objects. All but one of the amnesiacs were worse at **(5)** .... **VISUAL**
future events than those without amnesia. The way they saw future
events was not as a 'whole picture' where all the images fitted
together, but as a collection of separate ones. And in **(6)** .... **COMPARE**
with their control counterparts, most amnesiacs said little about how
they felt in the **(7)** .... scenario. Although there is some **FICTION**
anecdotal evidence to suggest that amnesiacs have problems picturing
future events, Maguire is the first to study it **(8)** .... **SYSTEM**
'The results show that amnesia patients are really stuck in the present,'
she says.

Vocabulary

Underline the correct alternative.

1 I'm afraid I have a *poor/weak/light/thin* memory for faces.

2 Clearly, you need to be a *thick/hard/strong/heavy* swimmer to be a lifeguard.

3 She seems to have a natural *hand/gift/present/art* for drawing.

4 Well, that didn't work. Got any more *accomplished/competent/expert/bright* ideas?

5 He has a very *prospective/promising/provided/proficient* career ahead of him.

6 I didn't *turn/put/fall/get* to sleep until after two this morning.

7 We've been sleeping *rough/light/badly/soundly* lately. It's far too noisy in our neighbourhood.

8 I didn't hear the storm last night. I was *fast/wide/hard/deep* asleep.

9 It is his versatility that *puts/makes/sends/sets* him apart from other actors of his generation.

10 There is little to *decide/choose/separate/divide* between the two films in terms of entertainment value.

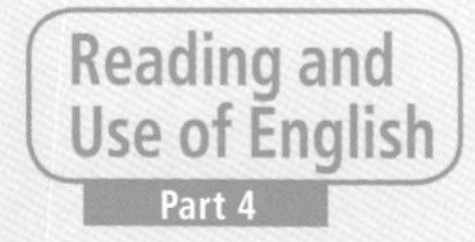

Key word transformation

For questions **1–6**, complete the second sentence so that it has a similar meaning to the first sentence, using the word given. **Do not change the word given.** You must use between **three** and **six** words, including the word given. Here is an example (**0**).
Write your answers **IN CAPITAL LETTERS**.

0 It may take several months to decide on the location for the new stadium.

MADE

It may take several months before ....A DECISION IS MADE.......... about the location for the new stadium.

1 They've postponed the meeting until January to give the management team longer to decide.

OFF

The meeting .... until January to give the management team longer to decide.

2 The police now think he invented the story to protect his girlfriend.

HAVE

He is now .... up the story to protect his girlfriend.

3 My parents are planning to pay someone to repair and redecorate their house next month.

UP

My parents are planning to have their .... next month.

4 He thinks his friends do not appreciate him.

GRANTED

He dislikes .... by his friends.

5 To help us run the exhibition next month, we need at least six people.

REQUIRED

No .... to help us run the exhibition next month.

6 A common belief is that British people cannot speak foreign languages very well.

WEAK

British people are commonly .... foreign languages.

Ready for Reading

Introduction

In this unit we will look at some of the techniques and approaches you should adopt in order to complete the four Reading tasks in the **Reading and Use of English** paper. For information on the Use of English tasks, see pages 42–45.

Part 5: Multiple choice

1 Part 5 contains one text followed by six 4-option multiple-choice questions. The task below is typical of those found in this part of the Reading paper.

2 Quickly read the article about researchers looking for signs of alien life. Does the article persuade you that aliens might exist? Why/Why not?

3 Read the article again. For questions **1–6**, choose the answer (**A**, **B**, **C** or **D**) which you think fits best according to the text. Underline the parts of the text which help you make your choices. ***Example:* 1B**

What to expect in the exam

- Each correct answer in Parts 5, 6 and 7 receives two marks.
- In Part 5 the questions follow the same order as the information in the text, although the final question may test understanding of the text as a whole.
- The questions may test detail, but also focus heavily on your understanding of the writer's attitude, opinion, purpose, tone and implication. You may also be tested on your understanding of text organization features, such as comparison (*question 3 on page 83*) and exemplification, when the writer mentions an example of something in order to make a point, (*question 6 on page 91 in Unit 7*).
- Many of the wrong options, or distractors, express ideas which are similar to, but not the same as, those expressed in the text.

Each of the highlighted sections in the text expresses an idea which might cause you to choose the wrong option for the question in brackets. As you answer questions 2, 5 and 6, match the highlighted section to the distractor and say why it is the wrong answer.

e.g. ***1 (D)*** *In the final sentence of the first paragraph, the writer explains that scientists are still struggling to resolve Fermi's paradox. This does not mean they are involved in disputes with each other, merely that they are finding it hard to understand and explain why there is no evidence of intelligent alien life in a universe with so many planets.*

First contact: will we ever hear from aliens?

Scientists have been listening for extraterrestrial transmissions since the 1960s, but all they have picked up is static. There are a lot of stars, and, by inference, lots of planets, on which aliens could evolve. So why hasn't one had the courtesy to make itself known to us? It is a good question, one originally posed by the Italian physicist Enrico Fermi, one of the founders of quantum physics. If intelligent life is common in the universe, we should have been contacted long ago, he argued. After all, Earth is relatively young in astronomical terms while alien civilizations elsewhere in the universe have had billions of years to rise, establish themselves and make themselves known to humanity. 'So where are they?' asked Fermi. (1) This is Fermi's paradox, and one which scientists, despite all their efforts, still struggle to resolve.

Much of their problem lies with the basic make-up of our galaxy. The Milky Way is an unremarkable group of stars, in a not very special part of the cosmos (2) that contains a hundred billion stars, a promising enough number if seeking the odd intelligent alien, you might have thought. However, most of these stars are going to be too big, too short-lived, too hot or too cold to support planets that might sustain intelligent beings. Thus the hunt to find the homes of clever extraterrestrials becomes less of a steady systematic search and more of a hunt for a planetary needle in a galactic haystack.

And there are other reasons why our galaxy is not alive with the sound of extraterrestrial twitter. From the perspective of US astronomers Peter D Ward and Donald Brownlee, Earth turns out to be prime galactic real estate. First, our

sun is a highly stable star unaffected by wild fluctuations in
30 radiation output. Furthermore, our solar system is situated in a safe suburban part of the galaxy, undisturbed by close neighbouring stars that could dislodge comets hovering at the edges of most solar systems. For good measure, our world is further blessed in having a relatively large moon which
35 helped stabilize Earth's rotation, preventing wild climactic swings. In other words, say these scientists, the primitive slime that evolved on Earth was blessed with conditions that allowed it, eventually, to evolve into the only intelligent creatures known to science, ourselves. So, while alien life may
40 be commonplace on other planets, a hostile environment may mean that only single-cell forms can be supported there.

Or it could be that extraterrestrial civilizations are ten a penny in our galaxy but doomed from the start. Aliens may simply be like us: just smart enough to invent technology
45 but not clever enough to control it. Thus they may be wiping themselves out round the galaxy almost as fast as they develop technology, an argument put forward by the evolutionary expert Stephen Jay Gould. 'Perhaps any society that could build a technology for such interplanetary travel
50 must first pass through a period of potential destruction where technological capacity outstrips social or moral restraint. Perhaps, no, or very few, societies can ever emerge intact from such a crucial episode.'

(5) Such arguments are rejected by other astronomers,
55 however. These scientists have argued that absence of evidence is very different from evidence of alien absence. For a start, says Seth Shostak, chief astronomer for the Search for Extraterrestrial Intelligence (SETI), alien hunting has been hindered – until recently – by a lack of equipment
60 and resources. Governments have consistently refused to finance SETI programmes and so its practitioners have had to borrow time on astronomical radio telescopes, usually for only a few days at a time. 'It's like trying to do medical research when you have to go next door to borrow a
65 microscope for a couple of hours at most,' adds Shostak. However, SETI scientists are now building their own telescopes, a classic example being the Allen Array, funded through a $11.5m donation from Paul Allen, co-founder of Microsoft®. 'When we do get a signal – we will follow
70 its source very carefully across the sky, as the Earth rotates,' says Shostak. 'Then we will ask other observatories to check it out, and if they back us, we will simply announce the existence of a message from E.T.'

However, the biology of aliens themselves is virtually
75 unguessable. An alien could be of almost any size or shape imaginable, though most scientists believe he or she (or it) is likely to be a carbon-based being like ourselves, from a world like ours, that is rich in water, the matrix of life. Indeed, the process of biological convergence, which produces similar
80 species from organisms from very different evolutionary origins, makes it plausible that aliens will be very similar to us, not just in design but in behaviour. (6) For the latter, we don't have a great record, having wiped out countless other species. So if aliens do call, it may be best not to pick up
85 the receiver.

1 The writer refers to physicist Enrico Fermi in order to
- **A** refute any claims that alien life forms have visited Earth.
- **B** highlight the nature of the challenge facing researchers.
- **C** show how alien life would be too remote to ever identify.
- **D** exemplify the kind of disputes arising between researchers.

2 When talking about the Milky Way, the writer puts forward the view that
- **A** the chances of finding alien life in our particular galaxy are minimal.
- **B** other galaxies have more potential to produce life than ours does.
- **C** the sheer number of stars that exist mean that alien life must also exist.
- **D** researchers should rethink their approach to exploring space for aliens.

3 In the third paragraph the writer draws a contrast between
- **A** conditions which will generate new life forms and those that will not.
- **B** the views held by certain people in space research and others in the field.
- **C** the way that life has developed on our planet and how it might develop on others.
- **D** beliefs that people held about the solar system in the past and in the present.

4 The writer uses the quote from Stephen Jay Gould to
- **A** highlight a flaw in a theory.
- **B** illustrate a particular point.
- **C** challenge majority opinion.
- **D** cast doubt on a previous argument.

5 What are we told about astronomer Seth Shostak?
- **A** He believes that proof of alien life may not have been recognized by scientists.
- **B** He resents having to compete with other researchers for financial support.
- **C** He is sceptical about the claims of other astronomers searching for alien existence.
- **D** He has been frustrated by government attitude towards his area of research.

6 In the final paragraph, the writer suggests that aliens
- **A** may find human behaviour aggressive.
- **B** could be wary of making contact with humans.
- **C** may share certain characteristics with humans.
- **D** will be superior in some aspects to humans.

4 Part 5 questions may include a **verb + noun collocation**, as in number 2 above: *puts forward the view*. Turn to page 206 and do the exercise.

Part 6: Cross-text multiple matching

1 Part 6 consists of four short texts by different writers on a similar theme followed by four multiple-matching questions.

The task requires you to read all four texts very carefully so that you can recognize the opinions and attitudes of each individual writer and see how these compare to the views of the other three.

2 Look at the photograph below together with the subheading for the four extracts from introductions to history books on page 85. Which group of historical people are the four authors discussing?

What do you already know about this group of people? Discuss your ideas with a partner.

Read the texts quickly. Are any of your ideas mentioned by the authors?

3 For questions **1–4**, choose from the authors **A–D**. The authors may be chosen more than once.

How to go about it

- Read the rubric, the title and the subheading carefully. This will give you a good idea about the central theme of the four texts; in other words, the one topic that the four different writers are all talking about.
- Read the four questions to identify the key information to focus on, e.g.

  aspects of the Viking legacy *common modern beliefs about Viking lifestyles*

  assessment of archaeological evidence *the extent of Viking exploration*
- Quickly read each of the four texts to get an idea of what each one is about.
- Read each text more carefully to locate a reference to each of the four questions.

  To help you for question 1, the references to the Viking legacy in each text have been underlined. (There is no such underlining in the exam.)
- Identify the opinion that each writer has on each question and compare it to that of the other writers. At this stage, you could look for:

  adjectives or verbs which indicate whether the writer's attitude is positive or negative,

  e.g. Text A in question 2: *two-dimensional caricatures, dismiss them we must*

  phrases or conjunctions which indicate the writer's support or disregard for particular ideas,

  e.g. *In fact (A), Despite (B), indeed (B), It is thanks to (C).*

A look back in time

Four authors introduce their history books on the theme of the Vikings

A

Ask people to think of a Viking and the image they would most likely conjure up is one of a huge, flame-haired Norseman in a horned helmet and brandishing a battleaxe. In fact, such ideas stem from romanticized 5 tales that took hold in the 18th century and which have evolved into the two-dimensional caricatures we are familiar with today. They may be captivating, but dismiss them we must. These myths have acquired such power that certain modern historians appear to 10 have been unable to resist turning assertion into fact, attributing purposes to relics for which there is no support, and imposing their interpretations of ritual when there is no truly reliable record. What has to be recognized above all else is the Vikings' technological 15 ability in boatbuilding and navigation, to which seafaring nations owe a debt of gratitude whether they realize it or not. On our own journey of discovery, we must stick with the facts, in particular when it comes to the limits of Viking territory. Reaching North 20 America was a triumph of sailing know-how, courage and ambition. To imagine that they went further is, at best, wishful thinking.

B

The Vikings were one of the world's greatest seafaring peoples, whose adventures and exploits have become 25 legendary, and who must be singled out because of their enormous influence on boatbuilding and navigation skills, even down to the present day. Their history stretches from the late 8th century to the mid 11th, and within this time the sight of their longships evoked terror in the hearts 30 of all that fled before them. Here we will be considering the stories of these Scandinavians and what they mean to us. We will examine the growing evidence which suggests that the achievements of these mariners were greater than is currently recognized, and that indeed, they 35 went beyond North America and Asia and reached the Australian continent long before other European explorers. Despite the refusal of many scholars to even consider this proposition, the proof is there, as we shall see in the coming chapter.

C

40 It is thanks to the perseverance of modern archaeologists at excavation sites, and the painstaking interpretation of written sources by fellow academics in the field, that our clichéd images of the Vikings as mere marauders can 45 be dispelled. This is vital if we are to admire these peoples for what they truly were; master boatbuilders whose technological know-how was a turning point for ship design and construction in Europe. They were able not only to sail around the 50 coastlines of Europe and North Africa but to reach distant Asia and North America. Some researchers have claimed evidence of Viking migration further afield, but this remains contentious speculation. Part of the problem facing Viking researchers is the 55 lack of hard evidence: Vikings often cremated their warriors and heroes, along with their weapons and navigational instruments. Furthermore, these early Scandinavian peoples were illiterate, and thus left no record of their own.

D

60 What would it be like to sight a fleet of Viking longships making silent progress up the river towards your settlement? To catch that first glance of a horde of Viking invaders surrounding your village? Ironically, it was not the Vikings that 65 recorded their own fighting prowess, but the people they attacked, often Christian scholars writing in Latin and perhaps centuries later as the stories grew with each telling. In this work, I hope to present a view of the Vikings, based on unbiased investigation 70 of original artefacts and objective interpretation of excavation sites. I choose such adjectives because the process of Viking research has not always been conducted in these ways. Even now, the current contention that the Vikings beat the Europeans to 75 Australia shows how keen some Viking 'experts' are to promote their own theories regardless of the truth. While the Vikings' seafaring techniques cannot be underestimated, it is their contribution to language and artistry that has, to my mind, made 80 the greater and more enduring impression on our European culture.

Which author

has a different opinion from the others on which aspect of the Viking legacy is most significant? 1 ____

shares author A's opinion on common modern beliefs about Viking lifestyles? 2 ____

takes a similar view to author D on the way previous archaeological evidence has been assessed? 3 ____

expresses a different view from the others on the extent of Viking exploration? 4 ____

Part 7: Gapped text

1 Part 7 consists of a text from which six paragraphs have been removed and placed in a different order after the text. You have to decide which gap in the text each paragraph has been removed from.

This task tests your understanding of text structure and your ability to predict how a text will develop. It is important, therefore, that you first familiarize yourself fully with the base text (the main text with the gaps) in order to gain an overall idea of the content of the text, and also its structure.

2 Look at the subheading for the newspaper article. How would pupils benefit from being *brave, resilient and kind*?

3 Read through the base text (ignoring the questions in *italics*). Are any of your ideas from exercise **2** mentioned?

4 Read the base text again. For each gap in the base text, read the paragraphs on either side of it, together with the questions in *italics*, to help you predict the general content of the missing paragraph.

How to go about it

- Read all the paragraphs before you start to make any choices.
- As you decide on your answers, underline ideas, words or phrases in the base text which show links with the missing paragraphs.
- Check your answers by reading through the whole article again to ensure that it makes sense. Check that the extra paragraph does not fit into any of the gaps.

5 For questions **1–6**, choose which of the paragraphs **A–G** fit into the numbered gaps in the article. There is one extra paragraph which does not fit any of the gaps.

A Rather, children seemed distracted, or else worryingly devoted to getting things 'right'. And when I started to ask teachers about this, I released a tsunami of anxiety about the everyday behaviour they were seeing in school.

B Reaction to both these publications was diverse, and it wasn't just parents who responded. And while they had much in common, there was one aspect of his research that seemed dubious to me.

C But when I got over myself and settled down to read his work, I realized we were approaching the same important territory from different angles. His is a brilliantly readable account of the growing evidence that inner resources count more than any amount of extra teaching when it comes to overcoming educational disadvantage.

D Meanwhile, universities were raising the alarm about how today's 'satnav' students seemed less able to think for themselves. A toxic combination of teaching to the test at school and parents hovering over their lives, was starting to mean that even those headed for the most prestigious universities were helpless when they first had to fend for themselves.

E This is the message of a new education book that has been topping the best-seller charts in the US. It has caused great debate by pointing out that over-assiduous parenting is associated with rising rates of anxiety and failure.

F My book, by contrast, is being written specifically for parents to show what strength of character consists of. It identifies six key values that, when knitted together, give a person deep-rooted focus, integrity and resilience, and suggests an outline for encouraging children to grow the 'backbone' of these qualities.

G But, as this book shows, character is badly in need of a comeback, and some pioneering schools are already starting to put it at the heart of their curriculum. It's a timely message, yet last summer, when the book was first published, it had me grinding my teeth in fury.

Better people make better students

Hilary Wilce explains the importance of teaching pupils to be brave, resilient and kind.

Character matters. In fact, it matters more than anything else when it comes to doing well in school – and life. Yet parents and schools are actively preventing children from developing their inner resources, either by being too neglectful, or by never allowing them to fail. 5

1 ______

↑ *What might 'It' refer to in the phrase 'It looks at why ...' in the sentence below?*

But its main concern is with poor children. It looks at why so many educational interventions fail to help disadvantaged students do better, and demonstrates that it is things like perseverance and determination that ultimately help children succeed. This old-fashioned 10 message would have been common once but appears to have vanished from the modern world.

2 ______

↑ *Look at the first sentence below. In the missing paragraph above, will the writer be expressing a positive or a negative reaction?*

This was not because I disagreed with its thesis but because I was deep into researching what seemed at first glance to be the same subject. US social affairs reporter 15 Paul Tough had produced *How Children Succeed: Grit, Curiosity and the Hidden Power of Character.* The working title of my book was *Backbone: What Children Need, Aren't Getting and How to Give it Back to Them.*

In the paragraph above, the writer uses the phrase 'at first glance'. What does this phrase usually indicate? How do writers or texts usually continue after using this phrase? ↓

3 ______

20 Drawing on neuroscience, economics, psychology and child development, Tough shows how qualities such as self-mastery and optimism are what make children succeed, and how, in the light of this, good parenting and character-based schooling can make all the difference. 25 It's a persuasive argument, and for anyone involved in creating educational policy, it should be forced reading, so they can see how fiddling with school structures can never, by itself, help pupils do better.

4 ______

↑ *In the paragraph below, is the writer talking about* Backbone *(her own book) or* How Children Succeed *(Paul Tough's book)? How do you know?*

On the way, it looks at the research showing how children 30 are becoming more self-absorbed and less able to deal with setbacks, and outlines how this in turn is making them less equipped to work with others and bounce back from disappointments. All this sprang out of the growing unease I felt as I spent time in schools. As a journalist, 35 I was usually there to write about 'development' in education – a revamped curriculum, or inventive method of teaching – yet it seemed to me that pupils' attitudes were too often sabotaging the very things designed to help them. And not, alas, in any exhilaratingly 40 rebellious way.

5 ______

↑ *Who might 'one' and 'another' be referring to in the paragraph below? How do you know?*

One said each new intake seemed less willing to share or even hang their own coats on their own pegs. Another complained about the staggering sense of entitlement many pupils now demonstrated – if he gave them poor 45 marks for a piece of work, they felt it was never because they could have done better, but only because he was 'picking on' them. (And often, he said, their parents agreed.)

6 ______

↑ *What do you understand by the phrases 'tomorrow's adults' and 'personal resources' in the paragraph below? (These are likely to be alluded to in some way in the missing paragraph above.)*

All this matters desperately because in a competitive 50 world, tomorrow's adults will have to draw deeply on their personal resources to navigate life's constant changes. A good life demands courage, resilience, honesty and kindness. This is the true spine of success, without which we are all jellyfish. And since no one wants their child to 55 be a jellyfish, our prime job as parents – and teachers – has to be to help our children build the backbone they need.

Part 8: Multiple matching

1 Part 8 consists of a longer text or several short texts preceded by questions or statements which you have to match with the corresponding information in the text.

The task requires you to scan the text in order to find the specific information you need. It is **not** necessary to read every word in the text to complete the task.

2 Read through the text on page 89 to get a general idea of its content.

What is the writer's attitude to biography at the beginning of the text? And by the end?

3 For questions **1–10**, choose from the text sections (**A–F**). The sections may be chosen more than once.

What to expect in the exam

Each correct answer in Part 8 receives one mark.

How to go about it

- Underline key words in the statements before the text. One of these has been done for you.
- Scan each of the texts, looking for information which matches that contained in the statements.

  The first statement for text A has been given and the relevant section in the text has been underlined. For the other statements, underline and label the relevant section, as in the example for number 2.
- If there are any statements you have not matched, scan the texts again looking for the information you need.

In which section are the following mentioned?

a biographer's use of items that had great sentimental value to the person written about	1
the writer's <u>confession</u> that she was <u>reluctant</u> to <u>reveal the nature of her job</u>	2
the view that we can only make sense of individuals by looking at their wider group	3
the possible reaction of readers today towards biographies they consider oversize	4
the advantage of omitting unnecessary detail from a biography	5
the view that the traditional structure of a biography does not accurately reflect reality	6
the ability of a biographer to incorporate the lives of many people into one work	7
the stimulus a biographer's subject required before finding his true vocation	8
a specific event being used as the focal point in a biography that deals with wider issues	9
examples of characteristics that often define poorly written biographies	10

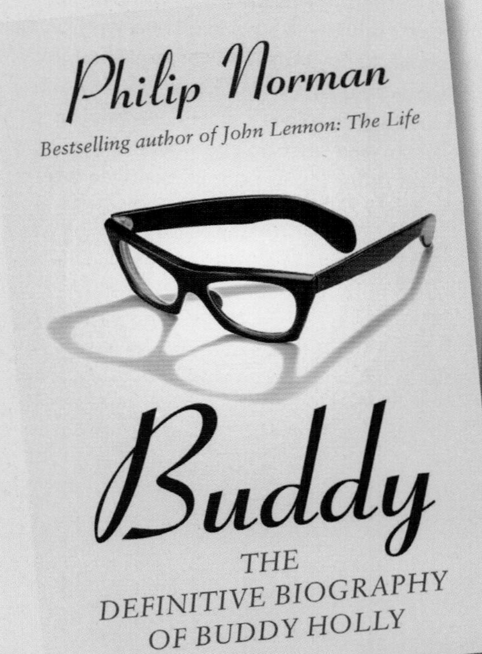

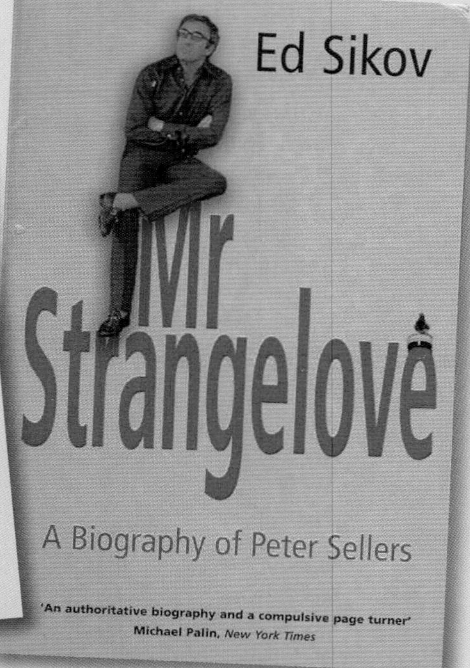

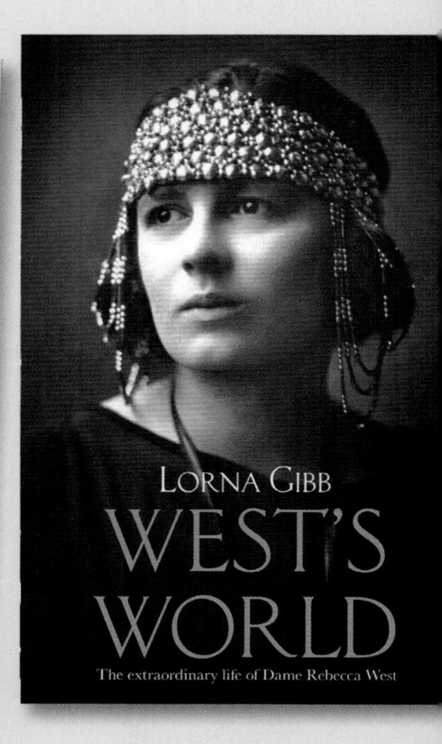

The art of biography

What is the future for this literary genre?

A

In 2008, I wrote a piece in which I declared that biography, if not quite dead, was in a terrible state. For years publishers had been timidly churning out versions of the last mega-hit, Amanda Foreman's excellent *Georgiana*, which had appeared a whole decade earlier. The endless counterfeit *Georgianas*, however, showed all the tendencies that the critic Janet Malcolm has identified as the mark of so much biographical writing: a sense that, as long as the facts are there, it doesn't matter how badly or baldly they are set out. The biographies Malcolm had in her sights were written in leaden prose, and entailed a marathon trudge from cradle to grave. I hesitated before telling people I was a biographer: it felt tantamount to admitting that I was a journalist incapable of original thought. (2)

B

But it turns out that biography wasn't in terminal decline after all. Last weekend the University of East Anglia hosted a conference entitled Turning Points at which masters and mistresses of the biographical genre took its pulse and made the cheering diagnosis that it is, in fact, in good health. What has happened, these expert practitioners explained, is that biography has changed its shape. This shift has emerged from a growing sense that biography as it used to be done was not getting us close to the experience it was trying to describe. We all know that life isn't actually comprised of a stately march through the decades in which loose ends, false trails, and those periods where nothing much happens are tidied away out of sight. Mostly our lives feel shapeless, coming into focus only when a particular occasion makes us feel, for a few minutes at least, fully ourselves.

C

One new approach to biography employs the presenting of something small – a deserted hamlet, two rusty muskets in a field – to tell a bigger story about the plague or the Battle of Culloden. Frances Wilson demonstrated how effective this approach can be in her recent *How to Survive the Titanic*. She focuses on the moment when J Bruce Ismay, the ship's owner, took the fatal decision to jump into a lifeboat while the rest of the first-class men gallantly allowed women and children to take the available spaces. Pressing hard on Ismay's split-second decision to leap to safety, Wilson tells a story not just about one man's lost honour, but about a layered drama of class, nationality and technological modernity. Another new way of doing biography is to organize your narrative around the objects that carried a particular emotional charge for your subject. In her book, *The Real Jane Austen*, for instance, Paula Byrne pulls out an East Indian shawl, a barouche and a bathing machine that figured in both Austen's own life and her fiction, and weaves a new narrative around them.

D

The new 'collective' approach to biography, meanwhile, acknowledges that people are always connected to others, even to those they can't stand or don't know personally, through familial and professional networks. It's an approach taken by Amanda Foreman in her follow-up to *Georgiana*. This time she opted to write *A World on Fire*, an epic history of two nations divided which tells the story of Anglo-American relations during the American Civil War by using mini-biographical case histories. Marshalling a vast cast of characters like this demonstrates an extraordinary degree of technical skill: like a juggler, she keeps many plates spinning while making it all look effortless.

E

The third type of new biography concerns 'the life in parts'; your subject's non-eventful schooling or the long holidays by the sea can be compressed into a few terse paragraphs so you can spend more time on the bits that matter. It was an approach showcased brilliantly by Matthew Hollis. In *Now All Roads Lead to France* Hollis concentrates on the defining moment when the Anglo-Welsh writer Edward Thomas gave up his unfulfilling journalistic career in favour of the poetry he had never quite got round to making. Under the pressure of the looming war, Thomas finally became the kind of writer he was meant to be, producing in the last five years of his life poetry that would change the music of the English language forever.

F

It would be disingenuous to claim that these new ways of telling lives are entirely driven by intellectual concerns. The pressures are commercial, too. People also have shorter attention spans which means that those doorstop biographies of 400 pages can start to seem like a looming threat rather than a delicious promise. But more and more interesting books are being published which deal with the lives of others. They may not announce themselves as 'biographies', but that doesn't mean they aren't. The genre is alive and well.

4 In Part 8, nouns or noun phrases may appear in questions 1–10, such as *the writer's confession that* or *the view that* in the reading task above. Adjectives might also be used to indicate opinion or attitude. Turn to page 206 and do the exercise.

7 Feeling good

Reading and Use of English 1
Part 5

Multiple choice

1 What is your reaction to the images shown in the pictures? How do you think these images might be associated with the theme of 'Feeling good'?

2 In the article below the writer talks about why people enjoy doing things that are potentially bad for them. Read through the article quickly. In which paragraph (**1–5**) does he refer to the ideas shown in the images?

3 Read the text again. For questions **1–6**, choose the answer (**A**, **B**, **C** or **D**) which you think fits best according to the text.

Chasing the highs

Why do people enjoy doing things which are potentially bad for them?

1

'That which does not kill us makes us stronger,' wrote Friedrich Nietzsche, the German philosopher, conceptualizing the idea that suffering is an inevitable and essential part of life. Is this still true when we bring the misfortune upon ourselves, and end up with metal pins in (5) our joints? A few weeks ago I heard of an old school friend (to be known here as Dave) who ended up with fractures in both ankles and his left wrist after failing to keep his grip while free climbing. My reaction, initially, was to grimace, but then I got round to wondering why a man (10) of his age would be risking life and limb on a sheer rock face. I can't help feeling he was showing off, under the delusion that at 40 he was at his physical peak. His mother refused to pay a hospital visit, reportedly disgusted at his egoistic risk-taking, although surely this is the person she (15) brought him up to be.

2

So what is the allure of extreme sports and living life on the edge? According to recent research, we can blame it all on dopamine, the chemical which helps control the brain's reward and pleasure centres. It's responsible for providing (20) a sense of contentment after a meal or that ecstatic feeling when our soccer team wins. It's also responsible for the high we feel when we do something brave, like swimming with sharks. Studies show that in the risk-taker's brain, there are fewer dopamine-inhibiting receptors. In other (25) words, the Daves of this world have brains more saturated with the chemical, meaning they'll keep taking risks and chasing the next high. The researchers are now working on a treatment, yet I don't envisage much uptake from the daredevils 'suffering' this condition. (30)

3

People don't just do this sort of thing in their free time, though. Last night, I happened across a battered Brad Pitt-lookalike flying across my TV screen, explosions still firing off in the background. This was 'Body Double', a cut-above-the-rest documentary about the lives of (35) stuntmen and women that stand in for the stars. Ironically, as a behind-the-scenes look at a career in Hollywood, nothing felt staged; rare for modern television. But it was the quieter moments of candid reflection that stood out, with some of the doubles expressing their anxiety to the (40) presenter over the longevity of their career. This is hardly surprising, given the amount of physical punishment that is continuously self-inflicted: neck injuries, burns, torn ligaments; the list goes on. The last word went to Jake, who'd quit his promising career as an actor, and had been (45) lured into stunt work because, as he put it, there'd be no dull moments. The famed camaraderie that exists amongst those in the profession was also a big drawcard, and perhaps it's this that keeps him signing contracts, despite his wife's protestations. (50)

4

While hurtling at 100mph towards the ground or leaping across rooftops will never be my thing, I confess to a love of horror movies. I take curious and enormous pleasure from being half-scared to death, to the point where I'm near-paralysed. Looking at the growth of the horror- (55) flick industry, I'm not alone. But why do we do it? One explanation is that when you're on the edge of your cinema seat, you can benefit from what seems a life-or-death situation, with the advantage of realizing, a mere

60 moment later and with joyful relief, that it's not. From the evolutionary perspective, it's been suggested that we've developed to find terrifying moments mesmerizing so as to ensure that we study would-be threats to survival. There's little research to back this up, though.

5

65 Taking pleasure from activities which are potentially harmful or terrifying to ourselves is one thing; deriving it from the misfortune of others is quite another. The Germans refer to this phenomenon as *Schadenfreude*, a concept that other languages may not have an equivalent 70 single word for, but which seems to be nonetheless understood by the inhabitants of today's 'global village'. What with the exponential rise of internet video clips, it is now possible to view the humiliation of thousands of strangers on demand. If you want to see someone diving 75 unwittingly into a frozen lake; it's online. How about a man being attacked by an angry deer? Click on 'Play'. As a form of entertainment, it says little for human evolution. But as life becomes more comfortable, and in a society where most of our basic needs are met, one has to wonder 80 what new thrills we'll seek out next, and what we're prepared to sacrifice for that ephemeral feel-good factor.

1 After the writer had reflected on the news about his old school friend Dave,
A he felt some disapproval towards his behaviour.
B he was envious of his active lifestyle.
C he felt the accident was undeserved.
D he was sympathetic to Dave's mother's point of view.

2 When discussing dopamine and extreme sports, the writer puts forward the view that
A the findings of the dopamine research are hardly surprising.
B a lack of dopamine cannot fully account for the desire to live dangerously.
C risk-takers are unlikely to want their dopamine levels reduced.
D dopamine has a greater effect on the human body than some people think.

3 According to the writer, what was the most impressive aspect of the documentary?
A the use of previously unseen film footage
B the director's innovative style
C the interspersing of drama and fact
D the interviews with the subjects

4 Why did Jake become a stuntman?
A He liked the idea of working within a group of friendly people.
B He had been encouraged to have a go by others in the field.
C He had had unrealistic expectations about the nature of the job.
D He had been unsuccessful in an earlier line of work.

5 In the fourth paragraph, the writer is
A encouraging readers to experience horror movies for themselves.
B questioning the claims of people studying horror movies.
C downplaying the effect of horror movies on audiences.
D suggesting explanations for why people find horror movies enjoyable.

6 The writer mentions internet video clips to illustrate his suggestion that
A there is an element of risk in everything we do.
B the kind of risks people take may well become more extreme.
C the majority of people are not amused by other people's suffering.
D it makes more sense to laugh at other people's embarrassment than our own.

Reacting to the text

Why do you think people take part in extreme sports or other potentially dangerous activities? Is it the kind of activity that you would enjoy?

Do you agree with the writer when referring to extreme internet video clips that 'As a form of entertainment, it says little for human evolution'?

Vocabulary: Risk and health

A Taking risks

1 Underline the correct word to complete the expressions in **bold**. Check your answers in the reading text on pages 90 and 91.

1. The company **brought** *struggle/misfortune* **upon themselves** through their own bad decisions.
2. You'll be **risking life and** *limb/soul* if you go up there without any safety equipment.
3. He was a musician that **lived life on the** *edge/brink*, so no wonder he died young.
4. I feel **scared to** *pieces/death* every time I'm a passenger in Jack's car.
5. It's because she hates her job that she's always **seeking out new** *pastimes/thrills* at the weekend.

B Complaints and injuries

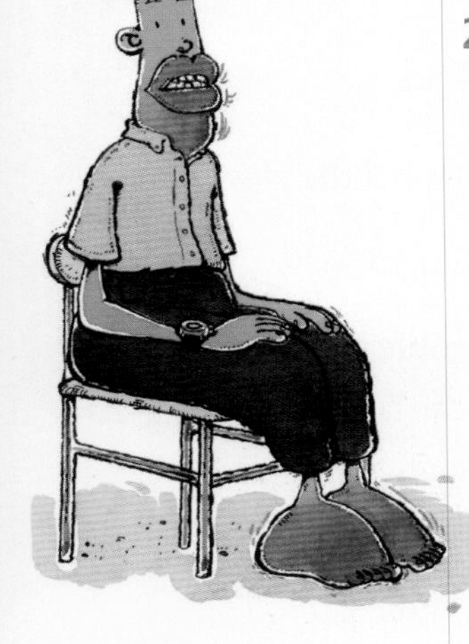

2 **a** For each of the adjectives on the left, underline the noun or nouns on the right which collocate with it. You may need to underline one, two or all three nouns. There is an example at the beginning (**0**).

0	torn	muscles/ligaments/cheeks
1	chipped	tooth/stomach/bone
2	sprained	nail/ankle/wrist
3	blocked	toe/nose/neck
4	dislocated	shoulder/hip/jaw
5	bruised	ribs/thigh/tooth
6	swollen	glands/lips/feet
7	upset	heart/stomach/brain

b Which of the complaints and injuries in **a** have you suffered? Tell your partner about them.

Collaborative task

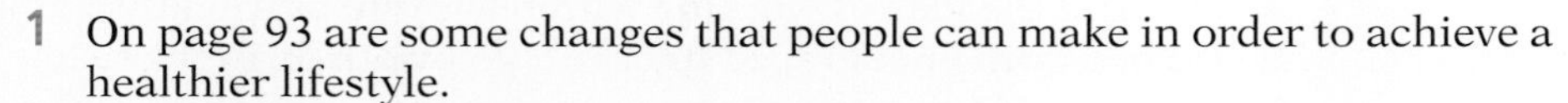

1 On page 93 are some changes that people can make in order to achieve a healthier lifestyle.

Talk to each other about how beneficial these changes might be in achieving a healthier lifestyle.

Useful language

1 a Which of the following adverbs is not normally used with the adjective *beneficial*?

reasonably	particularly	hugely	lowly	enormously

beneficial

b Which of the following adjectives **cannot** be used to mean *beneficial*?

helpful	advantageous	valuable	detrimental	useful

c Which of the following adjectives **cannot** be used to mean *very difficult*?

tricky	challenging	daunting	straightforward	problematical	tough

Now do the exercises on page 205.

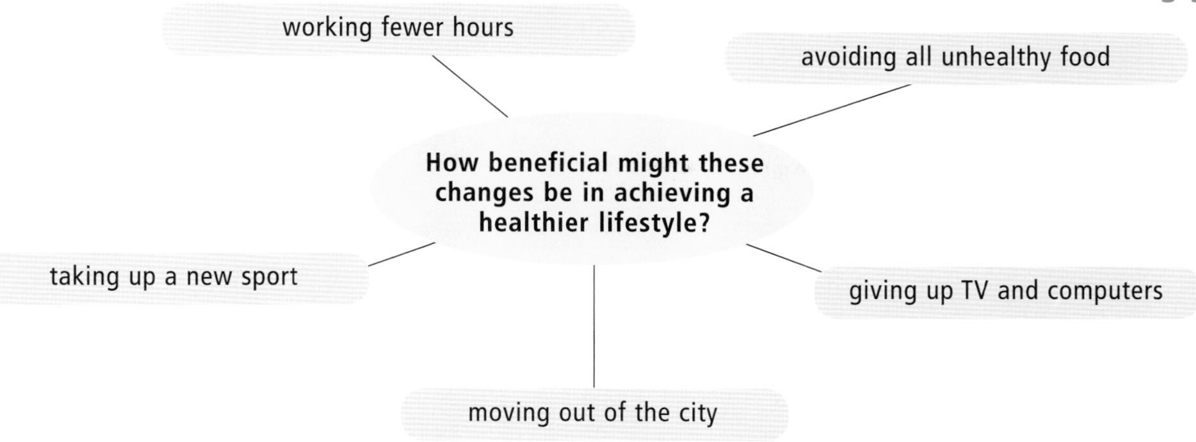

2 Now decide which change would be the most difficult to make.

3 Turn to page 207 for Speaking Part 4: Further discussion.

Reading and Use of English 2
Part 1

Multiple-choice cloze

1 Read the following text quickly, ignoring the gaps for the moment. Have you seen this phenomenon in your own language?

2 For questions **1–8**, read the text again and decide which answer (**A**, **B**, **C** or **D**) best fits each gap. There is an example at the beginning (**0**).

VIRTUAL DOCTORS

Clare Harrison rarely **(0)** .... ill and hates going to the doctor's when she does. So when she recently **(1)** .... out in a painful rash down one side of her body she emailed her symptoms, which also included a **(2)** .... fever, to e-doc, the internet medical service. Two hours later she was diagnosed as having shingles (*Herpes zoster*) by her online doctor, who **(3)** .... a special cleansing solution for the rash and analgesics to help **(4)** .... the pain.

Health advice is now the second most popular topic that people search for on the Internet, and online medical **(5)** .... is big business. Sites **(6)** .... enormously in what they offer, with services ranging from the equivalent of a medical agony aunt to a live chat with a doctor via email. They are clearly **(7)** .... a demand from people who are too busy or, in some cases, too embarrassed to discuss their medical **(8)** .... with their GP.

	A	B	C	D
0	**A** <u>falls</u>	**B** stays	**C** goes	**D** turns
1	**A** came	**B** passed	**C** worked	**D** ran
2	**A** small	**B** weak	**C** mild	**D** calm
3	**A** determined	**B** concluded	**C** prescribed	**D** intended
4	**A** relieve	**B** disappear	**C** improve	**D** lighten
5	**A** attendance	**B** appointment	**C** meeting	**D** consultation
6	**A** alter	**B** distinguish	**C** change	**D** vary
7	**A** meeting	**B** serving	**C** creating	**D** establishing
8	**A** complaint	**B** story	**C** hardship	**D** harm

3 Do you/Would you consult a medical service on the Internet? What do you think are the potential dangers of online medical advice?

Writing
Part 1

Essay

1 Look at the following chart showing statistics for obesity. Which countries have the highest and lowest rates of obesity? Why do you think these countries suffer/don't suffer from this crisis?

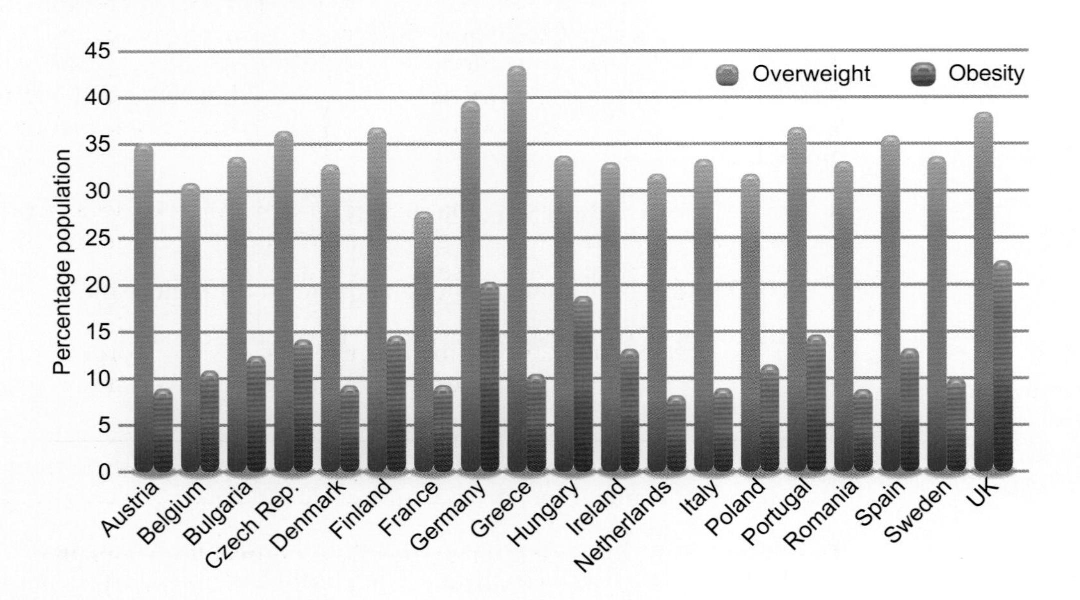

2 Read the following Part 1 task and a student's answer (ignoring the gaps). Has the student responded to all parts of the task?

Your class has recently attended a lecture on what methods governments should use to tackle obesity in schoolchildren. You have made the notes below:

Methods governments should use to tackle obesity in schoolchildren

- lessons on nutrition
- sports facilities
- legislation

Some opinions expressed in the lecture:

'If parents don't provide healthy meals, there's not much schools can do.'

'Schoolkids should be getting more exercise.'

'We need new laws so that people are less likely to buy junk food.'

Write an essay for your tutor discussing **two** of the methods in your notes. You should **explain which method you think is more important** for governments to consider, **giving reasons** in support of your answer.

You may, if you wish, make use of the opinions expressed in the discussion, but you should use your own words as far as possible.

Obesity: how do we tackle it?

Obesity has become a major issue for many developed countries. **(1)** ________ does it affect the quality of life of millions of people, but it has serious consequences for a country's economy and health services. It is evident, **(2)** ________ , that this is a problem that demands urgent action. There are many practical steps that governments could take to tackle it, but the following two would probably be the most effective.

Firstly, governments need to impose stricter laws **(3)** ________ the sale and marketing of fast food to young children. Fast food chains should **(4)** ________ be allowed to operate near schools nor advertise at times when children are likely to be watching television. Food companies, cafés and restaurants should also be required to show the calorie content of meals on labels or menus. **(5)** ________ , parents would be better able to make an informed choice about their children's diet.

Secondly, it is a sad fact that many children are not getting the kind of exercise that older generations benefited from. Many urban families live in environments which provide no opportunity for outdoor activity. For **(6)** ________ , governments need to make sure that schools have the kind of facilities that allow children to exercise and keep fit. They should also be ensuring that school timetables include regular sessions of physical education.

In the 21st century, it is ironic that for many children, it is *overeating* that is responsible for bad health, not starvation. If governments continue to ignore this crisis, the long-term consequences may be worse than we can imagine.

3 When you write your essay, it is important to use linking words and phrases to connect your ideas. Put the words/phrases in the box into gaps **1–6** in the model answer.

with regards to	that reason	in this way	not only	neither	therefore

4 The model contains some strong adjective + noun collocations that you could use for similar essays. In the table below, add the missing nouns to the extracts from the model. Then add a synonym for each noun.

	from the model	synonym
1 *has become a* ***major***	________	________
2 *that demands* ***urgent***	________	________
3 *impose* ***stricter***	________	________
4 *make an* ***informed***	________	________
5 *has* ***serious***	________	________
6 *take* ***practical***	________	________

5 Read the Essay task below and write your answer in **220–260** words in an appropriate style.

Your class has recently watched a documentary on what methods governments should use to tackle cyberbullying amongst schoolchildren. You have made the notes below:

Methods governments should use to tackle cyberbullying amongst schoolchildren

- school campaigns
- social media regulation
- punishment

Some opinions expressed in the documentary:

'If parents don't monitor their kid's online activity, there's not much schools can do.'

'Social media sites should do more to stop cyberbullies.'

'The government should introduce tougher penalties for this kind of bullying.'

Write an essay for your tutor discussing **two** of the methods in your notes. You should **explain which method you think is more important** for governments to consider, **giving reasons** in support of your answer.

You may, if you wish, make use of the opinions expressed in the documentary, but you should use your own words as far as possible.

Reading and Use of English 3
Part 6

Cross-text multiple matching

1 Which of the following 'self-help' themes would you be most and least interested in reading about?

- ways to improve your self-esteem
- strategies for making people like you more
- a set of 'rules' for finding and holding on to the perfect boyfriend/girlfriend
- tips for surviving in life-threatening situations
- methods for enhancing your business negotiation skills
- techniques for memorizing information

2 You are going to read four reviews of a book about self-help. For questions **1–4**, choose from the reviews **A–D**. The reviews may be chosen more than once.

Improving your self-esteem

Four reviewers comment on Oliver McPherson's self-help book called Journeys and Horizons

A

The latest publication in the self-help genre is *Journeys and Horizons*, a guide to improving self-esteem and achieving personal goals. In this, we are presented with a series of case studies, based on the interviews writer Oliver McPherson has carried out with his subjects. While there is a story that will reflect most people's experience, there are occasions when extreme claims are left unsubstantiated, as are unlikely statistics for areas such as 'the vital link between self-worth and longevity'. Then one wonders how much McPherson has relied on the work of others in the field in order to lend his book more substance. He can also be harsh when it comes to the reasons why people end up 'demotivated and drifting', placing the blame solely on an inadequate upbringing and absolving the individual from any personal responsibility, although the rationale for this line of thought is hard to pin down. Nonetheless, this is an accessible read, offering practical steps for confidence-building along the way.

B

Each chapter of *Journeys and Horizons* begins with an extract from an interview with 'a traveller'; which is how writer Oliver McPherson refers to the people whose lives, decisions and accurate/erroneous evaluation of self form the basis of this self-help work. According to McPherson, the choices they have made, or neglected to make, place them somewhere along the spectrum of 'highly effective' to 'extremely dysfunctional', with the latter condition apparently the fault of poor parenting skills. (Why this should be the case – when the opposite is not – is a point that McPherson does not back up with hard evidence.) Chapters conclude with an analysis of the behaviours that reinforce each person's positive self-image, or impair it, and a set of sensible key strategies for 'appreciating your own worth' that can readily be put into practice. Unlike certain previous authors in the field, McPherson offers some genuinely refreshing insights into what creates a balanced 'whole' person, taking the reader with him on a journey of honest self-reflection.

C

In *Journeys and Horizons*, Oliver McPherson draws on earlier research into the area of self-esteem and how it influences our responses to opportunities that present themselves in life: do we seize or dismiss them? While not a particularly pioneering work, it is still mostly an engaging one. The case studies of people 'on the road to personal success or the path to personal defeat' are well-constructed and the interviews are poignant. Less convincing are some of the strategies McPherson puts forward for dealing with self-confidence issues within the family hierarchy. Is it really worth challenging older siblings or confronting ageing parents with a list of their behaviours you find detrimental to your well-being? McPherson has also rather limited his readership by focusing on the middle-class and employed, a misjudgement, to my mind. Surely in times of recession it's the underprivileged and long-term out-of-work that need a boost?

D

With the wealth of new titles jostling for position on the self-help shelf, it can be a challenge to pick out something really worth your attention. Oliver McPherson's *Journeys and Horizons* may well be that candidate. An evaluation of the requirements for positive self-image and personal achievement, the book offers little that is new in terms of theory and concept, but readers will appreciate McPherson's unique blend of frank assessment and consistent optimism. Life skills will be enhanced by following his simple recommendations; strategies we already suspect may be effective but have never quite managed to put in place. For my part, if the case studies presented had reflected a wider section of society, McPherson's work might indeed merit a public service award. All the same, an intelligent and inspiring read.

Which reviewer

expresses the same opinion as reviewer C regarding the scope of McPherson's book? 1 [ ]

has a different view from the others on the originality of McPherson's ideas? 2 [ ]

shares reviewer A's opinion about the support McPherson offers for his beliefs? 3 [ ]

expresses a different view from the others concerning the extent to which McPherson's ideas are workable? 4 [ ]

Reacting to the text

Do you agree with the idea that 'an inadequate upbringing' is solely responsible for the way that a person's character develops?

Are there any other factors that might play a greater role in a person's character development?

Listening Part 3

Multiple choice 1.30

1 You will hear a radio programme about a treatment for removing frown lines and wrinkles from the forehead.

What do you think motivates people to have this type of treatment?

2 For questions **1–6**, choose the answer (**A**, **B**, **C** or **D**) which fits best according to what you hear.

1 Dr Evans says most of his patients prefer receiving the treatment at parties because
- **A** it is not complicated to administer.
- **B** they do not want to risk being seen by the media.
- **C** they are too busy to go to his surgery.
- **D** they enjoy socializing.

2 What do we learn from Lynnie about the injections?
- **A** The effects are temporary.
- **B** They are quite painful.
- **C** There are no side effects.
- **D** They can lead to addiction.

3 Dr Evans says that he has botulism injections himself in order to
- **A** advertise his business.
- **B** look good for his wife.
- **C** help him feel more confident.
- **D** impress the media.

4 Lynnie says of the treatment that it
- **A** is comparable to meditation.
- **B** is beyond the means of most people.
- **C** offers good value for money.
- **D** has become a routine.

5 How have other people reacted to Lynnie's treatment?
- **A** They cannot understand why she has the injections.
- **B** They have become accustomed to her appearance.
- **C** They are glad it has helped her overcome depression.
- **D** They have apologized for comments they made earlier.

6 Dr Evans says that people at the parties
- **A** are normally more talkative than usual.
- **B** compliment him on his appearance.
- **C** are surprised at how hard he works.
- **D** are unaware how tired he feels.

3 Lynnie says of the treatment: *It's a way of growing old gracefully. We all use moisturizer, we all take care of ourselves. I think it's just an extension of that.* To what extent do you agree with her?

Under what circumstances, if any, would you have either this type of treatment or cosmetic surgery?

Language focus: Reported speech

A Direct and reported speech

1 In the following example, an extract of direct speech from the listening has been reported. What tense changes have been made after the reporting verbs in **bold**?

Presenter: 'Have other people noticed the effects?'
Lynnie: 'Yes, they have. And they've grown used to my new look now.'
The presenter **asked** Lynnie if other people had noticed the effects and she **replied** that they had, and **added** that they'd grown used to her new look.

What other changes do you notice?

Read more about these changes in Part A of the Grammar reference on page 220.

2 For questions **1–4** below, refer to the direct speech to help you complete the gaps in the reported version. Use the reporting verbs in the box. **Do not write more than two words in each gap.** The exercise begins with an example (**0**).

warned	announced	reminded	~~repeated~~
pointed out	predicted	~~conceded~~	
admitted	stressed	concluded	

0 'Yes, I do accept the situation is critical, but let me say once again that we are doing our best to find a solution.'
The Prime Minister *conceded* that the situation *was* critical, but *repeated* that the government *was doing* its best to find a solution.

1 'Yes, I did sell the stolen paintings, but I would like to mention that I have given all the proceeds to charity.'
The defendant ___________ that she ___________ the stolen paintings, but ___________ to the court that she ___________ all the proceeds to charity.

2 'I think there'll be more than 250 000 taking part in the protest. There might be some violent activists – so be careful!'
The police chief ___________ that there ___________ over 250 000 taking part in the protest. He ___________ his men that there ___________ some violent activists and urged them to be careful.

3 'The result of all this is that we must increase profits. Remember – if we don't, the company will go bankrupt.'
The Managing Director ___________ that they ___________ increase profits and ___________ the board that if they ___________, the company ___________ bankrupt.

4 'I'd just like to tell everyone that I intend to resign at the end of this season. I should emphasize that I have not been asked to leave.'
The manager has ___________ that he ___________ to resign at the end of this season. He ___________ that he ___________ been asked to leave.

B Alternative verb patterns

1 Many reporting verbs can be followed by alternative verb patterns to the 'that' clause seen in section **A**.

Example:
'I should have started younger,' said Dr Evans.
Dr Evans regretted that he had not started younger.
Dr Evans regretted not starting/having started younger.

2 Match the groups of verbs **A–D** with the corresponding verb patterns **1–4**.

1 doing something
2 to do something
3 someone to do something
4 (that) someone (should) do something

A	C
urge	suggest
remind	deny
warn	admit

B	D
promise	suggest
agree	insist
refuse	agree

3 Add each verb in the box to the appropriate group **A, B, C** or **D**. Some verbs belong to more than one group, as with *suggest* in groups **C** and **D**.

threaten	recommend	persuade	
ask	encourage	demand	offer

C Verbs and dependent prepositions

Complete each gap with an appropriate preposition. Use the same preposition for both gaps in each sentence.

Example:
0 Management were able to discourage workers from *going on strike, but the union would not be dissuaded* from *taking legal action.*

1 I apologized _____ arriving late, but she thanked me _____ turning up at all.
2 He congratulated me _____ passing my driving test and insisted _____ buying me a drink.
3 She accused him _____ deception and spoke _____ reporting him to the police.
4 The union protested _____ the decision to sack him, but his own colleagues supported the move and argued _____ reinstating him.
5 She consented _____ the interview but objected _____ being photographed.

Read more about the points in sections **B** and **C** above in Part B of the Grammar reference on page 220.

Word formation: Verbs

The following verbs from the listening are formed using the affixes *-ize*, *-ify* and *en-*.

social + -ize *they enjoy socializing*
pure + -ify *the botulism toxin which is purified*
en- + able *to enable them to get work on television*

1 In **1–5** below, the affix at the beginning of each line can be used to form verbs with all of the words in the line, except one. Underline the odd one out and write down the verb forms of all the words. The exercise begins with an example (**0**).

0	**-ize**	special *specialize*	summary *summarize*	valid *validate*	modern *modernize*	commercial *commercialize*
1	**-ify**	class	example	simple	identity	general
2	**-ate**	difference	qualification	captive	value	assassin
3	**-ize**	character	stable	familiar	dominant	computer
4	**-en**	strong	sad	rich	deaf	high
5	**en-**	large	wide	sure	danger	courage

2 For each of the verbs in box **A** below, decide which of the prefixes in box **B** can be used to form new verbs.

Example: *cook – recook (cook again), overcook (cook too much)*

A cook appear read number load hear use

B re- dis- over- un- mis- out-

3 Complete each gap with an appropriate form of the word in capitals at the end of the line. The exercise begins with an example (**0**).

0 I see they've finally got round to *widening* the Shoreham Road. **WIDE**

1 Each employee's performance is __________ at least once a year. **VALUE**
2 We could barely hear ourselves speak above the __________ roar of the sea. **DEAF**
3 He was fined £500 and __________ from driving for three years. **QUALIFY**
4 They lost the battle, despite __________ the enemy by two to one. **NUMBER**
5 I spent my first two weeks back at work __________ myself with all the new procedures. **FAMILIAR**
6 Arnold died in 1953: his wife, who __________ him by almost half a century, passed away on the last day of the millennium. **LIVE**
7 Before enrolling on a course, you should first ensure that it has been __________ by an officially recognized body. **VALID**
8 New 'Deluxe' moisturizing cream smooths out wrinkles and __________ that your skin stays young-looking. **SURE**

4 Write similar gapped sentences for three more of the words in exercises **1** and **2**. Then give your sentences to your partner to complete.

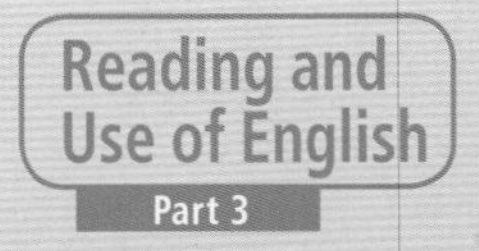

Word formation

For questions **1–8**, read the text below. Use the word given in capitals at the end of some of the lines to form a word that fits in the gap **in the same line**. There is an example at the beginning (**0**). Write your answers **IN CAPITAL LETTERS**.

HOLDING BACK THE YEARS

No need to suffer **(0)** ......PAINFUL...... , expensive cosmetic surgery. Here are some tips to combat the ageing process and make you look and feel better.	**PAIN**
Drink the right liquids	
Drinking two litres of water a day helps fight **(1)** .... , headaches,	**TIRE**
stiff joints and dry skin and eyes – especially if you work at a computer. Juices	
made with **(2)** .... of fruit and vegetables such as carrot and apple	**COMBINE**
will also give you a lift and your energy levels will increase **(3)**	**NOTICE**
Detox diets	
Regularly cleaning up your diet to clear out **(4)** .... toxins is the best	**WANT**
way to wash away the blues. A detox diet **(5)** .... and re-energizes	**PURE**
your body, **(6)** .... your mind and works wonders for your skin.	**SHARP**
Learn to laugh	
Laughter beats stress, boosts **(7)** .... and improves your ability to	**IMMUNE**
learn and **(8)** .... facts, say scientists.	**MEMORY**

Vocabulary: Health crossword

Across
2 a minor medical _____
6 a swollen _____
7 a sprained _____
9 a blinding _____
11 come out in a _____
12 a bruised _____
13 a blocked _____

Down
1 an upset _____
3 relieve the _____
4 a chipped _____
5 fall seriously _____
6 a mild _____
8 a torn _____
10 prescribe a _____

Reported speech

1 In each of the following sentences there is one grammatically incorrect word. Underline the unnecessary word. There is an example at the beginning (**0**).

0 Paul said that if he had known we were moving house last week, he would have offered <u>us</u> to come and help.

1 She confessed to being a little unfit and in need of exercise, and she agreed to having run in the local half marathon in April.

2 He complained about he was suffering from hay fever and claimed that a vase of flowers in the school entrance had brought it on on Monday.

3 The teacher reminded us that we should read more and virtually insisted we need buy an English newspaper; I haven't got round to doing it yet, but I will.

4 The Transport Minister commented to reporters on the need for greater safety on the roads and pointed them out that a number of measures were about to be taken.

5 Mrs Jacobs mentioned that she had had the car repaired five times in the last year and added that she regretted of ever having considered buying one in the first place.

2 Report the following sentences without using the verbs *say* or *tell*. The exercise begins with an example (**0**).

0 'I didn't take your pen so please don't shout at me.'
He denied taking her pen and asked her not to shout at him.

1 'You really must come and visit us sometime. You'll love it here, you can be sure of that.'

2 'I'm sorry I haven't phoned earlier – I've been very busy.'

3 'It's a very dangerous part of town, so please, please, don't go there on your own.'

4 'You ought to wear your gloves on the run tomorrow, and don't forget to do some warm-up exercises beforehand.'

5 'It might rain at the weekend, but if it doesn't, I'll take you all to the funfair.'

8 This is the modern world

Listening 1
Part 2

Sentence completion 1.31

1 Why do people play video games?

In what ways do you think video games might have changed over the years?

2 You will hear a man called Andy Brown, the owner of a video games development company, giving a talk on the gaming industry. For questions **1–8**, complete the sentences with a word or short phrase.

The Gaming Industry

Andy refers to modern games as a product of a '**(1)** .... of art and science'.

Andy says that gaming is now part of **(2)** .... , rather than being an activity just for young men.

Andy explains that **(3)** .... is currently providing developers with inspiration.

Andy's team are using **(4)** .... to help create different moods in a game.

In Andy's opinion, the themes of combat, problem-solving and **(5)** .... are essential in game design.

Andy blames the **(6)** .... for some people's negative opinion of gaming.

According to Andy, parents and teachers are unaware of the **(7)** .... within the gaming industry.

Andy emphasizes how a young person's creativity and **(8)** .... can be developed by gaming.

3 Which of Andy's beliefs below do you agree with?

- Modern games engage the player emotionally and intellectually.
- Gaming is no longer just an activity for young men.
- Gaming helps develop a young person's creativity and their use of logic.

Language focus 1: Determiners and pronouns

1 Complete each of the gaps in the following extracts from the listening with one of the words in the box. You will need to use one of the words twice.

another	both	every	many	one

In **(1)** ________ respect, the older games and modern games are similar, but they're very different in **(2)** ________ .
(3) ________ modern games engage the player emotionally and intellectually.
Whether it's a Sony PlayStation® or Xbox®, pretty much every household has **(4)** ________ .
It's no longer black and white – but **(5)** ________ shade of grey.
... parents and teachers **(6)** ________ seem to overlook something important about the gaming industry ...

2 **Determiners**, which come before nouns, are often used to talk about quantities and amounts.

Example:
*I don't think we've got **enough** evidence to show that gaming can improve your reaction time.*

Many words which are determiners can also be used on their own as **pronouns**. Pronouns are used instead of nouns.

Example:
*We need more evidence to show that gaming can improve your reaction time. We haven't got **enough**.*

Look at the extracts in exercise **1** and decide whether each of the words you have written is used as a determiner or a pronoun.

3 a Determiners can be used before either singular nouns, plural nouns, uncountable nouns or nouns of more than one type. In **1–3** cross out the grammatically incorrect word. There is an example at the beginning (**0**).

0 '*All/~~Much~~/Some/No* mobile phones have this facility.'
1 '*No/Each/All/Neither* player is allowed to handle the ball in this game.'
2 'This happens on *many/very few/every/most* days of the year in my country.'
3 '*A lot of/Very little/Several/No* fruit is this colour.'

b For each correct alternative in the sentences in **a**, discuss what the speaker might be referring to.

Example:
'All mobile phones have this facility.' All mobile phones can be used to speak to people and send text messages.

4 a Sometimes more than one determiner can be used before a noun. In **1–3** cross out the incorrect alternative.

1 I go swimming *every many/every few* weeks.
2 I'll be on holiday in *another one month/another few months*.
3 There are *no other/no many* languages I'd like to learn.

b How true are the sentences in **a** for you?

Read more about determiners and pronouns in the Grammar reference on pages 220 and 221.

Practice

1 Each of the paragraphs **1–4** contains **two** mistakes in the use of pronouns and determiners. Find the mistakes and correct them. You will need to change the pronoun or determiner, or one of the words which follows.

Example:
I tried on no fewer than ten coats, and didn't buy ~~either~~ any of them. Each one ~~were~~ was either too long or too short and none of them would have been suitable for work.

1 Every other years I meet up with a few of my old school friends. All of us are married with children now and we have very little free time, but we do our best to keep in touch with each another.
2 This is one of the few pubs where you can still have a quiet drink. There are quite a few others I enjoy going to, but most of they play loud music and neither is very welcoming.
3 Alan's been working at Crabtree's for some 30 years, and there's all likelihood he'll be there for another 20. Most people in his profession change company every five years or so, but he has none intention of moving on.
4 Both of my daughters use the computer, but they're each restricted to an hour a day on it. Several of my friends' children, on another hand, spend as most as 20 hours a week playing games or surfing the Net.

2 Complete each gap with one word from the box to complete the common expressions in **bold**.

all	lot	none	any	one	
few	little	most	each	every	either

1 We've got **an awful** ________ to do and **precious** ________ time to do it in, so let's get started now!
2 The service in the restaurant is first class and the quality of the food **second to** ________ .
3 He gave five concerts in London and I went to ________ **single one** of them.
4 You can get there by bus or train. ________ **way**, it'll cost you a lot of money.
5 ________ **too often** students fail to read the instructions properly, and **few, if** ________ , get full marks.
6 We had to queue **a good** ________ hours to get the tickets, but we **made the** ________ **of** our time, reading, talking and playing cards.
7 She turned the pages ________ **by one**, carefully studying the information on each one.
8 I'd like to thank ________ **and every one** of you for all your hard work.

3 Choose four of the expressions in exercise **2**. Have a three-minute conversation with your partner on one of the topics on page 204, aiming to include all four expressions. At the end of the three minutes, tell your partner which expressions he or she has used.

Vocabulary 1: Amount

1 The underlined words in the following sentences from the listening refer to cost or amount.

In large part, I feel this is down to the media.

... they don't know about the great number of career opportunities ...

And this is an industry that now turns over huge profits annually ...

In **1–6** below, use the information in the first sentence to complete the gaps in the second, more formal sentence. You should write two words in each gap; one from box **A** and the other, a noun, from box **B**. The exercise begins with an example (**0**).

A | small | ~~extra~~ | full | great | high | large | no |

B | limit | cost | deal | refund | number | ~~charge~~ | discount |

0 We can do this if you pay a little bit more.
This can be arranged for a small ___extra charge___ .

1 You can send in as many entries as you like.
There is ________________ to the number of entries that can be submitted.
2 If so, we'd give you all your money back.
If this were the case, you would be entitled to a ________________ .
3 The press are really interested in the event.
The event has attracted a ________________ of media interest.
4 It's a bit cheaper if you pay cash.
We offer a ________________ if you pay cash.
5 We've put up the price because it's very expensive to send it by rail now.
The current ________________ of rail transport has resulted in a price increase.
6 A lot of customers have complained.
We have received a ________________ of complaints from customers.

2 For **1–6** above, discuss with your partner the possible context for each of the sentences you have completed.

Example:
0 *This could be an announcement by a company or a shop which charges extra for delivery of products or purchases.*

Reading and Use of English 1
Part 2

Open cloze

1 You are going to read a text about a real experiment in which six men (three Russians, an Italian, a Frenchman and a Chinese) were sealed inside a fake spacecraft. The aim of the experiment was to see how they would cope with being cut off from the real world for 18 months – about the time it might take to get to Mars.

What issues and challenges do you think astronauts would face on a real flight to Mars?

Which of these do you think the men in the experiment experienced?

2 Read the text below, ignoring the gaps. Are any of the points you discussed in exercise **1** mentioned?

3 For questions **1–8**, read the text again and think of the word which best fits each gap. Use only **one** word in each gap. There is an example at the beginning (**0**). Write your answers **IN CAPITAL LETTERS**.

Getting ready for Mars

The 'Mars500 project' **(0)**...*WAS*... an experiment that simulated a return mission to Mars. Spending 18 months in a sealed facility in Moscow **(1)** .... access to natural light or fresh air, six men were monitored as they attended **(2)** .... their daily duties. A study into **(3)** .... each of them coped with the psychological and physical constraints of the mission has found that there were wide differences in their wake-sleep patterns. For example, **(4)** .... most of the crew began to sleep for longer periods as the mission progressed and boredom set in, one individual slept progressively less, resulting **(5)** .... him becoming chronically sleep-deprived towards the end of the mission. Identifying bad sleepers could be important on a real Mars mission, during **(6)** .... people are required to be constantly alert even when days are tediously similar. Researchers warn that for any astronaut heading to Mars, exciting as the trip might initially seem, **(7)** .... could be problems with stress brought on by the monotony of routine. However, they also report that **(8)** .... some personal tensions between crew members, there was overall harmony within the group.

4 Do you think you would be a good candidate for a mission to Mars? Why/Why not?

Which of the following statements is most similar to your attitude towards space exploration? Explain why.

It's a waste of money.

It's vital that we continue to invest in space exploration.

I'd seize the chance to go up in space!

It's too dangerous to even think about!

I'm not remotely interested.

Do you think people will have reached Mars in your lifetime? Why/Why not?

Reading and Use of English 2
Part 7

Gapped text

1 You are going to read an article that was written in 1999. In the article, the author talks about his experience of computers, email and the Internet.

How do you think that computers, email and the Internet have changed since 1999?

Think about size, speed, cost, functions, etc.

2 Quickly read the base text only. How does the writer feel about the technology available to him in 1999?

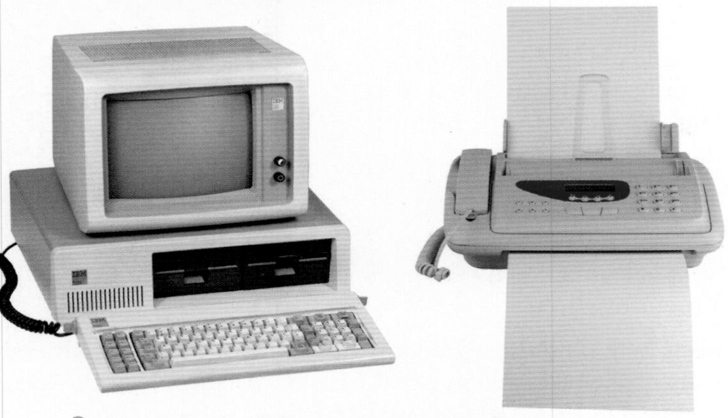

3 Now do the following Part 7 task:

You are going to read an article about someone who does not have a computer. Six paragraphs have been removed from the extract. Choose from the paragraphs **A–G** the one which fits each gap (**1–6**). There is one extra paragraph which you do not need to use.

UNPLUGGED

Martin Newell explains why he shuns computers and remains a devotee of 'snail mail'.

I am an Internot. That is, I have no desire to be on the Internet. I am, of course, well aware of the Internet. Boy, am I aware of the Internet! The world is being overtaken by people setting 5 up websites, talking www-slash-dot.coms and worrying about updating and upgrading.

1 ______

In fact, if I wanted to, I could sit in front of the computer, ordering whatever I wanted, whenever I wanted, 24 hours a day, and pay for it all 10 electronically. But I don't have a computer. My friends, who look upon me as a 'technological oddity', find it hard to believe that I can still find work. I can't drive a car, won't fly and won't travel abroad anymore. I don't even have a mobile 15 phone.

2 ______

As a congenital sender and receiver of snail mail, I can only remember about two occasions in 20-odd years when a letter has gone astray. Exactly how many bits of info has your machinery 20 swallowed this month, brave internaut? There is the access to information, though. While doing some research on a fairly esoteric subject earlier this year, I was told by a friend that 37 internet pages existed upon the matter. He downloaded 25 them for me.

3 ______

As for the actual equipment itself, computers are so unattractive and bulky. Buying a laptop I can understand, because you can put it away. But all that dreadful grey-white office junk in your 30 living space?

4 ______

I almost upgraded to a computer once but decided that a piano would be more fun, so I spent the money having one fork-lifted up into my first-floor living room. While others are 35 getting neck-ache and headaches and running up their phone bills, I've almost figured out how to play the first few bars of *Return to Sender*.

5 [ ]

It strikes me, though, that the main reason the Internet exists is not as a medium for spreading 40 the joys of music, but more for the purpose of shopping and advertising. Now I know a little bit about shopping, because I get on my bicycle and go to the greengrocer's every once in a while.

6 [ ]

45 But perhaps by doing things in this quaint, old-fashioned way, I'm missing out on some of the financial benefits of the whole computer culture. Companies are constantly undercutting each other. Full-page newspaper 50 ads are currently offering me the whole kit and caboodle and telling me that I can get myself connected and surfing, all for under a thousand pounds. Wow! What a bargain. I could get an electric organ fork-lifted up here for that.

55 Seriously, though, there is, I suppose, an outside chance I will be forced onto the Internet one day. By that time, however, it will have devolved into one tiny little module about the size of an answering machine, cost about 50 quid, and be 60 instant, as well as idiot-proof for people like me.

A There's also this marvellous little alternative to buying books on the Net: it's called my local bookshop. It has human beings working in it. Whenever I want a particular book, I just walk down there or telephone them, and they find it for me. Within a day or two I always have it.

B Friends like these will spend hours, days even, in front of their ugly state-of-the-art computers. As they listen to music being broadcast online from all four corners of the globe, they are subjected to a constant bombardment of advertisements encouraging them to buy, buy, buy. Well, bye-bye, friends.

C It has not escaped my attention that you can buy and sell houses on the Internet. You can book holidays, buy a pool-table and, so I hear, even get a divorce on the Internet. Were my dog to fall seriously ill, I could even consult a vet on the Internet. Or maybe he's called the Intervet.

D The information was largely superficial and in one or two cases, written by someone who I suspect was not entirely of this planet. In the end I went to the local reference library, where a reassuringly stern librarian plonked a huge pile of books on the table in front of me and said: 'That should be a start.' I had everything I needed within an hour.

E While we're on the subject, I hear that we can now download our music from the Net. I have only recently completed the costly operation of replacing my vinyl record collection with CDs. I hope this does not mean that these, too, will soon be obsolete.

F My own word processor, with VDU, keyboard and printer all in one unit, is much more compact. It can be quickly shoved in the cupboard when I'm not using it. In fact, even this is too ugly for me so I glued a piece of tapestry on the space between the keyboard and the screen to make it look more homely.

G 'But how will we get hold of you?' people ask, in a tone I usually associate with anguished parents pleading with a runaway daughter calling from a phone box. Well, you can telephone me. Or fax me. Or you could try writing me a letter.

Reacting to the text

Do you think it's possible for a person to manage without the Internet today? Why/Why not?

Which of the following are best done with a computer and which in the *'quaint, old-fashioned way'*? Give reasons for your opinions.

consulting reference works	shopping	writing letters	booking holidays
storing photographs	playing games	reading fiction	
raising capital for new business ventures		promoting your talents	

Since you first started using the Internet, what advances do you think have been made? Is there anything about using the Internet that you find frustrating?

How do you think computers or similar communication devices will develop in the future?

Vocabulary 2: Verbs formed with *up, down, over* and *under*

Up, down, over and *under* can be used to form a number of verbs.

Examples:
The world is being ***overrtaken*** *by people … worrying about* ***updating*** *and* ***upgrading****.*
We can now ***download*** *our music from the Net.*
Companies are constantly ***undercutting*** *each other.*

Complete each of the gaps with the correct form of one of the verbs in the box.

uproot	uphold	overthrow	overrule	~~overhear~~
downplay	downsize	undergo	undertake	

Example:
We closed the door to prevent anyone overhearing *our conversation.*

1 The military government was ____________ by a popular uprising and democratic elections were held.
2 The American-based company has been ____________ its operations, leading to the closure of a number of European factories.
3 The Court of Appeal had been expected to ____________ the judge's decision, instead of which it was ____________ and Jenkins had to serve out his sentence.
4 The two leaders ____________ to find a peaceful solution to the crisis and arranged to meet again.
5 The 28-year-old actress is rumoured to have ____________ emergency surgery, although doctors are ____________ the seriousness of the problem, suggesting she will be out of hospital soon.
6 During the war, thousands of children were ____________ , forced to leave family, home and school.

Language focus 2: Modal verbs 2: *will, shall* and *would*

1 The following examples from the reading text on pages 106 and 107 show three different uses of *will/won't*.

Habit
Friends like these *will* spend hours, days even, in front of their ugly state-of-the-art computers.

Refusal
I … *won't* fly and *won't* travel abroad anymore.

Prediction
There is, I suppose, an outside chance I *will* be forced onto the Internet one day.

2 The sentences in **1–6** all contain the modal verbs *will, shall* or *would*. Match each pair to the idea they both express.

Assumption	Habit	Annoying behaviour
Request for advice/instructions		~~Offer~~
Willingness	Refusal	

Example:
0 *I'll set* ***it*** *up for you if you like. It's the same as the one I use at work.*
Shall I show you how to draw graphs on ***it****?* Offer

1 **It** won't start – I think the battery's flat.
I asked him to park **it** somewhere else, but he wouldn't move **it**.
2 I wish he would turn **it** down.
We can watch the match on the balcony if you'll just help me take **it** out there.
3 **It** would keep her amused on long car journeys – but we insisted she have the sound off.
He'll play with **it** all morning, his eyes glued to the tiny screen.
4 That'll be Mike. Don't answer **it**!
They'll have got there by now. Give **it** to me – I know their number.
5 He will keep forgetting to turn **it** off. It gets so hot in the kitchen!
It would go wrong now, wouldn't **it**! Just as I put the meat in to roast.
6 There's no more room in **it**. Where shall I put the chicken?
Shall I defrost **it** now or when we come back?

3 What do you think **it** might refer to in each pair of sentences in **1–6** on page 108?

Example:
0 computer

 Read more about the modal verbs *will, shall* and *would* in the Grammar reference on page 221.

4 a Think of three domestic appliances, machines or other electronic devices and write two sentences for each, without mentioning the name of the object. Each sentence should include one of the above uses of either *will, shall* or *would.*

b Show your sentences to your partner, who will
- say which three objects you have written about.
- tell you the idea expressed by the modal verbs.

Speaking Part 2

Long turn

Here are some pictures showing people who are learning in different ways.

Student A:
Compare **two** of the pictures, and say why the people might have chosen to learn in these ways, and what the advantages are of learning like this.

- Why might the people have chosen to learn in these ways?
- What are the advantages of learning like this?

Student B:
In which situation does the learner have most control over their education?

Now change roles. Follow the instructions again using the pictures on page 207.

Writing
Part 2

Report

1 How useful do you think computers and the Internet are for language learning?

Some language schools or universities have multimedia rooms or learning centres where students can do extra study. In your opinion, what would the ideal multimedia room/ learning centre offer in terms of technology and services? Add to the table below.

Technology e.g. *really fast broadband*	**Services** e.g. *appointments with teachers for individual learning advice*

2 What do you think these student comments might refer to?

1 'It's stuffy and crowded.'

2 'Most of them are in American English.'

3 'I think some of it is out-of-date.'

4 'You can never get on them because people are just writing to their friends.'

5 'The recordings are poor quality.'

6 'It would be good to have a wider range.'

7 'The memory is too small for so many programs.'

8 'I can't hear myself think!'

9 'There's no one available when something goes wrong.'

3 Read the following Part 2 task and discuss

- who your target reader is.
- what the tone of your report should be (e.g. critical, persuasive, complimentary).
- what the general content would be for each paragraph of your report.
- what headings you would choose.

> You help out in the multimedia centre at a language school called Highford Academy. The school's director has asked you to write a report on the centre with a view to making improvements.
>
> Your report should
>
> - refer to the opinions of students.
> - make suggestions for improvements.
> - say in which areas spending could be reduced.

4 Reports are often based on information you have collected. In this case, you might collect your information from students and/or teachers.

Cross out the word or phrase which is **least** appropriate.

The **(1)** *aim/point/purpose* of this report is to **(2)** *mention/propose/recommend* ways in which facilities and services at the multimedia centre can be **(3)** *enhanced/improved/increased*, and also to **(4)** *outline/describe/suggest* where savings can be made. The recommendations are based on the opinions of students that **(5)** *carried out an investigation/completed a questionnaire/responded to a survey*.

5 Now write your **report** in **220–260** words, using some of the ideas from your discussion in exercises **1** and **2**. For more information on writing reports, see pages 34 and 35 in Unit 3 and page 201 in Ready for Writing.

Listening 2
Part 4

Multiple matching 1.32–1.36

1 How far do you agree with each of the statements **A–H** in Task One below? Consider the future 15 years from now when giving your opinions.

2 You will hear five short extracts in which people are predicting what life will be like in 15 years' time.

Don't forget!

- Concentrate mainly, but not exclusively, on Task One the first time you listen.
- The second time you listen, give more attention to Task Two.

TASK ONE
For questions **1–5**, choose from the list **(A–H)** the prediction each speaker makes.

TASK TWO
For questions **6–10**, choose from the list **(A–H)** the feeling aroused in each speaker by the future they predict.

While you listen you must complete both tasks.

	Task One			Task Two	
A	We will live longer.	1	A	amusement	6
B	Houses will be smaller.	2	B	annoyance	7
C	Life in the workplace will be very different.	3	C	worry	8
D	There will be more technology in the home.	4	D	nostalgia	9
E	There will be too many people.	5	E	amazement	10
F	Technology will be smaller.		F	enthusiasm	
G	We will lead healthier lives.		G	distrust	
H	There will be less traffic congestion.		H	indifference	

3 What are your own feelings about the future? How optimistic are you?

Language focus 3: Talking about the future

Both *will* and *going to* can be used when making predictions.

Examples:
It's *going to* change the way they do things here completely.
Life in the workplace *will* be very different.

1 In the following sentence from the listening, which of the verb forms in *italics* refers to
   - **a** an activity that will be in progress at a certain time in the future?
   - **b** an event that will be finished before a certain time in the future?

Of course, *I'll have left* long before then, and *I'll probably be enjoying* a long and healthy retirement somewhere.

2 For each pair of sentences **1–10**, decide if the meaning is similar (**S**) or different (**D**). If the meaning is different, explain what is meant by each sentence.

1 I hope she passes.
I expect she'll pass.
2 We're going to meet at seven.
We're meeting at seven.
3 Will you come to the show on Friday?
Will you be coming to the show on Friday?
4 The parcel should arrive tomorrow.
The parcel might arrive tomorrow.
5 The Brighton train is due to leave at 6.20.
The Brighton train leaves at 6.20.
6 I'm about to lose my temper.
I'm on the point of losing my temper.
7 She's bound to get the job.
She's likely to get the job.
8 He's confident of success.
He's assured of success.
9 They're thinking of getting married.
They're planning on getting married.
10 The government is to spend £45 million on health care.
The government is expected to spend £45 million on health care.

Read more about ways of talking about the future in the Grammar reference on pages 221 and 222.

3 Write five true sentences using different structures from exercises **1** and **2**.

4 Discuss your sentences with your partner.

8 Review

Determiners and pronouns

For **1–10**, complete each of the gaps with a word from the box. You do not need to use all the words.

little	few	other	others	another
much	many	all	either	neither
both	each	every	any	

1 I've nearly finished it – I just need ___________ couple of weeks.
2 My computer class is every ___________ day: Monday, Wednesday and Friday.
3 This is my favourite cheese, but there are one or two ___________ I really like as well.
4 It took us a good ___________ hours to drive to Leeds.
5 I was very tired, but there seemed ___________ point in going to bed until the storm had passed.
6 I have to go to the dentist's three times a year, about once ___________ four months.
7 I've got two brothers and ___________ of us is different in some way.
8 Where have you been ___________ this time? We've been worried sick!
9 You can pay as ___________ as £20 000 for a mobile phone number.
10 Has ___________ of you two got a pen you could lend me?

Key word transformation

For questions **1–6**, complete the second sentence so that it has a similar meaning to the first sentence, using the word given. **Do not change the word given.** You must use between **three** and **six** words, including the word given. Write your answers **IN CAPITAL LETTERS**.

1 Jake used his month's free membership really well by going to the gym every single day.
MOST
Jake .... his month's free membership by going to the gym every single day.

2 The Japanese are the best at making pocket-sized technology.
SECOND
The Japanese .... when it comes to making pocket-sized technology.

3 Each and every one of our employees has contributed to the great success of our company.
SINGLE
The great success of our company is due to the contribution .... our employees.

4 Can we please stay on one channel when we're watching TV?
KEEP
I wish you .... the channel when we're watching TV.

5 It's likely they were delayed in a traffic jam.
PROBABLY
They will .... up in a traffic jam.

6 The company does not intend to create any redundancies amongst employees even though profits are down.
NO
Even though profits are down, the company .... any of their employees redundant.

Multiple-choice cloze

For questions **1–8**, read the text below and decide which answer (**A**, **B**, **C** or **D**) best fits each gap. There is an example at the beginning (**0**).

GADGETS FOR THE FUTURE

This year's Future Product of the Year Award has attracted a number of unusual entries, including the Inculpable Mousetrap and an alarm-clock duvet and pillow. Stuart Penny and Gianni Tozzi **(0)** .... the Inculpable Mousetrap as an 'exercise in morality' and accept it is unlikely to **(1)** .... commercial success. You **(2)** .... the trap, wander off to the café and wait to see what happens. If a mouse approaches the trap, a transmitter **(3)** .... to it sends a signal to your mobile phone. You are then **(4)** .... to send back a text message with your decision whether to activate the trap or not.

Rachel Wingfield's alarm-clock duvet and pillow could **(5)** .... the end for alarm clocks. The sleeper **(6)** .... programmes the alarm clock on their mobile phone, plugs it into a socket on the duvet or pillow and is woken at the correct time – with light. The whole effect is **(7)** .... to replicate the break of day because the duvet and pillow are woven through with electro-luminescent cords. At the **(8)** .... time the mobile phone sends a tiny electric current through them and they begin to glow, waking the individual sleeper rather than the whole household.

	A	B	C	D
0	**A** projected	**B** held	**C** <u>conceived</u>	**D** evaluated
1	**A** favour	**B** enjoy	**C** appreciate	**D** support
2	**A** fix	**B** put	**C** set	**D** shut
3	**A** enclosed	**B** attached	**C** collated	**D** united
4	**A** offered	**B** asked	**C** urged	**D** let
5	**A** say	**B** speak	**C** write	**D** spell
6	**A** uniquely	**B** simply	**C** plainly	**D** purely
7	**A** pretended	**B** assumed	**C** supposed	**D** suggested
8	**A** said	**B** stated	**C** announced	**D** specified

9 Going places

Multiple matching

1 Where would you go for your ideal holiday? What would you do there? Who would you go with?

2 Imagine you are going to spend a week in Uganda climbing Mount Stanley and attempting to reach its highest point, Margherita Peak (5109 metres).

- What would you need to take with you on the climb?
- What difficulties do you think you might face?

3 Now read an article about a climbing group's experience of ascending Mount Stanley. For questions **1–10**, choose from the sections (**A–E**). The sections may be chosen more than once.

In which section of the article are the following mentioned?

the fact that the group did not consider an alternative and easier route	1
the writer conceding that his group caused problems for the people helping them	2
the participation in the climb having a positive effect on relationships	3
the writer's recognition of the skill involved in certain construction work	4
a reservation concerning the ability of the people assisting the group	5
the writer's acknowledgement that a name is particularly appropriate	6
the writer's melancholy feeling about the end of a relationship	7
the writer being inspired by the view despite his physical exhaustion	8
the writer expressing doubt about the likelihood of the group's success	9
the writer feeling that his success on this climb made up for earlier failures	10

Climbing Margherita

The Rwenzori Mountains have long cast a spell on visitors, and recently John McKinnell became one of its victims. Here is his tale of conquering Mount Stanley's highest peak.

A

Ptolemy's 2nd-century maps were the first to label them as the Mountains of the Moon, yet they are not remotely arid or colourless. However, as the mountains on the Rwenzori 5 range convey such a sense of total inaccessibility, strangeness and wonder due to hosting large tracts of snow and ice in equatorial Africa, it's understandable how the moniker has lasted almost two millennia. And so there we were, 10 our intrepid group of seven setting out to attempt the eight-day trek that would take us to Margherita Peak on Mt Stanley, accompanied by 18 support people. Although conditions were idyllic, I soon had a sense of foreboding – it 15 stemmed from an exhausted party of Russian climbers we ran into on that first day. They had failed to attain the summit of Margherita, despite attempting it in perfect conditions. Would we be as lucky with the weather, I 20 wondered, and would we be skilled and strong enough to reach that sign at 5109m saying, 'Welcome to the highest point in Uganda'?

B

Unfortunately, one of those questions was soon answered: tropical heat gave way to heavy rain. 25 Still, on the first day, I found the paths excellent considering that Mother Nature is determined to convert them into streams and rivers – they are a testament to huge effort and proficiency on the part of their builders. On day two, we 30 reached the fringes of the alpine zone. On day three, we were squelching through swamps as the trail took us up to 4000m. It is at this point that altitude sickness often kicks in. The escape option involves completing a lower altitude 35 circuit that skirts the main peak and reaches camp five a day ahead of schedule. This was not something we contemplated.

C

By day five, we were ready to tackle the Stanley Glacier. Crampons were strapped to boots, and 40 the ice axes came into their own as we set off in two groups of four climbers, each linked by a 60m rope. Our guides, Jeremiah and Sebastian, were supremely confident in finding the best route, but less wonderful in their technical 45 guidance. Perhaps halfway across the ice we unexpectedly encountered a 20m rock step in the white-out conditions. Ahead of me a desperate cry rang out as Rebecca plunged nearly vertically. The guide below her wasn't 50 in position to stop her fall, but fortunately Andrew and I managed to hold her on the rope. Crunching across the glacier was otherwise enormously enjoyable. Things steepened up as we approached the final rocky prominence, and 55 the summit of volcanic rock turned out to be a lung-bursting climb. But as I stood puffing and panting at the summit cairn the swirling mist parted sufficiently for a brief glimpse of nearby Alexandra Peak, which lifted my spirits further.

D

60 For all of the team, standing on top of that summit was close to a religious experience. For David and Rebecca and their dad Stephen Viljoen, this was an amazing bonding experience, an achievement sweetened by its 65 sharing. Furthermore, Rebecca (17), as the only girl on the team and under the constant scrutiny of 24 males, had proved a point. Andrew Kenny, at 60-plus, had constant, nagging doubts about this adventure, yet won through with his 70 dogged perseverance. I choked back tears as I stepped up to the very top, which represented vindication for two very gruelling and unsuccessful attempts to climb Batian, (Mount Kenya's summit) in similar poor weather.

E

75 On the way down, as we explored exquisite waterfalls, rushing rivers and silvery mists, I knew our hike was nearing its end. While comforts like hot showers and fresher food beckoned, I was already regretting the imminent 80 parting from our guides and porters, with whom we had forged friendships. An endearing evening ritual at every hut along the trail was a pep talk from the guides – they'd praise our efforts and exhort us to maintain our excellent 85 job of working together. In reality, in terms of cohesion, we must have been a guide's worst nightmare as we tended to string ourselves out ahead, behind, and in between our guides and porters. Back home, my wife met me at the 90 airport and asked about the trek. 'It was wet,' I said. 'Wet, long, difficult and cold. But it was the achievement of a lifetime.'

Reacting to the text

What character traits do you think you would need to take part in this kind of trip?

Would *you* be prepared to take up the challenge?

Vocabulary 1: Describing an adventure

1 In the article, the writer uses a great deal of descriptive language to make his account more vivid.

Which noun does not usually collocate with the adjective on the left?

a	arid	desert/island/landscape/jungle
b	intrepid	traveller/scenery/group/voyage
c	idyllic	spot/companion/conditions/setting
d	gruelling	hike/climb/stroll/race
e	swirling	mist/water/wind/sun
f	exquisite	waterfalls/flowers/earthquakes/views

2 **a** Use context to guess the meaning of the highlighted phrasal verbs in the reading text on page 115.

Example:
setting out: this probably means they are starting something (the eight-day trek) in order to achieve their goal (climbing Margherita Peak)

Now turn to page 207 and do exercises **2b** and **3**.

Listening 1
Part 2

Sentence completion 2.1

1 Here are some images from Queenstown, New Zealand. What kind of tourists do you think might choose to go there?

2 You will hear a student called Amelia Pond talking about her work placement at the front desk of a hotel. For questions **1–8**, complete the sentences with a word or short phrase.

Amelia says that **(1)** .... has little impact on the hotel she chose for her placement.

Amelia realized the importance of an employee's **(2)** .... in creating the right first impression.

The front desk clerk said that knowing a guest's **(3)** .... helps him meet their needs.

Amelia was impressed with the way the front desk clerk kept each **(4)** .... constantly updated.

The front desk clerk said that changing **(5)** .... was a task he did not enjoy.

According to Amelia, it is the **(6)** .... that draw young people to Queenstown.

Recommending **(7)** .... was something Amelia hadn't anticipated she'd be asked to do.

Amelia learnt that increasing **(8)** .... is vital to the hotel's success.

3 Discuss the following questions about your own attitude to travel. Give reasons for your opinions.

How much research do you do before going on holiday?

What kind of souvenirs are you likely to buy?

How important is it for you to stay in touch with 'the outside world'?

Language focus: Creating emphasis

1 2.2 Listen to these three extracts from the listening and write the missing words in each gap.

a **What** really impressed me about Andre was ________________ .

b **It** was ________________ that he said he had problems with.

c **It** ________________ that I realized how huge its hospitality industry actually is.

2 The words you wrote in exercise **1** are given emphasis by the use of *What* and *It*. Sentence **a** without emphasis would be as follows:

I was impressed by how Andre managed to inform every department in the hotel about those changes.

Now rewrite sentences **b** and **c** without emphasis.

3 Here are some other ways of creating emphasis. Complete each of the explanations by writing one item from the box in each gap.

a noun	a moment in time	a prepositional phrase
an action or series of actions		'the only thing that'

a *What* can be used to emphasize ____________ ;

Examples:

I couldn't find my key, so ...

what I did was (to) *try and climb in through the window, but ...*

what happened was (that) *a passer-by saw me and phoned the police.*

or ____________ ;

Example:

What I need is *a cup of strong, black coffee.*

b *All* can be used instead of *What*, meaning ____________ ;

Examples:

Don't make a fuss. ***All I did was (to)*** *spill some milk.*

He's so boring. ***All he (ever) talks about is*** *football.*

c *It* can be used to emphasize ____________ ;

Example:

It was in France*, not their native England,* ***that*** *they first became famous.*

or with *when* to emphasize ____________ ;

Example:

It was only when I got home that *I realized someone had stolen my wallet.*

4 Transform the following, emphasizing the part of the sentence which has been underlined. There is an example at the beginning (**0**).

Example:

0 I find it amazing that he can't even fry an egg.
What I find amazing is that he can't even fry an egg .

1 How old is she? That's what I'd like to know.
What ________________ .

2 He lost his job, so he started up his own business.
He lost his job, so what he ________________ .

3 What I enjoyed most about the film was the music.
It ________________ .

4 They got married in June, not July.
It ________________ .

5 I didn't recognize him until he took his hat off.
It was only ________________ .

6 I only found out she'd moved when I spoke to Jerry.
It wasn't ________________ .

7 I don't know what that noise is. I just switched it on, that's all.
I don't know what that noise is.
All ________________ .

8 He thinks about his precious car and nothing else.
All ________________ .

Read more about creating emphasis in the Grammar reference on page 222.

5 Complete each of the following sentences so that they are true for you.

a What worries me is ...

b What I like most/least about school/my job is ...

c What I'd like to know about ... is ...

d It was in ... that I ...

e I didn't enjoy ... lessons at school. All we ever did was ...

6 Compare and discuss your sentences with another student.

Writing Part 1

Essay

1 Where are the main tourist destinations in your country? Why do tourists go there?

2 In what ways has tourism benefited your country or region? In what ways has it had a negative effect?

3 Use the words in the box to complete the sentences below. There is one word you do not need.

mass	urban	community	traditional	waste	endangered
cultural	environmental	living	unregulated	employment	

1 The **tourism industry** is ________, which means that neither local people nor tourists are protected by the law.
2 ________ **tourism** does not exist here; people come in small numbers to get away from it all and have a quiet time.
3 Certain **species** have become ________ due to the destruction of their habitat by the development of tourist resorts.
4 Tourism provides many ________ **opportunities** for young people looking for work.
5 Some areas of natural beauty have been destroyed by ________ **sprawl**, as uncontrolled development encroaches upon the surrounding countryside.
6 Our ________ **legislation** generally protects our air and water quality.
7 ________ **standards** have improved for people residing in popular tourist areas, where the income from tourism has been reinvested in improving amenities for residents.
8 The development of hotels in some regions has caused ________ **displacement**, with local people being forced to move out of their homes.
9 ________ **material** from hotels and resorts creates more landfill in the surrounding area.
10 Foreigners sometimes violate ________ **taboos** without realizing it, for example, when they enter places they are not supposed to visit.

4 Choose two or three statements above which are true for your country. Talk about them in further detail.

5 In what way might the following people or groups be connected to the tourism industry?

developers	researchers	conservation groups	residents
contractors	stakeholders	activists	policy-makers

Example:
A stakeholder is a person, group or organization that has an interest in, or will be affected by, the process or outcome of a project. So if a new resort is being built in a mountain village, the stakeholders will be the people who already live there, the people who are investing in the new resort, people who might later be employed in the resort and so on.

6 Read the Part 1 task on page 119. Before you write your essay, read the section on **Planning** below it.

Your class has viewed a documentary on ways that sustainable tourism might be achieved. You have made the notes below:

Ways that sustainable tourism might be achieved

- providing employment
- protecting local culture
- preserving the environment

Some opinions expressed in the documentary:

'Local people must benefit financially from tourism.'

'All too often tourists have no idea how their behaviour affects local people.'

'Natural resources like the local water supply often suffer when resorts are created.'

Write an essay for your tutor discussing **two** of the ways in your notes. You should **explain which way is most likely to benefit both the host country and the tourists, giving reasons** in support of your answer.

You may, if you wish, make use of the opinions expressed in the documentary, but you should use your own words as far as possible.

Write your answer in **220–260** words in an appropriate style.

Planning

1 Choose two of the ways that sustainable tourism might be achieved. Then look at the 'opinions expressed in the documentary'. Do they provide you with any further information or ideas? Now write down two or three specific examples for each way.

e.g. *providing employment:*

1 Property developers should be legally obliged to hire builders from the region; this would benefit not only the individual builders but also the families that depend on them.

2 Resorts could support the local economy by selling locally-sourced crafts, rather than imported products.

2 Plan an introduction: think about an opening statement that will grab the reader's attention, then a sentence with your definition of sustainable tourism, with a final sentence that indicates the purpose of the essay.

3 Remember to choose one way that you think is likely to benefit both the host country and tourists; you can describe it in either the second or third paragraph, but you must use language that clearly shows that this is the way you believe is the most mutually beneficial.

4 Decide which of the language from exercises **3** and **5** on page 118 you could use in your essay.

Now write your **essay**.

Don't forget!

This is an academic piece of writing, and the target reader is a tutor; the register should be formal and your tone should be objective, not emotional, even if you feel strongly about some of the issues you mention.

Listening 2
Part 3

Multiple choice 2.3

1 Read the dictionary definitions and the newspaper headlines.

Why do you think people become so aggressive in cars and aeroplanes?

Have you witnessed or read about any examples of road rage and air rage?

air rage n [U] an airline passenger's verbal or physical assault of crew members or other passengers

road rage n [U] the uncontrolled anger of a motorist incited by the actions of another driver and expressed in aggressive or violent behaviour

Driver accused of 'road rage' shooting

Passenger faces two-year jail sentence for head-butting flight attendant

2 You will hear a radio interview with a road safety expert on the topic of road rage. For questions **1–6**, choose the answer (**A**, **B**, **C** or **D**) which fits best according to what you hear.

1 James says that drivers become angry if
A they think they will be delayed.
B other drivers threaten them.
C other people don't drive as well as they do.
D they lose control of their car.

2 Revenge rage can lead motorists to
A chase after dangerous drivers.
B become distracted whilst driving.
C deliberately damage another car.
D take unnecessary risks.

3 Most 'revenge ragers' are
A young male drivers.
B drivers of large vehicles.
C inexperienced drivers.
D people who drive little.

4 James says that passengers become angry when buses are
A slow.
B expensive.
C crowded.
D uncomfortable.

5 What, according to James, does the experiment with grass show?
A People living in country areas are better drivers.
B Strong smells help us drive more safely.
C Our surroundings can affect the way we drive.
D Regular breaks on a journey keep drivers calm.

6 James thinks the hi-tech car
A sounds less irritating than a passenger.
B is not very reliable.
C could cause further anger.
D would be difficult to control.

3 Do you have any suggestions for keeping calm in the car?

Does the public transport system in your area provide a viable alternative to the car?

How might the problem of traffic congestion in cities be solved?

Vocabulary 2: Anger

1 The following expressions were used in the listening to talk about people getting angry. Which two are more informal?

lose one's temper	blow a fuse	get worked up	become irate

2 Complete each of the gaps with an adjective from the box. The words in **bold** are common collocates of the adjectives.

seething	cross	heated	berserk	irate

1 They had a rather ________ **argument** about hunting, each with very different views on the topic.
2 The waitress was attempting to calm an extremely ________ **customer** who was complaining loudly about his bill.
3 Mummy's a little bit ________ **with you**, Peter. You know you shouldn't tell lies.
4 Her face showed no emotion, but inwardly she was absolutely ________ **with anger and indignation**.
5 He **went** completely ________ , shaking his fist at me and screaming blue murder.

3 Complete each of the gaps with a noun from the box.

outburst	rage	steam	tantrum	top

1 My dad would **blow his** ________ if he found out I'd been driving so fast.
2 When I refused his request, **he flew into a** ________ and stormed out of my office.
3 I was taken aback by her **sudden** ________ **of temper**.
4 I was furious; I had to go for a long walk to **let off** ________ .
5 If she doesn't get what she wants, she **throws a** ________ , stamping her feet and screaming her head off.

4 What sort of things make you angry?
What do you do when you lose your temper?
What do you do to calm down?

Speaking
Part 2

Long turn

Look at these pictures. They show people who are angry for various reasons.

Student A:
Compare **two** of the pictures, and say what might have happened to make these people angry and what might happen next.

Student B:
When your partner has finished talking about the pictures, say which of those situations is the more unpleasant for the person on the receiving end of the anger.

Now change roles. Follow the instructions again using the remaining pictures.

Before you do the task, complete the exercises in the Useful language box at the top of page 123.

- What might have happened to make these people angry?
- What do you think might happen next?

What to expect in the exam

- One student speaks for a minute about two pictures from a set of three. The other student has about 30 seconds to answer an additional question on the same set of pictures.
- Both students are then given a second set of pictures and the roles are reversed.

Useful language

1 For each picture, decide which of the words and expressions from the Vocabulary section on page 121 you could use when talking about it.

2 Complete each of the gaps with one of the pairs of words in example at the beginning (**0**).

looks as	looks like	may well	~~seems quite~~
very likely	fair chance	might have	

0 She *seems quite* cross.

1 He ______________________ been put in the wrong room.
2 She ______________________ have done something dangerous.
3 He ______________________ if he's about to burst into tears.
4 There's a ______________________ they'll come to blows.
5 They're ______________________ to go their own separate ways.
6 It ______________________ an example of road rage.

Word formation: Alternatives from the same prompt word

In these two extracts from the listening on page 120, the underlined adverbs are both formed from the same root, *consider*.

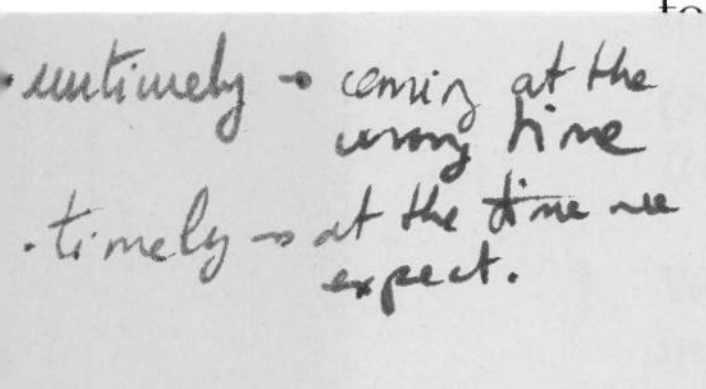

country roads there is *considerably* *less traffic.*
lso praises them when they are driving *considerately*.

ıich other noun, apart from the one underlined, can be formed from the word :apitals?

suggestions as to how we can maintain our *composure* *in the car.* **COMPOSE**

..derline the appropriate alternative in the following sentences. Each alternative is formed from the same prompt word given in capitals at the end of the sentence. Pay attention to the words in **bold**; these words are collocates of the correct alternative.

Example:
First prize is **the not** *inconsiderate/inconsiderable* **sum** of £500 000. **CONSIDER**

1 *The Lord of the Rings* is *a timeless/an untimely* **classic**, as fresh today as it was when it was first published. **TIME**
2 I grew up in England, but Spain has become my *adopted/adoptive* **country**. **ADOPT**
3 **Appearances** can be very *deceitful/deceptive*. **DECEIVE**
4 He produced a wealth of *supporting/supportive* **evidence** to substantiate his claim. **SUPPORT**

There has been **an** *appreciative/appreciable* **increase** in global temperatures over the last two decades. **APPRECIATE**

Police have refused to **reveal the** *identification/identity* of the man detained in connection with the murder. **IDENTIFY**

The appointment with my GP was at 8.30, but it wasn't until 9.15 that I was finally shown into her *consulting/consultative* **room**. **CONSULT**

The *Macmillan English* ***Dictionary*** *for Advanced Learners* contains over 100 000 *entrances/entries*. **ENTER**

Millions of innocent civilians **suffered great** *hardness/hardship* as a result of the war. **HARD**

10 He's retired and now works for the company **in an** *advisory/advisable* **capacity**. **ADVISE**
11 The gardens contain a wealth of plants and flowers **of every** *imaginary/imaginable/imaginative* **colour**. **IMAGINE**
12 My two brothers, Pat and Eric, were both given heavy prison sentences **for their** *respectable/respective/respectful* **crimes**. **RESPECT**

9 Review

Word formation

For questions **1–8**, read the text below. Use the word given in capitals at the end of some of the lines to form a word that fits in the gap **in the same line**. There is an example at the beginning (**0**). Write your answers **IN CAPITAL LETTERS**.

ANGER

We've all felt anger at some time, whether as faint **(0)** ANNOYANCE or blind rage.	**ANNOY**
Anger is a normal, sometimes useful human emotion, but uncontrolled outbursts of	
temper can be **(1)** .... 'People who give free rein to their anger,	**DESTROY**
(2) .... of the offence this may cause, haven't learnt to express themselves	**REGARD**
constructively,' says Martin Smolik, who runs weekend **(3)** .... courses in	**RESIDENCE**
anger management. 'It is important to maintain your **(4)** .... and put your	**COMPOSE**
case in an assertive, not aggressive, manner without hurting others. Being assertive	
doesn't mean being pushy or demanding; it means being **(5)** .... of	**RESPECT**
yourself and other people.' He adds that people who are easily angered are	
intolerant of **(6)** .... and frustration and, not surprisingly, find	**CONVENIENT**
(7) .... to other people very difficult. But what causes people to behave	**RELATE**
like this? There is evidence to support the idea that some children may be born	
(8) .... and prone to anger. However, research also suggests that	**IRRITATE**
they are simply modelling their behaviour on that of older family members.	

Vocabulary

1 In **A** and **B**, form expressions by matching each of the beginnings **1–6** with an appropriate ending **a–f**. The first one has been done for you.

A Sustainable tourism

1 provide employment	**a** the environment
2 improve living	**b** tourism
3 violate cultural	**c** an industry
4 achieve sustainable	**d** standards
5 preserve	**e** taboos
6 regulate	**f** opportunities

B Anger

1 lose	**a** off steam
2 fly	**b** a tantrum
3 let	**c** your temper
4 throw	**d** berserk
5 blow	**e** into a rage
6 go	**f** a fuse

2 Complete sentences **1–6** using the expressions in exercise **1**. You may need to change some of the words. You may need to write more than one word in each gap.

1 I have a large cushion at work, which I punch every time I need to ____________ .
2 All I did was ask him how old he was and he ____________ absolutely ____________ .
3 If the adventure tourism ____________ is not more strictly ____________ , further accidents are inevitable.
4 We need restrictions on fishing in this area if ____________ is to be ____________ ; otherwise there'll be no fish left for visitors to catch.
5 Rather like a small child who ____________ , she will scream, shout and stamp her feet to get what she wants.
6 The creation of a new wildlife park should ____________ many ____________ for local people looking for work.

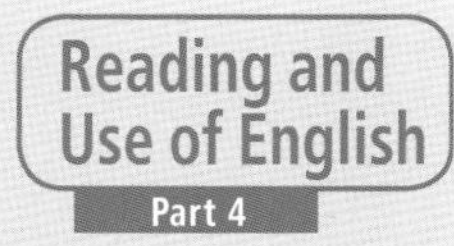

Key word transformation

For questions **1–6**, complete the second sentence so that it has a similar meaning to the first sentence, using the word given. **Do not change the word given.** You must use between **three** and **six** words, including the word given. Write your answers **IN CAPITAL LETTERS**.

1 It was only when Paul got angry that I realized something serious had happened.
UNTIL
It .... his temper that I realized something serious had happened.

2 Strangely enough, we only experienced problems when the weather improved.
RAN
Strangely enough, it was only when the weather got .... problems.

3 In the end, the holiday was better than I thought it would be.
TURNED
The holiday .... be better than I thought it would be.

4 We just sat on the beach all day.
DID
All .... on the beach the whole day.

5 We probably won't leave to go to the airport until midday.
LIKELY
We are .... off for the airport until midday.

6 It seems his aim was to disrupt the meeting.
SET
It looks .... out to disrupt the meeting.

Open cloze

For questions **1–8**, read the text below and think of the word which best fits each gap. Use only **one** word in each gap. There is an example at the beginning (**0**). Write your answers **IN CAPITAL LETTERS**.

Travelling on a student budget

There's no nicer activity **(0)** ...*THAN*... planning adventures. Dreams of sun, sand, lively people and freedom **(1)** .... responsibility can be a welcome break from all the essays and exams **(2)** .... thrown our way at this time of year. **(3)** .... is more, there are a variety of ways that students can travel **(4)** .... having to sell old games consoles and textbooks in search of extra cash. A popular choice is interrailing around Europe; there are InterRail passes for a week and up to a month, ranging from as **(5)** .... as £152 to £365. Interrailing is an amazingly social experience, **(6)** .... , in my opinion, is unlike any other. Then there is backpacking. You could, should you wish to, hitchhike and set **(7)** .... camp on the sides of roads, but in many countries, travel is cheap **(8)** .... to suit even the most economically-minded globetrotter and it's possible to stay in pleasant accommodation for no more than you'd be paying for rent at university.

Ready for Listening

Introduction

The **Listening** paper lasts approximately 40 minutes and contains four parts with a total of 30 questions. In all four parts the recordings are heard twice. At the end of the **Listening** paper, you will have five minutes to transfer your answers onto the separate answer sheet. Each correct answer is awarded one mark.

Part 1: Multiple choice

1 In Part 1 you will hear three short extracts from conversations between two or more people. The recordings, which are all on different themes, may be taken, for example, from radio broadcasts, conversations that you overhear, discussions or interviews. There are two multiple-choice questions for each extract. You will hear the same extract twice before moving on to the next one.

2 2.4–2.6 You will hear three different extracts. For questions **1–6**, choose the answer (**A**, **B** or **C**) which fits best according to what you hear. There are two questions for each extract.

Extract One

You overhear two journalism students talking about the issue of global warming.

1 Why does the man compare articles on war with articles on global warming?
- **A** to show that journalism is not truly objective
- **B** to emphasize that global warming has dangerous consequences
- **C** to suggest that public protest is growing

2 The woman says that people will do less harm to the environment when
- **A** they are obliged by legislation to be more considerate.
- **B** they see how they can personally benefit from this.
- **C** they are given information which is more accurate.

Extract Two

You hear part of an interview with Andy Marsden, the owner of a chocolate manufacturing company and shop.

3 What made Andy decide to buy Kiss Chocolates?
- **A** He had once been employed there.
- **B** His wife and the owner were old friends.
- **C** He thought it would provide a safe future.

4 What does Andy like most about working at Kiss Chocolates?
- **A** testing the chocolates
- **B** dealing with customers
- **C** making a steady profit

Extract Three

You hear two people on a book review programme talking about a book called *The Children of Hurin.*

5 The two speakers agree that *The Children of Hurin*
- **A** is hard to put down.
- **B** has a sad feel to it.
- **C** ends in a surprising way.

6 What slight criticism does the man make about the book?
- **A** It contains different styles of writing.
- **B** The characters are not complex enough.
- **C** The themes may not appeal to modern readers.

3 Check your answers by looking at the listening script on pages 233 and 234. Underline the part or parts of each extract which indicate the correct answer. The first one has been done for you.

Part 2: Sentence completion

1 In Part 2 you will hear a monologue lasting approximately three minutes. The recording will be taken from one of a possible number of sources including presentations, talks, lectures and anecdotes.

There are eight questions testing your understanding of specific information and people's opinions. You are usually required to complete sentences with a single noun or a noun phrase, e.g. social media, diploma course. You will *not* be tested on phrases that require hyphens (-).

2 **2.7** You will hear part of a talk by Amanda Tyler, who is a waxwork sculptor. For questions **1–8**, complete the sentences with a word or short phrase.

What to expect in the exam

- For Part 2 tasks you have 45 seconds to read the questions. Use this time to think about the kind of information you might hear and the language structure you might need to complete each question.
  e.g. *1 A noun will be needed here, possibly preceded by an adjective. It will probably be a part of the building, but the preposition 'in' can't be followed by 'first floor', 'second floor', etc.*
- For some of the questions you will hear distractors, words which might at first seem relevant, but which do not complete the questions correctly. For question 2, for example, you will hear Amanda mention two courses she took. Only one of these, however, is a degree course; the other is a distractor.
  As you read each question, underline key words to help you focus on the exact information required. The first two have been done for you.

WAXWORK SCULPTOR

Amanda's studio is situated in the **(1)** .... of the wax museum.

She took a degree course called **(2)** ....

She particularly enjoys the part of her job which requires her to take **(3)** .... of a subject.

She uses the clay model of a famous television **(4)** .... to explain how a waxwork figure is made.

The frame of a figure consists of wire netting and rods made out of **(5)** ....

Amanda says that the **(6)** .... of a figure is essential for conveying realism.

She can take up to **(7)** .... to complete a waxwork figure.

The make-up artist applies a combination of **(8)** .... and cosmetics to colour the wax head.

3 On page 205 you will find one student's answers to the listening task above together with relevant advice about what to do and what not to do.

Did you make any similar mistakes?

Part 3: Multiple choice

1 Part 3 consists of a conversation between two or more speakers lasting approximately four minutes. There are six multiple-choice questions, mostly testing your understanding of the attitudes and opinions of the speakers. The questions follow the same order as the corresponding information in the recording.

What to expect in the exam

- For Part 3 tasks you have one minute to read through the questions.
- As with the other Parts of the Listening paper, you will hear words and ideas which may cause you to choose the wrong answer.

2 You will hear an interview with Sandra Peyton and David Sadler, who work as partners in the media company, Advert Eyes, making TV commercials. For questions **1–6**, choose the answer (**A**, **B**, **C** or **D**) which fits best according to what you hear.

3 Before you answer questions **1–6**, here is an example (**0**). Read the question and the shaded section of the recording on page 234. Decide on the correct answer, underlining the part or parts of the text which justify your choice.

0 Why did Sandra leave her job with the satellite TV company?
A She was unhappy with the salary.
B She felt she was too old for the job.
C She predicted she might lose her job.
D She did not get on with her colleagues.

4 With your partner, explain with reference to the text why the other options are wrong.

5 **2.8** Now read questions **1–6**. Then listen to the recording and choose the correct answers.

1 What did David learn from his time with Trenton TV?
A the need to work as part of a team
B the importance of having a positive outlook
C the advantages of working under pressure
D the need to question existing practices

2 What impressed Sandra about David when they first met?
A his experience
B his appearance
C his future plans
D his enthusiasm

3 What made David accept Sandra's proposal to go into partnership?
A He had always enjoyed taking risks.
B He felt they had a similar way of thinking.
C She had relevant directing experience.
D She was familiar with the business world.

4 How did Sandra feel when she was having problems raising money for the business?
A puzzled
B depressed
C angry
D worried

5 What does David consider to be a drawback of directing TV commercials?
A He does not achieve enough recognition for his work.
B He does not have enough control over content.
C Money has too great an influence on the process.
D Many clients have unrealistic expectations.

6 What do Sandra and David say about the future of their company?
A They would prefer to keep their plans a secret.
B Their aim is to expand at some time in the future.
C They are unsure how the company will develop.
D They hope to move into other areas of directing.

6 Look at the listening script on pages 234 and 235 and for questions **1–6** follow the same procedure as in exercises **3** and **4** above.

Part 4: Multiple matching

1 In Part 4 you will hear five short monologues which are all related in some way. For each speaker there are two separate tasks. For each task, you are required to select the correct option from a choice of eight.

2 **2.9–2.13** You will hear five short extracts in which people are talking about living abroad.

Concentrate mainly, but not exclusively, on Task One the first time you listen. The second time you listen, give more attention to Task Two.

3 Check your answers using the listening script on page 235. Underline those parts of each extract which guide you to the correct answers.

What to expect in the exam

- You have 45 seconds to read through the tasks.
- Listen to the whole of each monologue to find the answers to both tasks. You may hear the answer to Task Two before the answer to Task One. This is the case with Speaker 4 below.
- Once again, you will hear distractors.

TASK ONE

For questions **1–5**, choose from the list **(A–H)** the main reason why each speaker went to live abroad.

TASK TWO

For questions **6–10**, choose from the list **(A–H)** what the speaker says about living abroad.

While you listen you must complete both tasks.

Task One		Task Two	
A to be with his/her partner	1	**A** I miss my family.	6
B for health reasons		**B** The weather can be depressing.	
C to speak the language	2	**C** I go home regularly.	7
D for work reasons	3	**D** Life is more exciting here.	8
E to earn more money		**E** I regret coming here.	
F to run away from a problem	4	**F** It's a cosmopolitan place.	9
G for a change of routine	5	**G** I feel like an outsider.	
H to study		**H** I won't stay here forever.	10

4 One student wrote the following **incorrect** answers for questions **6–10** in Task Two.

6 D **7** A **8** C **9** B **10** H

Identify the distractor in each extract which may have caused the student to choose the wrong answer.

Example:
6 Speaker 1: *Plus it seemed so exciting when I came here two years ago.*

10 House and home

Vocabulary 1: Describing rooms and houses

1 Some adjectives for describing rooms are often used in partnership with others which have a similar or related meaning. Match each adjective **1–6** with another **a–f** to form appropriate partnerships. The first one has been done for you.

1 bright and —	**a** tidy
2 light and	**b** dingy
3 neat and	— **c** cheerful
4 dark and	**d** cosy
5 warm and	**e** airy
6 cramped and	**f** cluttered

2 All three adverbs in each group **a–e** below collocate with one of the adjectives in the box. Write an appropriate adjective from the box in each space.

furnished	built	situated	decorated	lit

a dimly
brightly ________
softly

b comfortably
sparsely ________
elegantly

c tastefully
newly ________
richly

d recently
poorly ________
solidly

e conveniently
ideally ________
pleasantly

3 Using the adjectives and adverbs from exercises **1** and **2**, describe your
- home and its location.
- bedroom.
- living room.

Example:
I live on the outskirts of the city in a rented flat. It isn't very conveniently situated – there are no shops nearby and as the underground doesn't go out that far, I have to walk or get the bus everywhere. It's solidly built, but the stairwell is rather dark and dingy …

4 Work with a partner. Each describe one of the rooms in the pictures below, saying what type of person the room might belong to and how you would feel about living there.

Reading and Use of English 1
Part 2

Open cloze

1 Why do many people hate doing housework?

2 Read the following text, ignoring the gaps for the moment. According to the text, why is housework so depressing?

HOUSEWORK GETS YOU DOWN

It may come **(0)** ...AS... no surprise to learn that household chores can make you feel depressed. There is evidence **(1)** .... suggest that the more housework men and women do, the more likely they **(2)** .... to suffer from mood swings. 'Any form of repetitive cyclical work **(3)** .... bound to be depressing,' says psychologist Nicholas Emler. 'Domestic chores are open-ended tasks, so there is no defined end point. People prefer tasks they can complete, and **(4)** .... a satisfactory conclusion they become stressed.'

Work in the home has no job description and family members rarely appreciate just **(5)** .... much work has gone into preparing an evening meal or cleaning the bathroom. Women still take responsibility **(6)** .... the lion's share of domestic chores, but with many in full-time jobs they can **(7)** .... longer pride themselves on having a spotless home. 'The concept of being houseproud is out of fashion,' says Prof Emler, who points **(8)** .... that the vast majority of men continue to shy away **(9)** .... doing the dishes. In other situations financial reward can go **(10)** .... way to compensating for dull, repetitive work, but housework is a strenuous job with no pay.

Writer Tracy Kerry believes that many people nowadays just don't know how to do housework. 'There are an awful **(11)** .... of inexperienced people whose mothers were **(12)** .... busy working to show them. Sweeping a room **(13)** .... seem an easy enough task to perform, but there's a right way and a wrong way to do it.' To make housework easier she suggests **(14)** .... get rid of possessions that are of no use to us anymore. 'Keep clutter **(15)** .... control and you will feel more able to cope.'

3 For questions **1–15**, read the text again and think of the word which best fits each gap. Use only **one** word in each gap. There is an example at the beginning (**0**). Write your answers **IN CAPITAL LETTERS**. Use the questions and advice in the box to help you.

1 Why is a relative pronoun not possible here?
2/3 See page 221 for the grammar of 'likely' and 'bound'.
4 Will the missing word have a positive or negative meaning?
5 Overall context and 'just' before the gap will help you make your choice.
6 Which preposition is required after 'responsibility'?
7 Look at the surrounding context. Can women 'pride themselves on having a spotless home' now?
8 This phrasal verb appeared on page 98.
9 A preposition is required to complete this phrasal verb.
10 Why is an adjective *not* possible here before the singular countable noun 'way'?
11 See page 103 for the expression 'an awful ____'.
12 Note the infinitive later in the sentence.
13 Note that 'seem' is the infinitive form of the verb, not the third person singular. What does this tell you about the type of word required in the gap?
14 See page 220 for the grammar of 'suggest'.
15 Which preposition is used in the expression 'keep something ______ control'?

4 Who does 'the lion's share of domestic chores' in your house? Why?

To what extent are you/your parents houseproud?

Do you follow the advice in the last sentence of the text? What other advice would you give to make housework less depressing?

What to expect in the exam

the *Advanced* exam ere are only eight gaps in e Open cloze.

Reading and Use of English 2
Part 5

Multiple choice

1 In what ways would your life be different if your house had no running water, no electricity and no central heating? How would you cope?

2 Read through the text quickly and answer the following questions:
What is your initial reaction to the story of Albert Juttus?
Do you feel sympathy for him? Why/Why not?

3 Now read the text again. For questions **1–6**, choose the answer (**A**, **B**, **C** or **D**) which you think fits best according to the text.

THE JOY OF PLUMBING

An elderly couple is brought into the 21st century.

I'm driving along a road in Leicestershire, in the tidy heart of the English countryside, where slick green fields roll out on either side to the horizon. I drive through the village of Shenton, a quiet place without so much as a pub, past prosperous-looking farms and neat brick houses. And then I pull up outside a rather shabby bungalow. Around the bungalow is a sea of mud. Between the road and the bungalow there is a ditch, choked with weeds, with a little muddy stream trickling along it. I push open the door of the bungalow to find Albert Juttus, a gentle-looking 73-year-old, sitting in his front room before a tiny heater running off a cylinder of Calor gas. He's lived in this house for 46 years, and in all that time his only source of water has been that muddy ditch.

Albert had lived his life in total obscurity until last week, when the local council awarded him its biggest-ever grant, over £40 000, to transform his tiny property. It will now be connected to running water, given a new roof, windows and doors, as well as a lavatory, a sink and a shower. His wife, Grace, has moved temporarily into a nursing home while the work is in progress. Since the announcement of that grant, the council has been rather shown up by the interest that Albert Juttus's belated journey into the 21st century has attracted: front-page coverage in the local paper and visits to his humble dwelling by television journalists. The council said they'd have acted sooner, had they known about the Juttuses, but the couple had obviously been slipping through the net for a long time.

But Albert Juttus's life isn't just an odd curiosity: it says something about communities and how they work, or don't work, in Britain today. Having become rather frail and vulnerable in the last few years, he and his wife were heavily reliant on the good nature of one neighbour, who declines to be named. Her tales of their neglected life strike a chill into your heart. 'Every time I came back from seeing them my son would say, "You've been down at Albert's". The stink was so bad in their house it would get in my clothes.' The couple, who have no family, did not realize they were entitled to an improvement grant. 'We have never had very much, but we have always had each other,' said Albert, 'and that's all we ever wanted. We've never been comfortable with the idea of handouts.'

And it would be wrong to see Albert Juttus as just someone to be pitied. In many ways he's a real survivor. Fleeing from Estonia in 1946, he came to Britain without knowing a word of English. After a succession of low-paid jobs on farms and in mills, he found work in a nearby tyre factory. He had friends there, but although he knew he was the only one without

running water and electricity, his only thought was of the bills they must have had to pay each month. 'I didn't think I could deal with those big bills,' he remembers. And didn't they tell you to get your life together? Juttus looks a little shocked. 'They wouldn't speak out of turn,' he says quietly. So this man, living on a labourer's wage, with a wife who didn't work, clearly believed he was just locked out of the lifestyle that everyone around him took for granted.

So how did change ever come to this little house lost in time? Albert Juttus, in his bizarrely modest but oddly practical way, decided that it was indeed pretty hard getting water out of the ditch, but that it would be easier if he had a proper well. So some time ago he asked a health worker whether they could get someone to dig a well and their case was referred to a charity called Care and Repair. Shocked beyond belief by what they saw when they visited the house, these people began to put pressure on the council to rectify the situation.

Doesn't Mr Juttus wish he'd managed to change it all much earlier? 'It's too late to wish now,' he says, stubbing out a cigarette. 'Times never return.' And clearly something in him even feels ambivalent about the new life that looms ahead. 'It's easy, isn't it, you just switch a button or turn a tap, it all just happens. But, I'll get spoilt. They'll be bringing me slippers and a pipe next.'

It would have been a lot easier for the council if he had agreed to move into a spanking new home on a smart estate, but he wouldn't do that. At the back of his house the view sweeps on and on over green fields and to the soft surge of low hills fringed with trees. 'That's the good thing about the country,' he says, looking out over the familiar prospect. 'You see long distances. I can sit out before sunset, when the birds start singing. I wouldn't like to move. What for?'

1 On arriving at the Juttus's bungalow, the writer was struck by

A its isolation from the rest of the community.
B the ease with which she entered it.
C the contrast it made with the surrounding area.
D the beauty of the countryside in which it was situated.

2 What does the writer suggest about the Juttus's case in the second paragraph?

A It has brought the couple a great deal of unwanted publicity.
B The media have helped to bring about the changes.
C The money paid out to the couple is excessive.
D It has reflected badly on the local authorities.

3 In the third paragraph, the writer puts forward the view that there

A has been a general decline in respect for elderly people.
B is a reluctance amongst older people to accept new circumstances.
C is a lack of unity among people living in the same area.
D may be generational differences in attitude towards self-sufficiency.

4 What does Albert imply about his workmates in the tyre factory?

A They were probably earning more than he was.
B They did not appreciate how lucky they were.
C They had more right to running water and electricity than he did.
D They were not the type of people to interfere in the affairs of others.

5 What does Albert feel about the changes to his house?

A He regrets not making them before.
B He is uncertain whether he will like them.
C He thinks the council could do more.
D He cannot believe how fortunate he is.

6 In the last paragraph we learn that Albert does not want to leave his house because

A a suitable new home has not yet been offered to him.
B he is mistrustful of the local authorities.
C the view reminds him of where he used to live.
D he is very attached to his surroundings.

Reacting to the text

How common is it for people in your country to live in conditions like those of the Juttuses? What can local authorities do to help such people?

'He came to Britain without knowing a word of English.' What difficulties would someone in this situation face? Would you be able to cope?

'I wouldn't like to move. What for?' How true is this for you? Where would you prefer to live if you had to move

a to another part of your town or city?
b to a different part of your country?
c abroad?

Language focus: Participle clauses

1 Participle clauses are clauses which begin with a present or past participle. They help to express ideas concisely and are more commonly used in written English.

Participle clauses can be used instead of relative clauses, as in this example from the reading text:

Between the road and the bungalow there is a ditch, (which is) choked with weeds ...

Which words have been omitted from the following sentence to create a participle clause?

So this man, living on a labourer's wage, clearly believed he was just locked out of the lifestyle.

2 Conjunctions like *and, so, because, as, when, after* and *if* can also be omitted to create participle clauses. Underline the sentences in the reading text which express the same ideas as **a–d** below.

- **a** *Because* they had become rather frail and vulnerable in the last few years, he and his wife were heavily reliant on the good nature of one neighbour.
- **b** He fled from Estonia in 1946 *and* came to Britain.
- **c** These people were shocked beyond belief by what they saw when they visited the house, *so* they began to put pressure on the local council.
- **d** 'That's the good thing about the country,' he says, *as* he looks out over the familiar prospect.

3 Explain the difference in meaning between the following pairs of sentences. Which sentence in each pair is more likely?

- **1 a** Driving home from the pub last night, the police stopped him.
  - **b** Driving home from the pub last night, he was stopped by the police.
- **2 a** The manager being ill, Elisa took over all his responsibilities for the week.
  - **b** Being ill, Elisa took over all the manager's responsibilities for the week.

Read more about participle clauses in the Grammar reference on page 222.

Practice

1 Sentences **1–6** contain participle clauses. Rewrite each one using conjunctions or relative pronouns. There is an example at the beginning (**0**).

- *0* *Not wanting to wake anyone up, she took her shoes off and tiptoed up the stairs.*
  <u>She didn't want to wake anyone up, so she took her shoes off and tiptoed up the stairs.</u>
- **1** Having won the silver medal in the 100 metres, he went on to take gold in the 200 metres and long jump.
- **2** Don't look now, but the woman sitting next to you is wearing shoes made of crocodile skin.
- **3** Drunk in moderation, red wine is thought to protect against coronary disease.
- **4** Wrapped in a blanket and looking tired after his ordeal, Mr Brown was full of praise for the rescue services.
- **5** Reaching for the sugar, he knocked over his glass, spilling orange juice over her new dress.
- **6** Having never been abroad before, Brian was feeling a little on edge.

2 Rewrite the following sentences using participle clauses.

- **1** Because I live within walking distance of the centre, I rarely use the car.
- **2** When I was cycling in to work the other day, I saw a deer.
- **3** As we'd never had so much peace and quiet before, we found living here a little strange at first.
- **4** Our bedroom, which is situated at the back of the building, has some superb views over the rooftops towards the docks.
- **5** If you play it at full volume, it really annoys the neighbours.
- **6** The house is a little off the beaten track, so it's not that easy to find.
- **7** After the children had all left home, we decided to move away from the hustle and bustle.
- **8** Although it is not known for its tourist attractions, our neighbourhood does have one or two treasures which are waiting to be discovered.

3 For each of the sentences in exercise **2**, say whether you think the speaker lives in a rural area or a city. Which would you prefer to live in? Give reasons.

Listening
Part 4

Multiple matching 2.14–2.18

1 You will hear five short extracts in which people are talking about noise from the neighbouring house.

TASK ONE

For questions **1–5**, choose from the list (**A–H**) what the cause of the noise was.

TASK TWO

For questions **6–10**, choose from the list (**A–H**) what the speakers say about the effect the noise had on them.

While you listen you must complete both tasks.

TASK ONE		TASK TWO	
A birds	1	**A** It changed my personality.	6
B people talking	2	**B** It taught me to be more tolerant.	7
C construction work	3	**C** My health was affected.	8
D a television set	4	**D** I was forced to move house.	9
E music equipment	5	**E** It destroyed a friendship.	10
F cars		**F** It didn't bother me.	
G a baby crying		**G** It prevented me from working.	
H singing		**H** I was forced to take legal action.	

2 Which of the speakers do you have most and least sympathy with? Why? Have you had any similar problems with neighbours? Are you a noisy neighbour?

Vocabulary 2: Noise and sound

1 Look at the following extracts from the listening. What type of noise is indicated by all three underlined words?

a *The <u>din</u> was unbearable …*

b *… it would start at five – this awful <u>racket</u> and it'd wake up the baby …*

c *Night after night he'd have it <u>blaring out</u> at full volume …*

2 In **1–3** below, each of the adjectives collocates with the noun in capital letters at the end of the line. Underline the adjective in each group of three which has a very different meaning to the other two. There is an example at the beginning (**0**).

0	squeaky	high-pitched	<u>deep</u>	**VOICE**

'Deep' describes a voice with a low pitch; the other two adjectives describe a voice with a high pitch.

1	loud	booming	hushed	**VOICE**
2	distant	unmistakable	muffled	**SOUND**
3	excessive	incessant	constant	**NOISE**

3 Cross out the word which does not normally collocate with the noun or adjective in capital letters at the beginning of each line. There is an example at the beginning (**0**).

0	**DOGS**	growl	~~roar~~	whine	
Noun + verb					
1	**NOISE**	dies down	fades away	goes off	
2	**DOORS**	slam shut	rustle open	creak open	
3	**BELLS**	hoot	tinkle	chime	
Adjective + noun					
4	**ROWDY**	behaviour	fans	engine	party
5	**PIERCING**	groan	cry	scream	shriek
6	**DEAFENING**	applause	cheer	silence	ear

Now do the exercises on page 207.

Reading and Use of English 3
Part 1

Multiple-choice cloze

1 How often do you talk to your neighbours? What do you talk about?

2 For questions **1–8**, read the text below and decide which answer (**A**, **B**, **C** or **D**) best fits each gap. There is an example at the beginning (**0**).

Don't forget!

Read the text through first before making your choices.

Answer these questions as you read:

What has caused the decline in communication between neighbours in Britain?

What has been one of the effects of this decline?

A LACK OF COMMUNICATION

Recent research has **(0)** .... that a third of people in Britain have not met their next-door neighbours, and those who know each other **(1)** .... speak. Neighbours gossiping over garden fences and in the street was a common **(2)** .... in the 1950s, says Dr Carl Chinn, an expert on local communities. Now, however, longer hours spent working at the office, together with the Internet and satellite television, are eroding neighbourhood **(3)** .... 'Poor neighbourhoods once had strong kinship, but now prosperity buys privacy,' said Chinn.

Andrew Mayer, a strategy consultant, rents a large apartment in west London, with two flatmates. 'We have a family of teachers upstairs and lawyers below, but our only contact comes via letters **(4)** .... to the communal facilities or complaints that we've not put out our bin bags properly,' said Mayer.

The **(5)** .... of communities can have serious effects. Concerned at the rise in burglaries and **(6)** .... of vandalism, the police have relaunched crime prevention schemes such as Neighbourhood Watch, **(7)** .... on people who live in the same area to **(8)** .... an eye on each others' houses and report anything they see which is unusual.

0	**A** exhibited	**B** conducted	**C** displayed	**D** revealed
1	**A** barely	**B** roughly	**C** nearly	**D** virtually
2	**A** outlook	**B** view	**C** vision	**D** sight
3	**A** ties	**B** joints	**C** strings	**D** laces
4	**A** concerning	**B** regarding	**C** applying	**D** relating
5	**A** breakout	**B** breakthrough	**C** breakdown	**D** breakaway
6	**A** acts	**B** shows	**C** counts	**D** works
7	**A** asking	**B** calling	**C** inviting	**D** trying
8	**A** put	**B** keep	**C** hold	**D** give

3 What findings do you think similar research in your own country would reveal? Do you agree with Dr Chinn that 'prosperity buys privacy'?

Informal email

1 Imagine a friend is coming to stay in your home for a few weeks while you are away. Which of the following things would you expect them to do?

- water the houseplants
- feed and walk the dog
- wipe down the shower
- replace any food they eat
- put out any bottles or tins for recycling
- only use the washing machine at set times
- limit the amount of hot water used
- clean up after themselves
- ensure the windows and doors are locked on leaving the house

Is there anything else you would expect your friend to do?

Would it depend on the season in any way?

2 Read the following Part 2 task and the two sample answers A and B below and on page 138.

Compare the two sample answers in terms of

- vocabulary.
- register and tone.
- grammatical structure.
- organization.

You receive this message from an English friend who is coming to stay in your home for a few weeks while you are away.

> Is there anything I need to know about keeping your home secure? And are there any household jobs or responsibilities that you need me to take care of? Also, what's the best way to get around in your area? Send me an email and let me know.

Write your **email** in **220–260** words.

A

Hi Steve

It's good to know that you'll be in the apartment while I'm away in Berlin. It's in a pretty safe area, but it's reassuring to have you keeping an eye on things.

First, you need to know how to get into the building. When you arrive, press the buzzer for number 15 – that's my neighbour, Eric Grueber. He knows you're coming and he'll let you in and hand over the keys to my apartment door. The next time you need to get into the building, just enter the security number, which I'll stick on the fridge. I'm on the third floor so I don't really care about windows being open.

There's a load of stuff in the fridge and food cupboard so help yourself. But if you run out, head down to the supermarket on the corner. Tuesday is bottle and tin collection day, so would you mind putting them in the green recycling box, and then making sure the box is outside on the pavement before 8am? My neighbours are fairly easygoing, but please keep things sweet by not playing loud music or using the washing machine after 9pm. Thanks!

As for getting around, all the good cafés and shops are just five minutes' walk away and the city centre is traffic-free, so I'd just use your legs! If you feel like going further, Lake Constance is a brilliant place to visit: there are good rail connections, and you can borrow my bike, too. I'll leave some tourist information leaflets and train timetable in the kitchen.

Get in touch if you need any more info.

Johannes

B

Dear Steve

Thank you for your email. I hope the following information will be of use to you.

Security matters

- On arrival: press the buzzer for number 15. You will be let into the building by my neighbour Eric Grueber, and then given the keys to my apartment door.
- Security number for the building: this will be on the fridge door.
- General security: windows can be left open at all times as the apartment is on the third floor.

Household responsibilities

- Food supplies: should you need to go shopping, the supermarket on the corner is reasonable.
- Recycling: bottles and tins must be placed in the green recycling box and placed outside on the kerb by 8am Tuesday at the latest.
- Noise control: please refrain from playing music or using the washing machine after 9pm.

Transport

- City centre cafés and shops: these can be accessed best on foot since the centre is free from traffic.
- Longer distances: the train is highly recommended and there is also a bicycle available for your personal use.

Johannes

3 In sample answer A, the writer does more than just provide the basic information that was requested. Find examples of

- how he makes his friend feel welcome.
- what he adds to make his friend feel positive about his upcoming stay.

4 Now write your answer to the task below.

You receive this message from an English friend who has agreed to help manage your shop for a day while you are away.

> Hi – I'm looking forward to helping manage the shop next Saturday. But is there anything I need to know about the staff? What about opening and locking up? Is there any other information I should know? Send me an email, please.

Write your **email** in **220–260** words.

Reading and Use of English 4
Part 6

Cross-text multiple matching

1 What do you think would be the pros and cons of living in these neighbourhoods?

What attracts residents to your neighbourhood? What facilities do you think are lacking?

How would you rate your local infrastructure, particularly with regard to roads and public transport?

Are there any improvements that could be made?

2 You are going to read four blogs in which the writers are talking about council proposals for the local area. For questions **1–4**, choose from the blogs **A–D**. The blogs may be chosen more than once.

Proposals for the Bayview area

Four writers comment on council proposals for the local area

A

Our council members, a hopeless group who demonstrated remarkable incompetence in the design process of Hillside Road, are now busily working on plans for the rest of Bayview, again behind closed doors. Only when these people finish will the public be 'invited' to submit comments, by which point none of these will make a difference. The council will simply go ahead despite our concerns. Where is the transparency in this process? When has anyone from the council ever taken responsibility for the vast sums of money wasted when their schemes fail? And now we have to prepare for further wastage as the council use taxpayers' money to 'develop' Bayview in ways that no local desires. The reason for this tirade is that, in my view, the problems we are faced with – the escalation of high-rise housing in single-storey areas, the road design, the connection to our city, these issues have to be addressed before our beautiful environment is damaged beyond repair.

B

The council has announced its intention to spend a figure approaching $20 million over the next few years improving facilities and transport in Bayview. This is not before time. Furthermore, they have apparently set aside further funds to improve traffic flow on Hillside Road, and to finance the design and building of an exhibition centre and renovation of the library. People who live and work here will have to face the inconvenience of noise, dust and blocked-off pavements as roads are widened and car parks are extended in downtown Bayview, but this is something we must tolerate if we aim to attract the tourist dollar and encourage residents to use local services and retail facilities. The housing issue is another matter altogether and council plans for introducing out-of-character multi-storey buildings to the suburb have been ill thought out.

C

As a suburb that draws more tourists than any other in the city, Bayview deserves the considerable investment that the council has proposed. However, it is not for the council to force upon us developments that people here object to, and which we recognize are fundamentally detrimental to the community. Many of us have asked the council for details concerning the anticipated population figures, should their high-density housing projected be enacted, but they appear reluctant to disclose them. We have thus been forced to work it out for ourselves. It has been estimated that by building apartment blocks of four to five storeys, the council will facilitate an exponential and undesirable growth in population: 400 homes are likely to rise to 1200 in the North Bayview area and 700 cars could turn into 2100; with the increased population impacting heavily on Hillside Road traffic.

D

When it comes to our homes and our offices, why do we seem so willing to accept workmanship that falls way below standard and architecture that is soul-destroying in its bland functionality? It is expert design in conjunction with durable materials and craftsmanship that deserves our attention. The particular number of storeys in a new building is hardly the point. But before proposals to increase housing and retail development are even considered, and the required investment made, the council needs to concede that the Hillside Road situation is intolerable. In order for traffic to actually 'flow', we need two lanes in each direction, on both sides of the junction. A 'park and ride' shuttle service into Bayview would also be of great benefit to the community: commuters would be able to get to their place of employment without the considerable inconvenience and cost of finding a long-term parking space in the downtown area; and in turn this would free up spaces for visitors and tourists, who we must recognize bring in much needed revenue.

Which writer

has a different opinion from the others concerning the proposed housing development? 1 ____

shares writer A's opinion about the accessibility of information to the public regarding the council proposals? 2 ____

expresses a different view from the others on whether council spending on the whole is justified? 3 ____

takes a similar view to writer D on why improved infrastructure is necessary? 4 ____

Reacting to the text

The four writers are all concerned about the impact that population growth might have on their local area.

How would a considerable rise in population affect the area where you live? Would it be a positive or negative development?

10 Review

Vocabulary

Match each of the sentence beginnings **1–8** with an appropriate ending **a–h**. The items in **bold** are all common collocations.

Example: *1 c*

1 The words of the new President were drowned out by the **deafening**
2 I sat in the shade of a tree and listened to the sound of the **rustling**
3 The former headmaster was an imposing figure, with a **big booming**
4 He moved nervously towards the door, with one eye on the **growling**
5 They walked through a landscape of fast-flowing rivers and **roaring**
6 Irritated by the noise of other campers and the din of their **blaring**
7 The full moon lit up his monstrous face, and Edna **let out a piercing**
8 She quickly fell asleep, only to be woken soon after by the **chiming**

a **radios**, we moved on to another, quieter site.
b **voice**, which struck fear into the children.
c **cheers** of some 3000 jubilant supporters.
d **waterfalls**, fed by the recent torrential rains.
e **clock** in the hallway as it struck midnight.
f **leaves** being blown by the breeze in the branches above.
g **dog** that was chained to a post in the garden.
h **scream**, which cut through the silence of the night.

Participle clauses

Rewrite the following story using participle clauses and replacing the word '**and**' to combine ideas.

Example:
Having grown up in the countryside, Charlie wanted to go back there to spend his retirement.

Charlie had grown up in the countryside **and** he wanted to go back there to spend his retirement. He looked through a newspaper one day **and** he saw a cottage for sale in a picturesque rural area. It was situated in a small village near the church **and** it had a conservatory and a large garden **and** the garden contained fruit trees; it seemed perfect. Charlie was not known for his decisiveness **and** he surprised everyone by putting down a deposit on it the very next day. He saw it once **and** he immediately made up his mind to buy it.

However, he moved into the cottage **and** he soon realized it was not the peaceful rural idyll he had expected. The church bells chimed every hour on the hour **and** kept him awake at night. Also, the village was in an area of outstanding beauty **and** coachloads of tourists arrived every weekend **and** disturbed the peace and quiet. Worst of all, the locals objected to the presence of outsiders in the village **and** they were very unfriendly towards him. Charlie lived there for six months **and** he decided to move back to the city.

Reading and Use of English
Part 3

Word formation

For questions **1–8**, read the text below. Use the word given in capitals at the end of some of the lines to form a word that fits in the gap **in the same line**. There is an example at the beginning (**0**). Write your answers **IN CAPITAL LETTERS**.

IRONING

Many people hate ironing and seek out modern fabrics that **(0)** CONVENIENTLY	**CONVENIENCE**
do not crease, but is it really such a tedious and **(1)** .... chore? When	**AGREE**
done in the **(2)** .... of your kitchen with your headphones on, it can	**PRIVATE**
be a fairly relaxing way of spending your time.	
Anyway, love it or loathe it, here are a few guidelines:	
• Before you start, **(3)** .... there is enough wardrobe space to allow	**SURE**
your clothes to hang once ironed.	
• Plug the iron in close to the ironing board. A **(4)** .... of cord stretched	**LONG**
across a room represents a serious hazard. Also keep cords beyond the reach	
of children, whose natural **(5)** .... may lead them to pull the cord –	**CURIOUS**
and the iron – onto themselves.	
• Read the care label on each garment for the recommended	
ironing **(6)** .... and the appropriate temperature	**PROCEED**
(7) .... If in doubt, start with a cool iron. If this proves to be	**SET**
(8) .... and the clothes remain creased, increase the temperature	**EFFECT**
as necessary.	

11 A cultural education

Listening 1
Part 1

Multiple choice 2.20–2.22

1 Discuss the following questions about the photographs. In which English-speaking countries do you think they were taken? What significance might the tattoos have for the young man? What hardships do you think Chinese migrants had to face in a new country? How do you think the children are feeling?

2 You will hear three different extracts. For questions **1–6**, choose the answer (**A**, **B** or **C**) which fits best according to what you hear. There are two questions for each extract.

Extract One

You hear part of a radio discussion in which two people are talking about working for Summer Camps USA.

1 According to the woman, non-Americans working at summer camp may
- **A** arrange to visit newly-made friends in their countries.
- **B** be surprised at who their colleagues turn out to be.
- **C** feel as though they are in a minority group.

2 The man compares summer camp to a military camp to suggest that
- **A** there are strict rules.
- **B** the facilities are basic.
- **C** the working hours are long.

Extract Two

You hear part of a radio interview with two Chinese Australians who took part in a documentary about Chinese migration.

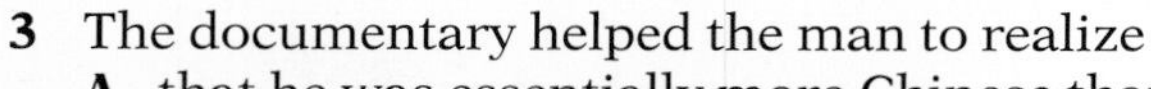

3 The documentary helped the man to realize
- **A** that he was essentially more Chinese than Australian.
- **B** how fortunate he was compared to other Chinese Australians.
- **C** what earlier generations of his family had endured.

4 According to the woman, Chinese Australians are now
- **A** working in a greater range of professions.
- **B** regarded as real Australians.
- **C** better educated than other ethnic groups.

Extract Three

You hear part of an interview with the organizers of an exhibition on the art of tattooing.

5 Both the organizers say that an aim of the exhibition is to
- **A** challenge beliefs about why some people have tattoos.
- **B** demonstrate how much variety of design there is in tattooing.
- **C** explain why tattooing is a growing phenomenon globally.

6 According to the woman, in Maori culture tattoos were worn
- **A** only by powerful men.
- **B** to indicate social status.
- **C** mainly on the face.

3 In what ways might children benefit from attending a summer camp? What can they learn?

Can you ever imagine emigrating to another country? If so, what would be your reason for going? Which country might it be?

If you were to have a tattoo, what would it show and why?

Vocabulary 1: Sight

1 Underline the correct alternative in the following extracts from the recording.

- **a** Make sure you *look/see* out for the advertisements in *The Globe*.
- **b** Our communities used to be hidden from *show/view* ...
- **c** You've now also got Chinese Australians performing as musicians, artists, writers – that was a rare *vision/sight* not so long ago.
- **d** ... the exhibition really does provide a fascinating *look/view* at the history of tattooing.
- **e** There's also a collection of tools on *view/sight* ...

2 Complete each gap with one of the nouns from the box. In each section **1–5**, the noun required for both spaces, **a** and **b**, is the same.

vision	sight	view	look	eye

1 **a** Looking out across the bay, she suddenly **caught** ________ **of** a dolphin.
b Stay here, don't say a word and **keep out of** ________ !

2 **a** A movement in the bushes **caught my** ________ and I moved closer to investigate.
b You'll need a good telescope, as the star is not normally **visible to the naked** ________ .

3 **a** He sprayed anti-government slogans on the ministry building **in full** ________ **of** the security guards.
b As we turned the corner the house **came into** ________ .

4 **a** You've probably sprained it or something. Let me **have a** ________ **at** it.
b Now it's time for *In Depth*, in which we **take a closer** ________ **at** an issue in the news.

5 **a** The mole, which spends most of its life underground, has very **poor** ________ . Nor can it hear or smell very well.
b Many of his short stories offer a dark and terrifying ________ **of the future**.

3 Talk to your partner about

- **a** **a familiar sight** in your town or the surrounding countryside at this time of year.
- **b** **a breathtaking view** you have seen.
- **c** someone **in the public eye** whom you admire.
- **d** a radio or television programme you know which provides **an in-depth look** at current affairs.
- **e** the advantages and disadvantages of having **X-ray vision**.

Reading and Use of English
Part 7

Gapped text

1 How often do you go to see a performance of a play, a classical music concert or an opera?

Are members of the audience expected to behave in a certain way?

What type of behaviour might other members of the audience find annoying?

2 You are going to read an article about the way people sometimes behave in the theatre or concert hall. Six paragraphs have been removed from the article. Choose from the paragraphs **A–G** the one which fits each gap (**1–6**). There is one extra paragraph which you do not need to use.

THE TROUBLE WITH MODERN AUDIENCES

Stephen Pollard believes that many of us need to be educated in the norms of social conduct – in particular, concert etiquette

According to the reviews, the performance of Mahler's *Sixth Symphony* that I went to last week was 'transcendent', 'emotionally perfect' and 'violently good'. A friend called me the following morning and told me that it was one of the most powerful experiences of her life.

1 ______

Sitting in the row in front of me, you see, was the family from hell. I don't know their names, but let's call them the Fidget-Bottoms. Mr and Mrs Fidget-Bottom spent the entire time stroking and kissing their kids, stretching out their arms across the backs of seats as if they were on the sofa at home and, just for good measure, bobbing their heads up and down in time with the music.

2 ______

I planted a well-aimed kick in the back of the seat but to no avail. A killer combination of the family's total self-absorption, and the seat's wooden solidity, meant that the only effect was a painful toe. So I resorted to another equally fruitless tactic; that of seething with righteous indignation.

3 ______

Now there is more of a *laissez-faire* attitude, which, whilst opening up cultural institutions to millions, has its own set of drawbacks. Today, you come as you please, and behave as you please. It's your right. If you want to flick through your programme, fine. If you want to use it as a fan, go ahead. If you want to cough, feel free.

4 ______

But we are not at home. The very point of the theatre is to be out of the house, and part of a crowd. And being part of a crowd has its obligations – not shouting 'fire' out of mischief, for example, in a crowded room. When travelling by bus, I do not suddenly begin to indulge myself by singing arias from Handel's *Messiah*. Nor do I whistle along to the music at weddings at which I am a guest. I behave as is expected of me.

5 ______

As a result we have forgotten – or more truthfully, never learnt – how to listen. When the *St Matthew Passion* was written, it was heard at Easter, once every very few years. A performance was an event, an event which we had no way of even attempting to recreate. Today, we can record the performance and then listen to it at our leisure in the bath. We can have its choruses playing as background music while we eat or converse with those around us.

6 ______

It's hardly surprising that we take that behaviour, and that attitude, into the concert hall with us. Mr and Mrs Fidget-Bottom, and the little Fidget-Bottoms, certainly ruined my concert last week, and I am fairly sure they are going to ruin quite a few others as they get older.

A This particular family may have been especially horrific, but they are merely grotesque extensions of the downside of the increasing accessibility of culture. Admittedly, the old formal rules of behaviour at the theatre, concerts and opera – dressing up in black tie and all that, and the feeling that unless you were part of a closed circle then on no account could you attend – were far too stifling.

B Rarely, if ever, do we sit down in our own home to listen to a full performance of a piece of music, with no other distractions. And if we do make an attempt, then no sooner have we settled into our armchair than we think of something else we could be doing – and we do it.

C Which is more than can be said for the Fidget-Bottoms of the world, who seem oblivious to the norms of social conduct. The problem stems from the fact that culture is now too readily accessible. We simply don't need to make an effort with it. You want to hear Beethoven's *Ninth*? Just go online. Fancy Vivaldi's *Four Seasons*? Which version?

D I felt then, as now, that my outburst of temper was justified. What these people, and people like them clearly need, is an education in how to behave in public, beginning with a basic introduction to concert etiquette. On no account should you kiss your children once the concert has started. Indeed, save that for when you get home.

E I wouldn't know. My body was in the concert hall, and my ears are in full working order. But neither were any use to me. The London Symphony Orchestra might as well have been playing *Chopsticks* for all the impact the Mahler had on me.

F Unwrapping sweets, fidgeting, wandering off to the toilet and chatting are also on the list of things you can do during a performance. When going out is as easy, and as normal, as staying in, then we behave the same in the theatre, or the concert hall, as we do in the living room. And so we don't have a thought for those around us.

G They were cocooned in their own world, with not the slightest concern for anyone around. I doubt that it even crossed their mind that they were doing anything wrong, so unabashed was their behaviour. The situation called for action.

Reacting to the text

Do you agree with the writer's views? Why/Why not?

There has been much debate in Britain in recent years about the 'dumbing down' of culture, a reduction in the quality and/or educational value of television and the arts, brought about by the desire to make them more accessible.

How true is this in your country? Do you think young people have greater or less cultural knowledge than previous generations?

Language focus: Inversion

1 Comment on the word order in sentences **a–d**, which are taken from the reading.
What effect is the writer hoping to achieve by placing the words which are written in **bold** at the beginning of the sentence?

a **Rarely**, if ever, do we sit down in our own home to listen to a full performance of a piece of music …
b **No sooner** have we settled into our armchair than we think of something else we could be doing …
c **On no account** should you kiss your children once the concert has started.
d When travelling by bus, I do not suddenly begin … singing arias from Handel's *Messiah*. **Nor** do I whistle along to the music at weddings …

2 Rewrite **a–d** in exercise **1** so that the words in **bold** do not appear at the beginning of the sentence.

Example:
a *We rarely, if ever, sit down in our own home to listen to a full performance of a piece of music.*

Read more about inversion in the Grammar reference on pages 222 and 223.

Practice

1 Rewrite the following sentences, beginning with the words given. There is an example at the beginning (**0**).
0 As soon as the group had gone on stage, it started to rain.
No sooner *had the group gone on stage than it started to rain*.
1 We only very rarely go to the cinema these days.
Only very rarely ________________________.
2 I have never seen such a terrible performance of *Hamlet* before.
Never before ________________________.
3 Bags must not be left unattended at any time.
At no time ________________________.
4 The identity of the murderer is not revealed until the very last page.
Not until ________________________.
5 They only realized the painting had been hung upside down when someone complained at reception.
Only when ________________________.

2 Rewrite sentences **1–5**, beginning with the word in *italics*.
1 He would *never* play in front of a live audience again.
2 She had *hardly* sat down to watch her favourite programme when the phone rang.
3 You will not be allowed to enter the auditorium *under* any circumstances once the play has started.
4 We *not* only went to the National Gallery, but we also saw a West End musical.
5 Amy had *not* enjoyed herself so much since she went to the circus as a child.

3 Complete the following sentences so that they are true for you.
a Only very rarely do I ________________.
b Under no circumstances would I ________________.
c Never again will I ________________.
d Not once in my life have I ________________.
e Not since ____________ have I ________________.
f Not until ____________ did I ________________.

4 Comment on and discuss your sentences with your partner.

Word formation: Nouns formed with *in, out, up, down* and *back*

1 The words *in, out, up, down* and *back* can be used to form nouns, as in this example from the text:

… they are merely grotesque extensions of the ***downside*** *of the increasing accessibility of culture.*

Complete the underlined words in the following sentences. Then check your answers in the text.

a Now there is more of a *laissez-faire* attitude, which, whilst opening up cultural institutions to millions, has its own set of draw________. (4th paragraph of base text)
b We can have its choruses playing as ________ground music while we eat … (6th paragraph of base text)
c I felt then, as now, that my ________burst of temper was justified. (paragraph D)

2 Complete each gap with an appropriate noun form of the word in capitals at the end of the line. Each of the nouns should be formed using one of the words in the box. The exercise starts with an example (**0**).

in	out	up	down	back

0 Organizers blamed the bad weather for the **low** *turnout*; fewer than 2000 people attended this year's festival. **TURN**

1 A **heavy** ________ before the start of the match left the pitch looking rather like a swimming pool. **POUR**

2 News of a **sharp** ________ **in** property prices will not please first-time buyers. **TURN**

3 The new tax legislation is designed to help those **on low** ________ . **COME**

4 There has been a **serious** ________ **of** cholera on the island, infecting over 50 000 people. **BREAK**

5 The exhibition **provides a fascinating** ________ **into** traditional farming methods. **SIGHT**

6 Whilst the government seems confident of victory, it is still too early to **predict the final** ________ **of** the election. **COME**

7 The government **suffered a severe** ________ in the election, losing its overall majority in the National Assembly. **SET**

8 There has been a 5% **fall in industrial** ________ this year, in contrast to agricultural production, which has risen by 3%. **PUT**

9 His parents were firm believers in discipline and **he had a very strict** ________ . **BRING**

10 There has been a **complete** ________ **in** law and order in the capital, with reports of widespread looting and violence. **BREAK**

Listening 2
Part 2

Sentence completion 2.23

1 You will hear part of a radio programme in which a writer called Gaby makes a confession. For questions **1–8**, complete the sentences with a word or short phrase.

Gaby says she spends a lot of time in **(1)** .... for research purposes.

As a teenager Gaby always had problems with her **(2)** ....

Most people attributed Gaby's A-level failures to **(3)** .... rather than lack of effort.

Gaby thinks that after leaving school she may well have appeared quite **(4)** .... to other people.

Gaby's reading helped her to develop an interest in different features of **(5)** ....

Some of her friends are in jobs which have a negative effect on **(6)** ....

According to Gaby, some of her friends have feelings of **(7)** .... because of her lifestyle.

A problem for many graduates is that they begin their working lives with large **(8)** ....

2 To what extent is having a degree in your country a guarantee of higher earnings?

What are the advantages and disadvantages of going to university?

In your country, how do students usually pay for their university education? (e.g. using family savings, getting a loan, a scholarship, an apprentice scheme) What are the advantages and disadvantages of these forms of funding?

Vocabulary 2: *Read* and *write*

1 What do the underlined words mean in these two extracts from the listening?

... the most versatile and prolific writer of her generation.
I also read voraciously and always seemed to have a book in my hand.

2 Complete each of the gaps with one of the words from the box.

neatly	widely	well	aloud	rough	plain	avid	good

1 My poem was **read** ________ to the whole class. It was so embarrassing!
2 My wife and I are ________ **readers** of your magazine and eagerly look forward to each month's issue.
3 This book's **a** very ________ **read** – I'd definitely recommend it!
4 As a student he **read** ________ and voraciously on a whole range of subjects from algebra to zoology.
5 Reproducing Goethe's style in English is no easy task, but this translation **reads** rather ________ .
6 I'd like you to **write a** ________ **draft** of the letter in this class, then you can **copy it** ________ into your notebook for homework.
7 I do wish these documents were **written in** ________ **English** – they're far too complicated to understand.

3 Do the speaking exercise on page 204.

Reading and speaking: Gap year

1 Read the following paragraph about gap years. Why do you think many UK universities and employers prefer students who have taken a gap year? Is the same true in your country?

Many young people in the UK take a gap year between leaving school and starting university in order to do something different before continuing with their studies. There are various options open to them, either in the UK or abroad, including travel, teaching, caring and conservation work, as well as academic and cultural study courses.

2 Read the following opinions, which were posted on a gap year website, and compare them with your ideas in exercise **1**.

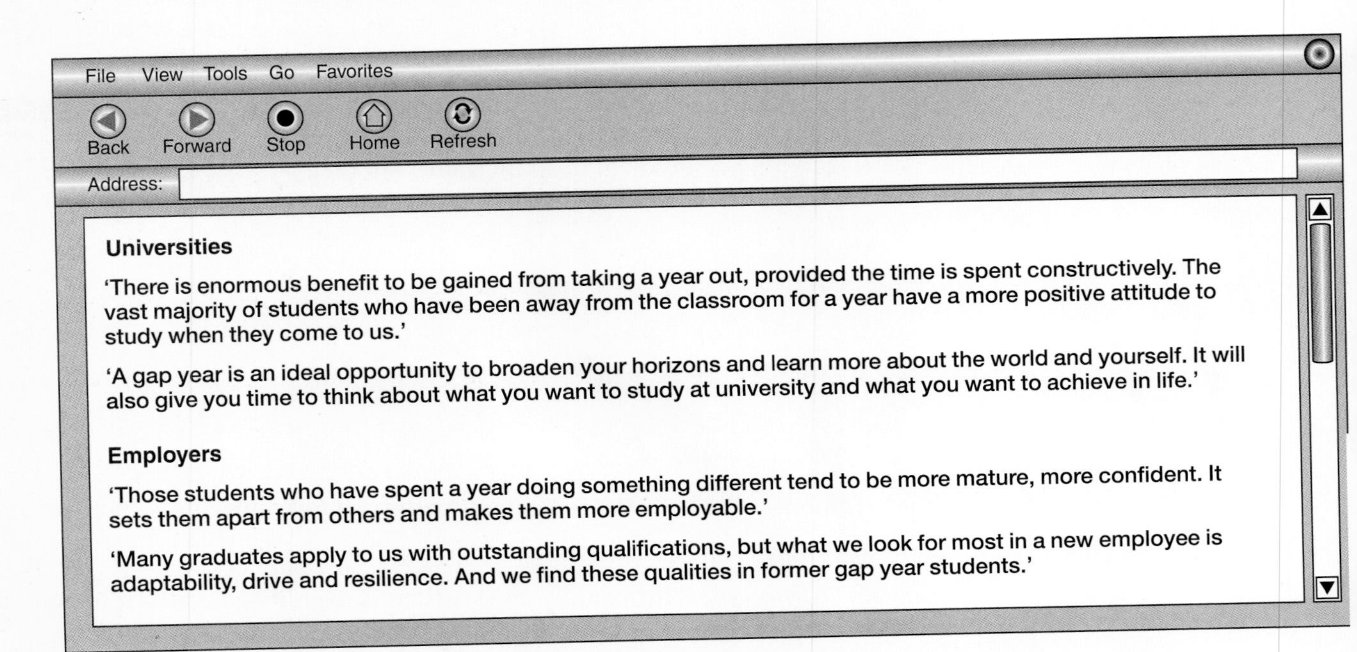

Universities

'There is enormous benefit to be gained from taking a year out, provided the time is spent constructively. The vast majority of students who have been away from the classroom for a year have a more positive attitude to study when they come to us.'

'A gap year is an ideal opportunity to broaden your horizons and learn more about the world and yourself. It will also give you time to think about what you want to study at university and what you want to achieve in life.'

Employers

'Those students who have spent a year doing something different tend to be more mature, more confident. It sets them apart from others and makes them more employable.'

'Many graduates apply to us with outstanding qualifications, but what we look for most in a new employee is adaptability, drive and resilience. And we find these qualities in former gap year students.'

Speaking 1 Part 3

Collaborative task

1 Here are some different experiences that students might encounter in their gap year. Talk to each other about what students might learn from these experiences.

2 Now decide in which of these situations a student would encounter most problems.

Useful language

When talking about the problems you might encounter, try to use some of the vocabulary in section **A** of the Wordlist on page 208.

Speaking 2 Part 4

Further discussion 

Discuss the following questions:

- How might parents feel about their children spending their gap year abroad?
- Do you agree that 'Experience is the best teacher'? Why/Why not?
- What has been your most valuable learning experience to date?
- What things can we learn from elderly people and what can we teach them?
- Some people think that young people have too many opportunities nowadays. What would you say to them?

Writing
Part 2

Proposal

1 Read the following Part 2 task, underlining key words in the instructions.

The committee of your college's Arts Club, of which you are a member, has decided to publish a monthly arts magazine for students. The leader of the committee asks you to draft a proposal

- suggesting what should be included in the magazine.
- outlining ways in which interest in the magazine could be generated.

Write your **proposal** in **220–260** words.

2 Here are some notes about what could be included in the magazine. Which ideas would you include? Expand the notes with further detail.

Notes

Reviews of ....

Promotions of events and services like ....

Q&A interviews with ....

Competitions about ....

Quizzes on ....

Articles on ....

Opinion pieces on topics like ....

Is there anything else you would include?

3 Here are some possible ways of generating interest in a new student magazine. Which, if any, of these would you choose and why?

posters	email	social media
a launch party	word of mouth	

4 Read the answer to the task on page 151.

Are any of your ideas from exercises **2** and **3** included?

Proposal for the new arts magazine

Introduction

The committee intends to produce a new arts magazine targeted at students attending college. The following are my suggestions for attracting the widest possible readership to the publication.

Reviews

Firstly, I recommend including several reviews per issue. In these, committee members or 'guest writers' could report on local concerts, especially when our own students were performing. We could also review exhibitions and comedy acts if they were offering student concessions.

Q&A interviews

In addition, it would be interesting to feature interviews with graduates who are now working in an arts-related industry. In particular, it might be useful for our current students to hear about the steps people took after leaving college, what their job involves, and to hear about any tips for 'getting your foot in the door'.

Online tutorials

A further idea would be to provide a digital edition of the magazine as well as the print version. This could feature video tutorials, for example, on using Photoshop® for 3D effects.

Launching the magazine

I propose that we promote the magazine via social networking sites and the college website as this will be the most cost-effective way to reach the widest audience. I also think that a promotional page should be running at least three weeks ahead of the first issue so people can contribute articles or use the site to promote their arts events.

Conclusion

I believe our arts magazine could attract a wide readership provided we focus on topics and events that are directly relevant and connected to our own student body.

5 Read the model again and underline examples of the following:

- structures and expressions for making suggestions,

  e.g. *I recommend including …, 'guest writers' could report on …*
- linking words and other cohesive devices, e.g. *Firstly, In these.*

6 Now read the task below and write your own **proposal** in **220–260** words.

You see the announcement below on the website of *The Far Horizons Club*, of which you are a member.

> *The Far Horizons Club* is seeking fresh ideas for events and activities that will provide new cultural experiences for members.
>
> The Club Secretary invites you to send a proposal
>
> - suggesting new events or activities that could be held over a weekend.
> - explaining how these events or activities would provide a cultural experience.

Write your **proposal**.

Don't forget!

- Plan your answer by making brief notes on the content of each paragraph.
- Make sure your reader is fully informed. Explain your ideas clearly and give reasons for your suggestions.
- Consider your target reader and use an appropriate register consistently.
- Include a range of vocabulary and structures.
- Use a variety of linking devices.

11 Review

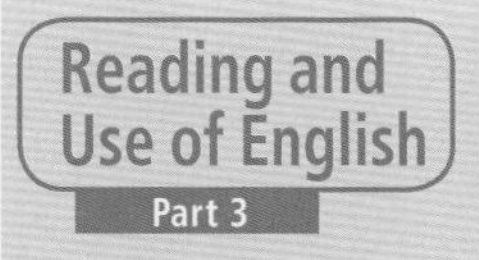

Word formation

For questions **1–8**, read the text below. Use the word given in capitals at the end of some of the lines to form a word that fits in the gap **in the same line**. There is an example at the beginning (**0**). Write your answers **IN CAPITAL LETTERS**.

ANTHONY MASTERS

Anthony Masters was a writer of **(0)** EXCEPTIONAL gifts and prodigious	**EXCEPTION**
energy. In 1964, at the age of 23, he published *A Pocketful of Rye*, a	
collection of short stories whose **(1)** .... of style earned him	**FRESH**
the distinction of being runner-up in the John Llewellyn Rhys Memorial	
Prize, an established and prestigious **(2)** .... award. He won the	**LITERATURE**
award two years later with his novel *The Seahorse*, after which he continued	
to display his **(3)** .... talent by writing both fiction and non-fiction.	**CONSIDER**
The **(4)** .... for many of his novels came from his experience	**INSPIRE**
helping the **(5)** .... excluded: he ran soup kitchens for drug addicts	**SOCIAL**
and campaigned for the civic rights of gypsies and ethnic **(6)**	**MINOR**
His non-fiction **(7)** .... was typically eclectic, ranging from	**PUT**
biographies to social histories, but it was as a writer of children's fiction that	
Masters outshone his contemporaries. His work contains a sensitivity which	
remains **(8)** .... by any other writer of the genre.	**EQUAL**

Vocabulary

Complete each of the gaps with the correct form of one of the verbs from the box. There is an example at the beginning (**0**).

look	turn	catch	come	read	~~have~~
suffer	take	keep	break	write	

0 Her parents were both lawyers and she _had_ a very comfortable middle-class upbringing.

1 One of the best ways to improve your English at this level is to ________ widely.
2 On tonight's programme we'll be ________ a critical look at education.
3 I've done the homework in rough – I'll ________ it out neatly tonight and hand it in tomorrow.
4 ________ out for a present for Luke when you go shopping tomorrow.
5 Their hopes of winning the championship ________ a serious setback on Sunday, when they lost at home to United.
6 She peered out into the audience, hoping to ________ sight of her mother.
7 A cheer went up on deck as the harbour ________ into view.
8 Toys should be ________ out of sight all the time a child is eating.
9 Thousands of people ________ out to catch a glimpse of the President as he toured the region.
10 Tensions grew between the two nations until finally war ________ out in March.

Reading and Use of English
Part 2

Open cloze

For questions **1–8**, read the text below and think of the word which best fits each gap. Use only **one** word in each gap. There is an example at the beginning (**0**). Write your answers **IN CAPITAL LETTERS**.

PHOTOGRAPHIC PORTRAITS

The most famous portraits are now created by photographers rather **(0)** ......*THAN*...... painters, and the people **(1)** .... the lens are as celebrated as the sitters in front. But are the images they produce of celebrities worthy of serious art exhibitions? Will they **(2)** .... looked back on as a true record of the age? Critics say fashion photographers lack artistic depth and integrity, **(3)** .... of which are necessary to be a true artist. Their defenders say their approach is little different from **(4)** .... of respected portrait artists throughout the ages, from the German Hans Holbein to English painter Sir Joshua Reynolds. Just **(5)** .... court artists in the past, photographers in modern times work to a tight timetable and commercial constraint and often have a very short time in **(6)** .... to get to know their sitter. For a painter like Reynolds, this was very much the case. It is known that he **(7)** .... hold up to eight sittings in a day to finish a work on time. Not **(8)** .... the 19th century did the idea emerge that art should not be commercially based.

Writing
Part 2

Review

You see the following announcement on a website, *Events 360*.

> Send us a review of an exhibition you have recently visited. What was the focus of the exhibition? How well informed were you by the end of your visit? Who do you think this exhibition would appeal to?

Write your **review** in **220–260** words.

12 The world about us

Listening 1
Part 2

Sentence completion 2.24

1 When you travel, do you usually take photographs? What kind of photographs do you prefer taking? How do you rate yourself as a photographer?

What do you think would be the highlights and downsides of a career in wildlife photography?

2 You will hear a photographer called Nina Christie, giving a talk about her work. For questions **1–8**, complete the sentences with a word or short phrase.

Nina says that determination and a strong **(1)** .... are needed to succeed as a photographer.

Nina says that her relationship with the **(2)** .... in Africa gives her an advantage over other photographers.

According to Nina, researching the **(3)** .... of animals before a trip is essential.

Nina always takes some simple **(4)** .... on her trips, as well as technical equipment.

In Nina's opinion, each of her photographs is a record of a **(5)** ....

Nina is conscious that the **(6)** .... can create a barrier between her and the wildlife she photographs.

Nina always makes sure she has **(7)** .... before taking photos of human subjects.

In the past, Nina has donated her photographs to organizations working on **(8)** .... projects.

Reacting to the text

Do you agree with Nina that

- taking photographs of strangers without their permission is offensive?
- using digital manipulation to alter a photograph is something to be avoided?

Vocabulary 1: Expressions and phrases with *work*

1 What do these underlined phrases or expressions from the listening mean?

a … so if you want (photography) to work out as a long-term career, you need real determination …

b … doing some groundwork really helps when it comes to predicting how the subject's going to move …

c … you're bound to end up being attacked by leeches … It's all in a day's work!

2 Fill the gaps using words from the box.

clock	dirty	dog	donkey	knowledge	order	skills	vigorous

1 Please reassure the client that we're **working around the** ______ to fix the problem.

2 I **worked like a** ________ for that company and for very little pay.

3 Employees must ensure that the machinery is **kept** clean and **in good working** ________ .

4 We need someone with **a good working** ________ **of** French.

5 The only thing that helps me de-stress is **a** ________ **workout at the gym**.

6 The manager didn't want to tell the staff about the redundancies, so he got his assistant to **do his** ________ **work** for him.

7 In my appraisal, they told me I had to **work on my presentation** ________ .

8 We **did all the** ________ **work** on that project, but Emre got all the credit for the finished product.

3 Choose three of the expressions from exercises **1** and **2** above. Use them to talk about situations which are true for yourself.

Example:

I can't remember the last time I had a vigorous workout. I've got a bit out of shape recently.

Reading and Use of English 1
Part 5

Multiple choice

1 Do you enjoy watching wildlife documentaries on television? Why/Why not?

The photographs show Sir David Attenborough, the presenter of many such programmes. What do you think are the qualities of a good wildlife documentary presenter?

2 Read the following magazine article about Sir David Attenborough. For questions **1–6**, choose the answer (**A**, **B**, **C** or **D**) which you think fits best according to the text.

DOING WHAT COMES NATURALLY

'This,' says a figure, addressing us from somewhere inside the world's thickest coat, 'is one of the coldest places. On Earth.' The emphases are heavy and deliberate, but the voice is like a piano played gently. You feel at home with this voice, you know where you are with it, which, on this occasion, is in the High Arctic, on the trail of the Arctic fox, with the temperature hovering somewhere around 50 below. The voice is unmistakably that of Sir David Attenborough. The words are those which open *The Life of Mammals*, Attenborough's latest *magnum opus* for the BBC.

We are familiar enough with Attenborough's work through previous documentaries to know that a number of things can be guaranteed. He will begin a sentence in, say, Australia and finish it in Brazil. And we will be variously appalled and intrigued by the ways in which mammals hunt, eat and form relationships. As Attenborough says in the introduction to the series, 'We will look at the lives of our closest relatives and they will lead us to ourselves.'

But will they lead us to David Attenborough? In *Life on Air*, he wrote a 400-page account of his career in broadcasting. It is one of the few books ever published to contain tips on handling a Gaboon viper. ('Push a pole under one, about a third of its length from the back of its head, and it will be balanced so that you can gently lift it. Then dump it in a box and slam the lid down very quickly.') However, its author is far less forthcoming for anyone seeking to know the private man. The death of his wife, Jane, which everyone close to Attenborough agrees devastated him, is approached in four sorrowful but guarded paragraphs. His brother Richard merits one mention in the book, and that in brackets. Attenborough, it seems, slams the lid down very quickly on subjects of intimacy.

Not surprisingly, perhaps, he keeps out of the limelight as much as possible, both on and off screen. His determination in this regard is founded in part on genuine anxieties he has about taking credit where it isn't due. Frequently, of course, Attenborough is present when the rare footage of, say, the naked mole rat is shot. But at other times he goes nowhere near the animal at all, adding his voice to the footage shot by a cameraman, who has been standing for months in a field in a pair of wet boots. Attenborough, too, has had his fair share of long nights spent on forest floors in damp sleeping bags, in disquieting proximity to leeches. Yet the elements of risk and discomfort in his work are things he would prefer to downplay. He considers himself a channel rather than the focus.

Attenborough could have had a quieter life. He went to Cambridge in 1945 to read natural sciences and considered becoming an academic. But he eventually gave up on the idea. 'I know someone who went looking for an animal in Sumatra,' he recalls. 'He didn't even see it for the first three years. Went out and looked for it every day. Saw footprints, occasionally a hair. And after he'd found it, that was all he was allowed to look at for another eight years. Another chap I knew had to count the number of bees that went into a certain kind of orchid between certain hours of the day. He was stuck out in the middle of the Panama Canal counting bees. A caricature of the intellectual life, really.'

So, in the hope of finding something more stimulating, he joined the BBC. He rocketed up through the ranks, lending the best of his energies to wildlife programming, which was then at an unpromisingly larval stage. In the 50s the technology wasn't readily available to film in the field, so the natural world had to be borrowed from London Zoo and brought to the studio in a sack.

'It gave you five minutes of very cheap programming, in which you showed a python.' In the classic tradition of these things, his becoming a presenter was entirely inadvertent, because the person who was to have done the show came down with something.

Ever since then, for over 50 years, he's been doing what comes naturally; entertaining and enlightening – and bringing comfort. For his programmes run reassuringly counter to the reflex of our times, which is to mull fearfully over a depressing prospect for the world about us. Seen through Attenborough's eyes, the planet tends not to be scalded and smoking, breathing its last. It teems and thrives, blossoms and grows. The future in Sir David Attenborough's world is big and bright.

1 The writer says that Sir David Attenborough's voice
- **A** is not immediately recognizable.
- **B** is comforting to the listener.
- **C** is distracting to an extent.
- **D** is authoritarian in tone.

2 What does Attenborough mean in lines 21–22 when he says 'they will lead us to ourselves'?
- **A** The mammals will remind us of the value of cooperation in survival.
- **B** We will realize how far humans have evolved compared to other species.
- **C** The mammals will help us gain an understanding of our own behaviour.
- **D** We will uncover more about ourselves than we will about the mammals.

3 In his book *Life on Air*, Attenborough
- **A** concedes to having a subjective viewpoint.
- **B** provides practical advice on taming animals.
- **C** appears indifferent towards family members.
- **D** reveals little in regard to his own emotions.

4 What are we told about Attenborough in the fourth paragraph?
- **A** He has sometimes underestimated the level of danger involved in filming.
- **B** He would rather not be the centre of attention in his documentaries.
- **C** He is equally fascinated by exotic animals and animals which are familiar.
- **D** He takes pride in sharing uncomfortable environments with the film crew.

5 Attenborough refers to the projects in Sumatra and the Panama Canal in order to
- **A** put the case forward for greater funding for scientific work.
- **B** highlight the dedication required to carry out valid investigations.
- **C** show which kind of studies have practical applications and which do not.
- **D** illustrate how futile some academic research can be.

6 What does the writer say about Attenborough's early days at the BBC?
- **A** He became the host of wildlife programmes by chance.
- **B** The company was reluctant to invest in certain technology.
- **C** His promotion in the company was a long time in coming.
- **D** His programmes were not always well-received by the public.

Reacting to the text

Do you share Sir David Attenborough's view of the world, as expressed in the last paragraph? Why/Why not?

What questions would you ask David Attenborough if you had the chance to interview him?

Language focus 1: Conjunctions and linking adverbials

1 The words in **bold** in the following extracts from the reading are all **conjunctions**; they connect two clauses in the same sentence.
The emphases are heavy and deliberate, ***but*** *the voice is like a piano played gently.*
He went to Cambridge in 1945 to read natural sciences ***and*** *considered becoming an academic.*
... the technology wasn't readily available to film in the field, ***so*** *the natural world had to be borrowed from London Zoo ...*

In sections **A** and **B**, complete each of the gaps with one of the conjunctions from the box.

A Reason and result

in case	otherwise	so that

a You'd better go now, __________ you'll miss your bus.
b Leave early __________ you don't miss your bus.
c Take some money for a taxi __________ you miss your bus.

B Contrast and concession

however	even though	whereas

a He went to see the match, __________ he doesn't like cricket.
b He went to see the match, __________ I watched it on TV.
c __________ you look at it, cricket is a boring game.

In less formal writing, conjunctions are sometimes used at the beginning of a sentence to connect it with the previous sentence, as in these extracts from the reading.
And *we will be variously appalled and intrigued by the ways in which mammals hunt, eat and form relationships.*
But *at other times he goes nowhere near the animal at all ...*
So*, in the hope of finding something more stimulating, he joined the BBC.*

2 However, normally **linking adverbials** are used to connect one sentence with another. They frequently appear at the beginning of a sentence, and are followed by a comma.
However*, its author is far less forthcoming for anyone seeking to know the private man.*
Ever since then*, for over 50 years, he's been doing what comes naturally ...*

In sections **A** and **B**, complete each of the gaps with one of the linking adverbials from the box.

A Contrast and concession

Despite this	By contrast	On the contrary

a He does not act hastily. __________ , he sometimes takes days to reach a decision.
b The song of the blackbird is melodious, but limited in range. __________ , the starling mimics other birds and has an extremely varied repertoire.
c The salary being offered was very low. __________ , there were over 650 applications for the job.

B Time

By that time	From that time on	In the meantime

a I hope to get a new computer next month. __________ , I'll use my husband's laptop.
b We finally reached the campsite at sunset. __________ , I was exhausted and went straight to sleep in the tent.
c The burglary affected us in other ways, too. __________ , we always made sure one of us was in the house.

In sections **C** and **D**, complete each gap in the linking adverbials with a word from the box. You will need to use one of the words more than once. All three adverbials in each section perform the same function.

as	for	from	in	of	on	to

C Reason and result

Her health had deteriorated significantly.

a ____ **a result,**
b ____ **account** ____ **this,**
c ____ **this reason,**

she decided it would be best to retire.

D Addition

Professional photographers will pack a range of lenses and filters for their assignments.

a ____ **addition** ____ **this,**
b ____ **well** ____ **this,**
c **Apart** ____ **this,**

they'll take all sorts of medicine with them.

Read more about conjunctions and linking adverbials in the Grammar reference on page 223.

3 Complete each of the sentences in an appropriate way. There is an example at the beginning (**0**).

0 You should start revising now,
  a otherwise *you'll start to panic nearer the exam* .
  b even though *the exam is in three months' time* .

1 The country was hit by torrential rain overnight.
  a As a result, ______________________ .
  b What is more, ______________________ .
2 This year's concert was held in a large indoor venue,
  a so that ______________________ .
  b whereas ______________________ .
3 He hadn't exactly had a stressful day.
  a On the contrary, ______________________ .
  b By contrast, ______________________ .
4 I wouldn't recommend it as a holiday destination,
  a unless ______________________ .
  b although ______________________ .

Multiple-choice cloze

1 Do you think wild animals should be farmed for their skin or meat? Give reasons for your views.

2 Read the first paragraph below, ignoring the gaps for the moment.

Why did Andy Johnson start his farm?

Are you surprised by his intended market?

3 For questions **1–8**, read the text again and decide which answer (**A**, **B**, **C** or **D**) best fits each gap. There is an example at the beginning (**0**).

CROCODILE FARMS

When Andy Johnson **(0)** .... Britain's first ever crocodile farm, he **(1)** .... under fierce criticism from animal rights groups, opposed to the factory farming of wildlife. However, Johnson **(2)** .... that his motivation for starting a crocodile farm was for **(3)** .... environmental reasons. He wants to protect wild crocodiles from being poached, and he is primarily interested in their meat, not their skins. 'By supplying Europeans with home-produced crocodile, we can **(4)** .... the market value of illegally supplied crocodile meat,' he claims.

In the last century, many species of crocodiles were hunted to the **(5)** .... of extinction as trade in their skins flourished. Some 300 000 Australian saltwater crocodiles were killed between 1945 and 1972. The alligator suffered a similar **(6)** .... , although both species are now protected and their **(7)** .... are slowly rising. Worldwide, the legal trade in crocodilian skins has roughly tripled since 1977. The majority of these are farmed animals, but upwards of 90 000 are killed annually in the **(8)** ....

	A	B	C	D
0	**A** put out	**B** gave off	**C** set up	**D** brought about
1	**A** came	**B** went	**C** met	**D** put
2	**A** insists	**B** ascertains	**C** insures	**D** convinces
3	**A** finely	**B** utterly	**C** cleanly	**D** purely
4	**A** downsize	**B** downplay	**C** undercut	**D** undergo
5	**A** frontier	**B** line	**C** side	**D** edge
6	**A** luck	**B** fate	**C** chance	**D** destination
7	**A** groups	**B** counts	**C** numbers	**D** volumes
8	**A** nature	**B** wild	**C** environment	**D** outside

4 Can you name any species currently threatened with extinction in your country?

What measures should be taken to safeguard these species?

5 Write four sentences, each including one of the wrong words from the text above. Leave a gap where the word should go, and give three options.

Example:

The new law _______ a significant change in the way animals were treated.
A *put out* ***B*** *gave off* ***C*** *brought about*

6 Ask your partner to complete the gaps in your sentences.

Your partner should also say why the incorrect options do not fit the gap.

Listening 2 Part 4

Multiple matching  2.25–2.29

1 What are the main issues involved in the following global concerns?

climate change   whale hunting   women's rights
child labour   human rights   GM foods

2 You will hear five short extracts in which people are talking about action they have taken on global issues.

TASK ONE
For questions **1–5**, choose from the list (**A–H**) the speaker's motivation for taking the action.

TASK TWO
For questions **6–10**, choose from the list (**A–H**) the effect that the experience had on the speaker.

While you listen you must complete both tasks.

A I hoped to change people's way of thinking.
B I was driven by feelings of guilt.
C I had always wanted to help others.
D A friend encouraged me.
E I wanted to prove a point to a friend.
F I had seen pictures of suffering.
G It would show me in a good light.
H I was impressed by other people's work.

1 ___
2 ___
3 ___
4 ___
5 ___

A I became disillusioned.
B It made me feel ashamed.
C It encouraged me to do more.
D It increased my self-respect.
E I suddenly became very popular.
F It made me regret what I had done.
G It helped me achieve an ambition.
H I felt I had not done enough.

6 ___
7 ___
8 ___
9 ___
10 ___

3 Have you ever taken action similar to that of any of the speakers? If so, what was your motivation and how did you feel afterwards?

Should individuals take more action on global issues, or is this best left to governments? Why?

Language focus 2: Modal verbs 3: *Must, need, should* and *ought to*

1 Which of the speakers in the listening said each of these two groups of sentences?

A 1 *We **had to** do exactly the same work.*
2 *There **must have** been about 500 of us altogether.*
3 *We **should have** done it years before.*

B 1 *I thought at first they might not accept me because of my age and inexperience, but I **needn't have** worried.*
2 *I **didn't need to** have any special skills.*

2 For each group of sentences, explain the difference in meaning between the words in **bold** as they are used by the speaker.

3 Which of the sentences in exercise **1** do **not** contain a modal verb? What are the main characteristics of a modal verb?
In which sentence could *ought to* be used instead of one of the words in **bold**, without changing the meaning?

4 Explain the difference in meaning between the words in **bold** as they are used in the following sentences.

a I really **must** be going – my son **should** be home from school soon and I **have to** take him to his swimming class.
b I know you **shouldn't** tell lies, but you **don't have to** tell him the whole truth, either. You **mustn't** let him know you've been here.

5 Usually, there is no difference in meaning between *needn't* and *don't need to*. However, *needn't* tends to be used to give permission not to do something, and *don't need to* is used more often to talk about general necessity.

*You **needn't** do it now – we're in no hurry.*

*You **don't need to** be tall to be a good basketball player.*

Rewrite each of the two sentences so that the meaning is positive. Is the modal or non-modal form of *need* required?

Read more about the verbs in this section in the Grammar reference on pages 223 and 224.

Practice

1 Underline the correct alternatives in the following sentences. Either one, two or all three alternatives may be possible.

1 I cleaned the flat specially for tonight, but I *mustn't/needn't/shouldn't* have bothered.
2 You really *must/need/should* do something about your handwriting.
3 What do you *have/ought/need* to do to become famous?
4 I'm meeting my partner's parents for the first time tomorrow. What *need/ought/should* I wear?
5 We're going into town, but you *needn't/don't need to/don't have to* come if you don't want to.
6 They *ought to/must/should* have got there by now. Why haven't they phoned?
7 I really *needed to study/must have studied/ought to have studied* hard at the weekend, but I did absolutely nothing.
8 If you *should/ought to/need to* happen to see my ex-boss there, can you give him my regards?

2 Choose four of the sentences from exercise **1** and have four separate conversations with your partner, using a different sentence to start each conversation. Remember to say your first sentence with one of the correct alternatives.

Vocabulary 2: Attitude adverbials

The adverbs in the following extracts from the reading text on pages 156 and 157 express the writer's attitude or opinion.

The voice is **unmistakably** that of Sir David Attenborough.
Not surprisingly, perhaps, he keeps out of the limelight as much as possible …
For his programmes run **reassuringly** counter to the reflex of our times …

In sentences **1–5** underline the best alternative.

1 Local residents have condemned the decision to build the factory, and *rightly/undoubtedly/clearly* so, in my opinion.
2 *Strangely/Apparently/Presumably* enough, I find myself agreeing with the government on this issue.
3 *Fortunately/Disappointingly/Conveniently* for us, it was an unusually warm winter and we couldn't go skiing on the hills as we'd hoped.
4 They chopped down vast areas of woodland with *believably/miraculously/predictably* disastrous results for the local bird population.
5 After such a wonderful holiday I *understandably/astonishingly/curiously* felt rather sad when we had to come home.

Key word transformation

For questions **1–6**, complete the second sentence so that it has a similar meaning to the first sentence, using the word given. **Do not change the word given.** You must use between **three** and **six** words, including the word given. Here is an example (**0**). Write your answers **IN CAPITAL LETTERS**.

0 The coral is going to die if we don't take immediate steps to protect it from pollution.
OTHERWISE
We must take immediate steps to protect the coral, OTHERWISE IT WILL BE KILLED off by pollution.

1 The government should have carefully considered the issue of global warming a long time ago.
ATTENTION
The government should .... the issue of global warming a long time ago.

2 There's a chance that you might find some interesting wildlife, so take a camera with you.
HAPPEN
You should take a camera with you in .... across some interesting wildlife.

3 It could be a long time before the dolphins swim past, so while we're waiting I suggest you relax.
MEANTIME
We could be waiting for a long time for the dolphins to swim past, so .... to relax.

4 Because that store sells clothes made by child labour in foreign factories, he doesn't shop there anymore.
ACCOUNT
He doesn't buy clothes from that store anymore, ... they sell clothes made by child labour in foreign factories.

5 I imagine it was tough for you to refuse every beggar that asked you for money.
TURN
It must .... every beggar that asked you for money.

6 It was a waste of time attending the protest march this afternoon, as the council had already made its decision in the morning.
PART
We needn't .... the protest march this afternoon, as the council had already made its decision in the morning.

Speaking 1
Part 3

Collaborative task 

1 Look at the photos of people learning to read and write in different ways. How do you think the people are feeling?

2 Here are some things that schools can do to help improve literacy standards in children.

Talk to your partner about how useful these approaches might be in improving literacy standards.

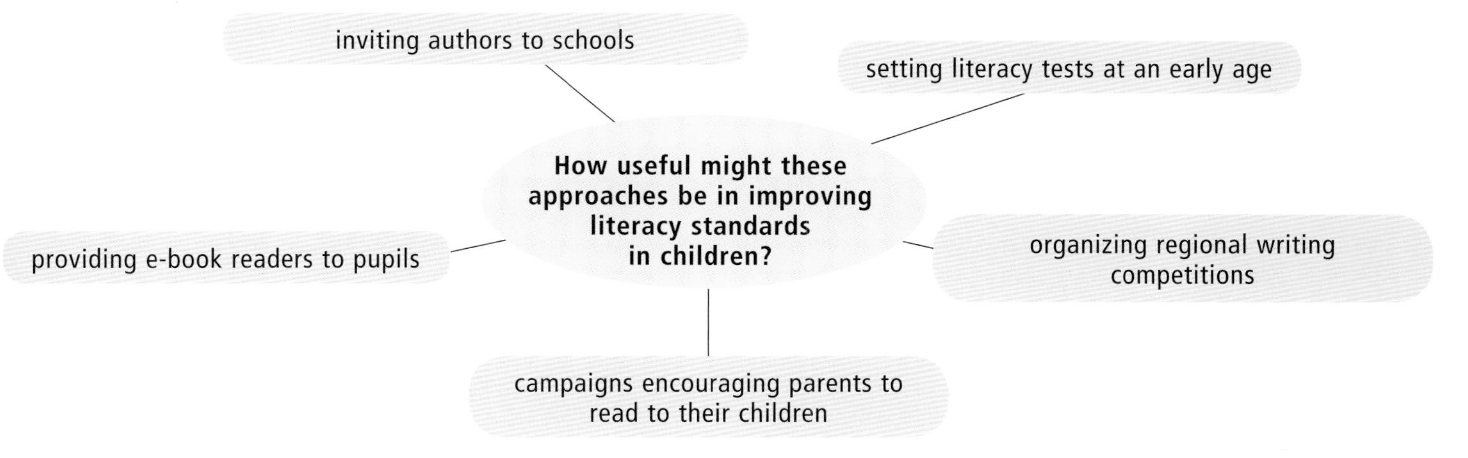

3 Now decide which approach you think children would most enjoy.

Further discussion 

Discuss the following questions:

- How important is it for children to spend time reading fiction?
- Whose responsibility is it to encourage children to read and write – teachers or parents?
- Do you think it is important to study literature at school? Why/Why not?
- Some people think that certain modern forms of communication have had a negative effect on people's writing ability. What do you think?

Essay

Read the following Part 1 Essay task below. Then, with a partner, decide which two methods you want to discuss. For each method, make notes on what specific points and suggestions you want to make.

Your class has attended a panel discussion on what methods schools should use to improve literacy standards. You have made the notes below:

Methods schools should use to improve literacy standards

- testing
- technology
- volunteer schemes

Some opinions expressed in the discussion:

'We want children to read and write for the pleasure of it, not because they have to.'

'The Internet allows children to access a great range of books.'

'Some companies already encourage employees to help out in schools with reading and writing programmes.'

Write an essay for your tutor discussing **two** of the methods in your notes. You should **explain which method you think is more important** for schools to consider, **giving reasons** in support of your answer.

You may, if you wish, make use of the opinions expressed in the discussion, but you should use your own words as far as possible.

Write your answer in **220–260** words in an appropriate style.

12 Review

Reading and Use of English
Part 2

Open cloze

For questions **1–8**, read the text below and think of the word which best fits each gap. Use only **one** word in each gap. There is an example at the beginning (**0**). Write your answers **IN CAPITAL LETTERS**.

CREATURE COMFORTS

Piglets must **(0)** ...*BE*... kept warm in their first few days to discourage them from snuggling up to their mother. That's because 80 per cent or so of piglet deaths occur during **(1)** .... period, and most of them are due to the sow rolling over and crushing her young. **(2)** .... an effort to tackle this problem, the trend in porcine interior design is away from unhygienic straw and **(3)** .... underfloor heating or infrared lamps. But these approaches leave piglets with only an uninviting concrete floor **(4)** .... lie on. The hard surface also aggravates the injuries that piglets often suffer while fighting for position at feeding time.

To find a solution, researchers studied the behaviour and weight gain of almost 1400 piglets held in pens with a variety of heating schemes. Very **(5)** .... all of the piglets preferred warm waterbeds to any of the alternatives, spending well **(6)** .... half the day lying about on them. Interestingly **(7)** .... farmers, the piglets on the waterbeds **(8)** .... only developed fewer skin lesions, but also gained significantly more weight than those kept on concrete.

Modal verbs

Complete each gap in **1–8** with either the positive or negative form of one of the modal verbs in the box. In each section, the verb required for both gaps is the same. There is one verb you do not need to use. There is an example at the beginning (**0**).

shall	should	will	would	~~can~~
could	may	might	need	must

0 She seems very pleasant, but she ___*can*___ be quite irritable at times.
I'm off to bed – I ___*can*___ barely keep my eyes open.

1 We __________ have caught that train if you'd run a bit faster.
I wish I __________ remember where I put my glasses!

2 She __________ have to phone now, right in the middle of my favourite programme!
After he retired, he __________ often go back to visit his old workmates.

3 You __________ have phoned to say you'd be late! I've been so worried.
No one seems to want the last piece, so I __________ as well eat it.

4 You __________ explain – John's already told me what happened.
I know you were angry, but you __________ have shouted.

5 That's very kind of you, but you __________ have gone to all that trouble.
He's just popped out to the shops, so he __________ be long.

6 Just a moment, I'll put you through. Who __________ I say is calling?
Let's go out for lunch, __________ we?

7 If you __________ tell me, I'll have to tickle you until you do!
Phone her a bit later – she probably __________ have got up yet.

8 Why __________ you always interrupt me when I'm speaking?
It __________ have been a huge explosion – it was heard up to 30 miles away.

Collocation revision: Units 1–12

1 In each of the spaces below write one word which collocates with all three of the other words or expressions. The question numbers also refer to the relevant unit of the book where the collocations appeared.

1 face a / take up a / rise to a __________

2 significant / far-reaching / sweeping __________

3 a faint / a musty / a strong __________

4 kick-off / injury / half __________

5 a close / a rocky / a stable __________

6 __________ soundly / rough / badly

7 a dislocated / a sprained / a bruised __________

8 reach a / uphold a / overrule a __________

9 spectacular / breathtaking / superb __________

10 a squeaky / a booming / a hushed __________

11 a rare / a familiar / a welcome __________

12 __________ like a dog / around the clock / on one's presentation skills

2 Use other collocations from the first 12 units of the book to help you create your own exercise. Write three words or expressions which can all be used with the same verb or noun, in the same way as in exercise **1**. Write four examples like this for another student to complete.

Ready for Speaking

Introduction

The **Speaking** paper consists of four parts and lasts 15 minutes. You will probably take the test with one other candidate, though it is possible to be part of a group of three. There are two examiners: the interlocutor, who conducts the test and asks the questions, and the assessor, who listens to the test and assesses your performance. The interlocutor also assesses and contributes to your final mark.

In the following advice to candidates, complete each gap with a word from the box.

repetition	ideas	pictures	opinion	attention	opportunity
~~range~~	silences	element	vocabulary	discussion	

There is an example at the beginning (**0**).

Demonstrating your abilities

- Use a **(0)** _range_ of language and show your ability to link your **(1)** _______ .
- Avoid long **(2)** _______ and frequent pauses as you organize your thoughts.
- If you cannot remember or do not know a particular item of **(3)** _______ , use alternative words to paraphrase.

Following instructions

- Always pay close **(4)** _______ to the interlocutor's instructions. In Parts 2 and 3, questions are printed on the same page as the pictures or the written prompts to help you remember what you have to talk about.
- Don't be afraid to ask for **(5)** _______ if you have not heard, or clarification if you have not fully understood, what has been said.
- Don't just describe the **(6)** _______ you are given; tasks based on visual material in Part 2 also involve a/an **(7)** _______ of speculation, opinion-giving and/or evaluation.

Taking turns

- Don't attempt to dominate a/an **(8)** _______ , but rather give your partner the **(9)** _______ to speak, and respond appropriately to what he or she says.
- If your partner appears reticent, try to involve them by asking questions or inviting them to give their **(10)** _______ .

Part 1: Social interaction

In Part 1 the interlocutor will ask you questions about yourself.

1 Work in groups of three. One of you is the interlocutor and the other two are candidates. You have two minutes to do the following task.

What to expect in the exam

- Part 1 lasts approximately two minutes.
- Questions will be asked from a range of topics including, for example, interests, daily life, family and holidays.
- You may respond to the other candidate's comments, though you are not actively invited to do so by the interlocutor.

Interlocutor

- Ask the candidates one or more questions from at least two of the categories on page 167. You may ask each candidate the same or different questions.

Candidates

- Answer the questions from the interlocutor as fully as possible, giving reasons for your ideas and opinions.

English
How long have you been learning English?
What are your main reasons for learning English?
Which aspect of learning English do you find hardest?

Travel and holidays
What is one of the most interesting places you have visited?
Do you prefer going on holiday with your friends or your family?
Where would you most like to travel to?

The past
What were you doing this time yesterday?
What are some of your earliest childhood memories?
What have been some of the happiest moments in your life?

Leisure time
What do you enjoy doing in your free time?
How important is sport and fitness in your life?
Do you like spending time alone?

House and home
What do you enjoy most about living where you do?
If you could afford your ideal home, what would it be like?
Would you ever consider living abroad?

Future plans
What are you most looking forward to doing in the next few months?
What do you hope to achieve in the next three years?
Do you usually plan your weekends well in advance?

When you have finished, change roles and repeat the exercise with different questions.

2 **2.30** Listen to two students, Jan and Ana, doing the Part 1 task and comment on their performance. Consider the following:

- how well each student develops their responses
- the range and accuracy of their language

Part 2: Long turn

In Part 2 you are given the opportunity to speak for one minute, without interruption, about some pictures. Your partner then has 30 seconds to comment briefly on your pictures by answering a question.

Your partner then speaks for one minute about a **different** set of pictures, after which you have 30 seconds to comment briefly on them.

What to expect in the exam

During your minute in Part 2, you have to compare two of the three photographs you are given, whilst at the same time speculating and giving your opinion about some aspect of their content.

Task One

1 Look at the following Part 2 task.

Work in pairs. Look at these pictures. They show people who are checking the time.

Student A:

Compare **two** of the pictures, and say why the people might be checking the time and how much influence time might have in their daily lives.

Student B:

When your partner has finished talking, answer the following question about all three pictures. For which person do you think time has the greatest influence in their daily life?

- Why might the people be checking the time?
- How much influence might time have in their daily lives?

Before you do the task, answer the question in exercise **2** on page 168.

2 How well does each candidate **a–c** approach the task in exercise **1**? Comment on each extract, giving examples to justify your opinions.

a *This woman is in the kitchen or perhaps the dining room with her son. She's checking the time because maybe she's late. I think she's a businesswoman. This woman is an athlete in a race. She's checking the time because she wants to know how fast she's running. I think time has a big influence in her life because …*

b *I'm going to talk about this picture here which shows an athlete, then this one here which shows a woman and her son. If I have time, I'll speak about the one here with the little girl and her toy watch. Well, all three pictures show women, well, women and a girl, checking the time. This woman is an athlete and I think she is looking at her watch to …*

c *The pictures of the working mother and the athlete both convey the idea of racing against the clock, a need or desire to do something within a certain period of time. The mother looks rather stressed, suggesting something unexpected has happened. She might be phoning the office to let them know she'll be late because her car won't start, or her son's fallen ill. The athlete, on the other hand, is probably …*

3 Now you are ready to do the task.

Don't forget!

- Avoid long silences and frequent pauses.
- Paraphrase if you cannot remember a particular word.

Task Two

1 Change roles from Task One. Turn to page 204.

2 **2.31** Listen to Jan and Ana doing the Part 2 tasks.

- How well do they each complete their main one-minute task?
- How varied is the language they use?

Part 3: Collaborative task

In Part 3, the interlocutor does not take part, but listens while you and your partner perform a problem-solving task together for about three minutes in total.

You are given written prompts, which form the basis for the task, and are asked to exchange ideas and opinions, make evaluations and/or speculate for about two minutes.

The examiner will then ask you a second, related question which requires you to try and reach a decision with your partner. You have one minute to do this.

How to go about it

- Don't simply agree with your partner or repeat his or her ideas. Express your own opinions or develop your partner's points by adding further comments of your own.
- In Task **1** you can talk about the different areas (in this case, jobs) in any order you choose. Try to talk about each one, developing your ideas and giving reasons for your opinions.
- In Task **2** you don't have to reach a final decision together, but it is important that the examiner hears you working towards an agreement.

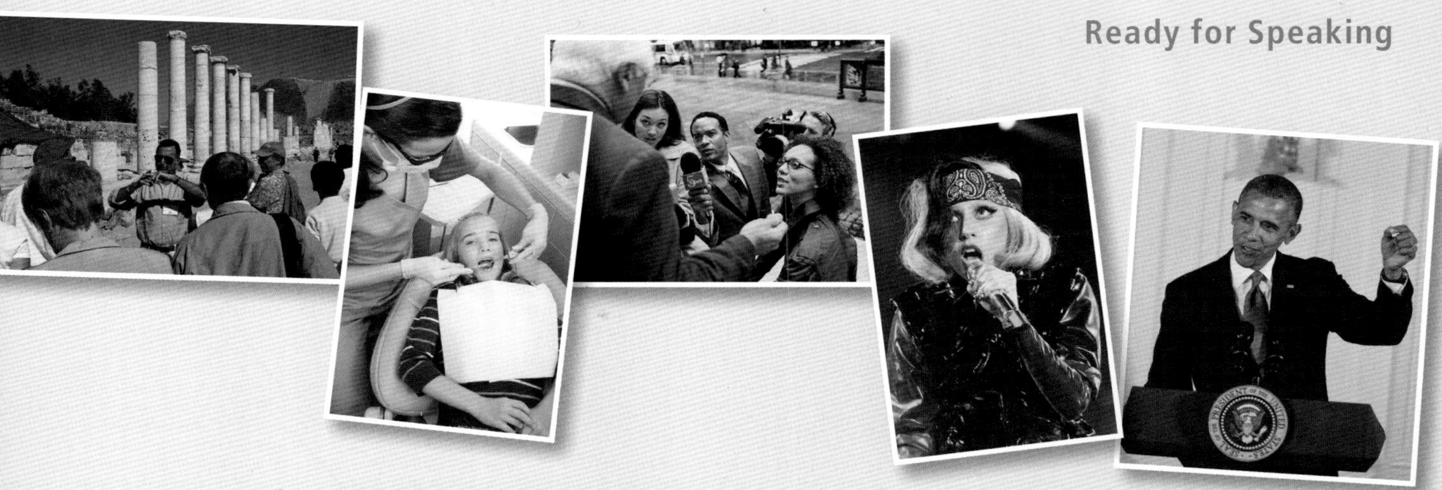

1 Here are some different jobs.

Talk to each other about what the most and least satisfying aspects of these jobs might be.

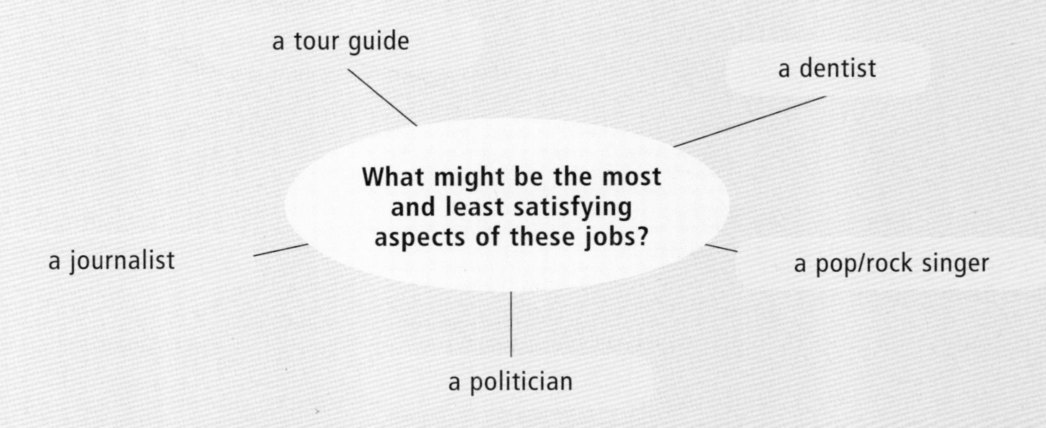

2 Now decide which job is usually regarded as having the most status.

3 2.32 Listen to Jan and Ana doing the Part 3 task and answer these questions.

- How well do Jan and Ana interact with each other in the two tasks?
- Do they reach a final decision in the second task?

Part 4: Further discussion

In Part 4 the interlocutor asks further questions related to the issues raised in Part 3. As well as responding to these questions, you should also interact with your partner and comment on what he or she says.

What to expect in the exam

- This section lasts approximately five minutes.
- The interlocutor's questions usually become broader and more abstract as the discussion develops.
- The interlocutor may direct a question to one candidate in particular, or else ask an open question for either candidate to answer.

1 Discuss the following questions with your partner:

- Which would you prefer to have: a job which is well paid but monotonous or one which is poorly paid but fulfilling? Why?
- Do you think that school prepares young people adequately for the world of work? Why/Why not?
- What difficulties do young people in your area face when searching for work?
- What do you think is the ideal age to retire? Why?
- How has computer technology affected the world of work?
- Do you think people who earn large amounts of money have a moral obligation to donate money to charity? Why/Why not?

2 2.33 Listen to Jan and Ana doing the Part 4 task.

- How well do they each react to what each other says?

A video of the Speaking test covered in this unit can be found on the Ready for Advanced Practice Online website.

13 Food for thought

Vocabulary 1: Eating and drinking

1 All the verb phrases in each of the groups **1–8** below can be used in combination with one of the nouns in the box. Write an appropriate noun from the box in each of the spaces. There is an example at the beginning (**0**).

food	drink	hunger	thirst	
meal	~~dish~~	stomach	appetite	eater

0 prepare your favourite *dish*
order a side

1 have a raging ________
quench your

2 feel faint with ________
satisfy your

3 pick at ________
gulp down

4 have a soft ________
go out for a celebratory

5 work up a big ________
lose your

6 be a fussy ________
be a big

7 do something on a full ________
do something on an empty

8 heat up a ready ________
have a square

2 Study the collocations in exercise **1** for two minutes. Then look at the nouns in the box and cover the exercise. How many collocations can you remember?

3 Use five of the collocations to write sentences about yourself and/or people you know.

Example:
Whenever I come home after a trip away, my mother prepares my favourite dish of lamb chops and fried potatoes.

4 Compare and discuss your sentences with another student.

Speaking Part 2

Long turn

1 Look at these photos. They show people who are eating meals in different situations.

Student A:

Compare **two** of the pictures, and say what considerations might have been taken into account when planning for the meals and how much the people might be enjoying them.

Student B:

When your partner has finished talking, say which meal you think would be more satisfying.

How to go about it

Student A

Some of the following considerations might be relevant to the photos you choose. Can you think of any more?

time	space	weight	
cost	taste	quality	health

- Note the use of modal verbs in the instructions: *might have been taken into account* and *might be enjoying*. Use a range of language to speculate about the photographs.

Student B

Your comment should be brief, but you do have time to give reasons for your feelings or opinions.

- What considerations might have been taken into account when planning for the meals?
- How much might the people be enjoying them?

2 Now change roles. Follow the instructions again using the remaining pictures.

Reading and Use of English 1
Part 3

Word formation

1 For questions **1–8**, read the text below. Use the word given in capitals at the end of some of the lines to form a word that fits in the gap **in the same line**. There is an example at the beginning (**0**). Write your answers **IN CAPITAL LETTERS**.

EATING IN THE RIGHT PLACES

Food researchers have discovered that the **(0)** APPRECIATION of a meal	**APPRECIATE**
lies not so much in what you eat as where you eat it. They served	
up exactly the same chicken dish in ten different places and found that	
the better the **(1)** .... , the better people said the food tasted.	**SET**
A meal of *chicken à la king*, which got low marks from **(2)**	**DINE**
in a **(3)** .... home for the elderly and a boarding school, was	**RESIDE**
given top marks when it was served up at a four-star restaurant, although	
it had been made from the same ingredients, cooked in the same kitchen,	
and accompanied by the same rice. These **(4)** .... will come	**REVEAL**
as **(5)** .... news to food snobs and celebrity chefs. According	**WELCOME**
to the researchers, the **(6)** .... demonstrate that food is	**FIND**
(7) .... and is often a great deal less important than the	**RATE**
environment in which it is eaten. The meal, which was assessed on its	
(8) .... , taste and texture, received the worst overall marks	**APPEAR**
when it was served at an army training camp.	

2 Tell your partner about three very different places in which you have eaten meals.

What kind of food did you eat? To what extent was your enjoyment of the food influenced by the surroundings?

Writing 1
Part 2

Informal letter

1 Read the following Part 2 task and the sample answer on page 173. Do you agree with the advice given? Is there anything else you would add?

A friend of yours has been given the task of organizing the food for a forthcoming event or activity and knows that you have some experience of a similar situation. The friend has written to you, expressing some anxiety about the task and asking for your help.

Write a **letter** giving advice on those aspects of the food arrangements which you consider to be most important and reassuring your friend of his/her ability to cope.

You should write **220–260** words.

Dear Graham

Great to hear from you! It's hard to believe that Luke's about to celebrate his fifth birthday. You're very brave to organize the party all by yourself! I'm not surprised you're a bit daunted by it all. Still, with Liz being away, I suppose you haven't got much choice.

I can certainly pass on some tips that I learnt from my own bitter experience in September. First of all, don't make the same mistake as I did and lay on a huge spread. Children are fussy eaters and tend not to have big appetites, so there's no point preparing vast quantities of elaborate food. They probably won't eat it. You'd be better off filling a few bowls with different flavoured crisps – they were the first things to disappear at Lara's party.

That's not to say you shouldn't put out other things for them to eat – some sweet, some savoury – but it's not worth going to a lot of trouble over it. And don't be surprised if they don't eat the birthday cake. Lara's friends hardly touched hers, so I wouldn't spend hours making one if I were you – buy one from a shop and you won't be disappointed.

And finally, whatever you do, make sure you don't let them have the food until after the games. Children running around on full stomachs is not to be recommended!

Anyway, I'm sure Luke and his friends will have a great time, even if it leaves you utterly exhausted. Let me know how it all goes, won't you?

All the best

Elisa

2 Does the answer address all aspects of the task?

3 Underline those expressions in the answer which are used to introduce advice.

What other evidence of a wide range of language is there?

4 To make the answer seem more natural, the writer
- shows interest in the forthcoming event.
- refers to her own experience.

Find examples of these features in the letter.

5 Now write your own answer to the task in exercise **1**.

How to go about it

- Choose an event or activity and list the advice you might give. Here are six possible situations; can you think of any more?

  camping holiday *hiking trip* *barbecue* *farewell party* *picnic* *family celebration*
- Select four or five pieces of advice which you consider to be the most important and write a paragraph plan.
- Imagine yourself in the situation described in the task. This will help you write a more natural answer.

  Remember to
  - show interest in the forthcoming event or activity.
  - make reference to your own experience.
  - offer your friend some words of reassurance.

Don't forget!

- Plan your answer carefully before you write. (See checklist on page 195.)
- Include a wide range of language.
- Write in a consistently informal register.

Reading and Use of English 2
Part 8

Multiple matching

1 What are the myths and facts related to the health benefits of drinking lots of water?

Why do people buy bottled water rather than drink tap water?

Is this a positive situation in your opinion? Why/Why not?

2 You are going to read an article about the trend of drinking bottled water. For questions **1–10**, choose from the sections (**A–E**). The sections may be chosen more than once.

In which section of the article are the following mentioned?

commonly held myths about the benefits of drinking bottled water	1
bottled water being responsible for a change in a social custom	2
the existence of cities having been dependent on the consumption of a particular drink	3
an explanation for why a temporary trend in bottled water sales occurred	4
the view that the role a particular person plays is largely redundant	5
the ability of a certain drink to provide comfort and bring people together	6
appreciation for an insight that supported the writer's own viewpoint	7
the desire to behave in a way that would highlight the absurdity of a situation	8
the potential uses of a drink to enhance physical well-being and mental performance	9
the habit of drinking bottled water being used to promote the image of its consumer	10

A nice cup of tea beats bottled water every time

Our writer tries to understand the appeal of fashionable plastic

A

I am occasionally engaged to speak in public, and the preliminary formalities are handled by a functionary who telephones to ask whether I will be needing a power point, and whether I have 'any special dietary requirements'. Sooner or later I'm going to answer both in the affirmative: 'Being a novelist, I will naturally be illustrating my talk with a series of graphs – and, as for the dinner, I will get my doctor to forward you the list of my allergies.' Immediately before the talk, the pointless man will stand up and say, 'A few housekeeping notes', before pointing out the exits, which, since they are usually the same as the entrances by which we came in, we already know. He then wastes further effort by marshalling before me some bottles of water. Again,

I am tempted to call his bluff. I ought to spend the first five minutes of my speaking time tipping the contents of these bottles down my throat. But, in practice, I never touch them. It just so happens that 20 I have never been gagging with thirst while being introduced as a speaker. Don't get me wrong, when I am thirsty, I have a drink: ideally, apple juice, because I prefer something with a taste. Above all, I drink tea – no fewer than half a dozen cups a day.

B

25 I find the bottled water fad to be a distressing instance of mass hypnotism, so when the remarks of an Australian scientist were reported last week, they represented to me a series of nails being hit firmly on the head. Dr Spero Tsindos 30 resoundingly pronounced that bottled water has become 'a fashion accessory and a token of instant gratification'. Unfortunately, the British public is not so sensible. Sales of bottled water have ascended continually since the 1980s apart from 35 a brief dip from 2006–2010. This was probably accounted for by a backlash against bottled water – at the glibness of the whole phenomenon, whose only tangible result is a mountain of landfill. Restaurants that refused to serve tap water were 40 condemned and often shamed out of the practice. But notwithstanding the fact that it doesn't flush toxins out of the body, improve the skin, or taste better than tap water, people now consume more bottled water than ever before.

C

45 I suspect that the appeal of a small bottle of water is that it is not a glass of wine. 'Look,' the water carrier proclaims, 'I am not drinking alcohol!' (at least, not right now). The water bottle is a priggish symbol of purity and piety, and insofar as this is radiated 50 externally, it is a reproof to the person daring to drink wine in the presence of the water-drinker. Insofar as it is not radiated, then the water-drinker is claiming moral points for being conscious of their own well-being. The other reason I can't stand 55 bottled water is that it seems unpatriotic. Since the 1980s, our traditional four cups of tea a day have apparently dropped to three. But let's quickly eliminate one suspect in the case of the lost cup. At first glance, it might appear to be coffee when we 60 notice the proliferation of high street coffee shops. But sales show that the culprit is actually bottled water, and to a lesser extent, fruit juice.

D

Why should we be celebrating tea? Being 99 per cent water, it has all the hydrating virtues of bottled 65 water but with a bonus, namely the tea itself, which provides a moderate dose of cerebrally-stimulating caffeine (the best thing you can do before an exam is drink a cup of tea). It is also rich in flavonoid antioxidants, which aid cardiovascular fitness 70 and tea leaves applied externally can act as an antiseptic, as monkeys in the jungle know very well. And unlike bottled water, tea requires the boiling of water, and it is said that tea consumption enabled the concentrations of population necessary 75 for urban living in the 18th century, when metropolitan water supplies were not clean.

E

As a child, I was involved in a serious car crash, and I could not speak from shock until a woman – a complete stranger, and angelic in my memory 80 – came up with a cup of sweet, milky tea. I doubt that a bottle of water would have done the trick. Tea is associated with an enjoyable and very social ritual, but imagine the sheer crassness of a host who inquired, 'More bottled water, anyone?' Tea is 85 our national common denominator, and it would be helpful in these uncertain times if it could be allied to our other such symbol, namely a certain Elizabeth. But I fear that Her Majesty is invariably accompanied on her travels by bottles of mineral 90 water.

Reacting to the text

To what extent do you agree with the statements below?

... the bottled water fad (is) a distressing instance of mass hypnotism ...

... bottled water has become 'a fashion accessory' ...

... it doesn't flush toxins out of the body, improve the skin, or taste better than tap water ...

What other food trends or fads do you see developing at the moment?

Imagine you worked for an advertising company. How would you promote a new brand of bottled water?

Language focus 1: Comparisons

A Comparisons

1 In these extracts from the Reading and Use of English texts on pages 172, 174 and 175, complete each gap with one word.

a The appreciation of a meal lies **not so** _______ in what you eat _______ where you eat it.

b _______ **better** the setting, _______ **better** people said the food tasted.

c The meal … received **the** _______ **overall** marks when it was served at an army training camp.

d **Sooner or** _______ I'm going to answer both in the affirmative. (A)

e Above all, I drink tea – **no** _______ **than** half a dozen cups a day. (A)

f People _______ consume more bottled water **than ever** _______ . (B)

2 Check your answers in the texts on pages 172, 174 and 175. The letters in brackets refer to the relevant section of the reading text.

B Qualifying comparisons

Many words and phrases can be used to qualify comparisons.

Examples:
Peaches are significantly/three times/slightly more expensive than last year.
There isn't nearly/half/quite as much on the menu as there used to be.

Underline the correct alternative in the following sentences.

a Food is often *a great deal/a large amount/a high number* less important than the environment in which it is eaten.

b My brother eats *a lot of/by far/far* more chocolate than is good for him.

c It claims to be a health cereal, but it contains *just/near/same* as much salt as ordinary cereals.

d I only weigh *slightly/little/bit* less than I did when I started this diet.

e It's *more/much/very* healthier to cook without salt.

C *Like* and *as*

Like is used with nouns, pronouns or gerunds to make comparisons.
As is used with nouns to indicate someone or something's job, role or function.

I got a job ***as*** *a waitress in a restaurant last summer. We worked* ***like*** *slaves.*
He found a piece of wood shaped ***like*** *a telephone and used it* ***as*** *a hammer.*

Both *as* and *like* can be used with clauses to make comparisons, although *like* is informal and considered incorrect by some.

She walked down the aisle of St Anne's, just ***as/like*** *her mother had done 30 years before.*

Complete each gap in these sentences with either *as* or *like*.

a Walking into the kitchen I noticed there was a strong odour, ______ the smell of milk that has gone off.

b ______ a safety measure, please ensure that hot oil is not left unattended.

c They seemed ______ normal customers, but in fact, they were food health inspectors.

D *So* and *such*

1 Complete each gap with either *so* or *such*.

a It's not quite _______ a hot curry as the last one you cooked.

b I'd never eaten _______ big a fish in all my life.

c The bar wasn't _______ crowded as we thought it would be.

2 What do you notice about the types of words which follow *so* and *such*?

E Further expressions

Complete each gap with one of the words from the box.

long	near	close	better
as	like	much	

1 She enjoyed eating out every day, and **if** the restaurant overlooked the sea, then **so much the** ___________ .

2 My host family was **nothing** ___________ **as** reserved as I'd been expecting and the food **nowhere** ___________ **as** bad.

3 I was rather disappointed by the size of the portions, ___________ **were** my two fellow diners.

4 Prices varied greatly, but the food was very ___________ **the same** in each restaurant.

5 This is the best meal we've had all holiday, **by a** ___________ **way**.

6 The lemon sorbet is delicious, but the chocolate mousse **comes a** ___________ **second**.

Read more about comparisons in the Grammar reference on page 224.

Practice

1 Select three of the following. Write three sentences for each pair, comparing and contrasting them. Use some of the language from sections **A–E** on this page.

- two restaurants you have eaten in
- two of your national or regional dishes
- two places you have been to on holiday
- two film actors
- two jobs you have done
- two pets you have had

2 Compare and discuss your sentences with your partner.

Listening
Part 1

Multiple choice 2.34–2.36

1 Where do people usually buy their fruit, vegetable and meat products in your country?

How popular are farmers' markets like the one in the photo?

In Britain, it's common for children to eat in a school canteen. What did you do for lunch when you were at school? What do you think of the meal in the bottom photo?

Why is it important for food to be packaged nowadays? What's your reaction to the photo of the packaged apples?

2 You will hear three different extracts. For questions **1–6**, choose the answer (**A**, **B** or **C**) which fits best according to what you hear. There are two questions for each extract.

Extract One

You hear part of a radio discussion in which two people are talking about farmers' markets.

1 The man feels that farmers' markets are gaining in popularity because
- **A** there has been a resurgence of interest in traditional foods.
- **B** people have come to prefer locally grown produce.
- **C** the produce sold here is perceived to be healthy.

2 Both speakers say that anyone hoping to set up a market stall
- **A** needs to consider what shoppers want.
- **B** should focus on the presentation of goods.
- **C** must offer diversity in their range of products.

Extract Two

You overhear two students talking about their presentation on the food industry.

3 What does the woman say about food packaging?
- **A** It must show the different ingredients of a product more clearly.
- **B** It should only be used on certain products.
- **C** It can generate a great deal of waste.

4 The man believes that the use of packaging is an essential means of
- **A** reducing advertising costs for food producers.
- **B** preventing contamination of food products.
- **C** conveying health-related facts to consumers.

Extract Three

You hear part of a radio interview in which two people are discussing a new policy concerning food at school.

5 What does the woman feel about the new policy?
- **A** It will be impossible to put into practice.
- **B** It will fail to achieve the desired results.
- **C** It will put additional pressure on schools.

6 What does the man believe is the main cause of childhood obesity?
- **A** poor role models at home
- **B** the wide availability of unhealthy food
- **C** a lack of information on healthy eating

3 How healthily do people generally eat in your country?

What changes have there been in eating habits in recent years?

Vocabulary 2: Deception

1 Look at the following phrases from the listening and complete the table.

*That's blatantly **deceptive**!*

*Nowadays, manufacturers are covering their products with **fraudulent** health claims ...*

*So it's all rather **misleading**.*

Noun	Verb	Adjective	Adverb
______	______	deceptive	______
______	______	fraudulent	______
——	______	misleading	______

2 Complete each of the gaps with the appropriate form of one of the words from the table in exercise **1**. In each section **1–3**, the words required for both spaces **a** and **b** are different, but from the same word family. There is an example at the beginning (**0**).

0 He has been charged with defrauding **the company of** £2 million.
Car insurance firms have expressed concern at the increase in the number of fraudulent **claims**.

1 a With their pointed snouts, fruit bats are often ______ **referred to** as 'flying foxes'.
b The tobacco company was found guilty of publishing ______ **information** on the effects of passive smoking.

2 a The device, which is ______ **simple in appearance**, is capable of performing a number of extremely complex functions.
b You're ______ **yourself** if you think you can pass without studying.

3 a He is serving a six-year jail sentence for **tax** ______ .
b The court heard how Smith had ______ **obtained money** by posing as a charity worker.

3 Complete each of the gaps in the following newspaper article with one of the words from the box.

through	into	out	in	for	for

Retired widow loses life savings

A retired widow has been **tricked (1)** ______ of her life savings by a bogus financial adviser. Sixty-five-year-old Grace Smedley was completely **taken (2)** ______ by the smooth-talking confidence trickster, who **deceived** her **(3)** ______ handing over nearly £20 000. Mrs Smedley expressed her frustration at allowing herself to **fall (4)** ______ the conman's trickery and failing to **see (5)** ______ his false promises of immediate high returns on her money. 'I've been **taken (6)** ______ **a ride**,' she complained. 'I feel a bit of a mug.'

The man, who is believed to be in his early 30s, claimed to have access to a high-yielding annuity scheme which would provide an ...

4 Underline and record any other words in the article which are related to deception.

5 Tell your partner about

- a time in your life when you or someone else **told a lie**.
- a television programme where **tricks are played on** people.
- a **swindle** you heard about in the news or saw in a film.
- someone you know who **cheated at** games as a child.
- a time when appearances proved to be deceptive.

Language focus 2: Adverbs of degree

1 Look at the following phrases from Extract One of the listening.

a I'm **absolutely delighted** that …
b … celebrity chefs have had a **fairly large** hand in this.
c … it's **a bit vague**, that label …
d … it's **very interesting** to see …

Absolutely is not normally used with the adjectives in **b**, **c** or **d**. Nor are *fairly*, *a bit*, *very* used with the adjective in **a**. Why is this?

What other adverbs of degree can be used with the adjectives in **b**, **c** and **d**?

2 Which of the following adjectives are gradable (used with *very*, *fairly*, etc) and which are non-gradable (used with *absolutely*)?

Example:
Gradable: tasty *Non-gradable: starving*

tasty	starving	frightened	pleased	huge
furious	dirty	ridiculous	tired	incredible

3 What is the meaning of *quite* in these two sentences?

a This fish is **quite** tasty.
b This fish is **quite** delicious.

4 There are a number of other adverbs which can be used to intensify or emphasize adjectives, as in these examples.

*The tap water here is **perfectly safe** to drink.*
*The water in this river is **highly toxic** to fish.*
*I am **fully conscious** of the risks involved in swimming here.*

In **1–6**, cross out the adjective which does not normally collocate with the adverb at the beginning of the line. There is an example at the beginning (**0**).

0	**perfectly**	clear ~~dependent~~	normal capable
1	**highly**	gifted talented	promising clever
2	**fully**	aware booked	worried equipped
3	**wholly**	informed inadequate	inappropriate unacceptable
4	**entirely**	free of charge old	different wrong
5	**utterly**	ridiculous qualified	opposed disgraceful
6	**totally**	unnecessary independent	unexpected intelligent

5 Tell your partner about a time when you were

- absolutely terrified.
- completely lost.
- utterly exhausted.
- highly motivated.
- totally wrong.
- extremely embarrrassed.

Report

You have been asked to write a report for an international survey about eating habits in your country. Your report should address these three questions:

- How have eating habits changed in your country in recent years?
- How positive are these changes?
- What developments may take place in the future?

Write your **report** in **220–260** words.

How to go about it

- Consider all three questions in the task and make notes under headings such as the following:
  Eating with family vs eating alone *Health foods*
  Traditional food vs fast food *Eating times*
  The headings you choose will depend on the situation in your country.
- Write a paragraph plan. Two possible alternatives are:

<u>A</u>	<u>B</u>
1 Introduction	1 Introduction
2 Changes	2 Eating with family vs eating alone - changes, how positive, future developments
3 How positive	3 Traditional food vs fast food - changes, how positive, future developments
4 Future developments	4 Eating times - changes, how positive, future developments

- For vocabulary of *Possibility*, see page 208 and of *Changes* see page 209.
- When you have finished the report, give it a title and add paragraph headings.

13 Review

Vocabulary

Decide which answer (**A**, **B**, **C** or **D**) best fits each space. There is an example at the beginning (**0**).

0 Don't judge a book by its cover – appearances can often be very ______ .
A mistaking **B** fraudulent **C** deceptive **D** tricky

1 He went for a walk to work _____ an appetite for breakfast.
A up **B** out **C** on **D** off

2 She had lost her appetite and could only ______ her meal, forcing down a mouthful or two.
A gulp down **B** bite off **C** eat up **D** pick at

3 How could I have allowed myself to be ______ by his lies?
A fallen for **B** taken in **C** tricked into **D** seen through

4 They eventually took the bronze medal, finishing a ______ third behind Poland.
A tight **B** final **C** close **D** late

5 I can't believe you ______ for a simple trick like that!
A swindled **B** trusted **C** fell **D** played

6 In ______ to my husband, I prefer to spend very little time preparing a meal.
A opposition **B** contrast **C** difference **D** disparity

7 I ordered a ______ salad to have with my spaghetti dish.
A side **B** spare **C** supplementary **D** part

8 She sat back in a ______ relaxed pose, her hands trembling slightly in her lap.
A trickily **B** fraudulently **C** deceptively **D** deceitfully

9 She went under ______ as a waitress to write an article on tipping.
A mask **B** act **C** pose **D** cover

10 ______ your child's hunger for knowledge with this downloadable version of our encyclopaedia.
A Satisfy **B** Quench **C** Fulfil **D** Meet

11 A copy of the booklet can be obtained ______ free of charge from your nearest chemist's.
A extremely **B** entirely **C** greatly **D** highly

12 The headteacher described his behaviour as '______ unacceptable' and defended her decision to expel him.
A wholly **B** fully **C** perfectly **D** deeply

Comparisons

Complete each of the gaps with **two words**. There is an example at the beginning (**0**).

0 She isn't anything *like as* unpleasant as people say she is.

1 He was nowhere __________ tall as I thought he'd be.
2 It isn't so __________ restaurant as a bar that serves food.
3 The village looks very much the __________ it did 200 years ago.
4 The longer I live in this house, __________ I realize how badly built it is.
5 This is by __________ best curry I've ever eaten.
6 This isn't quite __________ nice hotel as the one we stayed in last year.
7 I'd like it by Friday, but if you can do it before, then so __________ better.
8 He went to Oxford University, as __________ father before him.

Key word transformation

For questions **1–6**, complete the second sentence so that it has a similar meaning to the first sentence, using the word given. **Do not change the word given.** You must use between **three** and **six** words, including the word given. Here is an example (**0**). Write your answers **IN CAPITAL LETTERS**.

0 The judge decided it was true that the four men had smuggled pirated Blu-ray Discs into the country.

GUILTY

The four men were ...*FOUND GUILTY OF SMUGGLING*... pirated Blu-ray Discs into the country by the judge.

1 With only three buttons to push, this new food processor looks simple, but that's deceptive.

IN

With only three buttons to push, this new food processor .... appearance.

2 The moment I saw the filthy state of the restaurant kitchen, I no longer felt hungry.

SOON

I lost .... I saw the filthy state of the restaurant kitchen.

3 This recipe is really a lot more imaginative than the others in this book.

MOST

This recipe is by .... in this book.

4 Since he was promoted to head chef, he has never been so stressed.

EVER

He is suffering .... since he was promoted to head chef.

5 I had expected the snake dish to be much worse than it actually was.

BAD

The snake dish was actually nowhere .... I had expected.

6 This isn't nearly as good as the chicken soup you make.

SECOND

This chicken soup doesn't even come a .... one you make.

14 Money matters

Collaborative task

1 Here are some areas in which money plays a role. Talk to each other about how money, or the lack of it, affects these areas of our lives.

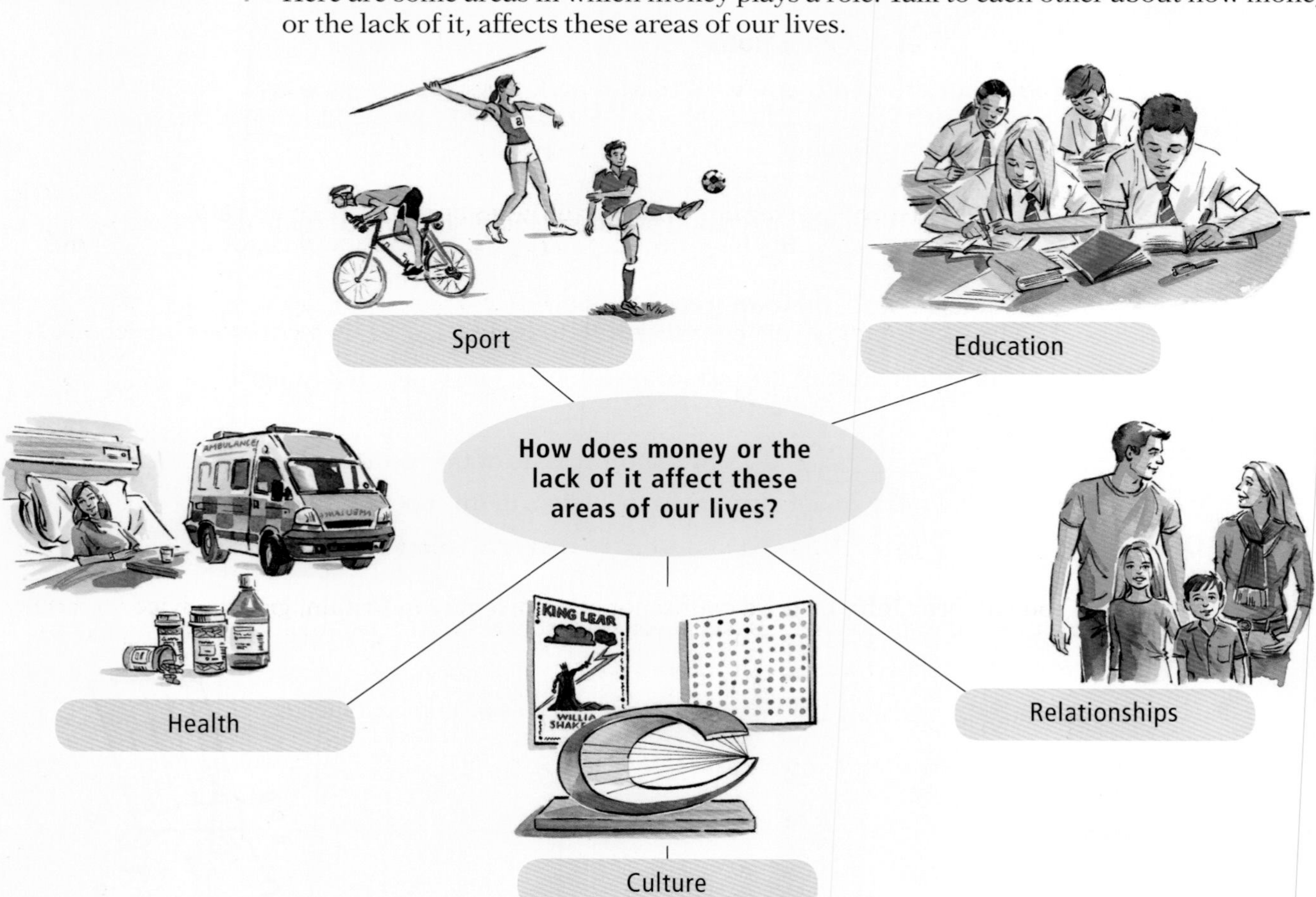

2 Now decide in which area money can have the most positive effect.

Useful language

Look at the adjectives to describe *Effect* on page 212 and write down two words in each of the following categories. Use some of these words in your discussion.

A negative effect   A positive effect
A small effect   A big effect

Vocabulary 1: Money

1 In **1** and **2** below, match each phrase **a–d** with an appropriate sentence **1–4**. The first one has been done for you.

1 They paid …
- **a** in advance
- **b** in arrears
- **c** in instalments
- **d** in full

1 They made regular payments over two years.
2 They paid all the money that was owing.
3 They paid for the hotel room before the holiday.
4 They settled the bill after the work was finished.

2 She bought it …
- **a** on impulse
- **b** on hire purchase
- **c** at auction
- **d** in the sales

1 Everything in the store was reduced by ten per cent.
2 She offered the highest price for the painting.
3 She saw the hat and immediately decided to buy it.
4 She hasn't finished paying for her new fridge yet.

2 Discuss the following questions with your partner:

In what situations do people or organizations usually pay
a in advance? **b** in arrears? **c** in instalments?

Do you ever buy things
a on impulse? **b** in the sales? **c** on credit?

Verb + adverb collocations

1 Complete each of the gaps with an appropriate adverb from the box.

hard	heavily	freely	generously

a 'Top sportspeople bring enjoyment to millions and deserve to be **paid** _______ .'
b 'There's no point being frugal when you're young – you should **spend** _______ and have fun.'
c '**Save** _______ , put down a deposit on a flat and leave home as soon as possible.'
d 'The government in my country needs to **invest** _______ in technology for schools.'

2 Do you agree with each of the statements in exercise **1**? Give reasons for your opinions.

Listening 1
Part 2

Sentence completion 2.37

1 How careful are you with your money? Are you able to make it last?

2 You will hear John Lister, a counsellor at a university in Britain, giving advice on money matters to a new intake of university undergraduates. For questions **1–8**, complete the sentences with a word or short phrase.

Students can borrow money for living expenses from the **(1)** ....

Payments are usually made to students each **(2)** ....

Students can obtain a personal **(3)** .... from the Internet.

He suggests choosing a bank with good **(4)** .... facilities.

John thinks that working **(5)** .... a week is enough.

Students are advised to talk to their **(6)** .... before buying books.

They should also consult the **(7)** .... in their department.

John tells students to make full use of their **(8)** .... card.

3 What further advice might John Lister give to the undergraduates in order to help them make their money last? Imagine that the students are living away from home for the first time. Consider the following categories:

food travel and transport **other**
clothes gas, electricity and phone bills

Writing
Part 2

Formal letter

1 Choose **one** of the following Part 2 tasks, **A** or **B**. Read the relevant Content advice for your chosen task.

A Your company has decided to offer a period of work experience to a student in a local school. You have been asked by your manager to write a letter to the principal of the school.

Your letter should explain
- what your company does.
- what the work experience would involve.
- what kind of student would be suitable.

Write your **letter** in **220–260** words.

A Content advice

When explaining what your company does, use this opportunity to use a wide range of vocabulary which is related specifically to your organization/field.

When describing the work experience, consider what kind of things the student would be asked to do, what kind of training might be given, and how the experience would benefit the student.

When writing about what kind of student would be suitable; think about the personal qualities and skills a young person would need to do the work you are offering.

B Your college is soon going to close for the summer and you would like to have some work experience during this time. You decide to write a letter to the manager of a local business to ask about possible work experience opportunities.

Your letter should explain
- why you are writing.
- what skills and qualities you have.
- what sort of work you are suited to.

Write your **letter** in **220–260** words.

B Content advice

Think about what kind of skills you have at the moment; for example, if you have computer-programming skills, then you might decide to apply to a business that needs help with computer programming. If you have good communication skills, you might apply to a business that needs help dealing with telephone enquiries.

What kind of qualities would make you attractive to the manager of a local business? For example, most managers would prefer someone who is eager to learn, reliable, hard-working, etc.

Remember that you are only enquiring about work experience, not a permanent job. Be realistic about the sort of work or duties you expect to be offered.

Useful language

Complete each of the following sentences with one of the phrases from the box.

assist staff members	attend an interview	offer the opportunity
adapt to new situations	enquire about the possibility	supervise the training

1 We are pleased to be able to ______________ of work experience at our company to a suitable student at your school.

2 The team leader will personally ______________ of the student for the two weeks.

3 The student will be required to ______________ with entering customer information into our software system.

4 I am writing to ______________ of work experience in your company.

5 I would say that I am a quick learner and that I can easily ______________ .

6 I could ______________ at any time that was convenient to you.

2 Now write your answer to **one** of the tasks in exercise **1**.

Reading and Use of English 1
Part 3

Word formation

1 Read the following text about the game of Monopoly, ignoring the gaps. Do you agree with the writer's view at the end of the text?

2 For questions **1–8**, read the text below. Use the word given in capitals at the end of some of the lines to form a word that fits in the gap **in the same line**. There is an example at the beginning (**0**). Write your answers **IN CAPITAL LETTERS**.

MONOPOLY

As a child, my experience of **(0)** ..FINANCIAL.. decision-making was usually limited	**FINANCE**
to deciding how to spend a **(1)** .... of small coins found under the sofa.	**HAND**
Imagine, then, how **(2)** .... I seized the opportunity to spend piles of	**ENTHUSE**
cash in any way I wanted; no matter that the money was fake and part of a board	
game. Although my siblings and I would always begin with a loud **(3)**	**AGREE**
over who would be 'banker' and continue with frequent **(4)** .... of cheating,	**ACCUSE**
we played it often. I well remember the thrill of exchanging that little row of	
plastic houses for a hotel, and **(5)** .... demanding the highest rent possible,	**MERCY**
knowing it would force another player into **(6)** .... I believe it was a great	**BANK**
(7) .... tool; counting my notes improved my maths no end. But it was	**EDUCATE**
inevitable, I suppose, given our **(8)** .... on technology these days, that an	**RELY**
electronic version of this game was developed, in which a credit card is, without	
mental effort, swiped through a machine. Will it enjoy the longevity of the original	
format? I think not.	

3 Do you enjoy playing board games? Why/Why not?
What other games have you played that involve money? Can you describe them?

Reading and Use of English 2
Part 7

Gapped text

1 Have you ever had an argument over money or spending?
What effect do you think money can have on people's relationships with others?

2 You are going to read part of an article about the psychological effect that money has on our behaviour. Six paragraphs have been removed from the extract. Choose from the paragraphs **A–G** the one which fits each gap (**1–6**). There is one extra paragraph which you do not need to use.

Money – that's what I want!

Money has a far more complex hold on us than most economists are willing to admit.
Mark Buchanan tries to find out why.

Cash, currency, greenbacks, dosh. Just words, you might say, but they carry an eerie psychological force. Chew them over for a few moments, and you will become a different 5 person. Simply thinking about money seems to make us more self-reliant and less inclined to help others. And it gets weirder; just handling cash can take the sting out of social rejection and even diminish physical pain, according to recent 10 psychological studies.

1 ______

Yet money stirs up more stress and envy than any other tool ever could. We just can't seem to deal with it rationally. But why? Our relationship with money has many facets. Some people seem 15 addicted to accumulating it, whilst others can't help maxing out their credit cards and find it impossible to save for a rainy day. As we come to understand more about money's effect on us, it is emerging that some people's brains can react to it 20 as they would to a drug, while to others it is like a friend.

2 ______

On the surface, this might seem unnecessary. Surely money is just cold, unemotional stuff? We know already that it takes a variety of forms, 25 from feathers of old, through gold coins, and dollar bills to data in a bank's computer. The value of $100 is supposed to lie in how much food or fuel it can purchase and nothing else. You should no more care about being short-changed 30 $5 at the supermarket checkout than losing the same amount when borrowing money to buy a $300 000 house.

3 ______

To understand how this affects our behaviour, some economists are starting to think more 35 like evolutionary anthropologists. Daniel Ariely of the Massachusetts Institute of Technology is one of them. He suggests that modern society presents us with two distinct sets of behavioural rules. Social standards of behaviour, which are 40 'warm and fuzzy', are designed to foster long-term relationships, trust and cooperation.

4 ______

Economic exchange has been going on throughout human history, so it is possible that our ancestors evolved an instinctive capacity for 45 recognizing the difference between situations suited to these different behavioural rules, and that this could have developed well before the invention of money. Alternatively, we may have learnt the distinction.

5 ______

50 Kathleen Vohs and colleagues at the University of Minnesota got student volunteers to complete an activity in which they had to arrange a series of discs into two patterns. But before doing this, they were asked to make sensible phrases either 55 from a group of words that had nothing to do with money or from a group of money-related words.

6 ______

Vohs suggests there is a simple dynamic at work here. 'Money makes people feel self-sufficient,' she says. 'They are more likely to put forth effort 60 to attain personal goals, and they also prefer to be separate from others.' The touchy-feely side of us may disapprove of such behaviour, but it is useful for survival.

A In reality we are not that rational. Instead of treating cash simply as a tool to be wielded with objective precision, we allow money to reach inside our heads and tap into the ancient emotional parts of our brain, often with unpredictable results.

B This is all the stranger when you consider what money is supposed to be: nothing more than a medium of exchange that makes economic life more efficient. Just as an axe allows us to chop down trees, money allows us to have markets that, traditional economists tell us, dispassionately set the price of anything from a loaf of bread to a painting by Picasso.

C The trick is to get the correct balance between these two mindsets. Psychological studies have found a general trade-off between the pursuit of extrinsic aspirations such as wealth and fame and intrinsic ones, such as building and maintaining relationships.

D Either way, we appear immediately and subconsciously to recognize the cues associated with the realm of market norms. Experiments published recently reveal that even a passing contact with concepts linked to money puts us into a market-oriented mentality, making us think and behave in characteristic ways.

E Then there is a set of market norms. These revolve around money and competition, and encourage individuals to put their own interests first.

F And, of course, whichever way we regard it, having a pile of money means that you can buy more things, so it is virtually synonymous with status – so much so that losing it can lead to severe depression. In these cash-strapped times, perhaps by developing an insight into the psychology of money, we can improve the way we deal with it.

G It turned out that those who had been primed with the latter set worked on the main task for far longer before asking for help. In a related experiment, these individuals were also significantly less likely to help anyone asking for assistance.

Reacting to the text

'Some people seem addicted to accumulating (money), whilst others can't help maxing out their credit cards and find it impossible to save for a rainy day.'

Do either of these descriptions apply to you?

How would you describe your own relationship to money?

Vocabulary 2: Quantifying nouns

1 Underline the following quantifying nouns in the text on pages 186 and 187. Which nouns are used after each one?

a series of *a group of* *a set of* *a pile of*

2 Complete each of the gaps with one of the words from the box. Use each word only once.

soft drinks	flames	salt	furniture
youths	biscuits	homework	water

a Add just **a pinch of** _________ to the mixture.
b The tap had been dripping and there was **a pool of** _________ on the floor.
c The plane crashed in **a ball of** _________ .
d We've been given **masses of** _________ to do tonight.
e We bought **a crate of** _________ for the party, but most of the children drank water.
f Police are hunting **a gang of** _________ in connection with the crimes.
g No, Johnny, the sea bed is not **a piece of** _________ .
h Don't eat them while you're speaking; you can't talk with **a mouthful of** _________ .

3 For each of the following groups of words, cross out the one which is not normally used with the quantifying noun, for reasons of collocation or meaning.

Example:
0 a bunch of flowers
keys
grapes
~~cheese~~

1 a set of criteria
children
guidelines
recommendations

2 a series of events
news
experiments
articles

3 a pack of cards
lies
words
wolves

4 a flock of bees
sheep
birds
geese

5 a handful of occasions
people
progress
companies

6 a scrap of paper
evidence
material
furniture

7 a piece of music
work
holiday
advice

8 a lump of coffee
sugar
coal
rock

9 a grain of truth
wool
salt
rice

10 a ray of hope
light
sunshine
sleep

4 Desribe five situations to illustrate five different collocations from exercises **1–3**. **Do not mention the collocations**; your partner will try to guess which ones you have illustrated.

Example:
There was a protest meeting at my workplace last week. The unions were expecting it to be well attended, but only four or five members of the staff bothered to turn up.
[Answer: *a handful of people*]

Long turn

The pictures below show people who are thinking about buying something.

Student A:
Compare **two** of the pictures and say what the people might be hoping to buy and what might affect their decision.

Student B:
Which of these people do you think will gain more satisfaction from their purchase?

Now change roles. Follow the instructions again using the remaining pictures.

- What might the people be hoping to buy?
- What might affect their decision?

Listening 2
Part 3

Multiple choice 2.38

1 You will hear an anti-consumerist, Chris Dawson, being interviewed on a local radio station about Buy Nothing Day. For questions **1–6**, choose the answer (**A**, **B**, **C** or **D**) which fits best according to what you hear.

1 Chris explains that one of the aims of Buy Nothing Day is to
A shock consumers into changing their ways.
B encourage participation in alternative activities.
C persuade shoppers to save more.
D force shops to shut for the day.

2 What does Chris say about the effect of Buy Nothing Day?
A For many people it has lasting consequences.
B Certain products experience a fall in sales.
C Some shops decide to offer less variety.
D Some products are reduced in price.

3 What does Chris say about Christmas presents?
A He buys them a long time in advance.
B He argues with his family on the topic.
C He never buys anything for his family.
D He always feels obliged to buy them.

4 For this year's Buy Nothing Day, Chris
A does not know yet what he will be doing.
B wants to keep his plans a surprise.
C will not be doing anything special.
D will be playing some type of sport.

5 According to Chris, how did most shoppers feel about his stunt last year?
A annoyed
B amused
C surprised
D pleased

6 Chris says that the current success of Buy Nothing Day is mainly due to
A good organization.
B the official website.
C television advertising.
D people telling each other.

2 Would you ever consider taking part in a Buy Nothing Day in your country? In what other ways might people protest against consumerism?

Do you spend much money on presents for members of your family? What type of presents do you usually buy?

Language focus: Noun phrases

1 Add each of the noun phrases from the listening to the appropriate column.

workers' rights	a threat to business
the January sales	the ethics of shopping
shopping malls	people's reactions
at the expense of the environment	

noun + noun
production methods

noun + *'s/s'* + noun
next week's Buy Nothing Day

noun + preposition + noun
a wealth of choice

2 In **1–10** below, decide which of the two underlined noun phrases is in the wrong form and correct it. There is an example at the beginning (**0**).

Example:
0 a *The boss's leg is still in plaster.*
b *He tripped over ~~the chair's leg~~.* the chair leg

1 a We drank several bottles of lemonade at the party.
b We ate nearly half a jam jar at breakfast this morning.

2 a Shall we have chicken's soup for lunch?
b This skirt is made of pure lamb's wool.

3 a I caught my jumper on the door handle.
b They've kicked the ball onto our house roof.

4 a I read it in last Sunday's newspaper.
b I always buy a Sunday's newspaper.

5 a I get four weeks' holiday a year.
b I'm going on a three days course on marketing.

6 a There's a lovely dress in that window of shop.
b I asked him what his source of inspiration had been.

7 a The restaurant is perched high on a mountain top.
b Write your name at the page top.

8 a Management has announced a member of staff from the catering department's dismissal.
b Management offered no explanation for the employee's dismissal.

9 a The town hall is a large brick construction from the 20s.
b Police are looking for an average height man in his 20s.

10 a Have you seen her children's new clothes? They won't thank her for buying those.
b We'll have some children's new clothes in stock after the January sales.

Check your ideas and read more about noun phrases in the Grammar reference on page 226.

3 Look back at each of the noun phrases in exercise **2** and discuss with your partner the rules governing the form of each one.

Example:
0 *The 's genitive can be used to talk about parts of the body, so The boss's leg is correct. It isn't normally used for objects, so the chair's leg is not possible: you could say either the chair leg or the leg of the chair.*

4 Match each sentence beginning **1–8** with an appropriate ending, **a–h**. The items in **bold** are all common collocations.

Example: *1 d*

1 Physical exhaustion gave way to an enormous **sense of**
2 After the lottery win money was no longer a **matter of**
3 A medical examination showed that his general **state of**
4 Market research surveys are still the principal **source of**
5 Regular reading of articles will increase your **chances of**
6 After the last place she had rented, this was the **height of**
7 The country was once again plunged into the **depths of**
8 He put his head round the door, but there was no **sign of**

a **health** was good, and there was no sign of heart disease.
b **luxury**, with its central heating and wall-to-wall carpet.
c **information** about people's shopping habits.
d **achievement** as she crossed the finishing line.
e **concern** to him and he took pleasure in spending freely.
f **life**, just the net curtain flapping in the open window.
g **success** in the exam, and improve your general language level.
h **recession** and many new businesses were forced to close.

5 You are going to write a similar exercise to the one in exercise **4** above. Student A should turn to page 206, Student B to page 205.

6 Discuss the following questions with your partner:

- The rich and famous receive a great deal of **media attention**. To what extent is this simply **the price of fame** and how much is it **an invasion of privacy**?
- We hear that money and power corrupt. Have there been any instances in your country recently of **an abuse of power** by someone in authority?
- How popular are **games of chance** with **money prizes** in your country? Give examples. Do you ever play?

14 Review

Noun phrases

Complete the gaps using noun phrases formed from the words in brackets. There may be more than one answer and you may need to change some of the words from plural to singular. There is an example at the beginning (**0**).

0 It isn't from a *recipe book* (book; recipes) – I got the idea for the dish from a *women's magazine* (women; magazine).

1 We're all still in a ______________ (shock; state) after ______________ (his resignation; announcement).

2 I found the ______________ (keys; car) at the ______________ (back; drawer).

3 Every evening we had a ______________ (cocoa; mug) made with fresh ______________ (milk; cow) from the farm next to the ______________ (site; caravans).

4 There was a ______________ (delay; seven hours) on our flight, so we spent most of Friday in the ______________ (airport; lounge; departures).

5 Police want to interview a 17-year-old ______________ (youth; average build) in connection with ______________ (robbery; yesterday).

6 He wears a thick ______________ (chain; neck; gold) and a ______________ (stud; nose; diamond). It's all a ______________ (personal taste; matter), I suppose, but it's not my ______________ (fashion; idea).

7 He was a real slave driver; we did ______________ (work; two months) for him and during that time we didn't have a ______________ (rest; day).

8 She gave a ______________ (talks; series) on a ______________ (topics; number) relating to the ______________ (environment; protection).

Vocabulary

Decide which answer (**A**, **B**, **C** or **D**) best fits each space.

1 There wasn't a ________ of truth in what he said.
A ray **B** lump **C** grain **D** pinch

2 Only a small ________ of volunteers turned up to help.
A armful **B** handful **C** fistful **D** earful

3 There's a ________ of dirty washing in the kitchen and none of it's mine.
A piece **B** pool **C** pack **D** pile

4 He didn't have a ________ of evidence to support his claims.
A sign **B** scrap **C** sense **D** state

5 It's the ________ of stupidity to go walking in the mountains in this weather.
A height **B** depth **C** source **D** matter

6 We had to save ________ for our holiday in Australia.
A long **B** hard **C** heavily **D** strongly

7 The company is known for paying ________, which is one reason why it retains staff.
A freely **B** largely **C** liberally **D** generously

8 The grant will be paid in three equal ________ over the course of the year.
A occurrences **B** episodes **C** instalments **D** inversions

9 It's normal for salaries to be paid monthly in ________, meaning you'll need to work four weeks first.
A advance **B** full **C** arrears **D** debt

10 I bought the chocolates on ________: I saw them while I was queueing up to pay.
A desire **B** urge **C** spontaneity **D** impulse

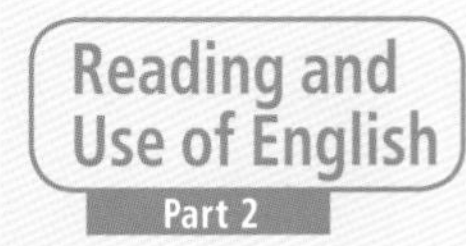

Open cloze

For questions **1–8**, read the text below and think of the word which best fits each gap. Use only **one** word in each gap. There is an example at the beginning (**0**). Write your answers **IN CAPITAL LETTERS**.

MONEY BUYS HAPPINESS

There has always been an assumption that **(0)** ..THE.. more money you have, the happier you are, but **(1)** .... now a direct link between wealth and joy has **(2)** .... been proven. However, findings from a study carried out by researchers at the University of Warwick prove **(3)** .... doubt that money does indeed buy you happiness. The study, based on interviews with 9000 families, looked at the effects of windfalls such as a lottery win or the receipt of an inheritance **(4)** .... people's well-being. At the end of a ten-year investigation, **(5)** .... the researchers found was that receiving just £1000 is sufficient to change the average person's outlook on life, although it would take at least £1 million to jump from feeling depressed and dissatisfied **(6)** .... being very happy and content. And, of course, a millionaire would require considerably more **(7)** .... the same effect to occur. However, it seems the happiness gained from money does not last, **(8)** .... the pleasure wearing off as you get used to it.

Ready for Writing

Introduction

In the **Writing** paper you have to complete two different writing tasks in 1 hour 30 minutes; the compulsory Part 1 task and another from a choice of three in Part 2. For each task, you are expected to write between 220 and 260 words.

In Part 1 you are asked to write an essay in response to a proposition to discuss. The proposition is accompanied by a text which takes the form of notes made during a seminar, lecture or panel discussion.

In Part 2, you could be asked to write one of the following: an email or letter, a proposal, a report or a review.

Marking

When marking answers in the **Writing** paper, as part of the general assessment criteria, examiners consider the features in the box. Match each feature to the general advice and information in **a–i** below. The first one has been done for you.

Content	Target reader	Accuracy
~~Range~~	Organization and cohesion	

1 *Range*	**a** Use a variety of language appropriate to this level. **b** Avoid repetition of vocabulary wherever possible.
2 ______	**c** Ensure that your answer addresses all the points in the task. **d** In Part 1 you do not always need to use all the information you are given.
3 ______	**e** Write in clear paragraphs of a suitable length. **f** Points need to be appropriately ordered and connected.
4 ______	**g** Write your answer in a register which is appropriate to the task and the intended audience. **h** Adopt a suitable tone for your piece of writing to produce the desired effect.
5 ______	**i** Avoid making too many mistakes, particularly basic ones or ones which prevent understanding.

Planning and checking

The sentences below show the stages to follow when planning and checking your written work. Match each stage **1–9** to the piece of general advice in **a–i** on page 194 to which it corresponds.

Example: *1 c*

1. Read the task at least twice, underlining key information and requirements.
2. Select appropriately from the information in the input material.
3. Decide whether you should use more formal or informal English.
4. Check whether the task requires you to achieve a specific aim such as persuading, reassuring, apologizing or justifying.
5. Make a list of ideas for your answer, then select the best ones and arrange them into logical groupings.
6. Note down words and expressions which might be suitable for linking your ideas.
7. Write down relevant words, collocations and structures which you might be able to include in your answer.
8. Think of synonyms for key words which are likely to occur more than once in your answer.
9. When you have written your answer, check spelling, punctuation and grammar.

Register

1 Below are two versions of the same letter, each one written in a different register. Use the information in the informal letter to complete the numbered gaps in the formal version. The words you need do not occur in the informal letter. Write **one word** in each gap. The exercise begins with an example (**0**).

INFORMAL LETTER

Dear Jilly
Thanks a lot for your letter – and congratulations on passing your exams! You did really well to get such a high grade.

You said you'd be interested in trying to get a job here with us in the family business. Believe me, we'd love to take you on. But because of the way the economy's been recently, I'm sorry to say we just can't offer you any work at the moment.

We'll certainly keep you in mind for when things get better – we'll be in touch as soon as they do. Until then, good luck with the job search!
All the best
Bob

FORMAL LETTER

Dear Ms Holden

I am writing with **(0)** *reference* to your letter of April 18th. I would like to congratulate you on your recent **(1)** ________________ in your examinations, and particularly on **(2)** ________________ such a high grade.

In your letter you **(3)** ________________ an interest in applying for a **(4)** ________________ here at Graves, Snipe and Wesley. I assure you we would be delighted to offer you **(5)** ________________. However, **(6)** ________________ to the current economic climate, we are unfortunately **(7)** ________________ to make any new appointments at the present time.

We shall, of course, keep your letter on our files in anticipation of an **(8)** ________________ in the situation. When this occurs, we shall **(9)** ________________ you immediately.

In the **(10)** ________________, I would like to wish you luck in your attempts to find work.

Yours sincerely

Robert Snipe

2 Use the two letters to identify some of the differences between formal and informal language.

Example:
The informal letter contains contractions such as 'you'd', 'I'm' and 'we'll' whereas the formal version does not.

Models and tasks

On the following pages you will find a model for each of the main task types, together with an additional task. You should answer the Part 1 task on page 197, and at least one of the Part 2 tasks. Read the relevant model, then follow stages **1–9** in the Planning and checking section on page 195. In order to help you demonstrate a good range of vocabulary you should select appropriately from the Useful language section.

Part 1: Essay

Your class has recently watched a television documentary on ways for governments to reduce traffic congestion. You have made the notes below:

Ways for governments to reduce traffic congestion
- public transport
- road building
- legislation

Some opinions expressed in the documentary:

'Maybe people would use buses if there were more of them.'

'We need fewer cars on the road, not more.'

'There should be limits on where and when you can drive.'

Write an essay for your tutor discussing **two** of the ways in your notes. You should **explain which way you think is more important** for governments to consider, **giving reasons** in support of your answer.

You may, if you wish, make use of the opinions expressed in the discussion, but you should use your own words as far as possible.

Model answer

Tackling traffic congestion: what should be done?

opening statement to engage the reader's interest

At the beginning of the 20th century, a car was a luxury that many could not afford, but since then, the number of vehicles on the streets of industrialized countries has soared. The simple fact is that most urban areas were never designed to cope with such high levels of traffic. It seems ironic that as car ownership has increased, the quality of life for people living in cities has, in some ways, diminished. Traffic congestion creates stress, pollution and many types of health problem. It is an issue that governments *must* address.

reasons for the proposition

clearly separate paragraphs help with organization

One approach that policy-makers could take is to introduce more legislation regulating the use of private vehicles. In certain countries, for example, drivers are required to pay a toll once they cross the boundary of the city centre. In some cases, car drivers are also restricted to using one lane only, leaving the other lanes for buses or taxis. Unfortunately, there is evidence that neither of these measures has reduced traffic to any significant extent.

a range of cohesive devices

An alternative approach would be to make public transport more attractive to potential passengers. According to a recent online poll, it is inconvenience rather than cost which deters people from using buses. Local authorities would therefore need to provide a much wider range of bus routes, and run far more frequent services.

formal register with impersonal language rather than first person pronouns

clear indication of which approach or method the writer considers more important

In conclusion, an improved public transport system would certainly require considerable financial investment, but in the long term, it might be a cheaper option than borrowing money to fund new road-building projects. This is the strategy that I would recommend governments adopt.

Task

Your class has attended a panel discussion on ways young people can be encouraged to keep fit. You have made the notes below:

Ways young people can be encouraged to keep fit

- school programmes
- sports clubs
- technology

Some opinions expressed in the panel discussion:

'Schools should be responsible for kids' fitness.'

'Maybe kids would do sport if they could choose one they liked.'

'Young people would be more motivated if a computer was involved somehow!'

Write an essay for your tutor discussing **two** of the ways in your notes. You should **explain which way you think is more important** for schools to consider, **giving reasons** in support of your answer.

You may, if you wish, make use of the opinions expressed in the discussion, but you should use your own words as far as possible.

Useful language for essays

Expressing an opinion
It is probably true to say that …
There can be no doubt that …
It is simply not the case that …

Commonly held views
It is widely believed that …
No one would dispute the fact that …
Few people would contest/dispute (the fact) that …
It is generally agreed that …

Saying what other people think
There are those who argue that …
It has been suggested that …
It is often claimed that …
Opponents/Supporters/Proponents of (hunting) argue that …

Referring to sources
All the evidence suggests that …
A recent survey proved that …
Judging by the comments made by …
Interviews with (students) have revealed that …

Part 2: Formal letter/email

You are the social secretary at Lambert College, a language school for international students. The local newspaper has recently made several negative comments on relations between international students and local people which you consider to be unfair. You decide to send an email to the editor of the newspaper. Your email should

- explain why the comments were unfair.
- invite local people to an event at the school.

Write your **email**.

Model answer

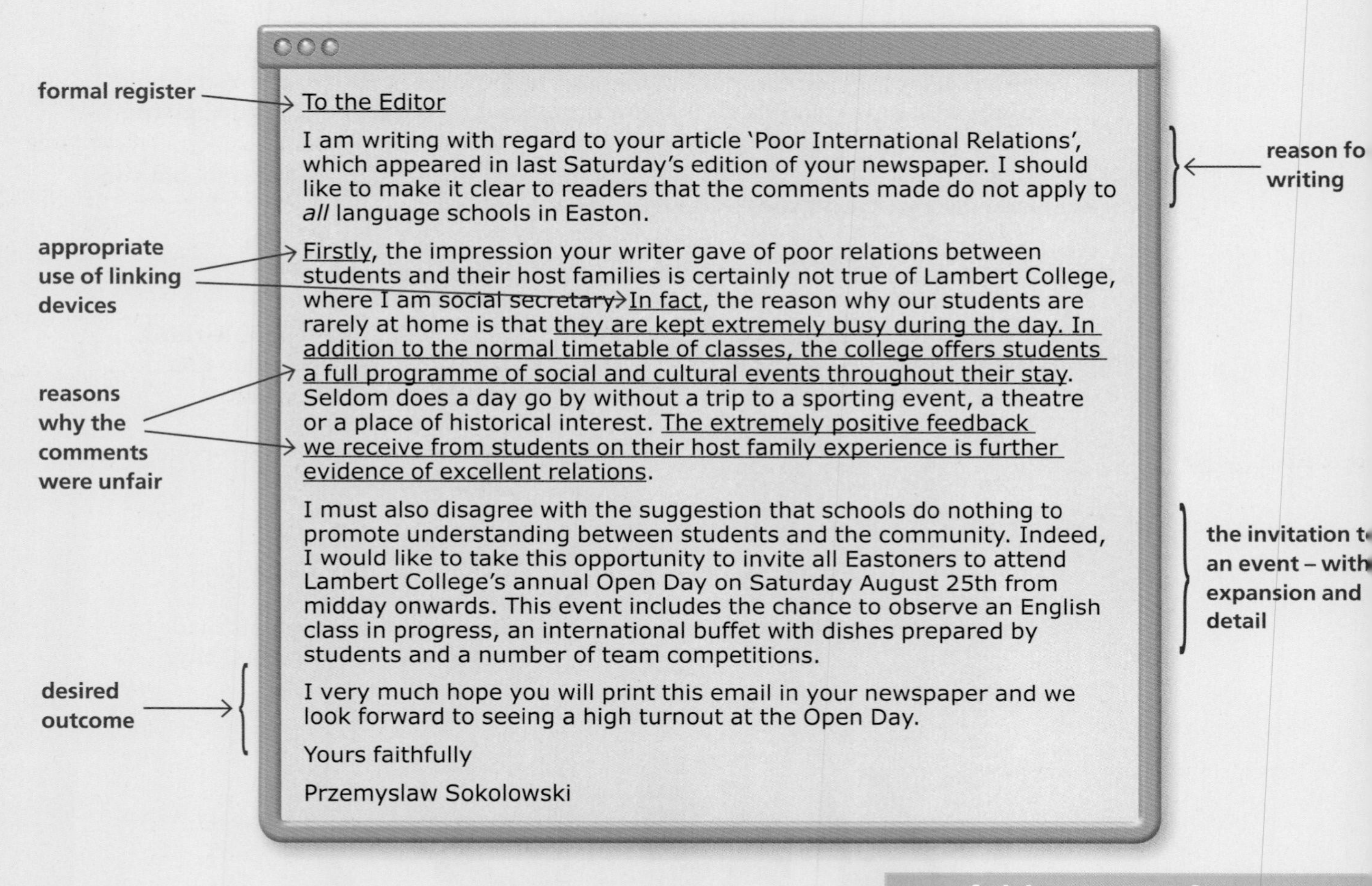

To the Editor

I am writing with regard to your article 'Poor International Relations', which appeared in last Saturday's edition of your newspaper. I should like to make it clear to readers that the comments made do not apply to *all* language schools in Easton.

Firstly, the impression your writer gave of poor relations between students and their host families is certainly not true of Lambert College, where I am social secretary. In fact, the reason why our students are rarely at home is that they are kept extremely busy during the day. In addition to the normal timetable of classes, the college offers students a full programme of social and cultural events throughout their stay. Seldom does a day go by without a trip to a sporting event, a theatre or a place of historical interest. The extremely positive feedback we receive from students on their host family experience is further evidence of excellent relations.

I must also disagree with the suggestion that schools do nothing to promote understanding between students and the community. Indeed, I would like to take this opportunity to invite all Eastoners to attend Lambert College's annual Open Day on Saturday August 25th from midday onwards. This event includes the chance to observe an English class in progress, an international buffet with dishes prepared by students and a number of team competitions.

I very much hope you will print this email in your newspaper and we look forward to seeing a high turnout at the Open Day.

Yours faithfully

Przemyslaw Sokolowski

Task

Last weekend you stayed at a hostel with a group of teenage students from the college where you work as Events Organizer. The hostel manager has emailed you complaining about the students' behaviour, and saying that students from your college will no longer be able to stay there.

You decide to send an email back to the hostel manager. Your email should

- explain what happened during the weekend.
- say why the manager should change his decision.

Write your **email** in **220–260** words.

Useful language for Part 2 formal letters/emails

Reason for writing

I am writing with regard/reference to …

I am writing to express (my concern about/disappointment with/disapproval of/apologies for) …

I would like to draw your attention to/point out …

Introducing points

(I feel) I must also (dis)agree with …

I should also like to point out that …

Your (article) states that … However, …

Request for action

I would appreciate it/be grateful if you would …

I look forward to receiving/seeing …

I trust/very much hope you will …

Informal letter

You recently took part in an activity which you enjoyed very much. A friend of yours has written to you expressing an interest in the activity and asking how it went. Write a **letter** telling your friend about the positive and negative aspects of your experience, encouraging him/her to take part in a similar event.

Model answer

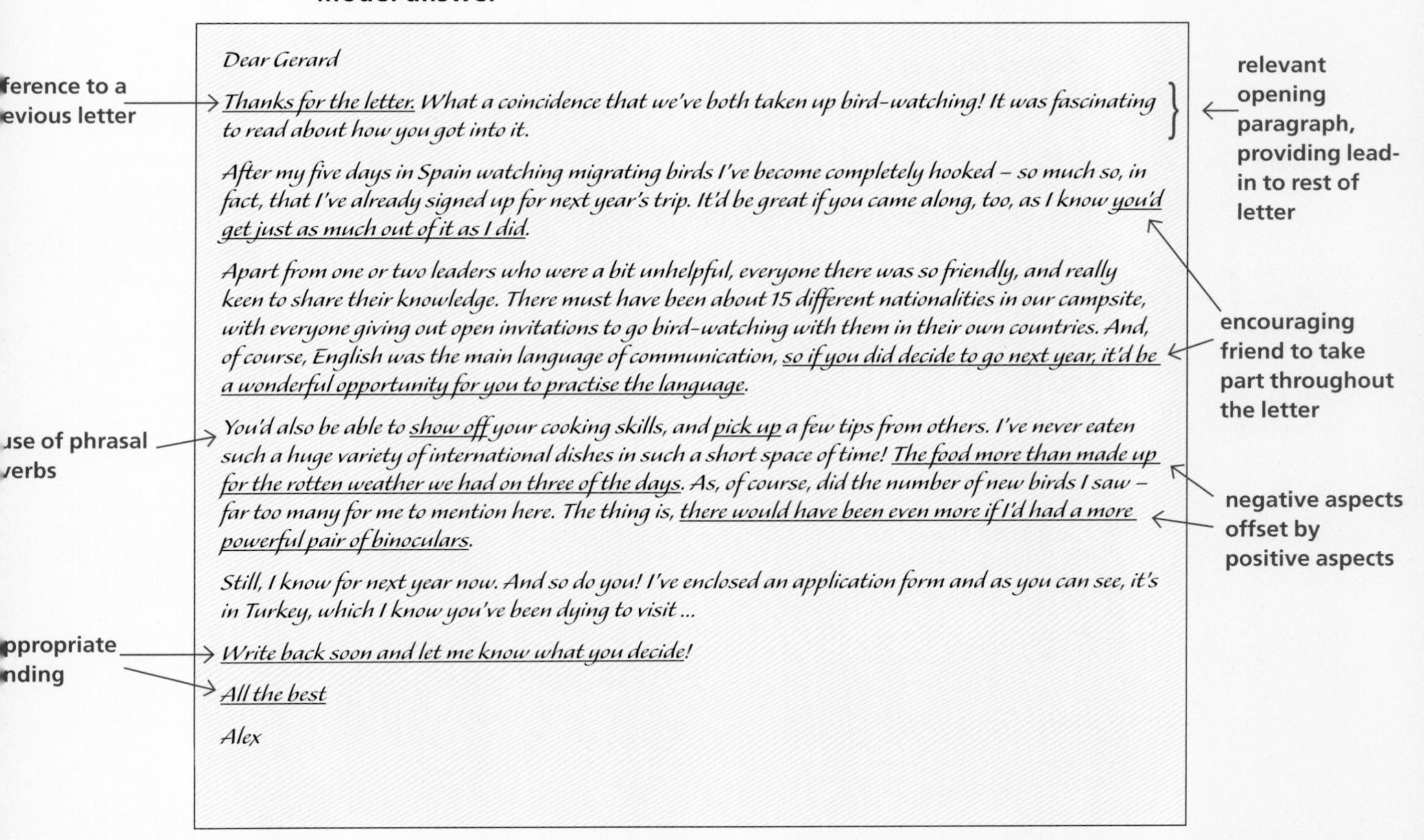

Dear Gerard

Thanks for the letter. What a coincidence that we've both taken up bird-watching! It was fascinating to read about how you got into it.

After my five days in Spain watching migrating birds I've become completely hooked – so much so, in fact, that I've already signed up for next year's trip. It'd be great if you came along, too, as I know you'd get just as much out of it as I did.

Apart from one or two leaders who were a bit unhelpful, everyone there was so friendly, and really keen to share their knowledge. There must have been about 15 different nationalities in our campsite, with everyone giving out open invitations to go bird-watching with them in their own countries. And, of course, English was the main language of communication, so if you did decide to go next year, it'd be a wonderful opportunity for you to practise the language.

You'd also be able to show off your cooking skills, and pick up a few tips from others. I've never eaten such a huge variety of international dishes in such a short space of time! The food more than made up for the rotten weather we had on three of the days. As, of course, did the number of new birds I saw – far too many for me to mention here. The thing is, there would have been even more if I'd had a more powerful pair of binoculars.

Still, I know for next year now. And so do you! I've enclosed an application form and as you can see, it's in Turkey, which I know you've been dying to visit ...

Write back soon and let me know what you decide!

All the best

Alex

Task

Either: **a** write your own answer to the task above;

or **b** answer the following question.

You recently went on holiday to a place which you enjoyed very much. A friend of yours has written to you expressing an interest in the place and asking what it was like there. Write a **letter** in **220–260** words, telling your friend about the positive and negative aspects of the place, encouraging him/her to go there next year.

Useful language for informal letters

Beginning the letter

Great/Lovely to hear from you (after so long).

Thanks (a lot) for the letter.

Sorry to hear about your ...

Sorry I haven't written/been in touch for so long.

Persuading

You'd get so much out of it.

It'd be a wonderful/marvellous opportunity for you to ...

Just think of (all the people you'd meet).

Just imagine how it would (improve your CV), not to mention (the money you could earn).

Advising

Whatever you do, make sure you ...

It's (not) worth/There's no/little point + gerund

I'd/I wouldn't ... if I were you.

You'd be much better off + gerund

Ending the letter

Write back soon and let me know how it goes.

Looking forward to hearing from you.

Can't wait to see you again.

(Give my) love/regards to ...

Signing off

Friends: All the best/Best wishes/Bye for now

Close friends or relatives:
Lots of love/All my love/Love

Proposal

Your town has been shortlisted to host a major international festival of folk music and dance next year. You have been asked to write a proposal for the festival organizers, stating why your town should be chosen from the list. You should include relevant information about accommodation, transport, concert venues and other leisure and entertainment possibilities.

Write your **proposal**.

Model answer

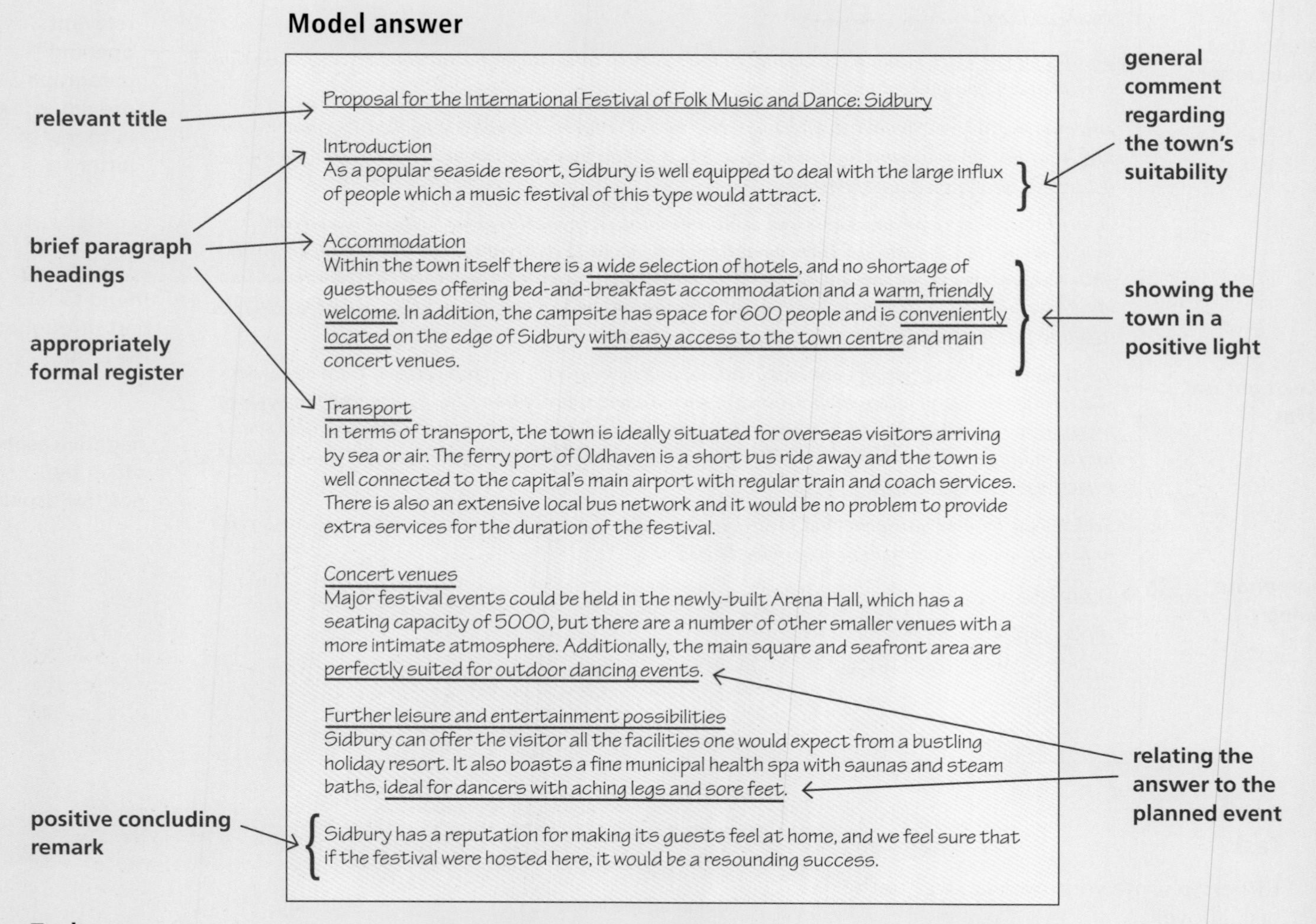

Proposal for the International Festival of Folk Music and Dance: Sidbury

Introduction

As a popular seaside resort, Sidbury is well equipped to deal with the large influx of people which a music festival of this type would attract.

Accommodation

Within the town itself there is a wide selection of hotels, and no shortage of guesthouses offering bed-and-breakfast accommodation and a warm, friendly welcome. In addition, the campsite has space for 600 people and is conveniently located on the edge of Sidbury with easy access to the town centre and main concert venues.

Transport

In terms of transport, the town is ideally situated for overseas visitors arriving by sea or air. The ferry port of Oldhaven is a short bus ride away and the town is well connected to the capital's main airport with regular train and coach services. There is also an extensive local bus network and it would be no problem to provide extra services for the duration of the festival.

Concert venues

Major festival events could be held in the newly-built Arena Hall, which has a seating capacity of 5000, but there are a number of other smaller venues with a more intimate atmosphere. Additionally, the main square and seafront area are perfectly suited for outdoor dancing events.

Further leisure and entertainment possibilities

Sidbury can offer the visitor all the facilities one would expect from a bustling holiday resort. It also boasts a fine municipal health spa with saunas and steam baths, ideal for dancers with aching legs and sore feet.

Sidbury has a reputation for making its guests feel at home, and we feel sure that if the festival were hosted here, it would be a resounding success.

Task

Your school has been shortlisted to host a two-day regional conference for students preparing for the *Advanced* examination. You have been asked to write a proposal for the conference organizers, stating why your school should be chosen from the list. Your proposal should include relevant information about the facilities within your school, accommodation, transport and other leisure and entertainment possibilities.

Write your **proposal** in **220–260** words.

Useful language for proposals

Suitability

The (town/centre/stadium) is well equipped to deal with/perfectly suited for (such events).

It is conveniently located/ideally situated/well connected to (the capital).

There is little doubt that it would be a resounding success/of great benefit to the (town/company).

Amenities

There is no shortage/a wide selection of (hotels/cinemas) to choose from.

The (town/conference centre/school) boasts an impressive range of (amenities/facilities).

Few (cities/schools) can offer such a large choice of …

Travel and transport

It is within easy reach/walking distance/driving distance of the (centre/hotel).

It is just a short walk/drive/bus ride/train ride from the (coast/station).

The (town) has easy access to (the motorway network).

Report

An international research group is carrying out an investigation into the housing situation for young people around the world. You have been asked by the group to write a report about your country, including the following points:

- the different housing options available in your country for young people in their early 20s
- the problems faced by young people with each option
- possible future changes in the housing situation for young people in your country

Write your **report**.

Model answer

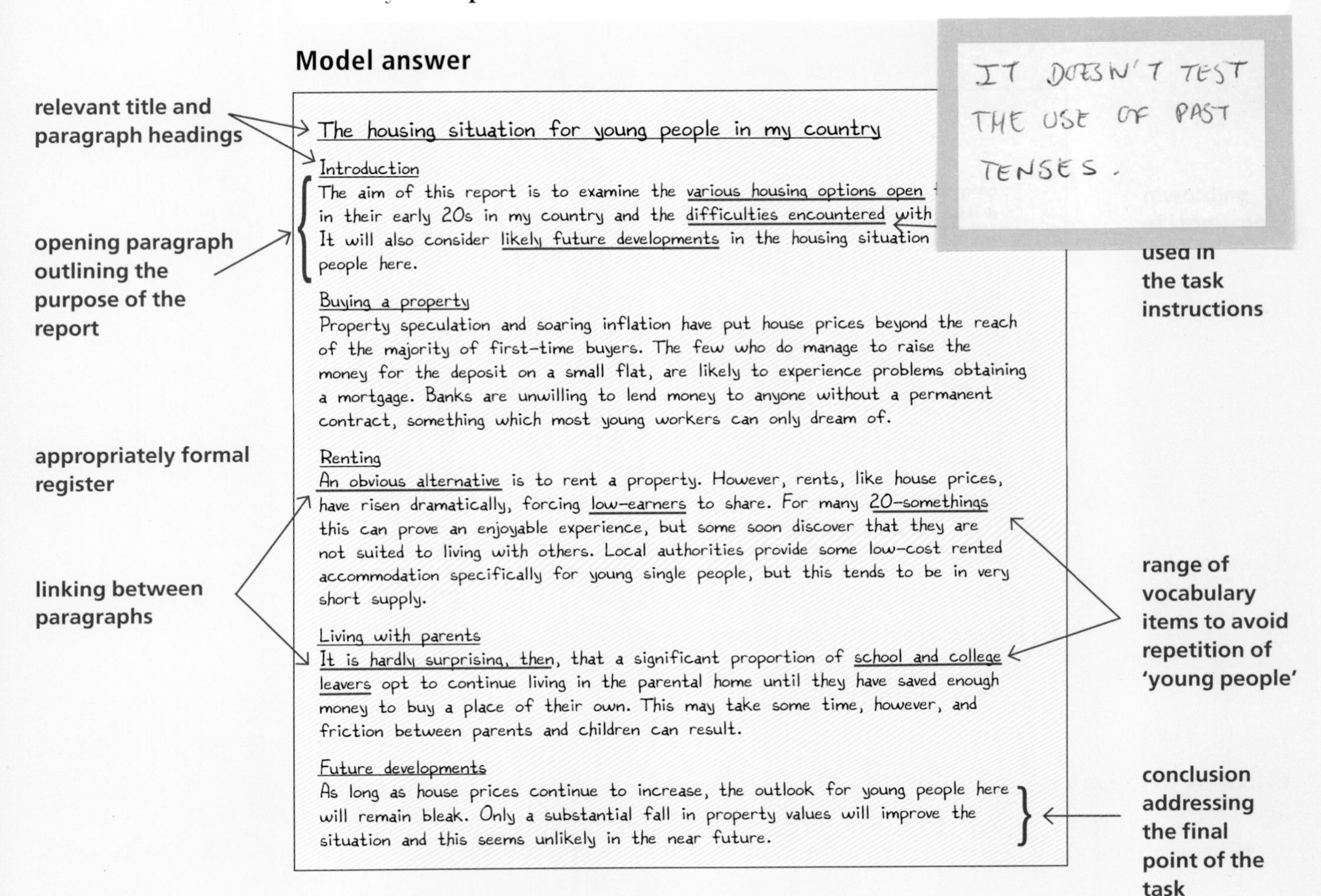

The housing situation for young people in my country

Introduction
The aim of this report is to examine the various housing options open
in their early 20s in my country and the difficulties encountered with
It will also consider likely future developments in the housing situation
people here.

Buying a property
Property speculation and soaring inflation have put house prices beyond the reach of the majority of first-time buyers. The few who do manage to raise the money for the deposit on a small flat, are likely to experience problems obtaining a mortgage. Banks are unwilling to lend money to anyone without a permanent contract, something which most young workers can only dream of.

Renting
An obvious alternative is to rent a property. However, rents, like house prices, have risen dramatically, forcing low-earners to share. For many 20-somethings this can prove an enjoyable experience, but some soon discover that they are not suited to living with others. Local authorities provide some low-cost rented accommodation specifically for young single people, but this tends to be in very short supply.

Living with parents
It is hardly surprising, then, that a significant proportion of school and college leavers opt to continue living in the parental home until they have saved enough money to buy a place of their own. This may take some time, however, and friction between parents and children can result.

Future developments
As long as house prices continue to increase, the outlook for young people here will remain bleak. Only a substantial fall in property values will improve the situation and this seems unlikely in the near future.

Task

An international research group is carrying out an investigation into employment prospects for young people around the world. You have been asked by the group to write a report abo[ut] your local area, including the foll[owing] points:

- the types of employment avai[lable] for young people in your area
- the difficulties faced by young people searching for work
- possible future developments in the employment situation for young people in your area

Write your **report** in **220–260** words.

Useful language for reports

Introducing the report

...eport is to
...e/outline ...
...er/suggest/

The report is based on a survey conducted among (college students).

Predicting the future

The outlook for young people/jobs/the country is (far from) bright/optimistic/depressing.

The future looks bleak/remains uncertain/is promising.

This seems unlikely in the near/foreseeable future. (See also vocabulary of Possibility on page 208 of the Wordlist.)

Making recommendations

I would (strongly) recommend that (the school/company) should ...

In the light of the results of the survey, I would (strongly) advise against ...

I feel it would be to our advantage if ...

Review

The magazine published by your school's English club is asking students to exchange information about non-fiction books they have enjoyed reading in English. Write a review of a non-fiction book you have read, saying what you learnt from it and encouraging others to read it.

Write your **review**.

Model answer

'Lost Cowboys' by Hank Wangford

Did you realize that there were no horses or cows in the Americas until Columbus introduced them on his return visit in 1494? Or that the first cowboys were not those of North America, but the 'gauchos', 'huasos', 'llaneros' and 'vaqueros' of Argentina, Chile, Venezuela and Mexico? I certainly didn't, until I read Hank Wangford's revealing study of cowboy culture from Patagonia in South America to the Alamo in Texas.

The book is full of interesting facts and stories about cowboy heroes who were previously unknown to me. One such man was Martín Miguel de Güemes, who in 1806 rode with 30 other gauchos into the waters of the River Plate and captured a British ship which had run aground there. The event is narrated with Wangford's characteristic sense of humour, which will have you laughing out loud from the very beginning of the book.

And if you're not a great cowboy fan, don't be put off by the title. 'Lost Cowboys' does more than simply trace the history of cattlemen on horseback: it provides a fascinating insight into the customs, food, music, geography and wildlife of a whole continent. There's something for everyone in the book, from enthusiastic and vivid descriptions of the scenery, to information on dances and singing traditions, such as the gaucho 'payadas' – I had no idea you could have a duel with the voice as your only weapon!

'Lost Cowboys' is an excellent read. It is both entertaining and educational and I highly recommend it to anyone who is interested in travel books.

questions to engage the reader's interest

what the reader learnt from the book

final recommendation

brief summary of the book's content

encouraging others to read the book

Task

Either: **a** write your own answer to the task above;

or **b** answer the following question.

The magazine published by your school's English club is asking students to give opinions on the coursebooks they have been using. Write a review of *Ready for Advanced*, giving your views on the following points:

- its content
- its design
- how well it prepares students for the exam
- how much it has helped you improve your English

Write your **review** in **220–260** words.

Useful language for reviews

Commenting critically

… provides a fascinating/valuable/revealing insight into …

I found the plot rather predictable/disappointing.

The acting is very impressive/convincing.

She gives a compelling/memorable performance as …

One particular strength/weakness of the film/book/CD is …

The design/characterization/production is second to none/is not its best feature.

Encouraging others (not) to read/watch/listen

Don't be put off by the title/critics/cover.

It will have you roaring with laughter/rushing out to buy the sequel.

It is a definite must-see.

I would definitely give it a miss.

I would highly recommend it to anyone interested in …

I would strongly advise you (not) to go out and buy/see it.

(For a list of adjectives used in reviews and the vocabulary of *Comparisons*, see page 211.)

Letter of application

You have seen this advertisement in an international magazine.

> **WRITERS REQUIRED**
>
> We are looking for people to write for this magazine about environmental issues in their local area that would be of interest to readers in other countries. We would like to hear from anyone who has
> - an interest in environmental concerns.
> - an awareness of environmental issues affecting their local area.
> - some experience of writing.
>
> Send us a letter of application, explaining why you think you are suitable and describing two environmental issues currently affecting your local area.

Write your **letter of application**.

Model answer

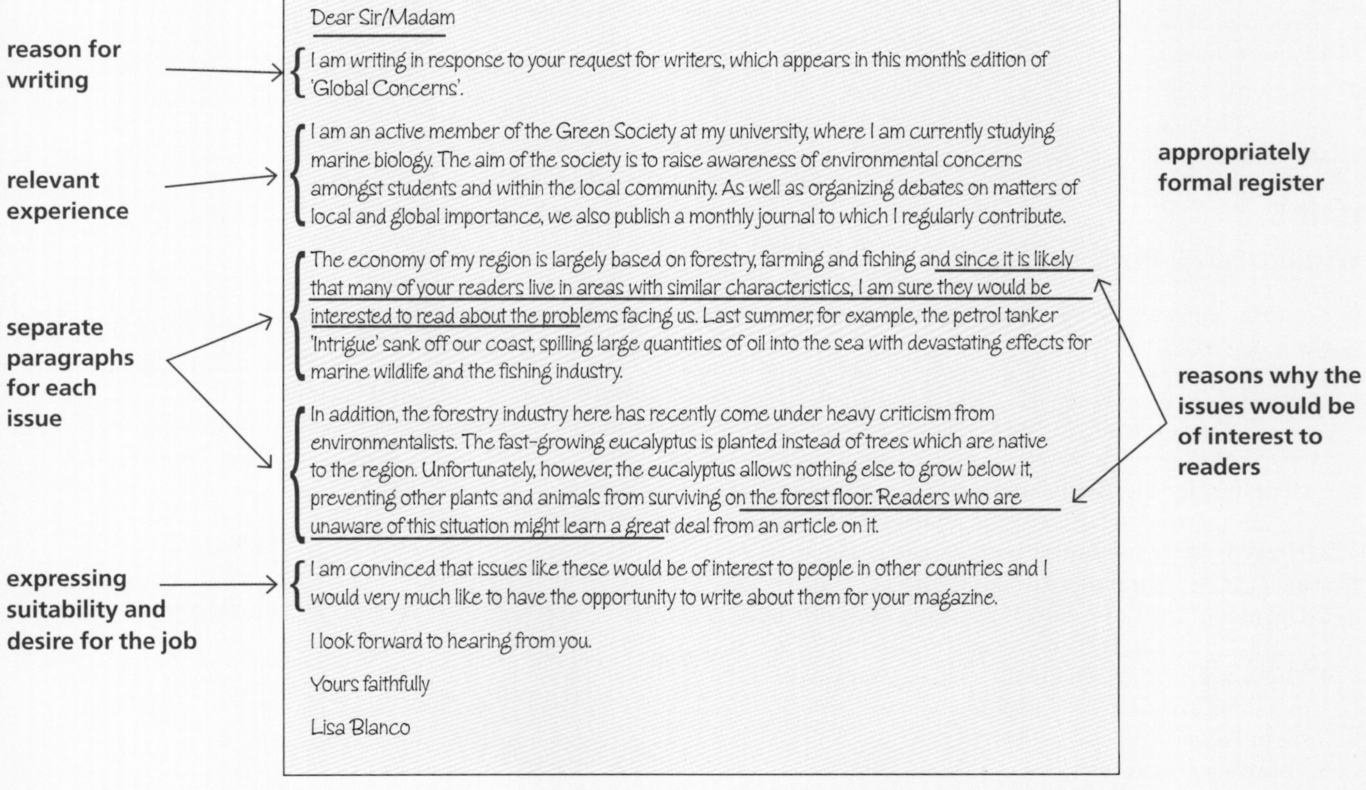

Dear Sir/Madam

I am writing in response to your request for writers, which appears in this month's edition of 'Global Concerns'.

I am an active member of the Green Society at my university, where I am currently studying marine biology. The aim of the society is to raise awareness of environmental concerns amongst students and within the local community. As well as organizing debates on matters of local and global importance, we also publish a monthly journal to which I regularly contribute.

The economy of my region is largely based on forestry, farming and fishing and since it is likely that many of your readers live in areas with similar characteristics, I am sure they would be interested to read about the problems facing us. Last summer, for example, the petrol tanker 'Intrigue' sank off our coast, spilling large quantities of oil into the sea with devastating effects for marine wildlife and the fishing industry.

In addition, the forestry industry here has recently come under heavy criticism from environmentalists. The fast-growing eucalyptus is planted instead of trees which are native to the region. Unfortunately, however, the eucalyptus allows nothing else to grow below it, preventing other plants and animals from surviving on the forest floor. Readers who are unaware of this situation might learn a great deal from an article on it.

I am convinced that issues like these would be of interest to people in other countries and I would very much like to have the opportunity to write about them for your magazine.

I look forward to hearing from you.

Yours faithfully

Lisa Blanco

Task

Either: **a** write your own answer to the task above;
or **b** answer the following question.

> **WRITERS REQUIRED**
>
> We are looking for people to write for this magazine about people in their local area whose work, achievements or lifestyle would be of interest to an international readership.
>
> Send us a letter of application, explaining why you think you are suitable and giving examples of two local people, living or dead, that you would write about.

Write your **letter of application** in **220–260** words.

(For useful language, see page 10 in Unit 1 of the Workbook.)

Additional materia[l]

Unit 1

Language focus 2: Spelling, page 14

4 Student A

1 Dictate the following ten items to your partner. When you have finished, your partner will check his/her spelling.

1. highly influential
2. desperately disappointed
3. utterly exhausted
4. comparatively unknown
5. fiercely independent
6. wholly unacceptable
7. academically successful
8. unnecessarily aggressive
9. extremely embarrassed
10. quite quiet

2 Now write down the ten items of vocabulary which your partner dictates to you. When you have finished writing, check your spelling on page 207.

Unit 6

Writing: Part 2 Review, page 74

6 Complete each of the spaces with one of the nouns from the box.

lines	terms	similarities
resemblance	difference	genre

1 Her latest novel, a tale of unrequited love, **bears little** __________ to her earlier, more philosophical work.

2 **There is little to choose from between** the two CDs **in** __________ **of** quality of production.

3 The plot of the novel **develops along very different** __________ **from** that of the film.

4 **There are** several **obvious** __________ **between** the two films, the first, of course, being that they are both set in Paris.

5 **There's a world of** __________ **between** the two records, despite their shared flamenco influences.

6 **What sets the film apart from others** of the same __________ is its ability to make us laugh.

Unit 11

Vocabulary 2: *Read* and *write*, page 148

3 Discuss the following with your partner. Give reasons in each case.

a Do you have **neat handwriting**, or do others find it hard to read?

b Are you a **fast** or **slow reader**?

c Are you **an avid reader** of any particular author, genre or magazine?

d Do you **read widely**?

e What was the last novel you read? Was it **a good read**?

Unit 3

Vocabul[ary: Smell, page 3…]

4 … from t… smells.

Examp…

yo… old b…

4 1. Your classroom: stale smell.
2. A Rose garden: pungent aroma.
3. Disinfectant: acrid odour.
4. Old books: pungent aroma.
5. Warm pizza: mouth-watering aroma
6. Your fav. cheese: " "
7. Decaying rubbish: rancid smell

Unit 8

Language focus 1: Determiners and pronouns, Practice, page 103

3 Choose one of these as the topic of your conversation:

Technology	Health and fitness
Schooldays	The media
Weekends	Relationships
The world of work	Entertainment
The natural world	

Ready for Speaking Part 2: Long turn, page 168

Look at these pictures. They show people reading.

Student A:
Compare two of these pictures, and say what and why the people might be reading, and how they might be feeling.

Student B:
When your partner has finished talking, answer the following question about all three pictures.
Which person is most interested in finding out what is written?

- What might the people be reading and why?
- How might the people be feeling?

Ready for Listening

Part 2: Sentence completion, page 127

3 Match each answer on the answer sheet to one or more of the pieces of advice in the box.

Example: *1 h*

1 *warehouse*
2 *Fine Arts course*
3 *mesurements*
4 *person who gives the news on television*
5 *position*
6
7 *five month*
8 *watercolours*

Advice for Part 2 Sentence completion tasks

a Check that your answer fits grammatically with the rest of the sentence.
b Check that your answer is spelt correctly.
c Do not leave any blank spaces on the answer sheet. If you are not sure of the answer, make a guess.
d Do not repeat information in your answer which is already contained in the question.
e Do not write long answers. You do not normally need to write more than three words.
f When you transfer your answers to the answer sheet, check that you have followed the numbering correctly.
g Try to write the words you actually hear on the recording.
h Beware of distractors.

Unit 14

Language focus: Noun phrases, page 191

5 Student B

Choose six of the following phrases and write a similar exercise to that on page 191. Then give the exercise to your partner to complete.

sense of smell	chances of promotion
matter of life and death	height of fashion
state of shock	depths of winter
source of energy	sign of age

Unit 7

Speaking: Part 3 Collaborative task, page 92

Useful language

2 Circle the collocate in *italics* which is different in some way to the other three and complete the gap with an appropriate preposition.

a This kind of change would have a *short-term/minimal/significant/limited* effect ______ people's overall health.

b A change like this would be *highly/reasonably/particularly/extremely* effective ______ reducing people's levels of stress.

c Would this be a/an *feasible/attractive/realistic/practical* option ______ most people?

3 Complete each gap with a preposition that can be used with all three verbs.

a Most people aren't able to *stick/adhere/keep* ______ a diet for long.

b It would be extremely hard to *do/go/manage* ______ TV!

c If people chose to *commit/devote/dedicate* less time ______ work, they'd have more time to spend with their family.

Ready for Use of English

Part 3: Word formation, page 44

4 Read through the text below quite quickly, ignoring the gaps, and check the predictions you made in exercise **3** on page 44.

Moths count!

Renowned conservationist Sir David Attenborough is launching a campaign today called 'Moths Count', to halt the **(0)** *DRASTICALLY* declining number of Britain's native moths and improve their poor image. A report **(1)** .... 'The State of Britain's Larger Moths' revealed last year that in some areas, the moth population has almost **(2)** .... since 1968. This has led the charity, 'Butterfly Conservation', of which Sir David is president, to develop a new strategy which will provide opportunities for real **(3)** .... to broaden their **(4)** .... and also generate appreciation among the wider public. Moths, he insists, play an essential role in the environment. Their loss **(5)** .... the species of of birds, bats and small mammals that feed on them, and the plants they pollinate. 'Moths Count' campaigner Richard Fox says 'Currently there's an image problem, partly because there's a **(6)** .... that moths are night creatures, although many are day-flying and only about half a dozen of Britain's 2500 species damage clothes.' Reasons for their decline include climate change and loss of habitat. Although the **(7)** .... of moths has increased with the establishment of new species in Britain, overall their numbers have dropped, and for some, extinction now seems sadly **(8)** ....

DRASTIC
TITLE
HALF
ENTHUSE
EXPERT
THREAT
PERCEIVE
DIVERSE
AVOID

Unit 14
Language focus: Noun phrases, page 191

5 Student A

Choose six of the following phrases and write a similar exercise to that on page 191. Then give the exercise to your partner to complete.

sense of relief	chances of survival
matter of personal taste	height of summer
state of emergency	depths of despair
source of income	sign of respect

Unit 5
Writing: Part 2 Proposal, page 67

5

Your college has a number of international students attending courses. Some of these students have experienced problems in adjusting to college life. You have been asked by your college director to propose ways to help students.

Your proposal should
- outline reasons for the problems.
- suggest ways to help the international students.

Write your **proposal** in **220–260** words in an appropriate style.

How to go about it

- Brainstorm ideas.
  Note down possible problems and their likely reasons. Then consider suitable solutions. Select the best two or three ideas.
- Write a paragraph plan.
  *Choose one of the plans from exercise **2** on page 67.*
- Write your proposal in an appropriate register.
  *Both questions in exercise **5** require a formal register.*
- Aim to use a wide range of relevant language.
- Give your proposal a clear title and write paragraph headings.

Ready for Reading
Part 8: Multiple matching, page 89

4 Complete each gap with one of the adjectives from the box. Use the collocates in **bold** to help you.

appreciate	cautious	disillusioned	reluctant
remorseful	resentful	resigned	sceptical

1 Young people have become **increasingly** __________ **with** politicians, who they feel have done little to solve the problem of youth unemployment.
2 The defendant apologized for his crime and seemed **genuinely** __________ **for** the suffering he had caused.
3 Sam had once again been overlooked for promotion, and was **quietly** __________ **to** the idea that she would probably never gain a management position.
4 The marriage began to fail as Williams became **bitterly** __________ **of** his wife's success.
5 The staff are **highly** __________ **of** the new director's claim that he can double profits within a year. It seems very unlikely.
6 Students are **understandably** __________ **to** spend a lot of money on new books, so the second-hand bookshop near the university does good business.
7 We are **greatly** __________ **of** all your hard work over the years and wish you all the best in your retirement.
8 Many children lack self-confidence and initiative as a result of parents being **overly** __________ **about** letting them play unsupervised.

Ready for Reading
Part 5: Multiple choice, page 83

4 Complete the following **verb + noun collocations** using the correct form of a verb from the box. The second sentence should have the same meaning as the first.

cast	~~challenge~~	lend	mock
point	question	refute	undermine

1 In his report, he disputes the belief that teleworking is more productive.
In his report, he *challenges* **the assumption that** teleworking is more productive.
2 The findings strengthen the theory that this is an ancient burial site.
The findings __________ **support to the notion that** this is an ancient burial site.
3 New research makes the earlier study seem less valid.
New research __________ **doubt on the validity of** the earlier study.
4 Young people are beginning to wonder if it's worth going to university.
Young people are beginning to __________ **the value of** a university education.
5 The professor reveals a fault in the government's arguments.
The professor __________ **out a flaw in** the government's arguments.
6 In her article, the journalist ridicules the view that travel broadens the mind.
In her article, the journalist __________ **the belief that** travel broadens the mind.
7 New unemployment figures weaken the assertion that the crisis is over.
New unemployment figures __________ **the claim that** the crisis is over.
8 The evidence proves the crater was not formed by a meteorite, as was suggested.
The evidence __________ **the suggestion that** the crater was formed by a meteorite.

Unit 1

Language focus 2: Spelling, page 14

4 Student B

1 Write down the ten items of vocabulary which your partner dictates to you. When you have finished writing, check your spelling on page 204.

2 Now dictate the following ten items to your partner. When you have finished, your partner will check his/her spelling.

1 mysterious disappearance
2 separate accommodation
3 eight-month guarantee
4 business arrangement
5 memorable occasion
6 unconscious decision
7 overall responsibility
8 frequent occurrence
9 guilty conscience
10 government committee

Unit 9

Vocabulary 1: Describing an adventure, page 116

2b Complete sentences **1–7** with the correct form of a phrasal verb from exercise **2a**.

1 In a fight-or-flight situation like this, the adrenalin will __________ very quickly.
2 A shot __________ and the race to get down the slope began.
3 We __________ to raise enough money for a six-week trek, but we ended up with twice the amount we needed.
4 It __________ that no one had remembered to pack the mosquito repellent.
5 Despite the storm, his sheer perseverance __________ and the boat arrived safely in port.
6 Unsure of our location, we split into two groups and __________ in different directions.
7 Five minutes after we left shore, we __________ trouble.

3 Tell your partner a brief anecdote – invented or true – about an experience or adventure you had. Use some of the language from exercises **1** and **2**.

Unit 10

Vocabulary 2: Noise and sound, page 135

4 Complete each of the gaps in **1–6** with a collocation from exercises **2** and **3** on page 135. There is an example at the beginning (**0**).

0 'Come in,' he said in a high *squeaky voice* that made him sound like a little mouse.

1 She spoke in a ______________ , anxious not to wake anyone up.
2 We could hear the ______________ of Bob's tractor in the valley below; it was faint, but unmistakable.
3 Wait until the ______________ a little before you give your speech, otherwise you'll have to shout.
4 Police arrested several ______________ who were clearly intent on causing trouble at the match.
5 His shock announcement that he was resigning met with ______________ ; no one knew quite what to say.
6 There was a sudden gust of wind and the ______________ behind her; she thought at first a gun had been fired.

5 **2.19** You will hear a sequence of sounds. Make notes as you listen.

6 Discuss with your partner what might have been happening. Wherever possible, use the vocabulary from exercises **2** and **3** on page 135 to describe the sounds.

7 What are your favourite sounds? Which sounds do you not like? Give reasons.

Unit 7

Speaking: Part 4 Further discussion, page 93

Discuss the following questions:

- How important is it for people to pay attention to nutritional advice?
- Some people find it difficult to stay at a healthy weight. Why do you think this is?
- Some people say that any advertising of junk food should be banned. What do you think?
- To what extent does the work you do influence your physical well-being?
- How far do you agree that the reason we sometimes help others is to make ourselves feel better?
- What are the positive effects of modern-day living? In what ways are we happier than previous generations?

Unit 8

Speaking: Part 2 Long turn, page 109

- Why might the people have chosen to learn in these ways?
- What are the advantages of learning like this?

Wordlist

Unit 1

A Problems

combat come up against confront encounter face face up to resolve rise above run into sort out tackle	a problem	a common a major a minor a potential a recurrent a serious a tough a trivial an unexpected an urgent	problem

B Challenges and achievements

accept face pose present rise to take up	a challenge	high/strong low/poor personal political staff student	motivation	admit be doomed to be resigned to end in meet with result in	failure	a burning my greatest a lifelong my main a personal a secret	ambition
a daunting an exciting a formidable a major a new a serious	challenge	achieve be assured of deserve enjoy guarantee meet with	success	complete continued dismal inevitable total	failure	a great a major an outstanding a remarkable a scientific a sporting a technological	achievement
improve increase lack lose strengthen	motivation	be a/an great huge overnight resounding roaring	success	achieve fulfil have pursue realize	an ambition		

C Possibility

There's every/little/no	chance likelihood possibility	of something (happening). that something will happen.

There's a (very)	distinct faint good real realistic remote slight strong	chance possibility	of sth (happening). that sth will happen.

They have/stand	every a fair a good little no an outside a slim	chance of doing sth

She is bound/certain/sure to do it.
She is highly likely to do it.
She may/might/could well do it.
She could easily/conceivably do it.
She is hardly likely to do it.
She's highly unlikely to do it.
It is highly likely/probable/unlikely/improbable that she'll do it.

We are going to investigate/look into One cannot ignore/rule out/exclude You should not overlook In order to reduce	the possibility that .../of ...

Unit 2

Changes

Verbs and nouns

bring about a call for a cope with introduce a lead to a resist welcome a witness a	change

adapt to/ adjust to	change/college life/a new job
adjust	clothing/the volume/the height of
alter	plans/clothes/ your appearance
amend	a law/a document
change	places/the subject/your mind/your tune/ your ways
convert	a building/ money/to a religion
modify	your behaviour/ your language/ a design
shift	the blame *or* responsibility for sth onto sb
switch	sides/(over) to a new currency/TV channels
transfer	money to another account/to a team or department
transform	(the appearance *or* character of) a person/a place/ a thing
vary	your diet/the menu/your routine/in price

Verbs and adverbs

adapt to/ adjust	automatically/ easily/effortlessly
alter	completely/ dramatically/ slightly
change	drastically/ overnight/ significantly
modify	slightly/ substantially/ subtly
transform	completely/ instantly/ radically
vary	considerably/ greatly/widely

Adjectives and nouns

a dramatic economic a far-reaching a pleasant political a refreshing a significant social a sudden a sweeping an unexpected a welcome	change

Prepositions and nouns

a change in	attitude(s) policy the law a patient's condition sb's fortunes the weather
a change of	address direction government heart luck mind mood pace plan scene

Unit 3

A Information

Verbs

access broadcast collect compile find gather get give obtain provide publish	information

Adjectives

(in)accurate (un)ambiguous (un)biased (un)clear comprehensive confidential limited misleading (ir)relevant (un)reliable up-to-date useful useless vague	information

B Smell

Verbs

detect get rid of give off leave notice remember	a/the smell (of sth)

smell good/bad

Adjectives to describe smells

acrid
distinct
faint
foul
fresh
mouth-watering
musty
overpowering
(un)pleasant
pungent
rancid
sickly
stale
strong
sweet
unmistakable

Nouns

aroma
fragrance
odour
perfume
scent
smell
stench

C Adjectives to describe methods and ways of doing things

controversial
convenient
(un)conventional
costly
cost-effective
effective
efficient
familiar
frustrating
handy
inexpensive
ingenious
innovative
novel
obsolete
old-fashioned
persuasive
rapid
(un)reliable
subtle
time-saving
traditional
tried and tested
unique
(un)usual

Unit 4

A Body idioms

be written all over one's face
find one's feet
get off on the wrong foot
get out of hand
give sb the cold shoulder
go over sb's head
go weak at the knees
have a good head for business
keep one's ear to the ground
(not) see eye to eye with sb
off the top of one's head
pick sb's brains
point the finger at sb
put sb's nose out of joint
talk about sb behind their back
turn a blind eye to sth

B Time

Verbs

allocate be pressed for devote find free up invest kill manage run out of set/put aside take up waste	time

Adjectives

free/leisure/spare kick-off/injury/half qualifying/winning/record-breaking arrival/departure/flying (off)-peak viewing/prime opening/closing/sale sowing/milking/harvest	time

Other expressions

at a specific/set/predetermined time
in the time allocated/allowed/available
extend/(fail to) meet/miss/set/work to a deadline
take time off work
time is against you
a matter of time
make time for oneself

Unit 5

A Adjectives to describe relationships

business close difficult family formal friendly intimate lasting love-hate personal professional prickly relaxed rocky solid stable strong uneasy working	relationship

B Adjective and noun collocations

heated/furious/fierce/pointless	argument
courting/elderly/married/young	couple
adoptive/extended/immediate/single-parent	family
inner/mixed/negative/strong	feelings
best/close/mutual/school	friend
brotherly/first/true/unrequited	love
family/heightened/rising/social	tension

C Further expressions

call sb names
call sb by their first name
fall for sb
fall out with sb
get on like a house on fire
get on sb's nerves
have it in for sb
keep oneself to oneself
keep in touch with sb
look up to sb
look down on sb
put a great strain on a relationship
put sb down
take after sb
take an instant dislike/liking to sb
take to sb
turn down a proposal of marriage
turn one's back on sb
turn to sb for help/advice
a relationship can turn sour

Unit 6

A Intelligence and ability

Adjectives and nouns

accomplished	dancer/pianist/singer
born	artist/teacher/writer
competent	driver/lawyer/skier
experienced	journalist/manager/professional
expert	cook/gardener/skier
gifted	musician/sportswoman/student
proficient	horsewoman/pilot/typist
promising	(young) athlete/player/student
skilful	card player/diplomat/footballer
skilled	craftsman/technician/worker
strong	swimmer
talented	actor/player/youngster

art/computer/wine expert

be brilliant/good/weak/terrible/hopeless at a subject, a sport or a skill

a brainy/brilliant/bright/gifted child
a whizzkid
a child prodigy

Expressions

be an ace at	solving puzzles/(playing) tennis
be good with your hands	
be a dab hand	at DIY/at painting/with a paintbrush
have a (natural) flair for	languages/design/improvisation
have a (natural) gift for	languages/music/writing
have an ear for	accents/language/music
have an eye for detail	
have a head for figures	
have a nose for a good news story	
have a good/poor memory	

Adverbs and adjectives

academically exceptionally highly intellectually musically naturally	gifted	enormously exceptionally highly hugely outstandingly	talented
highly incredibly remarkably	intelligent	extremely highly very	promising

B Adjectives for reviews

action-packed
atmospheric
clichéd
compelling
credible
disappointing
entertaining
excruciating
exhilarating
fast-moving
gripping
implausible
impressive
innovative
memorable
moving
overhyped
powerful
predictable
sentimental
stunning
tedious
unconvincing

C Comparisons

a considerable/huge/marked/slight difference
a close/remarkable/striking similarity

be common to all/both
be (not) dissimilar from/to
be very much alike
be unlike another thing
bear a close/a striking/a strong/a slight/little/no resemblance to
differ from
one thing compares (un)favourably/well/badly with another
develop along different lines/in a different way from
have a great deal/little/nothing in common with
resemble each other
there is little to choose between them in terms of
there is a world of difference between
there are obvious/striking similarities between
what sets him/her/it apart from others is

D Sleep

Adverbs

sleep	badly fitfully heavily lightly peacefully rough soundly well

Verbs and expressions

be a heavy/light sleeper
be fast asleep
be/feel wide awake
doze off/drop off/nod off
fall asleep
fall into a deep sleep
get a good night's sleep
get to sleep
have/take a nap
have a sleepless night
have an animal put to sleep
keep sb awake
lie/stay awake
lose sleep over sth
my arm/leg went to sleep
send sb to sleep
sleep like a log
sleep on it
sleep through the night
sleep through a storm
snooze
stay up
suffer from insomnia
toss and turn
wake up to the fact that

Unit 7

A Health

Adjectives and nouns

aching	joints/limbs/muscles
blocked	nose
bruised	ribs/thigh
chipped	bone/tooth
dislocated	hip/jaw/shoulder
sprained	ankle/wrist
swollen	glands/feet/lips
torn	muscles/ligaments
upset	stomach

blinding	headache
high/low	blood pressure
high/low/mild	fever
(highly) infectious	disease
medical	complaint
serious	illness

Phrasal verbs

break/come out in a rash
a disease breaks out
sth brings on a heart attack
bring sb round
an illness clears up
carry out tests
come down with an illness
come round
come through a serious illness
come up with a cure/treatment
pain eases off
get over an illness
pass on an illness
pass out
pick up an illness
put one's back/shoulder out
put sth down to sth
the effects of a drug wear off
wear sb out

Other verbs

diagnose sb as having/with (an illness)
fall (seriously) ill with sth
have/undergo an operation (on sth)
prescribe a drug/medicine
relieve pain

B Effect

have a/an: adverse, beneficial, catastrophic, damaging, dramatic, far-reaching, good, harmful, immediate, important, lasting, limited, long-/short-term, minimal, noticeable, side, significant — effect (on sb/sth)

Unit 8

A Amount

a full refund
a good few (hours)
a great deal of sth
a large number of things
a small/no extra charge
an awful lot of sth/things
no limit to sth
precious little (time)
the low/high cost of sth/things

B Verbs with *up, down, over* and *under*

downgrade	overrule	update
download	overthrow	upgrade
downplay	undercut	uphold
downsize	undergo	uproot
overhear	undertake	upstage

C Adjectives with *in, off, on, out* and *over*

inborn	oncoming	overcast
incoming	ongoing	overnight
inland	outdoor	overseas
off-duty	outgoing	
offhand	outlying	

D Plans

Adjectives

audacious, bold, brilliant, clever, controversial, cunning, daring, detailed, devious, elaborate, emergency, impracticable, ingenious, intricate, (un)feasible, (un)viable, (un)workable — plan

Verbs

abandon, announce, carry out, conceive, devise, draw up, jettison, oppose, put forward, reject, reveal, scrap, shelve, unveil — a plan

Unit 9

A Describing an adventure

Adjectives and nouns

arid	desert/island/landscape
exquisite	flowers/views/waterfalls
gruelling	climb/hike/race
idyllic	conditions/setting/spot
intrepid	group/traveller/voyage
swirling	mist/water/wind

Phrasal verbs

kick in
(shots/cries) ring out
run into (sb/a storm/trouble)
set off (on a journey)
set out to do sth
turn out to be
win through

B Anger

Adjectives and nouns

heated	argument/debate/discussion
irate	customer/letter/parent
sudden	outburst of temper

Expressions

become irate
be cross/furious with sb
be seething with anger/indignation/rage
blow a fuse
blow one's top
calm down
fly into a rage
get worked up about sth
go berserk/mad
let off steam
lose one's temper
maintain one's composure
make one's blood boil
scream blue murder
shake one's fist
stamp one's feet
throw a (temper) tantrum

C Criticism

arouse, attract, be impervious to, be unmoved by, be upset by, come in for/under/up against, draw, express, give rise to, ignore, meet with, overcome, respond to, voice — criticism

considerable, constructive, fierce, growing, mounting, severe, strong, unjust, valid, widespread — criticism

Unit 10

A Describing rooms and houses

Adjectives

bright and cheerful
cramped and cluttered
dark and dingy
light and airy
neat and tidy
spic(k) and span
warm and cosy

colourful
dull
elegant
gaudy
roomy
spacious
tasteful
tasteless
twee

Adverbs

badly/newly/poorly/solidly	built
lavishly/newly/richly/tastefully	decorated
comfortably/elegantly/simply/sparsely	furnished
brightly/dimly/poorly/softly	lit
centrally/conveniently/ideally/pleasantly	situated/located

B Noise and sound

Voice, sound and noise

booming, deep, hesitant, high-pitched, hoarse, hushed, loud, low, monotonous, rough, shrill, squeaky	voice
lose, lower, raise, shout at the top of	your voice
buzzing, crashing, creaking, distant, distinctive, faint, muffled, rumbling, rustling, unmistakable	sound
detect, emit, make, produce, utter	a sound
background, banging, constant, continuous, excessive, incessant, loud, traffic	noise
noise	dies down, fades away, grows, increases, reverberates

Other noises

deafening	applause/cheer/explosion music/roar/silence
piercing	cry/scream/shriek/whistle
rowdy	behaviour/crowd/fans/party
bells	chime/ring/tinkle
doors	slam shut/click shut/creak open
dogs	bark/growl/whimper/whine

music/a radio/a television blares out

Unit 11

Sight

give sb a/an angry/blank/cold/knowing	look
take a/an close/critical/fascinating/in-depth	look
a/an familiar/impressive/rare/welcome	sight
a breathtaking/spectacular/superb	view
have blurred/double/poor/twenty-twenty	vision
a/an clear/idealistic/realistic/terrifying	vision
high/good/reduced/low/poor	visibility

be hidden from view
be (in)visible to/with the naked eye
catch a glimpse of sb/sth
catch one's eye
catch sight of sb/sth
come into view
have/take a look at sth
keep one's eye on sb/sth
keep one's eyes open
keep out of sight
lose sight of sb/sth

at first sight/glance
in full view of sb
in the public eye
in sight/view
on view/show/display

Read and write

a/an good/excellent/exciting	read
a/an avid/fast/slow/voracious	reader
a freelance/prolific/struggling/talented	writer
distinctive/familiar/legible/neat	handwriting

read	aloud/avidly/voraciously/widely
write	clearly/legibly/neatly/in rough/in plain language

put sth (down) in writing
read sth out
read too much into sth
read up on sth
write a debt off
write off to sb for sth
write notes up
write out a cheque for (an amount)
write sth into a contract or law

Unit 12

A Expressions and phrases with *work*

administrative / casual / charity / conservation / construction / consultancy / freelance / social / voluntary — work

work — environment / experience / incentive / permit / schedule

be all in a day's work
do all the donkey work
do sb's dirty work
do some groundwork
have a good working knowledge of sth
have a vigorous workout
keep sth in good working order
work around the clock
work like a dog
work on one's (presentation, telephone, etc) skills

B Attitude adverbials

amazingly
apparently
astonishingly
(un)believably
clearly
conveniently
curiously
disappointingly
disturbingly
evidently
(un)fortunately
funnily
happily
indisputably
inevitably
interestingly
ironically
laughably
luckily
miraculously
naturally
obviously
personally
predictably
presumably
reassuringly
regrettably
ridiculously
rightly
sadly
sensibly
strangely
(not) surprisingly
understandably
undoubtedly
unexpectedly
unmistakably
(un)wisely
worryingly

Unit 13

A Eating and drinking

Verbs

eat/drink up
finish off
gulp (down)
munch
nibble
pick at
polish off
sip
swallow
swig
wolf down

Adjectives and nouns

favourite/side dish
celebratory/soft drink
big/fussy eater
ready/square meal
raging thirst

Further expressions

be famished/peckish/full up
I could eat a horse
do sth on a full/an empty stomach
eat into one's time/money
eat like a bird
eat one's words
eat sb out of house and home
feel faint with hunger
hardly touch one's food
have a sweet tooth
have sb eating out of your hand
lose one's appetite
quench one's thirst
satisfy one's hunger
work up an appetite

B Deception

Collocations

appearances can be deceptive
fraudulent claims/practices/trading
misleading impression/information/statement

deceptively easy/simple/straightforward
fraudulently obtain/use
misleadingly referred to as/termed/called

credit card/electoral/tax fraud

Verbs

be fooled/deceived/tricked by sb
cheat at sth
deceive sb into doing sth
fall for (a trick)
see through sb's lies/promises
swindle sb out of sth
take sb for a ride
take sb in
tell a lie
trick sb into doing sth
trick sb out of sth

C Intensifiers

acutely	aware/conscious/embarrassed/sensitive
bitterly	cold/disappointing/opposed/resentful
deeply	committed/concerned/moving/suspicious
desperately	disappointed/keen/lonely/worried
entirely	different/free of charge/new/wrong
fully	aware/booked/clothed/equipped/justified
highly	gifted/influential/promising/talented
hugely	expensive/popular/successful/talented
perfectly	acceptable/capable/clear/good/normal/safe
seriously	affected/ill/injured
totally	different/(in)dependent/unexpected/unnecessary
utterly	disgraceful/exhausted/opposed/ridiculous
wholly	inadequate/inappropriate/unacceptable/unexpected

Unit 14

Money

counterfeit / housekeeping / pocket / prize / ransom / redundancy / sponsorship — money

pay for sth — in advance / in arrears / in cash / in full / in instalments / on expenses

buy sth — at auction / in the sales / on credit / on hire purchase / on impulse

borrow	heavily
pay	generously/handsomely
save	carefully/hard
spend	extravagantly/freely/wisely
invest	foolishly/heavily/wisely

borrow	an idea/a phrase/a word
pay	attention/a compliment/one's respects/tribute
save	effort/energy/time
lend	assistance/credibility/support/weight
owe sb	an apology/an explanation/a favour

Grammar reference

Unit 1

Modal verbs 1: *might, could, may* and *can*

1 ***might, could*** and ***may*** can be used to express present, future and past possibility:
Try the shop on the corner – they ***might have*** *what you're looking for.*
Economists warn that house prices ***could rise*** *even further next year.*
She ***may not have received*** *your letter yet.*

The addition of *well* after the modal verb expresses more probability.
Take an umbrella – it ***may/could/might well rain*** *later on.*

2 ***might*** and ***could*** can be used to express:
- past possibility which did not happen
  We ***could have won*** *the game, but Joe missed a penalty.*
  It's a good thing I was wearing a crash helmet. I ***might have been*** *seriously* ***injured****.*
- annoyance
  You ***could at least say*** *you're sorry!*
  He ***might have told*** *me he was going to be late!*

3 ***might*** and ***may*** can be used to:
- express concession
  He ***might have failed*** *his degree, but he's earning much more than me.*
  (= Although he failed his degree, he's earning much more than me.)
  She ***may be*** *very famous, but that doesn't give her the right to behave like that in public.*
- suggest what one should do when there is no better alternative
  I might as well go *shopping with my parents – I've got nothing else to do.*
  You'll find out the truth sooner or later, so I ***may as well tell*** *you now what happened.*

4 ***can*** and ***may*** (more formal) can be used to:
- give or refuse permission
  You ***may/can borrow*** *up to three DVDs at any one time from the library.*
  You ***can't/may not go*** *until you have finished.*
- make offers
  May I be *of assistance?*
  Can I carry *that for you?*

5 ***can*** and ***could*** can be used to:
- make requests
  Can/Could you give *me a hand, please?*
- ask for permission
  Can/Could I open *the window?*

The more formal *may* can also be used.
May I ask *a personal question?*

6 ***can*** and ***could***, in the negative form, can be used to express certainty:
She ***can't be*** *more than about 20 years old.*
It ***couldn't have been*** *a bear that we saw – it was far too small.*

7 ***can*** can be used to express:
- theoretical possibility
  The new concert hall ***can seat*** *over 3000 people.*
- ability or inability
  I can understand *some Italian, but I* ***can't speak*** *it very well.*
- criticism
  She ***can say*** *some very hurtful things sometimes.*

8 ***could*** can be used to express:
- ability or inability in the past
  My late grandfather ***could play*** *the banjo, but he* ***couldn't sing*** *very well.*

When we talk about ability to do something on one occasion in the past, *could* is not possible. Instead, *was/were able to, managed to* or *succeeded in* have to be used.
I managed to speak *to Frank last night, but I* ***couldn't persuade*** *him to come to the opera with us.*
- permission or prohibition in the past
  When I was at school the boys ***couldn't wear*** *earrings, but the girls* ***could****.*

When we talk about permission to do something on one occasion in the past, *be allowed to* has to be used.
I was allowed to leave *work early yesterday to go and meet my husband at the airport.*

Unit 2

Talking about the past

1 Past simple
The past simple can be used to refer to:
- completed actions, events or situations which happened at a specific time or over a specific period of time in the past
  I sold *my car about three months ago.*
  When we ***lived*** *in York, my father* ***ran*** *a small bakery.*
- habitual actions or behaviour in the past
  Did you bite *your nails when you were a child?*
  When I was a teenager, my mum ***got*** *really angry if I* ***didn't tidy*** *my bedroom.*

Used to + infinitive can also be used to refer to past situations and habitual actions. *Would* + infinitive can be used to refer to past habitual actions, but not situations.
Every summer we ***used to/would go*** *to Scotland to visit my grandmother.*
I used to *(not would)* ***have*** *a parrot, but he escaped.*

2 Past continuous
The past continuous can be used to refer to:
- situations or actions in progress at a particular moment in the past
  This time last year I ***was taking*** *the Advanced exam.*
- a past situation or action which was in progress when another action occurred
  We ***were*** *still* ***having*** *breakfast when Mark and Marian called round.*
- past actions or situations occurring at the same time
  She ***was working*** *hard to earn some extra money and he* ***was spending*** *it all on new gadgets.*
- repeated past actions, which the speaker finds annoying
  She ***was*** *always* ***complaining*** *about something.*

3 Present perfect
The present perfect links past events and situations with the present.

A The present perfect simple can be used:
- to talk about recent past events which have some relevance to the present
  *They can't afford to go on holiday – they'****ve just bought*** *a new car.*
- to describe situations which started in the past and continue to the present
  *We'****ve had*** *these saucepans since we got married 43 years ago.*
- to talk about events which occurred at some time between the past and present. The exact time they occurred is either unknown or unimportant.
  I've *already* ***seen*** *United play three times this season.*

- after the expression *this/that/it is the first/second/third,* etc *time ...*
  This is the fourth time ***I've seen*** *United play this season.*
- after the expression *it's (two/three,* etc*) years/a long time since ...* The past simple is also possible.
  It's years since ***I've had/I had*** *bacon for breakfast.*
- with another present perfect to describe two states or actions which have existed or occurred together.
  *We****'ve been burgled*** *twice since we****'ve lived*** *here.*

B The present perfect continuous is used with verbs which describe actions (e.g. *give, play, take*), but not with verbs which describe states (e.g. *be, know, like*). It can be used to:
- emphasize the duration of a situation or activity
  *He****'s been working*** *on his first novel for over ten years.*
- suggest that a situation or activity is temporary
  My kitchen's being redecorated so ***I've been eating*** *at my mum's.*
- suggest that a situation or activity is incomplete
  I've been reading *that book you lent me – I think I know how it's going to end.*
- focus on the repetition of a situation or activity. The number of times it is repeated can only be included with the simple, not the continuous form.
  *Someone****'s been phoning*** *you.*
  *She****'s phoned*** *about six or seven times this morning.*

C Both simple and continuous forms of the present perfect can be used to talk about the present effects of a past event.
I'm exhausted! ***I've been cleaning*** *the house all morning.* (an activity)
*Sally can't drive for a while; she****'s broken*** *her leg.* (a single action)

4 Past perfect

A The past perfect simple can be used:
- to show that a past event or situation occurred before another past event or situation
  As soon as the film started, I realized I ***had seen*** *it before.*
- to describe situations which started in the past and continued to a later point in the past
  They ***had known*** *each other for several years before they got married.*
- after *that/it was the first/second/third,* etc *time ...*
  *We went to Switzerland last summer; it was only the second time we****'d been*** *abroad.*
- after *it was (two/three,* etc*) years/a long time since ...*
  It was a long time since she ***had*** *last* ***seen*** *her old school friend.*
- after certain time linkers, e.g. *after, before, by the time, as soon as, once, when, until*
  It was dark by the time I ***had finished*** *repairing the roof.*

The past simple can be used if the order of events is clear:
I had a relaxing bath after I ***got*** *home from work last night.*
or if the second event occurred as a result of the first.
When the music ***started****, everyone got up to dance.*

Participle clauses can sometimes be used in place of clauses with *when* or *after* and the past perfect.
Having eaten *his sandwich, he put his coat on and left.*
(*= After he* ***had eaten*** *his sandwich, he put his coat on and left.*)
For more information on participle clauses, see Unit 10 on page 222.

B The past perfect continuous can be used in similar ways to the present perfect continuous, but instead of linking past events and situations with the present, it links them with another point in the past. It is not used with stative verbs (e.g. *be, know, like*).
I'd been waiting *for over an hour when she finally arrived.* (duration)
She found out that her son ***had been using*** *her credit card to buy computer games.* (repetition)
*You only had to smell his breath to know he****'d been smoking****.* (effects of a past event)

5 Unfulfilled past events

The following structures can be used to talk about events which were intended to take place, but which did not happen.

I was going to send *you an email, but I had a few problems with my computer.*
I was about to call *the doctor, but then the pain suddenly disappeared.*
She ***had been/was thinking of going*** *to Iceland, but changed her mind and went to Norway, instead.*
The meeting, which ***was to have taken*** *place last weekend, was unexpectedly cancelled.*

6 Expressing preferences about the past

The following structures can be used to express how we would like the past to have been different.
- *would like/love/prefer to* + perfect infinitive, or *would have liked/loved/preferred to* + infinitive or perfect infinitive
  We ***would like to have stayed*** *longer, but we had to catch the train.*
  She ***would have loved to tell/to have told*** *him what she thought of him.*

If the subject of *would like,* etc is not the same as the subject of the verb which follows, an appropriate noun or object pronoun is inserted before the infinitive.
She would have preferred him to say *it to her face, rather than put it in a letter.*
- *would rather/sooner* + perfect infinitive
  We stayed in a hotel, but ***I'd sooner have slept*** *in a tent.*

If the subject of *would rather/sooner* is not the same as the subject of the verb which follows, the past perfect is used.
Would you rather I hadn't said *anything about it to Matt?*

For information on using *wish/if only* and conditional sentences to describe imaginary situations in the past, see section **A** in Unit 3 below.

Unit 3

Hypothetical situations and conditionals

Past tenses can be used to talk about unlikely, imaginary or impossible situations in the present, past or future.

A Past situations

- *wish/if only* + past perfect can be used to express wishes, regrets and criticisms about the past
  I wish I hadn't eaten *my dinner so quickly. I've got indigestion now.*
  If only you had listened *to my advice. You wouldn't be in this mess.*
- *should* + perfect infinitive can also be used to express regrets and criticisms about the past
  We ***should have brought*** *an umbrella. We're going to get soaking wet now.*
  You ***shouldn't have spoken*** *to him like that. I'm not surprised he's upset.*
- Third conditional sentences (*if* + past perfect, *would/might/could* + perfect infinitive) can be used to speculate about how things might have been different in the past
  If *you* ***had been paying*** *attention, you* ***might have understood*** *what I was saying.*
  (= You weren't paying attention, so you didn't understand.)
  If it hadn't been for *that traffic jam on the motorway, we* ***would have got*** *here on time.*
  (= Because of the traffic jam we arrived late.)

A more formal variation is to omit *if* and begin with *Had*:
***Had she known** about his criminal past, she **would never have employed** him.*

- Mixed conditional sentences can be used to speculate about how a different situation in the past might have had different results in the present
  *If you **hadn't stayed** up to watch the film last night, you **wouldn't be** so tired now.*

or, alternatively, how changes to a present situation might have influenced the past
*If I **weren't** so broke at the moment, I **could have bought** you something decent for your birthday.*
The past simple is used in this last sentence to describe an unreal, or imaginary, situation in the present. The past simple can also be used in conditional sentences to describe real situations in the past:
*If I **arrived** late at the office, my boss used to get really angry.* (*If = Whenever*)

For information on *would like/love/prefer* and *would rather/sooner*, see section **6** in Unit 2 on page 216.

B Present and future situations: conditionals

1 Zero conditional: *if* + present simple, present simple
- We use the zero conditional to talk about situations which are always true
  *If I **eat** too much spicy food, I start to feel ill.*

2 First conditional: *if* + present simple, *will/going to/may/might/could* + infinitive
- We use the first conditional to talk about possible future situations and their probable results
  *If you **don't water** that plant soon, it'**ll die**.*
- *if + should/happen to/should happen to* makes the event seem more unlikely or more of a chance possibility
  *If I **happen to see** Mr Dee there, I'**ll ask** him for you.*
  *If you **should happen to miss** the train, I **could drive** you there myself.*
- A more formal variation is to begin with *Should*
  ***Should** you wish to change your holiday arrangements, we will do all we can to help.*

3 Second conditional: *if* + past simple, *would/might/could* + infinitive
- We use the second conditional to talk about imaginary, unlikely or impossible situations in the present and future
  *If I **had** an extra pair of hands, then I **could help** you!*
  *I **might work** harder **if** they **paid** me more.*
  ***If it weren't for** my savings, I **wouldn't be** able to survive.* (= Thanks to my savings I can survive.)
- *if + were to* + infinitive makes the event seem more unlikely
  *If you **were to walk** in that direction for another thousand miles, you'**d** eventually **arrive** in Warsaw.*
- A more formal variation is to begin with *Were*
  ***Were** they to break the contract, we would, of course, take legal action.*
- *Suppose/Supposing/Imagine* can be used instead of *if*, particularly in speech
  ***Supposing** you ran out of money, what would you do?*
  ***Imagine** you lost your job. Do you think you'd be able to find another?*

4 *if* can sometimes be followed by *will, would* or *going to*, for example when making polite requests or describing the result of a course of action.
*If you **would take** a seat for a moment, **I'll tell** Mr Graydon you're here.*
*If it **is going to be** more profitable for the company, then I think we should do it.*

Unit 4

Punctuation

1 Commas

- Commas are normally used after subordinate clauses when these come first in a sentence.
  ***If I have any problems,** I'll let you know.*
  They are not normally used when the subordinate clause follows the main clause.
  *We'll phone you **as soon as we get there**.*
- Commas are used after linking adverbials at the beginning of a sentence (see Unit 12).
  ***Meanwhile,** darkness began to fall.*
  ***For this reason,** I have decided to resign.*
  They are also used before adverbials if these are inserted in the sentence.
  *The workers**, however,** have refused to accept the offer.*
- Commas are used to separate items in a list or series. They are not normally used between the last two items.
  She got up, had a shower, got dressed and went out.
- Commas are used with non-identifying relative clauses but **not** with identifying relative clauses (see Unit 5).
  *My father**, who is a lawyer,** advised me on the legal matters.*
  *The man **who bought our house** is a lawyer.*
- Commas are used to separate direct speech from the reporting verb.
  'Empty your bag,' he said. She replied, 'It's already empty.'
  They are not used before *that, if, where*, etc in reported speech.
  She replied that it was already empty.

2 Apostrophes

Apostrophes are used:
- to indicate where letters have been omitted from contracted forms
  *I **don't** think **it's** fair.*
- to indicate possession
  *the **boss's** office*　　*my **parents'** house*
  *the **children's** books*

Apostrophes are **not** used with possessive pronouns or adjectives.
***Yours** is here.*　　***Its** tail is white.*

3 Semicolons

Semicolons can be used:
- in place of full stops where two sentences are closely related in meaning
  Some storks fly south in winter; others stay put, using local rubbish dumps as their food source.
- to separate items in a list, particularly long or grammatically complex ones
  There were several reasons why Jeremy chose not to go abroad on holiday: he had an acute fear of flying (even though he had never flown before); long periods of exposure to the sun brought him out in a rash; he was suspicious of any food which was not 'good home cooking'; ...

4 Colons

Colons can be used:
- before explanations
  We moved to a different area: the noise from the traffic was becoming unbearable.
- to introduce a list
  The park boasts several different species of trees: oak, ash, elm, beech, alder and a wide variety of conifers.

5 Dashes

Dashes are used in informal writing:
- in place of a colon
  We've bought a new car – the old one kept breaking down.
- to create a pause in order to emphasize what follows
  I took my driving test yesterday – and I passed!

Gerunds and infinitives

A The infinitive with *to* is used:

- to express purpose
  I went out ***to get*** *some fresh air.*
- after some adjectives
  It's not ***easy to find*** *work these days.*
- after the verb *to be,* to give orders or to express an arrangement
  *You****'re to stay*** *here until I get back.*
  The President ***is to visit*** *Poland next month.*
- after *would hate/like/love/prefer,* with or without an object
  Would you like me to do *it now?*
- after the following verbs
  agree, appear, arrange, ask, attempt, choose, decide, demand, deserve, expect, help, hesitate, hope, learn, manage, offer, prepare, pretend, refuse, seem, threaten

  If you need any help, don't ***hesitate to contact*** *me.*
- after the following verbs + object
  advise, allow, ask, challenge, enable, encourage, expect, force, get, help, intend, invite, order, persuade, recommend, remind, teach, tell, urge, warn

  My family ***encouraged me to go*** *to university.*

  If *advise* and *recommend* are used without an object, the gerund is used.
  I ***recommended her to apply*** *to King's College.*
  I ***recommended applying*** *to King's College.*
- after the following nouns
  ability, attempt, capacity, chance, decision, desire, determination, effort, failure, intention, need, opportunity, permission, plan, proposal, refusal, right, tendency, way, willingness

  It was the director's ***refusal to accept*** *his proposals that led to his* ***decision to resign****.*

B The bare infinitive (without *to*) is used:

- after modal verbs
  I ***shouldn't eat*** *this really, but I* ***can't resist*** *it.*
- after the following verbs
  had better, help, let, make, would rather/sooner

*We****'d better go*** *home now – it's very late.*
Can you ***help me tidy*** *up, please?*

In the passive, *make* is followed by the infinitive with *to.*
We ***were made to do*** *all the dirty jobs.*

C The gerund is used:

- as the subject, object or complement of a clause or sentence
  Playing *golf helps me relax, but I find* ***watching*** *it on television rather boring.*
- after prepositions
  We thought ***about going*** *to France this year.*
- after the following expressions
  have difficulty/problems, there's no/little point, it's no good/use, it's (not) worth

  It's no use asking *him – he won't know the answer.*
- after the following verbs
  admit, adore, advise, anticipate, appreciate, avoid, can't help, can't stand, consider, delay, deny, detest, dislike, dread, enjoy, feel like, give up, imagine, involve, keep, (don't) mind, miss, postpone, practise, prevent, propose, put off, recommend, resent, resist, risk, suggest

  I ***resent having*** *to do all the housework myself.*
- after the following verbs + the preposition *to*
  adapt/adjust to, admit to, confess to, get round to, get used to, look forward to, object to

  She ***confessed to being*** *surprised by her success.*

Where the subjects of the main verb and the gerund are different, an object (pronoun) or possessive adjective is used.

I couldn't ***imagine him eating*** *something like this.*
We ***appreciate your coming*** *to tell us so quickly.*

D The following verbs can be followed by the gerund or the infinitive with *to* with no change in meaning:
begin, can't bear, continue, hate, intend, like, love, prefer, start

She suddenly ***started singing/to sing****.*

The infinitive is common for specific situations. Compare the following sentences:
I ***hate to say*** *this, but your breath smells.*
I ***hate getting up*** *early every morning.*

E The following verbs can be followed by the gerund or the infinitive with *to,* but with a change in meaning:
forget, mean, regret, remember, stop, try

- The infinitive is used with *remember, forget, regret* and *stop* when the act of *remembering*, etc comes first. The gerund is used when it comes second.
  I must ***remember to post*** *this letter later.*
  I distinctly ***remember posting*** *the letter yesterday.*
  Her car broke down and no one ***stopped to help*** *her.*
  I've ***stopped eating*** *chocolate.*

When *regret* is followed by the infinitive with *to*, it is normally used with verbs such as *say, tell* and *inform*. This use is formal.
We ***regret to inform*** *you that your application has been unsuccessful.*

- *try* + infinitive with *to* means *attempt. try* + gerund means *experiment with*.
  Please be quiet – I'm ***trying to sleep****.*
  If you can't sleep, ***try using*** *earplugs.*
- *mean* + infinitive with *to* means *intend. mean* + gerund means *involve*.
  I've been ***meaning to write*** *to you for ages.*
  Changing jobs also ***meant changing*** *house.*

Unit 5

Reference

1 *This, that, these* and *those* can be used to refer back to previously stated people, things, events or ideas. *This* and *these* are more common than *that* and *those*.

This and *that* can be used:

- before nouns or on their own
  … and he left school at 16. ***This (decision)*** *did not please his parents.*
  He hated school. ***That****'s why he left at 16.*

These and *those* are more commonly used before nouns.

- *… the mobile phone and the computer.* ***These two inventions*** *have revolutionized communications …*
  … during the 1930s. In ***those days****, of course, people didn't have computers.*
  You've got so many toys. Let's get rid of ***those*** *that you don't play with anymore.*

2 A number of other words can be used to substitute and avoid repetition of previously used words and phrases.

- *do/does/did* to replace a verb
  Paul didn't want to go, but I ***did****.* (= I wanted to go.)
- *do so* can also be used to replace a verb + object
  He told her to lock the door, but she had already ***done so****.*
- *so/nor/neither* + auxiliary verb + subject
  She likes dogs and ***so do I****.* (= I like dogs, too.)
  I've never been to Paris and ***nor/neither has he****.* (= He hasn't been to Paris either.)
- *so/not* to replace a *that*-clause after *expect, hope, seem, suppose, think*
  'Is he coming?' 'I ***think so****.'* (= I think that he's coming.)
  'Do you think it'll rain?' 'I ***hope not****.'* (= I hope that it won't rain.)

Note that *I don't think so* is more common than *I think not*.

- *if not/so* to replace whole clauses
  *Are you free on Friday? **If so**, do you fancy going to the cinema? **If not**, how about next week?*
- *one/ones* to replace countable nouns
  *What sort of **ice cream** would you like? **A plain one** or **one with chocolate sauce** on?*
  *Those red **apples** are much tastier than **these green ones**.*

Ellipsis

Ellipsis involves omitting words to avoid repetition.

1 It is common to omit words after *and* and *but*.
*I live and (**I**) work in Madrid.*
*John was impressed, but I wasn't (**impressed**).*
*We play tennis on Saturdays and (**we**) sometimes (**play**) on Sundays, too.*

2 The main verb can be omitted after an auxiliary verb.
*I'd do it myself if I **could**.* (= if I could do it myself)
*She said she would phone, but she **hasn't**.*
*He said he saw her there, but he **can't have**.*

Adverbs can be placed before the auxiliary.
*'Can you turn the heating on?' 'I **already have**.'*

be cannot be omitted after a modal verb.
*'Is the shop open yet?' 'It **might be**.'*

been can be omitted in a perfect passive, except after a modal verb.
*'Has she been promoted?' 'Yes, she **has**.'*
*He wasn't sent to prison, but he **should have been**.*

3 Instead of repeating a full infinitive expression we can simply use *to*.
*I don't **eat much cheese** now, but I **used to**.*

Relative clauses

A Defining relative clauses

These contain essential information which identifies the person or thing being talked about. *Who* and *which* can be replaced by *that*, and the relative pronoun can be omitted if it is the object of the verb in the relative clause. No commas are required at the beginning or end of the relative clause.

*The woman **who/that** used to babysit for us has just got married.*
*It's not the kind of novel **which/that** appeals to me.*
*I know a boy **whose** father is a professional diver.*
*Just a quick note to thank you for the flowers (**which/that**) you sent me.*

When and *why* can also be omitted in defining relative clauses.
*I'll never forget the day (**when**) Geoff resigned.*
*The reason (**why**) he left is still unclear.*

Where cannot be omitted. Compare the following:
*That's the shop **where** we bought our bed.*
*That's the shop (**which/that**) we bought our bed in.*

In more formal English, prepositions can be placed before the relative pronouns *whom* and *which* (but not *that*).
*They returned to the shop **in which** the bed had been purchased.*

B Non-defining relative clauses

These contain non-essential information: we can identify which person or thing is being talked about without the information in the relative clause. *That* cannot be used and the relative pronoun cannot be omitted. Commas are required at the beginning and the end of the relative clause (except when the end of the relative clause is also the end of the sentence).

*Our former babysitter, **who** got married last year, has just had her first child.*
*His first novel, **which** was largely autobiographical, became an overnight success.*
*Alan Smith, **whose** father is a professional diver, is the only boy in our class who can't swim.*

Which is used in non-defining relative clauses to refer to a whole clause.
*He works 12 hours a day, **which** must be very tiring.*

What is **not** used to refer to a whole clause. It means 'the thing that'.
*Let me know **what** you decide to do.*
***What** I need right now is a cup of tea.* (see Unit 9)

Unit 6

Passives

A Form

The passive is formed with the appropriate tense or form of the verb *to be* and the past participle of the main verb:

*We should **have been told** earlier.*
*A full investigation **is** currently **being carried out**.*

The passive cannot be used with intransitive verbs.
The rabbit was disappeared by the magician. ✗

B Use

The passive is used to focus attention on the action or the person or thing affected by the action, rather than on the agent, the person or thing that performs the action.

Smith was jailed for three years.

If the agent is mentioned, the preposition *by* is used:

*The President was criticized **by members of his own party**.*

The choice between active and passive is often influenced by context. 'Given' or previously mentioned information usually comes at the beginning of a clause or sentence and new information towards the end. In the following example, *The letter* is 'given' information: it is referred to in the previous sentence (*Albert Einstein wrote to President Franklin Roosevelt*). Since it is not the agent of the verb *'compose'*, the passive form is necessarily used.

*In 1939 Albert Einstein wrote to President Franklin Roosevelt, urging the United States to develop an atomic bomb. **The letter was composed** by the Hungarian-born physicist and biophysicist Leo Szilard, a former colleague of Einstein, who felt it would have more influence if it were signed by his eminent friend.*

There is also a tendency to place long phrases towards the end of the clause. If, as in the above example, the agent is a long phrase (*the Hungarian-born physicist*, etc) this appears at the end of the clause and the passive form is necessarily used. Also:

*The meeting was attended **by representatives of the five permanent members of the UN Security Council.***

C Not mentioning the agent

The agent is not usually mentioned in passive constructions:

- if the agent is unknown or unimportant
  *Lunch **will be served** from one o'clock in the canteen.*
- if it is obvious who the agent is
  *The musician **was arrested** at his home on Friday.*
- if the agent is 'people in general'
  *The passive **is not used** with intransitive verbs.*
- to avoid the use of 'you' in official notices
  *Unsold tickets **must be returned** by 16th August.*

D Further passive constructions

1 The infinitive or perfect infinitive with *to* can be used with certain verbs to give generalized opinions or facts. Verbs used in this way include: *allege, believe, consider, estimate, expect, know, report, say, think, understand*, as well as *be rumoured* and *be reputed*.
*She **is expected to make** a statement later today.*
*He **is rumoured to have sold** it for a six-figure sum.*
*A million people **were estimated to have taken** part in the demonstration.*

2 *have* + object + past participle can be used to show that the subject arranges for the action to be done by someone else. *Get* is a more informal alternative to *have*. Compare:
I'm going to develop the photos myself.
*I'm going to **have/get the photos developed** at the shop on the corner.*

The same structure can be used for events which are outside the speaker's control.
*I **had my passport stolen** on holiday.*

3 *get* can also be used as an informal alternative to *be* in passive sentences.
*We **got knocked out** of the Cup in the first round.*

It is commonly used with the following past participles: *burnt, caught, dressed, hurt, involved, left, lost, stuck*

*She **got caught** shoplifting.*
*Do as I say and no one will **get hurt**.*

Unit 7

Reported speech

A Changes

Some words and features of grammar used in direct speech may have to be changed in reported speech.

1 Tense changes
- Present tenses change to past; present perfect and past tenses change to past perfect.

'I'm having a great time,' said Paul.
*Paul said he **was having** a great time.*

'I've never ridden a horse,' said Clare.
*Clare said she **had** never **ridden** a horse.*

'We were trying to phone you,' she said.
*She said they **had been trying** to phone us.*

- The modal verbs *will, must, may* and *can* change to *would, had to, might* and *could*.
Would, might, could, should and *ought to* do not change, nor does *must* when it is used for deductions.

'It must be done by tomorrow,' she said.
*She told me it **had to be done** by the following day.*

'It must be raining,' she said.
*She said it **must be raining**.*

2 Other changes
Pronouns and certain words indicating time and place may have to change when we use reported speech.
*'**I** saw **you here yesterday**,' said Alan.*
*Alan said **he** had seen **me there the day before**.*

3 Tense changes are not necessary:
- if the statement being reported is still true
'I intend to retire next year,' he said.
He told me he intends to retire next year.
- if the reporting verb is in the present or present perfect
'We are going to get married.'
They have announced that they are going to get married.

'I never tell lies.'
She says she never tells lies.

4 When questions are reported:
- auxiliary verbs *do, does* and *did* are not used
- the word order is the same as for statements
- *yes/no* questions are reported with *if* or *whether*
- question marks are not used

'Where's Paul?' *He asked where Paul is/was.*
'Did you enjoy it?' *She asked if I (had) enjoyed it.*

B Verb patterns

Several different verb patterns can be used in reported speech. Some reporting verbs can be used with more than one verb pattern. For example:

*He **asked to leave**.*
*He **asked them to leave**.*
*He **asked that they should leave**.* (Formal)

1 verb + *that* clause
e.g. *add, admit, announce, assure, claim, complain, concede, conclude, confirm, emphasize, estimate, explain, mention, point out, predict, reassure, remark, remind, repeat, say, state, stress, tell, warn*
Note that *assure, reassure, remind* and *tell* are followed by an object.

*Critics **predicted that the film would be** a success.*
*My daughter **reminded me that I had promised** to take her to the zoo on her birthday.*

2 verb + *(that) sb (should) do sth/sth (should) happen*
e.g. *advise, agree, ask, demand, insist, propose, recommend, request, suggest*

*They **demanded that** he **should resign**.*
*We **suggested he apply** for the job.*

3 verb + infinitive with *to*
e.g. *agree, ask, claim, demand, offer, promise, refuse, threaten*

*He **claimed to be** an expert on ghosts.*

4 verb + object + infinitive with *to*
e.g. *advise, ask, beg, convince, encourage, forbid, instruct, invite, order, persuade, recommend, remind, tell, urge, warn*

*She **urged him not to** get involved.*

5 verb + gerund
e.g. *admit, advise, deny, recommend, regret, suggest*

*He **denied taking/having taken** the money.*

6 verb + preposition + gerund
e.g. *advise, argue, protest, warn* ***against***
apologize, blame, forgive, praise, tell off, thank ***for***
discourage, dissuade ***from***
accuse, speak ***of***
congratulate, insist ***on***
admit, confess, consent, object ***to***

*She **admitted to feeling** rather nervous.*
*He **told me off for singing**!*
*I **insisted on his/him wearing** a suit.*

7 Some reporting verbs can be used in the passive after *it*. This structure can be used if the speaker does not wish to take responsibility for a statement or is reporting the views of others. Verbs include: *announce, believe, claim, confirm, estimate, rumour, suggest* and *think*.
***It is thought that** she may have left the country.*
***It has been suggested that** the minister took bribes.*

Unit 8

Determiners and pronouns

A Determiners

1 The following words are determiners: they come before nouns and can be used to indicate which thing(s) you are referring to, or to talk about quantities and amounts.

all, another, any, both, each, either, enough, every, (a) few, fewer, less, a lot of, (a) little, many, more, most, much, neither, no, one, other, several, some, this, that, these, those

2 Determiners can be used:
- before singular countable nouns
  e.g. *another, any, each, either, every, neither, no, one, some, this, that*

Can I have ***another*** *sandwich, please?*

Either and *neither* are used to talk about two things. *Each* is used to talk about two or more things; *every* is only used to talk about more than two. All four determiners are followed by a singular verb.

It's an exciting final, which ***neither player*** *deserves to lose.*

Each/Every *song sounds the same.*
- before plural nouns
  e.g. *all, any, both, enough, (a) few, fewer, a lot of, many, more, most, no, other, several, some, these, those*

We haven't got ***enough*** *eggs to make an omelette.*

Few means 'not many' or 'not as many as desired or expected'. *Very* can be used before *few* to emphasize it.
There are ***very few*** *apples left. We need to buy some.*

A few means 'some' or 'more than expected'.
We've still got ***a few*** *eggs – enough to make an omelette.*

Quite can be used with *a few* to mean *a fairly large number.*
We've got ***quite a few*** *kiwis – we need to eat them before they go rotten.*
- before uncountable nouns
  e.g. *all, any, enough, less, (a) little, a lot of, more, most, much, no, some, this, that*

He's nearly bald – he's got ***very little*** *hair left.*

Some can be used to mean 'approximately' or 'a large amount':
I was waiting for ***some two hours*** *– that's quite* ***some time****.*

3 Sometimes more than one determiner can be used before a noun.
every few/five days *every other week* *another few drinks*
no other town/books *many more/other ways*
these few examples

B Pronouns

1 Most of the determiners above can also be used as pronouns. Pronouns are used instead of nouns. *Every, no* and *other* cannot be used as pronouns: *each* is used instead of *every*, *none* instead of *no*, and *others* instead of *other. A lot of* becomes *a lot* as a pronoun.

Bad reviews are better than ***no*** *reviews.* (Determiner)
Bad reviews are better than ***none****.* (Pronoun)

2 Pronouns can be used:
- on their own
  'Would you like sugar on it?' 'Just ***a little****.'*
  'Do you prefer tea or coffee?' 'I don't like ***either****.'*

One another and *each other* are used as objects of verbs.
Bob and Alice loved ***one another/each other****.*
(Bob loved Alice and Alice loved Bob.)
- with *of* + pronoun
  They've got two boys – ***both of them*** *are blond.*
- with *of* + *the, this, that, these, those, my, your,* etc + noun
  Try ***some of my*** *wine.*
  Neither of these *books is mine.*

of is optional with *all* and *both* before a noun
All (of) my clothes/Both (of) my socks *are wet.*
- after a determiner
  There are no others. I've got a few more. Look at this one. Try each one. Would you like any more?

All and *both* can also be used
- after a noun or pronoun
  My parents both work at home.
  Jazz, pop, rock … I listen to them all.
- after a modal or auxiliary verb
  We've all/both seen that film.

Modal verbs 2: *will, shall* and *would*

1 ***Will*** and ***would*** can be used to express:
- present and past habits. This use is not possible with stative verbs (e.g. *be, know, like*).
  She ***will*** *often* ***fall*** *asleep in front of the television.*
  He ***would*** *always* ***read*** *us a story at bedtime.*
- typical annoying behaviour. In speech, *will* and *would* are stressed.
  He ***will keep interrupting*** *when I'm talking.*
  I ***would get a cold*** *now, just as the holiday is starting!*
- willingness to do something. This includes requests.
  *If you****'ll/would follow*** *me, Ms Ray will see you now.*
  Will/Would *you open the door a little, please?*
  I wish he ***would try*** *a bit harder.*
- refusal to do something in the present and the past.
  Mummy! Eva ***won't let*** *me play with her dolls!*
  I asked him, but he ***wouldn't*** *tell me.*

2 ***Will*** can also be used to express assumptions about the present.
*'There's someone at the door.' 'That****'ll be*** *Lydia.'*

3 ***Shall*** can be used:
- to make a request for advice or instructions
  I'm very worried about Peter. What ***shall we do****?*
  What time ***shall we meet****?*
- to make an offer or a suggestion
  Shall I help *you carry that?* ***Shall we go****?*

Talking about the future

1 *will* and *going to* can be used to make predictions.
I don't think ***I'll be/I'm going to be*** *well enough to go to work tomorrow.*

2 *going to* also describes intentions or plans.
I'm going to work *really hard this year.*

3 The present continuous describes fixed arrangements.
I'm having *lunch with Brian tomorrow.*

4 Modal verbs express different degrees of uncertainty about the future.
Dave ***should be*** *here soon.* (Probability)
We ***might have*** *a party next week.* (Possibility)
may/might/could well + infinitive without *to* expresses probability.
We ***might well be moving*** *in the next few weeks.*

5 Verbs of thinking, such as *believe, doubt, expect* and *think*, are followed by *will* when referring to the future. *Hope* can also be followed by a present tense.
I ***expect I'll lose*** *again – I always do.*
I ***hope they (will) keep*** *in touch with us.*

6 *be (un)likely to* + infinitive expresses probability.
The situation ***is likely to get*** *worse.*

7 *be bound to* + infinitive expresses certainty.
*It's a ridiculous plan and it****'s bound to fail****.*

8 *be (just) about to* + infinitive/*be on the point of* + gerund can be used to talk about the immediate future.
I'll call you back – ***I'm just about to go*** *into a meeting.*

9 *be due to* + infinitive refers to scheduled times.
The new supermarket ***is due to open*** *in April.*

10 The present simple also refers to scheduled times.
Hurry up! The bus ***leaves*** *in ten minutes.*

11 *be* + *to* + infinitive can be used to talk about arrangements.
Next year's tournament ***is to be held*** *in Frankfurt.*
(See also section **A** of Gerunds and infinitives in Unit 4 on page 218.)

12 The future continuous is used:
- to talk about actions or events which will be in progress at a certain time in the future.
  *Don't call after eight – I'**ll be watching** the match then.*
- to talk about a future action that will happen because it is regular or decided. It can be used to ask about someone's plans politely.
  ***I'll be seeing** Joe later – I'll give this to him then.*
  ***Will you be coming** out with us tomorrow night?*

13 The future perfect is used to talk about actions and events which will be completed by, or which continue until, a certain time in the future.
*I think we'**ll have finished** the job by Friday.*
*Next month **I'll have been working** here for ten years.*

Unit 9

Creating emphasis

If we want to give particular importance to a person, a thing or a clause in a sentence, we can use these structures: *It is/was … that …* or *What … is/was …*

***It was** Norman's incredible sense of humour **that** first attracted me to him.*
***What** I find strange **is** (the fact) that he never talks about his father.*

In each case, the underlined part of the sentence is being emphasized.

1 *It is/was … that …* can be used:
- with *(only) when, while* or *not until* to emphasize a (period of) time
  ***It was while** he was in Spain **that** Lennon wrote* Strawberry Fields Forever.
  ***It wasn't until** he took off his hat **that** I recognized him.*
- with *because* to emphasize reasons
  *Perhaps **it's because** I'm a chef **that** people never invite me to their dinner parties.*
- to emphasize prepositional phrases
  ***It was on the radio that** I first heard the news.*
- to emphasize a thing or a person
  'who' can be used in place of 'that' if we are referring to a person.
  ***It was** Gary **who** broke the chair.*
  ***It's** his left arm **that**'s broken, not his right one.*

Modal verbs can be used instead of *is* and *was*.
***It can't be** my mobile phone **that**'s ringing – it's switched off.*
***It might have been** the fish **that** made me feel ill.*

2 *What … is/was …* can be used to emphasize:
- a noun
  ***What** I most wanted to see in The Louvre **was** the* Mona Lisa.
- an action or series of actions
  ***What** you do then **is (to)** add the flour and stir it in thoroughly.*
  ***What** happened **was (that)** I left my wallet in the café and had to go back.*

All can be used instead of *What* to mean *'the only thing that'*.
***All** he (ever) did during the school holiday **was (to)** play on his computer.*
***All** I really want **is** a little house in the countryside.*

Unit 10

Participle clauses

Participle clauses are clauses which begin with a present or past participle. They help to express ideas concisely, and add variety to written English.

1 Participle clauses can be used:
- instead of relative clauses

  *I recognize that man **standing** over there.* (= who is standing)
  *Three of the people **injured** in the crash are still in hospital.* (= who were injured)
- instead of certain conjunctions

because/so
***Not wishing** to offend my host, I ate everything on my plate.*

as/while
***Looking** out of the window last night, I saw a shooting star.*

when/once/after
***Having worked out** how much you can afford to pay for your computer, you need to decide on the model.*

and
*He fell off the ladder, **breaking** a leg and three ribs.*

if
***Cooked** in their skins, potatoes retain most of their nutrients.*
- after the objects of the following verbs: *see, hear, watch, notice, feel* and *find*

*Police **found him lying** unconscious on the kitchen floor.*
*I could **hear something moving** in the bushes.*

2 Note that:
- Stative verbs (e.g. *be, want, know*) are not normally used in continuous tenses, but the *-ing* form can be used in participle clauses.
  I am being a very shy person, so I never enjoy going to parties. ✗
  ***Being** a very shy person, I never enjoy going to parties.* ✔
- The subject of a participle clause is usually the same as the subject of the main clause.
  ***Working** as a waitress, **I** have all my meals in the restaurant.*

However, it is possible to have a participle clause with a different subject. Instead of:
***Having been damaged** by vandals, **Helen** had to walk rather than go on her bicycle.* ✗
we can say:
Her bicycle having been damaged by vandals, Helen had to walk. ✔
- *with* is sometimes used to introduce a different subject.
  ***With both my parents working** all day, **I** have to cook my own lunch.*

Unit 11

Inversion

Certain adverbs and adverbial phrases with a negative or restrictive meaning can be placed at the beginning of a sentence for emphasis. In this case, the position of the subject and verb is reversed, as in question forms. This occurs mainly in written English or more formal speech.

1 Where the main verb is used with an auxiliary verb, the position of the subject and auxiliary verb is reversed.
I will never lend money to Richard again. (Normal word order)
***Never again will I** lend money to Richard.* (Inversion)

Where no auxiliary verb is present, either *do, does* or *did* is inserted.
Steve hardly ever turned up on time for his lectures.
***Hardly ever did Steve** turn up on time for his lectures.*

2 Inversion is used:
- after certain phrases with *not*
  ***Not since** I was little **have I** enjoyed myself so much.*
  ***Not until** we got to my parents' house **did we** realize we'd left all the Christmas presents at home.*
  ***Not only did he** leave dirty footprints all over our carpet, **but** he **also** sat on my glasses.*

- after certain phrases with *only*
  ***Only when** I tell you **can you** put your books away.*
  ***Only then was I** made aware of the potential dangers.*
  Further examples: *only recently, only later, only in the last few weeks, only at the end of the lesson*
- after certain phrases with *no*
  ***On no account must you** speak to other candidates.*
  ***Under no circumstances should the door** be left open.*
  ***In no way will we** give in to their demands.*
  ***At no time were you** in any danger.*
- after certain frequency adverbs
  ***Never have I** seen such an ugly building.*
  ***Rarely/Seldom does one** find antique furniture of this kind in such perfect condition.*
  ***Hardly ever is he** in his office when I phone.*
- with *No sooner ... than ...* and *Hardly/Barely/Scarcely ... when ...*
  ***No sooner had I** got into the shower **than** the phone rang.* (= As soon as I got into the shower ...)
  ***Hardly had we** finished breakfast **when** we were told it would soon be time for lunch.*
- after *Little*, meaning *not at all*
  ***Little did they realize** that their conversation was being recorded.* (= They had no idea ...)

Unit 12

Conjunctions

Conjunctions connect two clauses in the same sentence.

Reason, result and purpose
e.g. *as, because, in case, in order (not) to, otherwise, so, so as (not) to, so that*

in case and *so that* can be followed by the present simple to refer to the future.
*Take an umbrella **in case it rains** later on.*
*I'll lend you some gloves **so that you don't get** your hands dirty.*

Contrast and concession
e.g. *although, but, however, (even) though, whereas, while/whilst*

As a conjunction, *however* means *'no matter how'*.
*You can decorate your room **however** you want.*

in spite of the fact that and *despite the fact that* can also connect two clauses.
*She continued to support him, **despite the fact that** he had treated her so badly.*

Time
e.g. *after, as, as soon as, before, by the time, hardly, no sooner, once, since, then, until, when, whenever, while*

Many of these conjunctions are followed by a present tense or present perfect to refer to the future.
***Once** it **stops/has stopped** raining, we'll go out.*

For information on *hardly* and *no sooner*, see Inversion in Unit 11 above and on page 222.

Linking adverbials

Linking adverbials connect one sentence with another. They frequently appear at the beginning of a sentence, and are followed by a comma.

Reason and result
e.g. *As a result, Because of this, Consequently, For this reason, On account of this, Therefore*

*There was a power cut this morning. **Consequently,** I couldn't do any work on the computer.*

Contrast and concession
e.g. *All the same, At the same time, By/In comparison, By/In contrast, Even so, However, In spite of/Despite this, Likewise, Nevertheless, On the contrary, On the other hand, Similarly*

On the contrary is used to introduce a positive statement which confirms a negative one.
On the other hand introduces a point which contrasts with a previous one.
*The lottery win did not bring happiness. **On the contrary**, it caused the breakup of his marriage.*
*It's a rather ugly city to live in. **On the other hand**, house prices here are very low.*

Time
e.g. *After that/Afterwards, Before that/Beforehand, By that time, Eventually, Ever since then, Finally, From that time on, Initially, In the end, In the meantime/Meanwhile, Until then*

*The bed's being delivered next week. **In the meantime,** I'm sleeping on the sofa.*

Addition
e.g. *Additionally, Besides (this), Apart from this, As well as this, In addition to this, First of all, Secondly, Finally, Furthermore, Moreover, What is more*

*... and the campsite shop rarely opened on time. **Furthermore,** the staff there were rude to me on a number of occasions.*

Modal verbs 3: *must, need, should* and *ought to*

A Must

1 ***must*** and ***have to***
must + infinitive is used to give orders or strong advice, or to tell oneself what is necessary. The authority comes from the speaker.
*All questions **must be answered.***
*You really **must see** Russell Crowe's new film.*
*I **must remember** to get some bread.*

Although not a modal verb, *have to* + infinitive is also used to talk about obligations. The authority comes from someone other than the speaker.
*We **have to wear** a swimming cap in the indoor pool.*

2 ***mustn't*** and ***don't have to***
mustn't expresses prohibition; *don't have to* expresses lack of obligation or necessity.
*You **mustn't touch** this, darling – it's very hot.*
*You **don't have to come** if you don't want to.*

3 ***must have done*** and ***had to do***
must have + past participle is used to speculate about past situations; *had to* + infinitive expresses past obligation or necessity.
*Sean's late – he **must have got** stuck in a traffic jam.*
*The bus broke down so I **had to walk**.*

B *Should/Ought to*

1 *should* and *ought to* + infinitive are used to give advice or express opinions about what is right and wrong. *should have* and *ought to have* + past participle can be used to criticize past actions, express regret or talk about things which were supposed to happen but didn't.
*You **shouldn't play** with matches – it's dangerous.*
*You really **shouldn't have shouted** at him like that.*
*We **ought to have asked** Jill if she wanted to come.*
*Where's Bob? He **should have been** here ages ago.*

2 *should* and *ought* can also be used to talk about probability.
*If you leave now, you **should be/ought to be** there by midday.*

C *Need*

1 ***need*** and ***need to***
need + infinitive is not used in ordinary statements and is very rare in questions; *need to* + infinitive is much more common for expressing necessity.
*I **need to get** some new shoes.* (not: *I **need get** ...* ✗)
*What **do we need to take** with us?*
*My brother-in-law and his family stayed with us at Christmas. **Need I say** more?*

2 ***needn't*** and ***don't need to***
Usually, there is no difference in meaning between *needn't* + infinitive and *don't need to* + infinitive: they both indicate a lack of obligation to do something.

However, *needn't* usually refers to immediate necessity and tends to be used to give permission not to do something; the authority comes from the speaker.
*You **needn't come** tomorrow if you don't want to.*

don't need to tends to indicate general necessity; the authority does not come from the speaker. *don't have to* can be used in the same way.
*You **don't need to/don't have to spend** a fortune to keep fit.*

3 ***needn't have done*** and ***didn't need to do***
needn't have + past participle is used to talk about an action which was performed but which was unnecessary.
*You **needn't have bought** those batteries – we've got plenty in the drawer.*

didn't need to + infinitive is used to talk about an action which was unnecessary. It usually indicates that the subject did not perform the action.
*I **didn't need to spend** very long on my homework last night – it was quite easy.*

Unit 13

Comparisons

A The following structures and expressions can be used to talk about similarities and differences.

1 Comparing past with present
***Where once** he was at the top of his profession, he **now** struggles to find work.*
*We **now** depend on technology **more than ever before**.*

2 *The* + comparative, *the* + comparative is used when one thing is the result of another.
***The more** he laughed, **the angrier** she became.*
***The easier** I find a subject, **the less** I enjoy it.*

3 *as* + auxiliary + subject
*He **lived** to a ripe old age, **as did** his wife and children.*

4 *Like* is used with nouns, pronouns or gerunds to make comparisons.
*She ran **like the wind** back to her flat.*
*Getting him to talk is **like getting** blood out of a stone.*

As is used with nouns to describe someone or something's job, role or function.
*She used her scarf **as a bandage**.*
*He's just started work **as a postman**.*

As is used with a verb phrase to make comparisons. *Like* is used informally, and is considered incorrect by some.
*She believes, **as I do**, that the President is wrong.*

5 *as* + adjective/adverb + *as* can be used to show similarities. *so* can be used instead of the first *as* in negative sentences.
*You're **as stubborn as** your father.*
*He's **not so silly as** he looks.*

so can be used in the following structures.
*He is known **not so much** for his singing **as/but** for his charity work.*
***If** you can park close to the station, then **so much the better**.*

Note the position of the article when *so* and *such* are used before nouns.
*Nothing gives **so bad an impression as** arriving late for your interview.*
*It is**n't** quite **such a cold winter as** last year.*

B The following words and expressions can be used to modify comparisons.

1 With comparatives
a bit, a little, slightly, much, (quite) a lot, far, significantly, considerably, three times, etc, *a great deal*
*I'm feeling **considerably better than** I did yesterday.*

2 With superlatives
by far, easily, by a long way
*China is the company's **largest** market, **by a long way**.*
*She is **by far the most gifted** musician in the band.*

3 With *as ... as ...*
not quite, (not) nearly, almost, just, half, twice, three times, etc, *nothing like, nowhere near*
*She earns **twice as much as** me and works **half as many** hours.*

4 With *the same ... as ...*
not quite, (not) nearly, almost, just, (very) much
*I have **much the same** opinion **as** my colleague.*

Unit 14

Noun phrases

A **Noun + noun** is used when referring to:
- what things are made of
  a silver spoon a metal door a stone wall
- products from dead animals
  a lamb chop a leopard skin a chicken sandwich
- things that occur or appear regularly
  the evening shift a Saturday job daytime television
- duration. The first noun is hyphenated and in the singular.
  a five-hour delay a 20-minute speech
  a two-week holiday
- containers
  a water bottle a tea cup a biscuit tin

Noun + noun is also used in a large number of commonly accepted compound nouns. The two nouns describe a single idea.
a shop window a door handle a fire engine

B **Noun + *'s/s'* + noun** is used when referring to:
- possession by a particular person or animal
  Sally's bicycle the dog's bone my children's toys
  An adjective can be placed between the two nouns.
  my children's new toys
- something that is used by people or animals in general
  children's shoes women's clothes an ants' nest
  Adjectives are placed before the two nouns.
  a monthly women's magazine
- an action done to or by a particular person
  Mr Smith's resignation her husband's murder
  the Labour Party's defeat
  The 'noun *of* noun' structure is preferred if the modifying noun is a long phrase.
  the resignation of several members of the committee
- products from living animals
  goat's milk a hen's egg sheep's wool
- things that occurred at a specific time
  this evening's newspaper yesterday's storm
  last Saturday's programme
- parts of people's and animals' bodies
  the boy's foot a sheep's head the dog's tail
- duration, as an alternative to the noun + noun structure
  two years' absence a day's work an hour's delay

C **Noun + preposition + noun** is used:
- for containers and their contents
  a bottle of water a cup of tea a tin of biscuits
- with words like *top, bottom, side, edge, back, front, beginning, middle* and *end* to indicate a part of something
  the top of the picture the back of the book
  the middle of the week
  There are a number of common exceptions, e.g.
  a mountain top, the day's end, the water's edge
- to describe the characteristics of a person or thing
  a man of average build a place of great beauty
  a ring of little value
- where no commonly accepted compound noun exists
  a book about parks the roof of the house
  a woman on the radio
- in a large number of collocations
  a source of inspiration an invasion of privacy

Listening scripts

Unit 1 (Page 12)

 1.1–1.3

Part 1: Multiple choice

Extract One

M = Man W = Woman

M: You know, when we heard we'd been nominated for an award – and we knew who the other nominees were – well, just for a brief moment, I guess we got a kick out of it. I mean, the other bands are guys we really respect, but we've always used our music to attack capitalism. It would be incredibly hypocritical to go to a ceremony sponsored by the corporate world.

W: Yeah, and we knew who had voted for us. We've been together for four years, and the people who liked our music from the start, the ones who've been coming to the gigs, they know what our principles are. And they wouldn't go in for that kind of thing. But you know, you get your first number one single and the mainstream music listeners think you're a new band and they go out and vote for you. For a moment in time your song's getting the biggest number of hits – and then the public move on.

Extract Two

OM = Older man YM = Younger man

OM: Well – obviously – I was gutted that the home team didn't come out on top, but it wasn't altogether a surprise. Three of the players were making their debut, and you can tell they were a bit overawed by the occasion, and it impacted on the overall team performance. You can't put the blame on the coach – giving the novices a chance was a management decision, and it backfired. That's all I've got to say on that game, but I have to say that I do have a problem with the way that a couple of the players only seem interested in offering their skills to the highest bidder. They've got no regard for the fans, apparently.

YM: That's what it looks like, certainly on the outside. It's a shame because those guys have inspired a generation. You have to wonder whether the newspapers are doing what they usually do and stirring up a bit of controversy – but if it's true the players are quitting and going overseas just for the big dollars, that's very disappointing.

Extract Three

W = Woman M = Man

W: *40-hour Famine* is about students not eating food for 40 hours. The idea is to promote a bit more awareness of what it's like for people who are starving through no fault of their own – say through crop failure or drought. Many students are too young to volunteer to go overseas and help out directly and they haven't got the cash to make monthly donations, but taking part in this is something they *can* do. And, of course, the sponsorship they get goes to excellent charities. This is my first year, but it's Tom's second, isn't it, Tom?

M: Yeah.

W: How did you do last year?

M: I only made it to 35, actually. I felt really dizzy and had to give up. But no one made me feel like I'd let them down; they were just concerned. I thought 'Oh, well, I'll make sure I manage it next time.' And look … in another four hours I will have reached that goal.

Unit 2 (Page 18)

 1.4

Part 2: Sentence completion

Hi. I'm Simon, and last week I got to spend a whole day at the National Museum where I was shown around by one of the curators. I'd only been there as a visitor before, so it was interesting to find out what goes on behind the scenes. The collections at the museum are quite diverse – there's a whole floor devoted to the natural environment, for example, and, of course, a large section for Pacific cultures. Melanie, the curator, told me she'd done a degree in anthropology, but when she applied to the museum, she decided to focus on social history, and she's been working in that area ever since. I thought it would be worth asking what sort of educational background most of the other curators had, and what sort of work experience you needed if you wanted a position there, but apparently it's your communication skills that really count. They're essential for all museum staff.

Then I asked Melanie to explain what kind of things she's personally responsible for. She said that whenever the museum acquired a new object, the first stage of the process was identification. That might involve, for example, finding out where and when something was made, that sort of thing. She would do that by herself, but she'd work with other specialists if the object was in any way damaged, and needed restoration of some kind. Then, we went on to talk about one aspect of being a curator that I know I'd be hopeless at if I had to do it – and that's when they have to write and maintain records. You obviously have to be meticulous about detail.

Melanie also spends some of her time preparing for conferences, and liaising with other curators or researchers working in the same field. She also has to reply to the correspondence and enquiries she gets from the public, and this can take up quite a bit of time.

I was also curious to know what Melanie liked most in the collection, and she said it was a series of letters sent by a soldier to his wife back home. I had a look and they were certainly very moving. What really caught my eye, though, and you can see them all along the walls, were a lot of advertisements from the 20th century. They really give you an insight into people's lifestyle at the time. Well worth a look if you go to the museum.

Melanie told me that many exhibits have been gifted, so, for example, most of the paintings have been donated not bought. Apparently, it's not just wealthy benefactors, but ordinary people who want to offer a family heirloom, say. So recently, for instance, a woman brought in an antique clock in perfect working order. Melanie has to say no to photo albums, however, because it's so hard to preserve them.

I'm going to finish by mentioning the biggest problem the museum has – and it's not something you'd automatically think of. When it comes to preserving the physical exhibits, the curators are confident that they've got that under control, but they're not so good at preserving digital data, and they're investigating new storage formats to ensure it's preserved for posterity.

Well, I hope I have given you a better idea of what it's like to work at the museum.

Unit 2 (Page 26)

 1.5–1.9

Part 4: Multiple matching

Speaker 1

I'd given up just about everything – the job, the house, the car – and gone to Spain to be with my husband. Then six months later it was all over. Both of us believed we'd rushed into marriage too soon and there was little that made us compatible as spouses. At the same time, we felt the friendship that had drawn us together in the first place was just too valuable to throw away and the only way to save it was by splitting up. The thing is, I remember hugging Alfonso at the airport, boarding the flight to Manchester and waiting to feel some kind of relief. It didn't come. By the time we landed, I had this awful sense that we'd rushed just as fast into a divorce. A year has passed and I still can't help wishing we'd put a bit more effort into staying together.

Speaker 2

I was a no-hoper at school, see. No one had heard of dyslexia in those days, so my teachers just classed me as an 'idiot'. I might have behaved myself later if I'd been given a bit more attention then, but I was told time and time again that I was going to be a failure. It surprised no one, including myself, that I ended up in prison, but all that time on my hands gave me the chance to think. I realized I'd turned out just how they said and I wanted to prove it could be different. I did a law degree while I was inside, and it was tough, I tell you, but since I got out, I've never looked back. I'm about to become a partner in a law firm and that's an achievement that gives me immense satisfaction.

Speaker 3

I'd always wanted to do voluntary work, ever since I qualified as a nurse. Marriage and children always got in the way of my plans, though, but now that the kids were older, there didn't seem any reason to put it off, even though I was coming up to my 50th birthday. And once I'd got their backing, there was no stopping me, really. Of course, I missed them all when I was there, but I just threw myself into my work. I had to, really. It was a very isolated rural area – there was no running water, no medicines and so much poverty. But I can't tell you how much I appreciate the fact that I was given the chance to go – it was a real eye-opener and I learnt so much about their culture and about myself – for that I'll always be thankful.

Speaker 4

I'd worked my way up to supervisor and got just about as far as I could go in the company. It was a responsible position and gave us a certain amount of security and, I suppose, that's why I stuck it for so long. Inevitably, though, it got to the point where the routine just got too much. I wasn't developing professionally and nothing about the job pushed me to better myself. So when Sue suggested taking over a café franchise, I jumped at the chance. Neither of us had a background in catering, but we refused to be daunted. We had to learn all aspects of the business in a very short time, but I found it all very thrilling, and still do. Even now I wake up every day really looking forward to going in to work – being in a new environment and dealing with the fast pace.

Speaker 5

I'd been biting my nails since I was a three-year-old, apparently. It had never really bothered me before, despite my parents' constant moaning. They made me put this liquid on them called 'No-bite'. Tasted horrible, it did – until I got used to it, that was. When I started work, though, I began noticing the looks of mild horror on the customers' faces. Every time I was wrapping up a present or was just resting my hands on the counter, I could sense them staring and it made me incredibly self-conscious. So I had these plastic tips put on and that gave my nails the chance to grow. No one notices them anymore so the problem is essentially solved, but it has nothing to do with my willpower. It's actually humiliating for a 23-year-old to be wearing plastic tips. It's a secret I would hate my boyfriend to find out.

Unit 3 (Page 32)

 1.10–1.12

Part 1: Multiple choice

Extract One

M = Man W = Woman

M: The last book I wrote was something my publisher *asked* me to write – about the River Thames, and its history – and it wasn't a passion of mine, that sort of thing – and to this day I'm not entirely sure why the publisher approached *me*, but I could imagine how *other* people might be interested, so I signed up. And once I'd got into it, I found the whole thing quite intriguing. I'd rather not have had to limit our investigation just to the inner city, but there's only so much you can pack into 400 pages. Now it's finished, I have to say I rather miss working on it. Do you enjoy the research side of things?

W: Not so much, but now we have the Internet, of course.

M: Indeed, but can you trust what you read?

W: The way I see it, the Internet's given us access to limitless knowledge. If only we'd had it when I was first starting out – it would have saved me countless trips to the library and a lot of time and effort. Sure you have to check and cross reference things, but I can live with that.

Extract Two

M = Man W = Woman

M: I don't know if you've heard, but I'm off to Greece once the term finishes. I'm joining up with this team of archaeologists – they need people to do the physical stuff – the digging, I mean. It won't be paid, but it'll give me some real experience in the field – even if it's not strictly relevant to the courses I'm taking next year – and it'll make a change from the tedious kind of jobs I normally end up doing during the holidays.

W: Well, I imagine you'll really get a lot out of it. After I finished my first degree – and we're talking, er, at least ten years ago now, I got offered a position with a really prestigious firm of architects – and I felt I couldn't say no, especially because we were all still waiting for the exam results to come out. And it was good there, but I still wish I'd given myself the chance to consider something else. Well, that's why I've come back to university, I suppose.

Extract Three

EM = English man

AM = American man

EM: If you only hang out with other game designers, if gaming is your entire world, that's actually going to work against your development. The people on top in this profession are the ones with, I'd call it, an 'insatiable curiosity' for, say, history, science, music – that kind of thing. Anyway, when I'm starting out on a new game, I'll work out what the goal is. That's my priority. So, for example, for my last game it was the idea that Man is a part of Nature, not separate, and I'll go from there. The people and the overall image come later down the line.

AM: I probably have a similar approach and I agree that whatever you're designing – be it a first-person shooter, action-adventure, role-playing, whatever ... if you want to become one of the great game designers, you need a great deal of general knowledge and an enquiring mind. A good grasp of behavioural psychology is also essential. Without this, you won't convince anyone, and playing a game without conviction is rather pointless.

Unit 3 (Page 36)

 1.13

Part 3: Multiple choice

P = Presenter H = Helena

P: With me today on *Infospeak* is journalist and writer, Helena Drysdale. Hello, Helena, and welcome to the programme.

H: Thank you. Good morning.

P: Helena, you spent the last two years travelling around Europe doing research for a forthcoming book. What were you trying to find out?

H: Yes, we went in search of Europe's minority languages to determine exactly what state they're all in, particularly given today's climate of mass culture and so on. We travelled right up to northern Scandinavia and the Arctic circle, where the Sami reindeer herders live, and we got down as far as Corsica and Sardinia in the sunny Mediterranean. Then there were the mountains of northern Italy where Ladin is spoken, and we had a rather wet and rainy time in Brittany in the west of France with its Celtic Breton. Thirteen countries and 15 minor languages in all.

P: By 'us' and 'we', you're referring to your family, of course.

H: Yes, my husband Richard, and our two young children, Tallulah and Xanthe – not forgetting the Mob, of course, our trusty mobile home.

P: What was that like? Two years together in a mobile home can't have been easy.

H: It got a little cramped at times, particularly when the weather kept us in. The kids couldn't run around, they'd start playing up, tempers would overheat, and everyone fell out. But apart from that, fine.

P: Yes, I can see. And how did you go about gathering your information? What were your sources?

H: I did some research in the library and on the Internet after we came back, but the only real way to get the kind of information I was looking for was by actually talking to people. We met writers, teachers and artists, who generally gave a more intellectual analysis of the situation, and we were able to balance that with the more down-to-earth, personalized accounts of people in the rural areas. That's where many of these languages are most frequently spoken and also where people, particularly the older generation, seemed less reluctant to open up and give us their honest opinion.

P: And I imagine they had some very interesting stories to tell about the past.

H: Yes, indeed. For example, we often heard stories of punishments that people received for speaking their own language at school. One old lady in the south of France told us how she used to have to wear a stone or a stick round her neck if she was caught speaking Provençal. She had to keep it on until someone else committed the same offence and then they'd have to wear it. And whoever had it at the end of the day was made to pay a fine, or sometimes even beaten.

P: Hard to believe, really.

H: Mm. She's able to laugh about it now, but at the time it was considered deeply shaming to have to wear *le symbole*, as she called it. Sometimes it could be a wooden shoe or a pottery cow, which represented the country bumpkin, someone to be despised.

P: And were these punishments effective? Did they contribute to the decline of some of these languages?

H: Yes, they lowered the status of a language. But sometimes they helped to keep a language going – at least in the short term, anyway. They caused resentment and made people more defiant towards the authorities. You know, it can be a bit like pruning a tree – if you cut it back, it grows much stronger. But there were and still are other more powerful forces which represent a much bigger threat to the survival of Europe's minority languages.

P: By that you mean globalization, I presume.

H: That's right. And tourism. Now although tourism can give a language status by attracting outside interest in it, it can also have a negative effect on local cultures. You know, in one place we visited, the natives moan about the influx of outsiders and how they buy up land at giveaway prices to build holiday cottages, and how it's destroying their culture, and so on. But then the very same people are selling up their farms so they can run hotels or open souvenir shops. Understandable, perhaps, but they're encouraging the very thing they're complaining about.

P: Are languages like Sami and Provençal endangered species, then?

H: Well, I think it's true to say that if no positive action is taken, they'll simply die out. The problem is that some people are indifferent, and even hostile to their own language. They think it's of no use in the modern world, which they so desperately want to be part of. Fortunately, though, there are enough people around who realize that to lose your mother tongue is like losing a part of yourself. Your language makes you who you are. And if you spoke a different language, you'd be a different person. But people on their own can only do so much. It really is up to the European Union to legislate to ensure the survival of minority languages.

P: And how exactly do you legislate to save a language?

H: Well, I think there are several things you can do. Firstly, of course, the EU would have to bring in …

Unit 4 (Page 47)

 1.14–1.18

Part 4: Multiple matching

Speaker 1

I was told the best way to prepare for an interview is by going to the company's website and finding out everything you can about them. The idea, of course, is that it creates a good impression and proves that you are keen on working for them because they can see you've done your homework. The trouble was that they hadn't done theirs – the web page hadn't been updated for over a year, so I asked all these questions about products they didn't produce and subsidiaries that no longer existed. They must have thought I wasn't very well prepared. It wasn't my fault, though, and I kind of lost enthusiasm for the job once I found out what had happened. I mean, it's a bit slack, isn't it?

Speaker 2

So there I was the night before, in the living room talking to the dog. A bit strange, you might think, and you'd probably be right. But I was getting ready for the next day, you see. The dog was the interviewer, and I was trying out all my questions and answers on him. I'm not sure that's what the writer of the article had in mind when she said, 'Rehearse the situation with a friend', but it seemed like a good idea to me. Anyway, it was all a bit of a waste of time, really. I overslept the next morning and by the time I got there they'd already taken somebody on.

Speaker 3

'Now you're not to get all uptight and on edge, like you normally do,' was what my mum said. And that's more or less what the careers teacher told us at school: 'Projecting self-confidence at an interview is vital for success'. Those were his exact words. So I put on my best suit to give me that confidence, cleaned my shoes and off I went. Well, my hands were shaking so much, you wouldn't believe it. I nearly spilt my coffee down my trousers. I think I managed to hide it, though. Course, what I couldn't hide was the fact that I'd failed my maths GCSE. They wouldn't take me on without it. Shame, really – the money wasn't too bad.

Speaker 4

'Don't lean back in your chair', he says. 'If you do that, it might look as though you're trying just a bit too hard to cover up your nerves. Either that or you're not interested in the job.' So according to this Dr Benson, it's advisable to lean forward, keep your legs uncrossed and smile confidently. Well, I did all that. In fact, I smiled so much my face began to ache. But they somehow seemed to realize that I don't normally walk around with a permanent grin from ear to ear – they said they were looking for lively, bubbly people for their sales team, and they weren't convinced that I fitted the bill.

Speaker 5

I saw this video in the university careers office where they recommended imagining the interviewer in the bath, playing with a plastic duck, of all things. The idea is that they're only human, so there's nothing to be frightened of. So, anyway, I thought about the type of questions they might ask me and I got to the interview about half an hour early so I could go over the answers I was going to give. But, bath or no bath, the interviewer turned out to be not so human after all. It was like an interrogation, and the things he asked were really tricky – nothing like what I'd prepared for. I just didn't know what to say. I felt pretty sick about the whole thing afterwards, I can tell you.

Unit 4 (Page 55)

 1.19

Part 2: Sentence completion

Time, ladies and gentlemen, is one of our greatest assets, and in this fast-moving competitive world, poor management of our time is a major cause of stress both in the workplace and at home. The first and most essential element of effective time management is forward planning. If you start the morning by mapping out what you hope to achieve during the day, you can go a long way to avoiding unnecessary frustration and wasted effort. Be realistic, though, in terms of what you hope to accomplish in the time available, and think through carefully how and when you will accomplish it. Unmet expectations will only serve to put you under more pressure, to create more stress – and you'll only have yourself to blame if that happens.

Of course, tiredness – rather than any lack of ability – can often present a major obstacle to our obtaining the goals we've set ourselves, or indeed to meeting the deadlines that others have set for us. If that's the case, stop, turn your computer off, take a break. If you feel you can't go on, or you're just too snowed under, don't make yourself ill. Work should always take second place to your health. It can be counterproductive to carry on regardless, particularly if the next day you have to phone in sick and take time off work.

And also, if time is against you, if you're pressed for time, be prepared to adapt to the circumstances – don't worry if what you produce is less than wonderful. We cannot, we should not always strive for perfection. It slows us down, it reduces productivity and means we have no time for other tasks. Good enough is still good, and in all probability no one will notice the difference. And this applies to the home as well as the workplace. A similar dose of self-discipline is needed when we take on the household chores. Limit the amount of housework you try to do in a day, lower your expectations and relax if the shirts you've just ironed still have creases. It doesn't matter.

Because ultimately, let's face it, what we all work for is to make time for ourselves, to free up time for the things we really want to do outside of work. It's essential to set aside enough time to pursue your interests, to do the things which are most fulfilling for you in life. Many people fail to achieve the right balance between work and relaxation and once again, stress is the outcome. And just a word of warning here – if by relaxation you understand slumping on the sofa in front of the television, think again. It is a poor use of time, and it usually ends up making you feel more tired, and time-pressured than before.

Now, technology has done a great deal to …

Unit 5 (Page 59)

 1.20

Part 3: Multiple choice

I = Interviewer   A = Adrian

I: My guest today is Adrian Mitchell, whose book *Who we are and what we want* on the subject of family relationships has been at the top of many best-seller lists for the most part of this year. Adrian, I know you've been lecturing in sociology for over 20 years. So, was the book an inevitable consequence of that?

A: Well, without that background, I don't suppose I'd be writing a book on social issues; but many academics have been in the game for a great deal longer than I have, and they don't feel the need to publish their thoughts for public consumption. I suppose for me it was more that I was talked into it by colleagues of mine who insisted that there was a market for that kind of subject. None of us, though, I don't think, had, er anticipated how well it would do.

I: And I believe that you've also put your experience as a counsellor to good use in the book.

A: I like to think so, although I have to admit that I quit counselling several years ago. I'd been doing it for years, and it was certainly something I was passionate about, but there were simply too many things going on. I was stretched to the point that I could no longer say I was fully committed to anything, and that wasn't something I could live with. It wasn't really fair on my wife and children, either.

I: In your book, you do take pains, I notice, to avoid presenting yourself as the ideal husband. I mean, you're not pretending to have all the solutions.

A: No, absolutely not. I think I'm a fairly typical 21st-century husband. I want to provide for my family, but I'm grateful that we have my wife's salary. It allows us to do so much more than one income would permit. And, um, like most husbands, I suspect, I'm handy about the house, but I don't insist on fixing the car or the computer myself – I leave that to the experts. I think I'm also typical in the way I tend to – er, shall we say – *overlook* certain domestic chores that need doing. I *will* do them, but I do need a bit of pushing from my wife. I would certainly argue against the idea that men have lost sense of who they are. Our roles may have *changed* over the years – but that doesn't mean we're *confused* about them.

I: Yes, but it's a notion that seems popular on daytime television. Um, in the book, you thank your children in the acknowledgements, but after that, there's no further mention of them. Did you make a conscious decision to exclude them?

A: Well, yes. If I'd written about them, it would have felt like a form of exploitation, I suppose. Even if they'd agreed to appear in the book, they would have done so just to make me happy because that's what children do – look for approval. Well, we all do, I suppose. And you don't know whether they're going to feel the same way once they're older and in a position to make a more informed decision. I can see why people draw from their own personal experiences when they're writing a research-based book, but this has to be weighed up against the impact your writing may have on others.

I: A chapter I found particularly interesting was the one on how the media reports on social issues. You refer to the way it portrays single parents, single *mothers* in particular.

A: Yes, unfortunately, many journalists are happy to cut and paste their information from other articles doing the rounds on the Internet; this doesn't necessarily mean that the bare facts, the *numbers*, are wrong, but there's a lack of balance. So in the case of single parents, it may be true that numbers are on the rise, but the stories presented to us fail to discuss how many of these parents are able to continue working or return to further education. They're still contributing to society. But headlines with this kind of positive development don't sell copies, I suppose.

I: So where do you see marriage as an institution in, say, 20 years' time? Do you think it will come to be seen as simply unnecessary?

A: Hardly. You only need look at the number of commercial ventures set up within the wedding industry. People are just as keen to get married as ever; just perhaps not in the way that their grandparents did. It doesn't have to be in a church, the dress doesn't have to be white and people no longer want towels and whiteware as gifts. One thing that hasn't changed is the fact that a high percentage of couples go into marriage not anticipating the kind of challenges likely to arise as a result of becoming a 'unit'. A lot of married life involves meeting halfway, and if you're not prepared to do that, then you're in for trouble. And don't forget, just because tradition is less important in *some* western countries, this isn't the case in others.

I: Adrian, thank you. We're going to take a break, but when we come back, Adrian is ...

Unit 5 (Page 65)

 1.21–1.23

Part 1: Multiple choice

Extract One

I = Interviewer M = Miriam

I: Miriam, your new play, which opens next week, is described as a black comedy – not something you're known for. Are you at all anxious or is opening night an occasion which no longer bothers you?

M: Well, it depends on the production, but in this case, I've been privileged again to have Malcolm Rush as a director. He doesn't care whether you're exhausted; mentally, physically, emotionally – it's immaterial, he'll just continue pushing until every scene is simply perfect. You don't just learn the part – you live it, which takes away any fears you might have of not being able to persuade an audience you're real.

I: Malcolm does have a reputation of being quite the dictator. No one dares voice their opinion, I hear.

M: Well, I do! Malcolm is entirely willing to listen to your point of view once you gain his respect. When we're working on a play, it's a two-way process in which one person comes up with an idea – we see how it works out – and then we don't hold back on any constructive criticism. Actors I've worked with, some of whom have been rather new to the stage, *know* that he's going to be tough with you – but once you've proved yourself, it's all about cooperation and being open to change.

Extract Two

M = Man W = Woman

M: We finally delivered our presentation this morning. The surprising thing, for me, I suppose, was that I actually got on all right with the other students in our group, even Simon, and he's usually so argumentative – and I'd thought that we'd never get *anything* done with him there. Our discussions generated ideas I hadn't even *thought* of.

W: There were three of us working together on our last project. And yes, I think that like that we were probably more creative than if we'd been working alone. I wasn't keen on the idea of collaboration at first, I mean, I didn't know what the other people were like to work with, but my worries came to nothing in the end.

M: So did you find the project easy to do?

W: Not at all – it was still a challenge. For *my* section, I volunteered to do the research on a German company and I had ample time to do it, if I'm honest. And there was plenty of information online which I could refer to. The feedback I got from the tutor, though, was that I needed to take a more critical approach and put my own views forward. I knew as I was writing the project that I wasn't doing that – but I'm just not used to it.

Extract Three

I = Interviewer D = David

I: So David, with the next rally less than 12 hours away, how confident are you of holding your position in front?

D: Well – the team has done an incredible job sorting out all the problems with the car – it's running at peak performance now. The big issue, as you may know, is that my co-driver, Scott King, broke his leg last week and so that's it – he's out for the foreseeable future. Fortunately for us, Eddy Houseman stepped in at the last minute, though, of course, he's never partnered me before, which is a bit of a concern. At least the conditions are favourable – the worst of the ice has cleared – just a few patches left we can deal with.

I: Scott's been with you from the start, hasn't he?

D: Yes, people often underrate the co-driver's role, the glory always goes to the driver. But it's Scott who has the map and the notes. Without him I'd be truly driving blind. You have to have complete faith that what he says is right, I have to know exactly how fast I can take a corner, and be sure that we don't end up rolling into a ditch. That's not to say that he's always to blame for every crash! And I don't know how Eddy's going to deal with my temper – Scott's got used to it after all this time ...

Unit 6 (Page 71)

 1.24–1.28

Part 4: Multiple matching

Speaker 1

I went to, if you like, 'normal' school Monday to Thursday, and I didn't particularly excel in anything, and if that'd been my sole form of learning experience, I probably wouldn't be where I am today, I mean, playing in front of huge European audiences. You see, on Fridays I went to an independent school, where they set up a project for the day, say something on volcanoes. You learnt the usual stuff, but then they encouraged you to respond in your own way. So, for example, the arty kids would make a sculpture, the practical-minded kids built models, and I used to get the instruments out and compose something, just in the corner by myself at first, but then I gained confidence. For me, that's what education should be about, getting kids to express themselves, to use their imagination as a means of developing their abilities.

Speaker 2

I think I got into this profession partly as a reaction to my own teachers. I wanted to show them how teaching should be done. You know, there's nothing worse than when a teenager has a go at something and then they're criticized for getting it wrong. It humiliates them, makes them reluctant to speak out in front of who they see as the brainy kids. My colleagues and I all have the attitude that participation should be rewarded. See – rather than just telling them, 'You're wrong' it's better to help them out with a few more leading questions that'll direct them to the right answer. In that way you're sending the message that it's better to have a go even if their answer isn't quite right than sit there in silence and be excluded.

Speaker 3

There was never any doubt that we were going to send Andrew to boarding school – it's a tradition that goes back four generations in our family – although Andrew is back with us at weekends and I only ever returned for the holidays. The academic advantage is clear – with far smaller classes you get greater individual attention. That allows you to really master a subject. But also, the reason why this kind of private education system works is that the whole ethos is about becoming self-sufficient – it is up to the individual student to ensure they spend a good amount of time on their homework or studying in the library. It is up to them to be in class on time and keep their rooms in order. That kind of discipline is invaluable when it comes to the real world.

Speaker 4

For the last 30 years or so, the majority of schools have allowed boys and girls to study side by side. Whereas their integration within the classroom may benefit them in terms of their social development, the studies we have carried out show that boys consistently underperform when learning alongside girls. Our investigations were based on observations within classrooms that we visited as well as the examination results from a hundred schools over the last three years. Many parents find the notion of educating their son or daughter separately from members of the opposite sex rather old-fashioned, but I believe that school should provide the opportunity for a learner to do as well as they possibly can. While not every child may be naturally gifted, it is possible to develop their intelligence to a far greater extent in the right learning environment.

Speaker 5

My father was rather unconventional and he took it upon himself to educate me at home. This often involved visiting castles, art galleries, and, of course, the wonderful Science Museum. And that's where it all began for me: I was fascinated by the models of atoms and by the early microscopes. I would read up about the stuff I'd seen at home and my father would always say 'When you're ready, we'll have a little test and see what you can remember,' but there was no strict schedule. He knew that it takes time to absorb information. In my laboratory I have to do everything with extreme care and it is vital you do not rush things, but the end result makes it all worthwhile. The same approach should be applied to education.

Unit 6 (Page 78)

 1.29

Part 2: Sentence completion

Good morning everyone. Today, as part of our investigation into sleep disorders, we'll be looking at the condition known as narcolepsy. Narcolepsy can be defined as a chronic neurological disorder which causes excessive sleepiness and frequent daytime attacks. It's not just a case of dozing off and snoozing in a lecture – narcoleptics actually can't stop themselves from falling asleep during inappropriate occasions. And possibly herein lies the problem – sleepiness can be caused by many factors so it can take many months, years even, before a diagnosis, a correct one, I mean, is eventually made by a doctor, but at the moment, narcolepsy is known to affect at least 2500 people in the UK. Perhaps there are more. The exact cause of narcolepsy is a matter of debate, but it's widely believed to be the result of a genetic mutation. The result is that the brain doesn't produce enough of the hormone that regulates a person's sleep-wake cycles. For many narcoleptics, the symptoms aren't just limited to nodding off when they shouldn't. They can also suffer a sudden loss of muscle control whenever they've just experienced a surge of emotion – perhaps they were angry, or fearful or were even just laughing at a good joke. Then, during the night, some narcoleptics suffer from sleep paralysis and during the day, in some cases, even hallucinations are possible.

Let's think about the consequences of this disorder. Not only do narcoleptics have to put up with the physical challenges, but they have to deal with the ignorance of other people. Sufferers are often mistakenly considered to be inebriated or lazy, for example. Narcoleptics report that one of the things that really begins to disappear as a result of their condition is their social life. It's simply too difficult to manage a day or evening out. And it's other people's prejudice again that prevents the majority of narcolepsy sufferers from getting a foothold on the career ladder – they can't even get an interview in many cases – not even an initial one. You can imagine how demoralizing this must be. And, in fact, the problem exists not just for narcoleptics hoping to pursue a white-collar profession, but also for those seeking manual work. Any job that requires a person to operate machinery will probably not be open to narcoleptics – ostensibly for reasons of safety. And there's another consequence of suffering from this disorder – perhaps the one that the families of narcoleptics find most difficult to deal with. Because narcoleptics have to keep as calm as possible – all the time – in order to avoid the sudden loss of muscle control we talked about earlier – it may involve a personality change – and this must be a hard thing indeed to bear.

Currently, there's no cure for …

Unit 7 (Page 97)

 1.30

Part 3: Multiple choice

P = Presenter
DE = Dr Evans L = Lynnie

P: In search of a more youthful appearance, many people nowadays are turning to Botox®, the botulism toxin which is purified and used in small doses to remove unwanted wrinkles. With me is Dr Duncan Evans, who regularly turns up at parties to inject the guests with the toxin, and Lynnie Highfield, one of Dr Evans' patients and a regular Botox partygoer. Dr Evans, perhaps I should begin by asking why this treatment takes place at parties, and not in a surgery?

DE: That's very simple, really. It's easier, and more convenient, for people to go to a social gathering at a friend's house, than to give up their valuable time getting into central London. When I first started out in this business, I'd often be asked to go to the homes of the rich and famous, the type of people who didn't want to get caught by the press going into a clinic. Now, though, it's mainly people who've simply got too much going on in their lives to justify making the journey in.

P: Is that your case, Lynnie?

L: Yes, it is. Plus, of course, we have a good time. I've been to several parties in the last couple of years and you tend to meet up with the same people. That's largely because the benefits of the injection tend to wear off after three or four months so we all keep going back for more.

P: Is it painful?

L: Nowhere near as painful as having your legs waxed, I can tell you! Just a slight discomfort as the needle goes in, that's all. And there are no serious side effects – or so Dr Evans tells us – just some minor bruising and an outside chance of getting some fluey, cold-like symptoms.

P: So, Dr Evans, how does it work? Why would anyone want to have a poison injected into their body?

DE: Well, yes, poison it most certainly is, and a deadly one at that. But injected in small quantities into the forehead it does nothing more than paralyse the muscles that cause frown lines and wrinkles. Different people use it for different reasons – to make them feel better, to look younger, to enable them to get work on television – whatever. Of course, I need to set a good example if I want to convince people of the benefits of the treatment, so I regularly hand over the needle to my wife, who does it for me. She's a qualified nurse, so I have every confidence in her.

P: Does it work for you?

DE: Well, I make a living, if that's what you mean, but perhaps I should have started younger – as you can see, I've still got one or two faint lines there.

P: And how about you, Lynnie? Why do you have the injections?

L: For me, it's a way of growing old gracefully. I mean, we all use moisturizer, we all take care of ourselves. I think it's just an extension of that. Many people might baulk at the price, but I think it's fairly affordable. It's certainly worth doing, anyway. I look upon it now as normal maintenance – something that needs doing on a regular basis. I also like doing meditation, as well. I want to feel beautiful on the inside as well as on the outside.

P: And have other people noticed the effects?

L: Yes, they have. And they've grown used to my new look now, of course, but when I first went for treatment, they didn't say, 'Oh, you do look younger', which is, of course, why I had it done. It was more of a 'you look less stressed' or 'you don't look so depressed'. Before the treatment, you see, I had these terrible hereditary lines, a kind of constant frown, which made it look as though I was permanently unhappy. I was always saying, 'I'm fine. Really. It's just the way I look'. Now I don't have to make excuses for my appearance anymore.

P: You must be very proud of your work, Dr Evans, knowing the effect it can have on people's lives. And it's fun, too, I imagine.

DE: It's certainly a wonderful feeling seeing people grow in confidence and self-esteem. I'm not a great one for being charming and chatty when I'm working, though – that would just be too draining. Dealing with 20-odd patients in one evening is not normal, by any stretch of the imagination, and it takes a lot out of you. But no one seems to notice that. I'm obviously so fresh-faced and young-looking ...

P: Now it's funny you should mention that, because I've been dying to ask you about your age ...

Unit 8 (Page 102)

 1.31

Part 2: Sentence completion

Good morning. My name's Andy Brown, and I'm the co-founder of Kingdom Games. It's a pleasure to be here – and I'm hoping that if you're not into gaming already, I will have convinced you that you're definitely missing out by the time I've finished this talk.

Well, the industry has come a long way since the basic pixellated formats of the 1980s. In one respect, the older games and modern games are similar: we play them for the thrill, for the victory – but they're very different in another. Many *modern* games engage the player emotionally and intellectually. As a product, I suppose we could describe them if you like, as a marriage, between art, when we consider their visual impact on us, and science; the technology that allows us to step inside these very different worlds. And in those days, back in the 80s – even up until the last ten years – we know that it was largely young men that were the target market. But today we have to acknowledge that gaming has been fully integrated into mainstream culture. The equipment has been moved into the living room for the whole family to play. Whether it's a Sony PlayStation® or Xbox®, pretty much every household has one. The way I see it, developers have both responded to and instigated this trend.

You might ask, where do developers get their inspiration from? Well, numerous sources, of course, but at the moment, we can see the definite influence of classic cinema. For example, in the past, good and evil could easily be recognized – through the characters you created, through the options they were offered. You knew which side you were on. Well, we're maturing now, along with our audiences. It's no longer black and white – but every shade of grey. And one of the consequences of this, for my team, anyway, is the need to establish mood – a sense of anxiety, of despair, for example, through the use of lighting. And this is something we're working on in our current projects with – I believe – great success.

Some things, I guess, won't change. There are the central and basic concepts, or themes, that create authenticity and purpose in a game. Combat is one – you'll always need a good fight whether it's between unidentified enemy soldiers, aliens, zombies ... whatever ... and the problem-solving element is also vital. And finally, and I think this is true for all forms of storytelling, you need the element of exploration. It's in our human nature to pursue this.

So why are some sections of society so anti-gaming? What is it that creates fear and ignorance amongst people – people who've usually never picked up a console for themselves? In large part, I feel this is down to the media. They never seem to miss an opportunity to focus on a story or a piece of research that shows the industry in a bad light. Look, it's basic common sense that if you let your kid play for 24 hours straight, they're missing out on other things – on *life* – but let's have some balanced reporting, please.

For a start, parents and teachers both seem to overlook something important about the gaming industry – they just don't know about the great number of career opportunities it offers. And this is an industry that now turns over huge profits annually – so worth getting into. And I think there's a feeling amongst some parents, a suspicion in fact, that gaming is somehow rotting their kids' brains. But the evidence is there to prove otherwise. Now I've got a vested interest in all this, of course, but if you look at the research, we know for a fact that not only do kids get more creative through game playing, but they also get better at logic. Surely that's something that most people would be happy to see developing in their child.

Now, one future development concerns crowd-funding, which ...

Unit 8 (Page 111)

 1.32–1.36

Part 4: Multiple matching

Speaker 1

I think a lot of the science fiction scenarios of miniature computers the size of a matchbox and phones you can wear like a button on your jacket are going to be too impractical to be put to general use. You only have to look at a widescreen TV to realize there's little chance of that happening. My own belief is that electronic gadgetry will actually take over our living space – you won't be able to move in your own home for fear of knocking into some device or other. That's a big shame, really – life was so much simpler before, so much more free of clutter. And I'm not talking about the dim and distant past here, but a relatively recent one.

Speaker 2

There's little doubt that the average lifespan will be greater, but I can't help feeling more than a little concerned about the quality of life we'll be leading when we reach the end of our days. I'm not sure, for example, that we'll have achieved what we need to in terms of finding cures for certain degenerative diseases such as Alzheimer's or Parkinson's. There's a great deal of enthusiastic talk about genetics and how absolutely marvellous it is that we've mapped the human genome. Now that's all very well, but I'm afraid I just can't see myself, or anyone else for that matter, playing tennis at the age of 120.

Speaker 3

It always irritates me when people go on about population growth and how it's getting out of control and so on. If you look at the figures, you'll see that predictions of exploding populations made 20 or 30 years ago are simply not coming true. It's probably the same people that worry about the number of vehicles on the roads, as well. Let's face it though, 15 years from now most of us will be working from home on a computer, which means fewer people getting stuck in jams on their way to work, and a consequent reduction in pollution. Now that's definitely something worth looking forward to, isn't it?

Speaker 4

They sent me on a computer training course last month – at my age! We had a right laugh about it in the office, I can tell you. Still, you've got to keep up with it all, else they won't keep you on, will they? There seems to be more and more technology every day – it's going to change the way they do things here completely, you know. In 15 years from now you won't recognize the place at all.

Of course, I'll have left long before then, and I'll probably be enjoying a long and healthy retirement somewhere. But it does make you wonder whether they're up to something – you know, Big Brother and all that. I've always been suspicious of change, me. Can't help it.

Speaker 5

Where I live, you'd be forgiven for thinking the size of the population is mushrooming. Every weekend there are more and more houses going up, and you see more and more traffic on the roads. But what's happening, of course, is that the existing population is financially healthier than it used to be, so more and more people can afford to buy themselves a second home in the country – which is where they're all driving out to on a Friday evening. And because the price of land is so expensive, these places are gradually shrinking in size – so much so that by the time I've raised enough money to buy my own place, I won't be able to swing a cat in it. Sounds funny, but it's a real nuisance, I can tell you.

Unit 9 (Page 116)

 2.1

Part 2: Sentence completion

Well, hello everyone. I think most of you know that I recently went to Queenstown for my work placement, um, at the Lake Hotel, and the person I was attached to for the week was the front desk clerk. So basically I was learning all about what a typical day for him involved and what kind of skills you needed to do that specific job. I had a choice of three hotels that I could work in for the placement – but I ended up deciding on the Lake Hotel because it isn't really affected by seasonal tourism. A high proportion of its guests are there for conferences and meetings – so it's pretty much fully booked on a continual basis – and I wanted a bit of a challenge. Anyway, as soon as I walked into the hotel, I suppose I was struck by how professional everyone seemed. Of course, your room and the hotel facilities are important, but actually, I realized it's the way the hotel staff are presented that you notice first, and in particular, how stylish and neat the uniform looks. I think I'll definitely have to smarten up once I start work for real. Well, getting back to the front desk clerk – his name was Andre, he was Swiss, and he'd been working at the hotel for about three years. As I watched him talk to the guests, I saw that he was using their names quite a bit, which is apparently the hotel policy – it's a way of building a professional relationship. Then later Andre explained that whenever he deals with a guest, he makes sure he finds out the nationality of that person, because that sort of information will tell him what their requirements are likely to be, and so enable him to give them the best service possible. So, for example, in his experience, German travellers tend to have done all their research before they arrive and only want basic advice, but Chinese travellers often expect everything to be arranged for them, apparently.

I worked from 7am to 3pm every day – under Andre's supervision, of course – and there was honestly a constant stream of people checking in all the time I was at the front desk. Then, of course, other guests would come and request a room move or extend their stay or something, and what really impressed me about Andre was how he managed to inform every department in the hotel about those changes, almost immediately in fact, no matter how busy he was. There's a daily meeting with management, too, but I didn't go along to that.

I asked Andre if there was anything he disliked about the job, and I thought he would have said something like guest complaints or working nights. (I don't know how people get used to the night shift.) It was dealing with foreign currency transactions, though, that he said he had problems with. He said he would always delegate it to an assistant if he could. I think he just preferred interacting with guests – and I don't think he was just making small talk with them – I think his interest in helping them was actually quite genuine.

I spent quite a bit of time giving guests information about things to do in Queenstown – including where to go shopping and buy decent souvenirs – that was more for the tour groups and older guests. The younger ones were there primarily for the adventure activities – that was the main attraction – and they wanted advice on which companies to book with. So part of my job was to promote some of the more established and reputable tour operators and I was fine with that because I'd expected it and got myself prepared. The local restaurants, though, were a different matter. I was surprised that guests were asking me about them because obviously there's one in the hotel and you really want the guests to be eating there. I just had to admit that I'd only just started work – and I'd have to get Andre to help them. I did ask him later why it would be in the hotel's interest to recommend other places for the guests to eat or visit, even. He said that in order for the hotel's profits to continue to grow, it was essential to keep on building up customer loyalty – and that meant providing the best service possible. I could see what he meant. I suppose a lot of hotels have a similar outlook and philosophy. Well, I would definitely recommend Queenstown if you haven't done your work placement yet. It wasn't until I began working there that I realized how huge its hospitality industry actually is.

Unit 9 (Page 117)

 2.2

Language focus: Creating emphasis

See page 117 Language focus: Creating emphasis

Unit 9 (Page 120)

 2.3

Part 3: Multiple choice

P = Presenter J = James

P: It started with road rage in the 90s, then we had air rage, and now it's trolley rage, surf rage, movie rage and even dot.com rage. Anger, it seems, is all the rage these days. But why? With us is James Frith, head of road safety at the British Automobile Club. James, what makes people so aggressive on the roads?

J: Well, it's all about control, really. Once people get in their car, they feel a false, a dangerous sense of security and control. They're in their own little world, their own safe environment where they can deceive themselves into thinking they're better drivers than they really are. But this, of course, contrasts with events that happen outside the car, events over which they have absolutely no control whatsoever.

P: And when they lose control, they lose their temper, right?

J: That's right. For instance, most people set deadlines for their road journeys, and if someone threatens to prevent them from meeting that deadline, from not getting where they want to, when they want to, they blow a fuse. And that's when we get road rage, or in many cases now, revenge rage.

P: Another rage! What's revenge rage, James?

J: Well, it's similar to road rage, but less active. People get worked up inside, but just think nasty thoughts about other road users, without actually doing anything. They imagine, for example, going after someone who's cut them up and forcing them off the road. The problem is they get so caught up in their angry dreams of revenge that they fail to concentrate on the essential task of driving safely. And there's more of a risk of them causing an accident themselves than there is for the driver who has offended them.

P: And who are these angry people, these so-called 'road' and 'revenge ragers'?

J: We carried out a study recently and we found it was mainly 18- to 25-year-old men who committed acts of road rage, and these people often had criminal records, histories of violence or drug or alcohol problems. In the case of 'revenge ragers', people who merely fantasize about violent acts, they are more evenly spread across the age groups and between the sexes. The majority, though, are low-mileage motorists, those who only average between 30 and 60 miles a week. And the people who are most likely to trigger revenge rage, the ones who cause these people to lose their temper, are inexperienced youngsters who drive quickly, elderly drivers, and drivers of big articulated lorries or vans.

P: Makes you wonder why people don't just get the bus! Surely that's a calmer, more comfortable way to travel? Or is there bus rage, too?

J: Not exactly. But people do get fed up, don't they, when the bus just crawls its way along the route because the driver's busy taking people's money, giving them change or answering questions. And other road users don't respect the bus lanes, so you can end up in the same congestion, the same anger-inducing situations that you tried to avoid by leaving the car at home.

P: So what is the solution? How can drivers keep their calm on the roads?

J: I'm not sure there are any easy answers. But in one experiment, Dr David Lewis, the man who coined the term 'road rage', gave 25 stressed out city drivers a kit containing real grass and a spray of grass scent. He told them to park their cars, take off their shoes and socks, and enjoy the sensation of grass beneath their bare feet.

P: The point being ...?

J: Well, changes in their heart rate and blood pressure were measured and they were clearly more relaxed with the smell and sensation of grass around them. Now, you'd expect a higher proportion of calm drivers on country roads, because there is considerably less traffic, but it's the combination of silence in the car, the smell of our immediate environment, and what we can feel that can really help calm us down and have a positive influence on our driving habits.

P: So can we expect grass kits to be on the market soon?

J: Possibly. I'm sure the research will be put to some use. What we do have already, though, is a kind of back-seat computer. Engineers have developed a hi-tech car which criticizes drivers when they are behaving rashly or have poor control of the car. A message comes up on the control panel. It also praises them for good road manners when they are driving considerately. If the driving becomes too erratic, the car stops.

P: Sounds like a good idea.

J: As long as drivers don't rely on it. We're always interested in technology that helps drivers' control, but not technology that takes it away from them. Certainly, though, we've all been in that situation with someone in the passenger seat telling us to calm down – it can be annoying, but very effective. And if this works in much the same way, then fine – though I can see stressed out drivers becoming even more irate when their car suddenly stops!

P: Yes, indeed! Now, James, some of our listeners have written in with their own suggestions as to how we can maintain our composure in the car. Alan Hammans writes in from Tooting telling us how he uses spoken word tapes ...

Ready for Listening (Page 126)

 2.4–2.6

Part 1: Multiple choice

Extract One

W = Woman M = Man

W: Did you see that programme on global warming the other day? I thought it was kind of irresponsible to present the views of a minority of scientists who think that man-made global warming doesn't exist.

M: Yes, but remember that one of the first things we were taught on the course is that you must have a balanced approach to reporting. That means allowing the public to hear both sides of the argument. At the same time, you and I know perfectly well that a real balance doesn't exist. You wouldn't, for example, give as many column inches to the enemy opinion in a war, would you? And the same goes for the global warming debate. I'd say that, realistically, far more attention is given to the scientific view that climate change *is* happening – and not to the few voices that deny it.

W: I guess so. After the programme I read a lot of comments posted on the channel's website. There was quite a bit of mixed reaction. Some people were making the point 'if global warming isn't man-made, why bother taking steps to save the environment?' That's why I thought the programme had been rather reckless. But I suppose that if the media *really* had a lot of influence, people would have changed their behaviour already, like stop using their cars so much. You know what people are like – only government regulations will stop them from polluting and messing up the natural world – that's what it'll take in the end.

Extract Two

I = Interviewer A = Andy

I: Andy, your company, Kiss Chocolates was established a good 20 years before you took over. What made you suddenly decide to take a leap into chocolate-making?

A: Actually a combination of random events. I was made redundant in 2002, and although I absolutely loved advertising, it was a relief to leave because it meant that all the uncertainty about whether the job would last was gone. At the same time, my wife had just happened to come across the chocolate shop and was buying a gift box, when she overheard the owner mention her desire to retire. We both thought the product was excellent – and we both knew there would always be a demand for chocolate.

I: Yes, indeed! And there are probably a lot of people listening who are very envious of you. What's the best part of the job for you, Andy?

A: Well, the product is certainly hard to resist! But because people come in to buy the chocolate as a gift, as a token of love or of appreciation for another person, you never have to face anyone in a bad mood. That's what makes it all so rewarding for me, even more than the prospect of long-term financial security.

Extract Three

J = Jennifer A = Andrew

J: I have to say that I found *The Children of Hurin* completely absorbing, far more so than I expected. But it's hardly uplifting, is it?

A: No. Even from the early pages, one has a great sense that all is not going to end well for the central character, Turin. He *is* a hero in the sense that he is a brave, honourable man on a mission, but fate delivers him one cruel blow after another. As events unfold, you can see how tragedy is inescapable.

J: Now the book is based on various manuscripts that JRR Tolkien never completed before he died. And it's taken his son Christopher 30 years to put them together as a single cohesive story.

A: That's right – and overall, he really has produced a thing of beauty. Readers will notice, however, that one passage may be written in some kind of ancient English and then the next in a more contemporary manner – as you'd expect in a book pieced together from manuscripts written over a 50-year period, and that can be a little distracting. Tolkien's characterization is sometimes underdeveloped but not so this time, as Christopher has given us a hero we can identify …

Ready for Listening (Page 127)

 2.7

Part 2: Sentence completion

Well, hello everyone. My name's Amanda Tyler and I've come to tell you something about my work as a waxwork sculptor. Um, I spend nearly all of my time hidden away with my colleagues in the studio at the wax museum. You might imagine we have a light and airy warehouse space. That would be nice. But actually we don't have much sun coming in at all because we're down in the basement. It feels a bit sad at times, to be honest! It makes a nice change to be here with so many people and some natural light.

I suppose I became interested in sculpting at school, where I was taking classes in art and design. My teacher was very encouraging and she encouraged me to go and specialize at Loughborough University on their course which was then referred to as Fine Arts. I suspect the title may have changed since I was there.

Well, firstly, I'd like to tell you a bit about the process that goes into making a waxwork figure. Um … the first stage is, in fact, the one I like most. That's when we get the measurements of our subject – the person we want to make a model of. This is a real highlight of the job, as you get to travel and meet celebrities. It's not easy though, getting them to sit still for two hours or more while you struggle to get the information you need.

Now, as you can't have failed to notice, there's a big clay head on the table and even at this early stage, I'm hoping that you can recognize the well-known newsreader, David Wainwright, from Channel 5. So at the moment, as I said, he's made of clay which I've moulded onto an 'armature'. That's this thing here, which is basically a frame made out of wire netting. Back in the studio I have an armature for his whole body – and that's got rods as well, metal ones, to give it support and strength, and I've cut those to size for his arms and legs.

Now, another thing that we sculptors have to bear in mind is that the public have certain expectations about the way a famous person might sit or stand or move, and if we don't get that right, then our wax figure won't be convincing. So it's really vital that the position we put the subject in looks authentic. When I've finished David here, he'll be sitting behind a desk, leaning back slightly.

The whole thing is a very slow process. It can take me about three or four weeks just to get to the clay model stage we have here, and I may need as much as five months to make one figure – from the time I start to the time it's ready to go on display.

So, what's next? Well, from this clay model I'll make a plaster mould and fill that with hot liquid wax. And when it's cooled, hey presto, we have our wax head. Um … then it's time for the eyes. What we do is select two acrylic eyeballs that are roughly the same size as the subject's.

Then we touch them up by hand with watercolours to get a more exact copy. That's usually my job. Then I hand it over to our make-up artist, who uses oil paint together with more conventional cosmetics for the rest of the head.

The hair is probably …

Ready for Listening (Page 128)

 2.8

Part 3: Multiple choice

I = Interviewer S = Sandra
D = David

I: On this week's *In Partnership* programme we talk to Sandra Peyton and David Sadler, who together run the successful media company, Advert Eyes, specializing in the making of TV commercials. Sandra, if I could start with you. What were you doing before you set up in partnership with David and what made you change?

S: Well, I was directing – er, drama mostly – for a small satellite TV company. It was an interesting, experimental time for me – they were a young, dynamic group and seemed to be going places. But these were troubled times for the business in general and they just weren't making enough money. Anyway, things weren't looking too good for me; as I'd been the last to arrive, I reckoned I'd probably be the first to have to leave.

I: So you jumped before you were pushed, so to speak.

S: That's right, and that was a great shame, because I'd never felt so comfortable working in a team as I did with that group of people.

I: David, you had a similar background, didn't you?

D: Yes, I'd also made a name for myself directing TV drama, but with the much larger Trenton TV. I left them because they were moving in a different direction to where I wanted to go. But the experience proved invaluable for the future – I can see that now.

I: In what way?

D: Working in close collaboration with others is an integral part of this business – that's always been clear to me – but I came to realize that you can't rely on other people to make things work. It's a tough old world and ultimately it's down to you – it's a question of attitude. Things only happen if you let them – and if you only see grey skies and gloomy days ahead, that's what you'll get.

I: So the whole thing focused you for your future with Advert Eyes.

D: That's right, I did a lot of growing up with Trenton.

I: Well, tell us how you met each other, Sandra.

S: We were introduced at a party by a mutual friend. I remember I was very wary of David at first. He already had quite a reputation in the business – his past work spoke for itself. And he looked so serious, so apparently indifferent to everything. He mentioned some vague idea he had for setting up a business, something to do with advertising – but that wasn't what struck me most. I just couldn't get over how animated, how passionate he became when he talked about – well, everything really. It was difficult not to be carried along by his words.

I: So when he asked you to join him, you had no hesitation in accepting?

D: Well, it was actually Sandra who asked me. And I was the one who had no hesitation. My colleagues at Trenton had warned me against going into business with a complete unknown – they said it was too much of a gamble. But when I met Sandra, it was like looking into a mirror. Here at last was someone on my wavelength, someone who looked at life through the same camera lens. And, anyway, I felt it was time to do something different, to live a little dangerously.

I: And has it been? Dangerous, I mean.

D: Anything but. Funnily enough, though, it's turned out that we do have quite a lot of differences, but these have all been to our advantage. Sandra, for example, has much more of a business brain than I do.

I: Is that right, Sandra?

S: Well, yes, it seems to be a hidden talent of mine. But I've had to learn the hard way. Raising money, for example, was an absolute nightmare – we just couldn't seem to get the finance.

I: That must have been quite disheartening.

S: Well, no, you can't afford to let things

like that get you down. It was no good getting upset about it; throwing a tantrum in a bank manager's office is never a good idea – you might need to go back there one day. No, I just couldn't work out what the problem was, given our experience and the way the advertising market was shaping up at the time. We were just a small concern, asking for a small amount of money.

I: But you obviously got the money.

S: Yes, I met an investor who understood what we were about – and then, once we'd made a couple of ads, money was easier to come by.

I: David, how does, er, advertising work compare with TV drama? Is it very different?

D: Well, for a start there's more money around than for normal TV work, and that can be very liberating. But the market's understanding of quality may not be the same as yours and you find your creativity stifled. Yes, it's our own company, and it may seem a creative business to an outsider. But an advert is not your own baby in the same way that a TV drama might be. There are too many people who have a say in what you do and what goes into the advert.

S: Yes, I'd go along with that, although for me, running a business can be incredibly creative.

I: So what does the future hold for Advert Eyes? What are your plans for the company?

S: Well, we can't really say too much at the moment. It's not that we're not willing to, it's just that we're not entirely certain how things will work out ourselves.

D: That's right. The normal thing might be to look at some type of long-term growth for the business, but at the moment we're concentrating on consolidating our position, rather than branching out. Who knows what the future will bring?

I: Sandra, David, the very best of luck for the future. There we must leave it. Thank you.

S&D: Thank you.

Ready for Listening (Page 129)

 2.9–2.13

Part 4: Multiple matching

Speaker 1

I could barely string two sentences together when I first arrived, and now I'm reasonably fluent. In that sense, then, I've achieved what I set out to do – just by being here and mixing with the locals. I've met some great people since I got here, especially the family I'm living with. But there's a big downside to all this. I decided to come here on my year out because it's so different to all the other places I could have gone to. Plus it seemed so exciting when I came here two years ago. However, that was on holiday and I realize now that living here is actually rather dull. I really wish I'd gone somewhere on the mainland now – my girlfriend's having a great time there.

Speaker 2

My father studied here as a young man, so I knew quite a lot about the country before I came. And when the head of my company's overseas operations told me our branch here wasn't doing too well, and would I please go and sort things out, I was very happy to accept. My husband came out shortly after I did and like me, immediately fell in love with the place. The pace of life suits us to a tee and the food is just out of this world. Ultimately, though, we're home birds and when this posting's over we'll want to go back to be nearer our grandchildren – if we ever have any, that is!

Speaker 3

I was working in the dullest job you can imagine – nine to five every day on the computer, answering customers' email queries. But it was thanks to that job that I got to know Patti, who was over on a work exchange programme in another department. She only stayed for three months, though, so after that nearly all our contact was by email. Of course, you can't keep something going like that indefinitely, so I took the plunge and moved out here. Life is fine – despite the overcast skies and regular downpours! I have to admit, though, it does get me down sometimes. I'd like to get back home more often, but it's just too far.

Speaker 4

I only wish I'd made the break earlier. It's so vibrant in this part of the world – there's so much more going on. I think if I was still back home, I'd be so depressed, what with the current climate there and so on. The fact is I was in a bit of a rut. I was sick of the same old thing, day in, day out and I thought, 'There's got to be more to life than this'. So I looked into the price of property in different parts of southern Europe, and this area was one of the cheapest. It didn't take me long to settle in – the language isn't much of a problem and I've even got myself a little part-time job. Keeps me out of trouble!

Speaker 5

A few years ago I set up in business with a friend of mine. Then I decided to go it alone and bought out my partner's share. Unfortunately, before long, things started to go wrong and I was up to my eyes in debt. Call it cowardice, but I just couldn't deal with it and I moved out here. It got me out of a mess, but I can't say I'm having the time of my life. I know a lot of different people here, but I just don't seem to fit in with them. We share the same language – more or less – but we're worlds apart in most other respects. One thing's for sure – if ever I do go back to face the music, it'll be for good.

Unit 10 (Page 135)

 2.14–2.18

Part 4: Multiple matching

Speaker 1

We used to live above a gym. I say 'used to' 'cause they had to close it down and go somewhere else. Some of the neighbours got together, see, and got someone from the council to come round. It wasn't so much the music because the place was pretty well soundproofed. It was more all the coming and going – especially at night, around 10ish, when it shut and the people would all leave at the same time and then one engine after another would start up. In the winter they'd leave them running for a bit – time to defrost the windows, I suppose – and the neighbours said it made too much of a racket. I can't say I noticed it much, though – live and let live, I say. We've all got to make a living somehow.

Speaker 2

Well, one day I was upstairs in my office and was just about to start on a new chapter when I heard this – noise. At first, I thought someone was actually in pain and I leapt up to the window – but then I saw my neighbour Sheila and I guess a couple of her friends in her back room. What they were doing, you see, was practising for the local amateur operatic group. The din was unbearable and it completely put me off my writing. And I've got deadlines to meet that I cannot put off and I was getting nowhere! It went on every morning for a fortnight and then just suddenly stopped. Perhaps they went to practise elsewhere. I live in dread that it'll start up again.

Speaker 3

Nothing but trouble, that man. Fancy bringing a cockerel to live in a residential area! That sort of thing you'd expect in the countryside, but not here. Being a cockerel, it would start at five – this awful racket and it'd wake up the baby and she'd start wailing so there was no way we could ignore it. We tried to reason with him but, he said we were making a fuss over nothing. Then that afternoon there was a whole bunch of hens clucking around his back garden, too. It got so bad that we realized the only course of action was to take him to court. Which we did and we won. It was expensive but worth it. He was ordered to have the cockerel destroyed or sell it. Whatever he did – we can now sleep peacefully.

Speaker 4

One of the benefits of working as a builder – all that physical activity knocks you out for the night. But since I did my back in and I had to take a desk job, it's harder for me to get off to sleep. This woman down the road has a teenage son, and every Friday and Saturday night their house seems to be the meeting point for all their mates. They hang around in the road and, and maybe they don't realize how far their voices carry – or maybe they just don't care. Why can't they have a conversation *indoors*? I used to be a laid-back kind of guy, but now I feel angry a lot of the time. That's not how I want to be – and I resent the effect it's had on me.

Speaker 5

Night after night he'd have it blaring out at full volume – news programmes and reality shows mostly – and all we could do was sit there, seething. He said he couldn't hear it if he had it on any lower. Deaf as a post, he was. It really brings out the worst in you, something like that, and it put a tremendous strain on our marriage. We were so stressed out by it all and we rowed like we'd never rowed before, often about the silliest of things. Anyway, we got so sick of it all, we sold up and bought a place in the country. Shame really, 'cause I like having people around me and there are days here when all I have for company are the pigeons and other birds we have nesting up in the trees across the road.

Unit 11 (Page 142)

 2.20–2.22

Part 1: Multiple choice

Extract One

W = Woman M = Man

W: It's traditional for American kids to spend part of their summer at camp, but the young people looking after them are often from other parts of the world, usually students on their *own* summer break. So someone, say, from Spain, will arrive at camp and as they get off the bus, they discover they'll be working with someone from Australia, for instance, rather than the American they expected. And then, of course, by the time camp's over, they'll have made travel plans to tour the USA together.

M: Yeah, it's the people you work with that make you want to go back. It's a fantastic thing to do when you're young. But I would say to anyone who's considering applying to work for a camp that it's not the equivalent of a luxury holiday in a hotel. It *is* a very satisfying experience – but it does feel a bit like military camp at times. That's not to say that you're taking orders and have no say – it's all very much about teamwork. It's more that you're often on duty for extended periods – including night supervision of the children. The food's not too bad, though. Make sure you look out for the advertisements in *The Globe*.

Extract Two

M = Man W = Woman

M: Before I took part in the documentary, I'm ashamed to say that I didn't know that much about that period of history – the 1900s, of course – when my great-grandfather came to Australia and worked, like so many other Chinese, in the gold mines. I've always seen myself as a Chinese Australian, but that was more to do with family values and some of our spiritual beliefs. I have to say that we grew up, my sisters and I, we grew up when my parents were already relatively wealthy, and I had a good education. But I know now that I took it all for granted then. Being involved in the film showed me what hardships our ancestors went through and the sacrifices they made.

W: I suspect we had the same kind of childhood. Strict Chinese parents. I bet you had to do more homework than other kids in your class.

M: Yes, but in all other respects, I think we were the same. If you have an Australian accent, you're seen as an Australian.

W: Hmmm, I think we've come a long way. Our communities used to be hidden from view, but now we're much more integrated. We're not hidden away in cafés and market gardens anymore. And it's no longer the case that every parent is insisting their kid becomes a doctor or a lawyer. You've now also got Chinese Australians performing as musicians, artists, writers – that was a rare sight not so long ago. But it still occasionally happens that when I'm introduced to a European Australian, they like to compliment me on my good English. It doesn't occur to them that my family may have been here longer than theirs.

Extract Three

M = Man W = Woman

M: In the West, tattooing is still not regarded as mainstream art, so one of the reasons for putting the exhibition together is to break down people's preconceptions about this art form. There's this stereotype of tattoos being worn by people trying to show that they're non-conformist in some way – but certain cultures have long been wearing tattoos to show exactly where they *do* fit in society.

W: Yeah, they're seen as sacred and the patterns are often incredibly intricate. But if you're from a culture that associates tattoos with antisocial behaviour – you might regard a tattooed person with suspicion, I suppose. That's the kind of mentality the exhibition hopes to confront, really. Um, a large part of the exhibition is dedicated to the Maori people of New Zealand; as with other Polynesian cultures, tattoos for Maori were an indication of a man's rank within the tribe. But unique to Maori was how facial tattooing also indicated his ancestry – that's why it's essentially taboo for non-Maori men to copy them. That's not to say that Maori women weren't tattooed – but it was often done on the chin. Anyway, the exhibition really does provide a fascinating look at the history of tattooing. There's also a collection of tools on view which are worth ...

Unit 11 (Page 147)

 2.23

Part 2: Sentence completion

P = Presenter G = Gaby

P: Now, in our regular *Confessions* spot, we listen to award-winning writer Gaby Longfellow, who was recently described as 'the most versatile and prolific writer of her generation'. So what is Gaby's confession?

G: People assume that because I'm a writer, because I come from Oxford, and because I spend hours poring over books in university libraries doing research for my work, that I must have gone to university myself. And the plain truth of the matter is, of course, that I didn't. I don't have a degree.

During my school years I had a very full social life: I was in a theatre group, I sang in a choir, I had a boyfriend, I went rock climbing. Right through my teens concentration was never my specialist subject at school. I'd always be looking out of the window, thinking of the hundred and one other things I could be doing.

And so it was with my A-levels. Which I failed, quite spectacularly. I could have retaken them, of course, but I was too worried the same thing might happen again. Failing once wasn't too bad – nearly everyone put it down to bad luck, as opposed to any lack of effort on my part. But if I'd failed again I would've been officially declared stupid. Or at least, that's how I saw it then.

But it never occurred to me that I was any less intelligent than my friends who did go to university. In fact, at the time I thought *I* was the clever one for not going, and I probably came across as being rather arrogant as a result. I went to live in London and had a wonderfully exciting time, experiencing many things that my undergraduate friends could not. It was a period that gave me ideas and inspiration for my writing. I also read voraciously and *always* seemed to have a book in my hand. My reading gave me a passion for language and all its various features; an aptly chosen word, a well-crafted phrase, a striking metaphor – these are all things I try to emulate in my own writing.

Do I have any regrets? No, none at all. Indeed, many of my friends agree that university was rather a waste of time. And some of them feel bitter because their degrees pushed them into the types of professions that are detrimental to family life, ones that keep them away from home. They always seem to be worried about losing their well-paid jobs and they have little time or energy to devote to the things, or rather the people, that really matter. I even detect a certain amount of envy from some quarters. A lawyer friend of mine is always asking if he can swap lives with me. I have a great deal of admiration and respect for lawyers, but not, I have to say, enough to want to become one.

But I wouldn't try to discourage young people today from going to university. It has its advantages as well as its drawbacks and people have to make up their own minds. But it doesn't help now that when graduates start work in their chosen profession, many of them have huge bank loans, because they've had to borrow heavily in order to pay their way through university. The idea is that those with degrees will have well-paid jobs and can easily pay back the money in the future. There's no guarantee of that, of course, and besides, it tends to convert money and the prospect of higher earnings into the main incentive for university education. And that, I confess, is not something I agree with.

Unit 12 (Page 154)

 2.24

Part 2: Sentence completion

Hello, my name's Nina Christie, and I'm here today to talk to you about the work I do, which is taking photographs of wildlife, mainly here in Britain and Africa, and also India – when I'm lucky enough to get a job there. Um, I'll start by saying that I get lots of enquiries from young people asking whether it's possible to make a living as a wildlife photographer – and yes, it is, but it's becoming an increasingly competitive world, and so if you want it to work out as a long-term career, you need real determination in the tough times, not to mention a really good business sense. A love of nature isn't going to be enough – not if you want to pay the bills. Um, nowadays, I tend to take on projects that are located in places where I've already done a lot of work – so, for example, some of the big national parks in Africa. Over the years I've built up a good relationship with the local authorities there, so it's relatively easy for me to get the right permits to work off-road and after hours, for example. That definitely gives me the edge over other photographers. So, before I go on a trip, there's quite a bit to sort out – booking guides and vehicles – that sort of stuff, and the other thing that you absolutely have to do in terms of research, is decide which animals you're going to photograph, and then study their behaviour. So, I'll spend time reading up on them, or watching anything available on film. So yeah, doing some groundwork really helps when it comes to predicting how the subject's going to move and react.

I know some of you will be keen to know what camera equipment I use and I've brought along some lenses and filters to show you, but we'll do that a bit later. Anyway, over the years I've learnt through experience that it's also worth packing some basic forms of medicine. If you're wading through swamps or lying in long grass – you're bound to end up being attacked by leeches or tics or some other creepy-crawly. It's all in a day's work!

I'd like to explain a little bit about my own personal attitude to photography. For me, I think that every time I take a photograph – that photograph is a means of capturing a real event. I'd rather spend a long time in the field waiting for the shots I want, than come back to the studio and get the perfect image through digital manipulation. Having said that, what you don't want to do is only regard your subject through a lens. It's important to look at the animal or bird with your own eyes and see what's going on around it – what it's reacting to. If you don't, there's a danger that you put up a barrier, or rather, it's the camera that does this, and you'll actually be isolated from your subject and you won't see the other photographic opportunities around you.

Mainly it's animals and birds, as I said, that I focus on, and sometimes a landscape shot, but very rarely human subjects. My reason for this, I suppose, is that all too often I see tourists snapping away and they haven't even asked permission first. That's something I always do – if and when I *do* want to take a photograph, say, of the tour guides or local people. It's common courtesy.

One other reason that I focus on wildlife photography is that I think it can help with people's awareness of environmental issues. If you want to do something to help save an endangered species, a picture is a good way to bring it to public attention. Over the last few years, I've worked for free for a couple of organizations involved in schemes connected to conservation, and my images have appeared on their websites and publications. It's the least I can do, I suppose.

Unit 12 (Page 160)

 2.25–2.29

Part 4: Multiple matching

Speaker 1

So there I was, the rich tourist in a developing country. Of course, you get people begging at home, but there it was on every street corner. The poverty is so evident, so widespread, and I couldn't help feeling, as a wealthy Westerner, that I was in some way to blame. So I decided to do something to help, despite the attempts of my friend and travelling companion to persuade me otherwise. Every day we were there I put aside a certain amount of money to give to beggars. My friend told me I was being overgenerous, but when I got back home I couldn't help thinking I should have given more.

Speaker 2

A mate of mine often complained about all the suffering in the world – but he never did anything about it. He said it was difficult for individuals to change things. Well, I just couldn't accept that. I took it as a kind of challenge and applied for voluntary work overseas in a school for street children. I thought at first they might not accept me because of my age and inexperience, but I needn't have worried – I didn't need to have any special skills or anything. In fact, that was part of the trouble. Most people were as green as me, so there was no real organization to talk of. Plus, I felt the government there could have done a lot more to help. A shame really, because I was so enthusiastic when I went out there.

Speaker 3

I did a concert last year to raise money for an international relief organization. My manager said it would be good for my image – you know, to be seen to be caring about other people's suffering and so on. I'd love to be able to say that I did it because I admired the work they were doing, and I was concerned about the issues they were fighting for. But that was more of an afterthought, really. I'm embarrassed to admit that my first instinct was to consider what was in it for me, what I stood to gain from it all. Sure, I did the concert for free and helped to raise lots of money for charity, but it's not something I boast about. I'm not at all proud of myself.

Speaker 4

I saw this photograph of activists in a small rubber dinghy moving up alongside one of those huge whaling boats. It was a striking image, and it made me think that if they can risk their lives in this way to stop the suffering of an animal, then I can surely risk some of my money to help them. The trouble was, though, I chose the wrong moment to be generous – I didn't realize just how little money there was in my account when I sent off the cheque. It left me with next to nothing, and I couldn't afford to go away on the weekend trip I'd planned with my friends. I wished afterwards that I hadn't been quite so willing to help out.

Speaker 5

Back in the sixties, of course, women's rights still wasn't much of an issue. People just seemed to accept that we got paid a lot less than men, even though we had to do exactly the same work. Amazing, really. I mean, if I'd been a man, I'd have felt so guilty about it all. I wanted to help put that right, to challenge existing perceptions. So, I got all the girls on the shop floor to go on a protest march through the town – there must have been about 500 of us altogether. We should have done it years before. They couldn't sack us, of course – there were too many of us – and when I realized that, it spurred me on. In fact, that's what made me go into politics, so I could continue the struggle.

Ready for Speaking

 2.30–2.33

Listening scripts in Teacher's Book.

Unit 13 (Page 177)

 2.34–2.36

Part 1: Multiple choice

Extract One

M = Man W = Woman

M: Personally speaking, I'm absolutely delighted that farmers' markets are becoming more popular and I'd say that celebrity chefs have had a fairly large hand in this. If you watch any cooking programme nowadays, there's an obvious bias towards sourcing and using food that's come from nearby farms, and that's had a direct effect on consumer choice, I believe. This is probably a trend that will outlast the craze for organic food, because no one's really clear what that means, anyway.

W: Yes, it's a bit vague, that label, isn't it? So, have you been going to your local farmers' market for a while?

M: Yes. And it's very interesting to see which stallholders are still there after a few years, and which have disappeared. My advice to people thinking about getting a market stall for themselves and selling something they've made or grown – do a bit of research into customer demand. Overpriced jars of home-made jams and sauces – forget it – no matter how much effort you put into making the bottles look pretty.

W: Indeed. People go to farmers' markets for the basics. Nothing has to come in a fancy wrapper. They're just after good quality, that's all. As you say, look at what sells if you want to have a go at running your own stall.

Extract Two

W = Woman M = Man

W: So, in the presentation, one thing we should mention is food packaging. Like this morning, I opened up a new box of cereal, and the bag inside was much smaller – the contents were only half of what you'd expect. That's blatantly deceptive! And, you know, when I look at the amount of plastic and cardboard that ends up in the bin, well, it's appalling, really. And paper's no alternative. That just gets chucked away, too. I'd really like to see the government impose some new policies that force producers and supermarkets to rethink the way they sell stuff.

M: In principle, I agree with you, but I don't know how it'd work in practice. For a start, for a lot of food, you need the wrapping to keep bacteria and stuff from spreading, so I can't see how we can do without it. And actually, the other thing is that producers rely on packaging as a means of showing off their brand to their customers, the shoppers. Think about it. They must invest an immense amount of money in research – what images to use, the colours, the wording – all that kind of thing. So if the government were to propose a change in packaging policy, I think they'd have a huge battle on their hands. But it's an issue we can raise in the presentation.

Extract Three

W = Woman M = Man

W: There's a bit of confusion about what the new policy actually requires schools to do. I've heard people saying 'how can teachers be expected to go around and confiscate fizzy drinks and chocolate bars?'

But from what I understand, pupils can still bring in their own choice of snack; it's just that school canteens have been asked to stop serving up fatty foods and come up with healthier options instead. I do think, though, that the government is a bit over-optimistic if it thinks this will have a significant impact on child health and fitness. But, anyway, at least it's a proactive stance against childhood obesity.

M: And I think most parents will welcome *anything* that tackles this problem. Nowadays, manufacturers are *covering* their products with fraudulent health claims – 'This'll give your child energy all day long.' 'This'll make your kid more intelligent.' – and really what's in there is just a load of sugar. So it's all rather misleading. Even if kids today *do* know about healthy eating choices – it's just hard to resist temptation when it's there in front of you. Junk food is everywhere – in the corner shop, the petrol station – you name it. Excluding school as an outlet can only be a good thing.

Unit 14 (Page 183)

 2.37

Part 2: Sentence completion

Hello, I'm John Lister from the Student Financial Advice Centre here on the university campus. My main aim today is to give you one or two bits of advice on money matters before you get down to the main task of studying next week.

As you may know, not so long ago you might have received a student maintenance grant from the Local Education Authority to pay for all your living expenses. Now, of course, these grants don't exist and you have to borrow that money from the Student Loans Company. If you haven't applied for your loan already, make sure you do it soon, otherwise you may have to wait several months for your first payment. If you have, then you can expect to receive the money once a term; in other words, in three equal instalments over the course of the year.

And that's the first problem, really. Many students find that their money disappears almost as soon as they get it – and it's often because they fail to plan their finances carefully. To prevent the same thing happening to you, you can download your very own budget planner from the university website. It'll help you record your expected income and expenses for the year and then calculate how much you've got left over for yourself each month. It's worth having a look.

Even then, you may still find that you need a bit of extra financial help, particularly in the first term when your outgoings will probably be quite high. So if you haven't already opened a bank account, bear in mind that some banks offer better overdraft facilities than others. Shop around a bit – find out how much you can go overdrawn without asking for permission from the bank, and without paying any extra interest.

You can, of course, supplement your income by working part-time, but you have to make sure you strike a balance between work and study. Some students here work over 20 hours a week in part-time jobs, but I personally wouldn't recommend any more than two evenings a week. That's for you to decide, of course, but I'd certainly wait a few days before applying for jobs, at least until you've got your timetable.

Now, it's clear that a major expense each year is going to be books. For that reason, it's well worth having a word with your course tutor before you rush out and buy everything on your reading list. He or she can advise you on which books are the most important to have. You might also find that you can buy some second-hand from students in higher years who don't need them anymore. Keep an eye on the noticeboard in your faculty building for that.

And when you pay for things, always make a point of asking for student discounts. Don't just assume the shop assistant knows you're a student – not even in the university bookshop. Get the most out of your student travel card and be very careful how you use your credit card. Every year dozens of students come to us at the Advice Centre with huge debts they can't pay off – and, in most cases, it's all down to their credit card.

Unit 14 (Page 190)

 2.38

Part 3: Multiple choice

I = Interviewer C = Chris

I: When was the last time you spent the whole day without buying anything? With us today on *Local Lookout* is Chris Dawson, a committed anti-consumerist who'll be taking an active part in next week's Buy Nothing Day. Chris, apart from buying nothing, what exactly is the aim of Buy Nothing Day?

C: Firstly, let me say that it is anything but a day of militant action with angry anti-government slogans and boarded-up shops closed for business. We're much more into persuasion than provocation as a means of bringing about change. We want to make shoppers question the need to consume and get them doing other things, like spending time with people, as opposed to spending money on them.

I: The obvious question here is 'Why?' What's wrong with shopping?

C: We're not saying people are bad because they go shopping. But they do need to think more about the products they buy. Whether, for example, their new trainers were produced using cheap labour in countries where workers' rights are virtually non-existent. What materials and production methods went into producing them, and the effect this might have on the planet. It's all very well for shopping malls to offer a wealth of choice, but this should not be at the expense of the environment or developing countries.

I: Indeed. But if people buy nothing on just one day, is it really going to change all that?

C: Well, for quite a few, Buy Nothing Day will indeed be a life-changing experience, not just a one-off thing. In previous years a lot of people have made long-term commitments to consuming less and recycling more. And that can only be a good thing.

I: So it's an annual event, then?

C: Yes, it is. In Europe it's always the last Saturday in November, while in the States they always have theirs on the day after Thanksgiving, at the start of the Christmas shopping season.

I: Presumably then, Chris, you're against Christmas shopping, too?

C: Good question! I'm afraid to say my family would never forgive me if I didn't get them anything, though they know how I feel about the whole thing. I just get so annoyed at the whole run-up to Christmas – already in October the shops have got their Christmas stock in, and the January sales start before you've even had a chance to finish your turkey. So it's handkerchiefs and socks if they're lucky, and maybe something special for my girlfriend.

I: Let's come back in time if we may, Chris, to next Saturday. What exactly will you be doing then, apart from not buying anything, that is?

C: Ah, well, erm, I'm not so sure I can tell you that, I'm afraid. Don't want to give the game away. Of course, there'll be the usual handing out of leaflets and putting up posters and so on. But as for the rest, I can't say. You'll have to wait and see.

I: Last year, then. Tell us about that.

C: Last year was all a bit surreal, really. A group of us – 15 altogether – all dressed up as sheep and went from shop to shop making loud sheep noises. And behind us we had a shepherd with a sign saying 'Don't follow them, follow your conscience'.

I: And what were people's reactions to it all?

C: Well, the shopkeepers were generally quite hostile, though we were expecting that. I suppose they saw us as a threat to business, and most of them moved us on. Quite a few of the customers saw the funny side of things and had a little chuckle – one or two of them even joined in – but on the whole they couldn't quite believe that someone was questioning the ethics of shopping. It certainly made them think – which is what we wanted, of course.

I: Is interest in Buy Nothing Day growing? How do you advertise yourselves?

C: It's getting bigger every year. Yes, we have our leaflets and posters – which you can download from the Internet, by the way – but up until now, at least, it's mostly been down to word of mouth. That may change, of course, as we get bigger and better organized. At the moment it's celebrated by about a million people in nearly 50 countries – and that's without the support of TV. In the US, for example, none of the major channels wanted to run the Buy Nothing Day commercial, because they said it went against the country's economic policy.

I: Yes, indeed. So, Chris, if we want to get involved in all this, how do we go about it? Who organizes it all?

C: That's the beauty of it all, really – you do. You just go to the Buy Nothing Day website and they give you ideas for what to do. You might want to dress up as something, set up a swap shop …

Answer key

Unit 1 Aiming high

Speaking: Long turn Page 6

Useful language
very happy: delighted, elated, thrilled, overjoyed
sad or wanting to cry: tearful, miserable, close to tears, weepy
nervous or worried: anxious, apprehensive, tense, on edge

Reading and Use of English: Multiple choice Page 7

1

the type of person who would take up such a challenge
Paragraph 1: He's now 17, he has impeccable manners and self-confidence.
Paragraph 2: He used to have no interest in outdoor pursuits.
Paragraph 6: He appears to be the kind of person who 'relishes a fight'.
their reasons for doing so
Paragraph 2: He formed a friendship with explorer Robert Swan, who invited him on a trip.
Paragraph 3: He wanted to become the youngest-ever person to trek to the North Pole and also raise awareness about melting ice caps.
Paragraphs 5 & 6: He's campaigning to raise awareness about climate change.
the preparation required
Paragraph 2: *He ate lots of chicken, spent a long time in the gym, …*
Paragraphs 3 & 4: raising money to fund his treks
the conditions or difficulties they experience in the Arctic and the Antarctic
Paragraph 3: *The Pole, … became virtually inaccessible, surrounded by patches of uncovered ocean.*
Paragraph 6: … *hauled a sled across hundreds of miles of frozen tundra, lived off freeze-dried food for weeks, and learnt how to ward off a hostile polar bear, …*

How to go about it
'etched': You usually see scars and broken veins carved into or marked on the faces of polar explorers.
'impeccable': Parker has perfect manners.
'escalated': The email correspondence between Parker and Robert Swan grew into a friendship.
'perplexed': Parker's friends and family were confused by his decision to go to the Antarctic.
'farce': When friends and family thought about the non-sporty Parker hauling a sled across the ice, they thought this was a ridiculous situation.

2

1 A Lines 15–20 … *he happens … boarding schools.*
2 C Lines 38–43 *Friends and … the least.*
3 A Lines 68–73 *The Pole … uncovered ocean.*
4 C Lines 95–105 *'By complete … or something.'*
5 D Lines 118–136 *His view … their fault'.*
6 B Lines 154–164 *It must … day's work.*

Language focus 1: Modal verbs 1: *might, could, may* and *can* Page10

1

1 annoyance
2 past possibility which did not happen
3 past possibility
4 future possibility
5 present possibility
6 lack of enthusiasm – 'might/may as well' is a fixed phrase
7 concession

2

Possible answers
1 I'm so angry with him. I do think he might have phoned to say he couldn't come.
2 We've missed the beginning, so we may as well go home and watch a DVD.
3 It was rather dangerous. Someone could have fallen over it and broken their leg.
4 I can't find it anywhere. I think I may have left it on the bus on my way home.
5 She might have a university degree, but she has no idea how to talk to the public.
6 Cheer up! It might stop raining later and then we can go out.
('Cheer up! It might never happen' is often said to someone who looks sad.)

3

1 theoretical possibility **2** criticism **3** request
4 inability **5** deduction **6** prohibition

4

Suggested/possible answers
2 This could be a girl telling off her boyfriend. It could be that he played a practical joke on her, but she didn't see the funny side of it.
3 This might be a magician, asking someone in the audience for help.
4 This could be a younger brother. He could be trying to retrieve a football from a tree.
5 This might be a parent trying to dissuade a teenager from eating a bar of chocolate.
6 This could be a parent refusing to allow their young child to stay up beyond their bedtime to watch something on TV.

Extension

1

a 'faint' suggests that it is not very possible. The other adjectives express the opposite.
b 'a fair' expresses a reasonable degree of possibility. The others suggest it is not very possible. Note that *could, might* and *will* can all be used with these two sentences. *may* is less frequent.
c 'good' is not correct. ('a good' would be correct)
d 'predictably' is not possible here. It is an attitude marker meaning 'as is to be expected', often found

at the beginning of a sentence and usually with past reference:
Predictably, house sales rose as a result of the cut in the interest rate.
He was predictably turned down for the job because of his poor health.
It is also often used to qualify adjectives.
He is predictably upset at what happened.

e 'highly likely' means 'very probable'.
f 'hardly likely' means 'not very probable'.

2

Possible sentences

1 I think I stand a good chance of passing the *Advanced* exam.
2 To improve my chances of doing so, I need to read a lot outside of the class.
3 In the world today we face the very real possibility that computers will one day replace books in schools.
4 There's an outside chance that I could be going to the States on holiday next year.
5 It seems highly unlikely that I will get a decent pay rise this year.

Vocabulary: Collocations Page 11

1

a success **b** ambition **c** motivation **d** failure **e** challenge
Note that 'an overnight success' means it is sudden and unexpected.

4

fulfil/realize an ambition
achieve/enjoy success
take up/rise to a challenge
end in/result in failure
improve/lack motivation

5

a challenge **b** ambition **c** failure **d** success **e** motivation

Listening: Multiple choice Page 12

2

1 A **2** B **3** A **4** B **5** C **6** B

Word formation: Nouns Page 13

1

achieve-ment motivat-ion fail-ure

2

1 refreshments **2** disapproval **3** eagerness
4 procedures **5** insignificance **6** simplicity **7** secrecy
8 membership **9** breakage(s) **10** likelihood
11 independence **12** anxiety

3

1 pleasure, exposure, closure
2 appearance, annoyance, reliance
3 storage, shortage, package
4 rehearsal, renewal, proposal
5 efficiency, intimacy, vacancy
6 enjoyment, requirement, commitment
7 prosperity, originality, familiarity
8 leadership, companionship, partnership
9 neighbourhood, fatherhood, adulthood
10 absence, persistence, evidence
11 selfishness, tiredness, carelessness
12 explanation, interpretation, application

4

advocacy, agency, appearance, awareness, coincidence, collection, confidence, correspondence, existence, friendship, hostility, legislation, location, mixture, reality
Also: champagners, emissions, explorer, leaders, tourists

Language focus 2: Spelling Page 14

1

Verbs ending in consonant + vowel + consonant double the final consonant if the final syllable is stressed or if there is only one syllable.

2

fulfilling, limiting, setting, upsetting, targeting (*targetting* is also used. This is true also of *focusing/focussing* and *benefiting/benefitting*), forbidding, writing, waiting, travelling (*traveling* in American English), panicking

3

1 pleasent – pleasant
Note the differences between the noun *appearance* (see example 0) and the adjective *apparent*.
2 neccessary – necessary
3 publically – publicly
4 definate – definite
5 irresponsable – irresponsible
6 leafs – leaves
Other examples with this spelling change are *calf – calves; half – halves; life – lives; loaf – loaves; self – selves; shelf – shelves; wife – wives*
7 preceeding – preceding (from the verb *precede*)
Note the spelling difference between *exceed/succeed/proceed* and *precede/recede/concede*.
8 bussiness – business
9 dissappointed – disappointed
disappear is also commonly misspelt by students.
10 recieve – receive
Seize and *weird* are correct, exposing the often quoted spelling 'rule' of 'i before e, except after c'. This only seems to be true (and worth learning) for words such as *believe, relieve, achieve* and *conceive, receive, deceive*.
11 influencial – influential
12 factery – factory

Writing: Formal letter Page 14

1

The answer addresses all aspects of the task and would have a positive effect on the manager reading it.

2

Paragraph 1: Reason for writing; description of project; need for money and reason
Paragraph 2: Description of the fundraising event; expected outcomes

Paragraph 3: How the company's sponsorship money will be used; benefit to company
Paragraph 4: Closing comments; suggestion for meeting

Linkers: As you may know, also, Unfortunately, therefore, Naturally

3

the way the writer describes the community centre and the event
In the first paragraph the writer suggests that the community centre benefits many local people, including adults, teenagers and children, and fulfils a range of purposes. This would be more likely to attract a potential sponsor's attention. The writer also provides a good amount of detail about the event to show that it will be well organised and interesting; this should also encourage a sponsor to help out.

the point at which the writer asks for money
The writer doesn't ask for money until the third paragraph – using paragraphs one and two to convince the potential sponsor that the community centre is a worthwhile cause.

the verbs and tenses used by the writer in the third and fourth paragraphs
The writer uses modal verbs 'would' and 'might', and a 2nd conditional *(If sponsorship from Fresh World were possible, I would be happy to arrange a meeting at any time that was convenient to you.)* because of the tentative nature of the request: there is no guarantee that the manager of Fresh World will agree.

4

we need assistance
to help finance our project
help us by paying for the hire
our key sponsor
If sponsorship ... were possible

5

Sample answer

Dear Sir/Madam,

I am writing to ask if you are interested in acting like a sponsor for a children's sports club.

The club was set out a year ago by local voluntaries and our goal is to encourage kids from different social enviroments to make sports. We've seen the advantages on the children's health from doing regular exercise and we also believe that team spirit in youngers will help to them in other aspects of their life.

Until now we have been using the playing fields at Wentworth College. However, some club members have problems getting to the college, so we would like to rent a field and changing rooms closer to the centre of town. Consequently we need obtain a quite large amount of money, so we are planning an event to earn money.

We will charge a small entrance ticket and there will be various activities which people will have to pay for. We would like to have a lottery for a pair of football boots, have an arching and a long jump competition. We also have baby photos of famous sports personalities which aspirants have to guess. There will be stalls selling second hand sports equipment and a healthy selection of food and drinks will also be served.

We would be extremely grateful if you could provide us t-shirts with the club logo on and some prizes for the competitions as different items of sports equipment.

I look forward to your reply.

Yours faithfully,

Katerina

247 words

Examiner's comment

Content: The writer addresses all three points successfully. Good realization of task.

Communicative achievement: Register is consistently formal and polite. The target reader would be well informed and would consider sponsoring the club.

Organization: The introductory paragraph introduces the purpose of the letter well and subsequent paragraphs are well organized.

Language: There are some grammatical errors – *acting like*, misuse of bare infinitive – *need obtain*, omission of preposition – *provide us t-shirts*. However, the writer shows a good control of tenses – *have been using, we are planning, will also be served*. Word choice is sometimes incorrect – *set out, aspirants*, and there are errors with word formation – *voluntaries, youngers, arching*, as well as some spelling mistakes – *enviroments*. However, the writer has used a range of vocabulary related to the theme – *sponsor, goal, playing fields, changing rooms, long jump, club logo*.

Mark: Good Pass

Review 1 Pages 16 and 17

Modal verbs
1 can, have **2** may/might **3** to, well
4 unlikely/improbable, may/might/could **5** at, no **6** in, to

Spelling
1 important **2** generally **3** objective **4** identifies
5 successful **6** themselves **7** of **8** to **9** confident
10 factors **11** were **12** interest **13** their
14 improvement **15** perceive

Reading and Use of English: Word formation
1 EXPECTATIONS
2 PAYMENT(S)
3 PERFORMANCE(S)
4 RECOGNITION
5 ABILITY
6 DIFFICULTIES
7 FAILURE
8 JUDGEMENT/JUDGMENT

Word combinations
1 strong **2** slightest **3** every **4** stand **5** tears **6** delighted **7** enjoyed **8** rose **9** lifelong **10** light

Unit 2 Times change

Listening 1: Sentence completion
Page 18

4
1 social history
2 communication skills
3 restoration
4 records
5 public
6 advertisements/adverts/ads
7 photo albums
8 digital data

Speaking: Collaborative task Page 19

Useful language
1 would not be complete without
2 is a part of everyday life
3 be intrigued to see
4 would demonstrate very clearly
5 might conceivably be obsolete
6 are unlikely to be using

Reading and Use of English 1: Open cloze Page 20

1
Mattel's Barbie dolls

2
1 AS **2** THAT **3** WITH **4** WAS **5** INTO **6** DID **7** SUCH **8** WHOSE

Language focus 1: Talking about the past Page 20

A Review
1 (had) never kissed, met *The past perfect of 'kiss' is optional since the sequence of events is made clear by 'until'.*
2 have had
3 has been crying
4 was always losing (*indicating irritation*)
5 ate (*first she ate the large meal, then she started to feel sick*)/was eating (*she started to feel sick while she was eating it*)/had eaten (*focus on the completed action: she had finished eating it before she started to feel sick*)/had been eating (*focus on the activity rather than the completed action*)
6 Marjorie left when Paul arrived: *She left after Paul arrived, possibly as a consequence of his arrival.* Marjorie had left when Paul arrived: *She left before Paul arrived.* Marjorie was leaving when Paul arrived/was arriving: *Both events occurred simultaneously.*
7 told/were telling (*no difference in meaning*), bought/have bought *The speaker may be situating in his/her mind the action of buying at some specific past time (e.g. last week), hence the possible use of past simple. The present perfect can be used to indicate a recent past event with a present result (the book he/she is holding now).*
8 didn't do/hadn't done, did (do)/had done *The past tenses in both these sentences are used to refer to past time. The past simple indicates a regular action. The past perfect can be used to emphasize the sequence of events.*

B Further ways of talking about the past
1 used to know/knew. *would* cannot be used with a verb which is used statively.
2 I've ridden/I rode
3 All three are possible.
4 I'd seen
5 hadn't made
6 going to work/to have worked (*thinking of/about working*)
7 After he'd done/Having done
8 All three are possible.

Reading and Use of English 2: Multiple matching Page 21

2
1 C **2** D **3** A **4** D **5** B **6** A **7** D **8** A **9** C **10** B

Language focus 2: Nouns in formal English Page 23

1
The main difference is the greater number of nouns in the first sentences from the text and the higher frequency of verbs in the second, alternative sentences.

2
1 disappointment, application
2 disapproval, suggestion/proposal/request, reduction
3 dissatisfaction, delay(s), claim/assertion/guarantee/assurances
4 failure/inability, importance, result/consequence, awareness/knowledge, education/teaching

3
The following features appear in **a** and are more characteristic of an informal style.
- contractions
- phrasal verbs *turned down*
- informal language such as *get* (3a), *a bit* (1a), *just* (2a)

Note also there are more words in **a** than in **b** e.g. (2a) 33 words (2b) 17 words.

Writing: Review Page 24

2
The New World (because this is a term often used first by 16th- and 17th-century Europeans to describe the Americas)

3
Paragraph 1: This provides an overview of the film and its genre.
Paragraph 2: This provides more detail about the characters in the film and the events that unfold.
Paragraph 3: This answers the question 'why it is worth watching, and in what ways it could have been better.'

4
It is in the third paragraph that the writer mainly focuses on 'why it is worth watching' e.g. The film is beautiful to watch (*a visually stunning epic*), and it doesn't represent the Native Americans in a clichéd way (*skilfully avoids the usual stereotyping of Native Americans*). The writer suggests the film could have been better by saying that the film does not show history as it really happened: there are details about Pocahontas which are simply not true.
The writer also shows support for the film by saying that the director has shown the real reason why Pocahontas saved Smith, and praising a scene in which Pocahontas and Smith teach each other new words.

5
The writer mainly uses past forms to describe real events, and present forms to describe the situation and events of the film.

6
Adjectives and adverbs/nouns in the text
legendary story, honest approach, complete wonder, genuine feeling, visually stunning, slightly idealized, masterful film

Adjectives in Wordlist
Some adjectives are open to interpretation

Positive
action-packed, atmospheric, compelling, credible, entertaining, exhilarating, fast-moving, gripping, impressive, innovative, memorable, moving, powerful, stunning

Negative
clichéd, disappointing, excruciating, implausible, overhyped, predictable, sentimental, tedious, unconvincing

7
1 performances
2 eyes
3 adaptation
4 development
5 clichés
6 objection
7 fact

8
Sample answer

This summer I have seen an entertaining historical film: 'The King's Speech'. Normally I don't like films about royal people, but this one was very captivated. I felt interested from the first scene.

The film is set in the 1920's epoch and tells a story of King George 6th and his problem with speaking. It also shows how George 6th brother didn't want to be king because he was in love with a divorced woman and he abdiquated.

Colin Firth is the perfect actor for this part. You feel very sorry for him with his affliction and you also get a good idea of how much his wife loved him, because despite she was a posh lady she asked a therapist who was not from the same class as her to help her husband.

Lionel Logue is also very convincing in the film, he is a failure actor who becomes a therapist. He is very bohemian and works with his patients in a dirty old office.

The filming gives a realistic picture of life at that time. You also see the beautiful English countryside and see how London changed since the 1920's. It also shows the beginning of the media image stage. Although some scenes are slow in general the film was perfect.

This is a great film for foreigner students because you can learn a lot about the British royal history and the actors are usually speaking slowly, so it is not too difficult to understand. I think you should include it in your top recommendations for a historic film.

261 words

Examiner's comment

Content: Generally good realization of task although there is not much mention of how the film could be improved.

Communicative achievement: Register is appropriately semi-formal as befits a film review. The reader would be informed and would consider using the piece in a magazine.

Organization: Well organized. Each paragraph covers a different point.

Language: There are a number of errors which suggest a lack of control, e.g. with the use of verbs – *I have seen, changed since, are usually speaking*, linkers – *despite*, word formation – *captivated, failure, foreigner*, and one misspelt word – *abdiquated*. However, none of these seriously obscure communication. The review includes some appropriate vocabulary – *entertaining, scene, set, convincing*.

Mark: Pass

Listening 2: Multiple matching

Page 26

1
1 C **2** E **3** F **4** D **5** A **6** B **7** F **8** E **9** A **10** C

Vocabulary: Changes Page 27

A Verb + noun collocations
Possible answers
your name you don't like it/you become a performer/you get married (some women in some countries)
your mind someone persuades you or you realize you're wrong/your opinion simply changes
your tune (= to express a different opinion or behave differently) when your situation changes and it no longer interests you to express a certain opinion
gear (on a bike or in a car) you want to increase or decrease your speed/you go up or down a hill
the subject (= to start talking about a different thing) what you are talking about is embarrassing or causing people to get upset or angry

sides you no longer share the opinions of the people or group (e.g. political party) you have previously supported
places to see a film, play, etc better/you want to sit next to someone else/you want to move to a non-smoking section
a tyre when you have a puncture or when the tyre is bald (= worn down)
your ways (= behave much better) after a period of time in prison or bad behaviour at school

B Adjective + noun collocations
1 c **2** d **3** a **4** b

C Other verbs of change
1 D **2** C **3** C **4** A **5** B

Review 2 Pages 28 and 29

Language focus: Talking about the past

1 had been/gone/travelled/worked
2 Having achieved/fulfilled/realized
3 has worn
4 have played
5 was taken
6 would … read/tell
7 been given/granted
8 did let

Vocabulary: Changes

1

1 Same: both mean 'to get used to a new situation by changing your behaviour and/or the way you think'.
2 Different: If you adjust a piece of clothing, you move it slightly and correct its position so that it is in the right place or more comfortable, e.g. *He looked in the mirror and adjusted his tie*. If you alter a piece of clothing, you make changes to it so that it fits better, e.g. *The jeans I bought are a bit too long, so I've asked my mum to alter them slightly*.
3 More or less the same: both mean to change a building in order to use it for a different purpose. ['Transform' perhaps emphasizes the fact that there has been a complete change.]
4 More or less the same: both express the idea of changing the negative aspects of your behaviour in order to make it more acceptable. 'Modify' usually suggests that these changes have been small.
5 Different: If you change your tune, you behave differently or express different opinions when your situation changes, e.g. *He always used to be criticizing management, but he soon changed his tune when he got promotion*. (See **4** for 'change your ways'.)
6 Different: If a restaurant varies the menu, it changes it regularly. If a restaurant adapts the menu, it makes changes to it to suit a particular situation or group of people, e.g. vegetarians, children, a wedding party.
7 Same: both can have the meaning of no longer sharing the opinions of the people or group you previously supported.
8 Different: If a country switches to the euro, the euro is adopted as the official currency of that country, replacing the previous one. If someone converts money into euros, they change a certain amount of the money of their own country, in order to use it, for example, on holiday or on a business trip.

2
2 convert **3** adjust **4** switch **5** modify

Reading and Use of English: Multiple-choice cloze

1
In the second paragraph, the writer is negative. In the final paragraph, the writer is positive.

2
1 B **2** A **3** D **4** A **5** C **6** B **7** C **8** A

Unit 3 Gathering information

Speaking: Long turn Page 30

Useful language

1 **Positive:** efficient, convenient, cost-effective, handy, time-saving, inexpensive, rapid
Negative: costly, unreliable, frustrating
2 **Positive:** relevant, reliable, accurate, clear, unambiguous, useful, comprehensive, up-to-date
Negative: irrelevant, unreliable, inaccurate, unclear, ambiguous, useless, limited, misleading, vague

Listening 1: Multiple choice Page 32

1
1 B **2** A **3** C **4** A **5** C **6** A

Language focus 1: Hypothetical past situations Page 33

A *Wish/If only* and alternatives

1
a Yes
b The speaker is very unhappy about this.

2
The sentences will refer to the present or future if the present infinitive is used.

Practice
1 have gone to France (instead)
2 you'd/you had phoned earlier
3 you hadn't done that
4 you'd/you had gone to university
5 have mentioned it before
6 to have stayed longer

B Past conditionals

2
1 c **2** f **3** a **4** e **5** b **6** d

3
1 Sentences 1, 2, 3 **2** Sentences 4, 5 **3** Sentence 6

Practice
Possible answers

1

1 He wishes he'd revised for his exams.
2 If I'd taken a few books with me on holiday, I might not have got bored.
3 If it hadn't been for Steve, we couldn't have got the car started.
4 I'd rather my parents had bought me an iPad (than an iPod).
5 I'd really like to have seen the film on telly last night.
6 I might have got the job if my French wasn't so bad/ was better.
7 I'd rather have watched the football than looked at all their holiday snaps.

Word formation: Adjectives and adverbs Page 34

1

1 countless/limitless/pointless
Note that the suffix *-ful* cannot be added to these three nouns.

2

1 approachable, applicable, believable
2 argumentative, administrative, provocative
3 introductory, contradictory, preparatory
4 chatty, muddy, rocky
5 luxurious, mysterious, monstrous
6 endless, priceless, sleepless
7 persistent, apparent, obedient
8 managerial, secretarial, territorial

3

1 imagin**ative** **2** **un**satisfact**ory** **3** increas**ingly**
4 **dis**courte**ous** **5** knowledge**able** **6** hope**lessly** **7** substant**ial**
8 strateg**ically**

Writing: Report Page 34

1

A is the better answer. The register is appropriately formal and shows a wider range of language.

How to go about it
How else could you structure your report?
Students could reverse the order of paragraphs 4 and 5. They might also have two recommendations paragraphs – one for each advertising medium.

3

Sample answer

Introduction

The aim of this report is to describe the situation of two of the most important ways of advertising in Spain: TV and the sponsorship of sports.

TV

Undoubtedly, TV is the most important mass media. An advertisement broadcasted at prime time can grab the people's attention in a way absolutely unthinkable for any other form of publicity.

Nevertheless, the high price of this kind of advertising is an inconvenience that prevents companies from offering their products through TV. Moreover, the interruption of the programs with the best audience rating by an advertisement usually annoyes the viewers who, frequently, switch channel until the end of the break.

Sport

Nowadays, sport is one of the preferred pastimes of people. Consequently, the sponsorship of sports events or even the existence of teams with commercial names, like it happens in cycling, is a very profitable way of advertising.

However, something to take into account is the great rivality and hatred around the world of sport; the presence of a brand's name in a football team shirt may be free advertising for the competitors among the rival team supporters.

Recommendations

Since the high cost of a TV commercial is a considerable problem, a good solution could be the making of shorter adverts. The saving would be significant without affecting the effectiveness. In fact, the most resounding successes in the last years have been achieved by marketing campaigns whose adverts lasted few seconds.

As far as the sporting world is concerned, the key point is probably the carefulness at the time of choosing the event or team to sponsor. This decision can led either to a huge success or to a total failure.

275 words

Examiner's comment

Content: The task has been completed reasonably well. It is informative and deals with each of the bulleted items. The introduction could be rather longer. More references could be made to the situation in Spain – this is, after all, the point of the report. In a few places, the report reads a little like a discursive composition.

Communicative achievement: The target reader would be fairly well informed (but see comments in *Content* section above). The register is appropriately formal throughout.

Organization: Report features are included and the writing is appropriately paragraphed. However, sentences are sometimes too long and slightly difficult to follow, – *Moreover, the interruption of the programs with the best audience rating by an advertisement usually annoyes the viewers who, frequently, switch channel until the end of the break.* It is not clear what is meant by the references to advertising for competitors.

Language: The writing is generally accurate despite a few errors of word choice and spelling, – *programs, annoyes, rivality*. There is evidence of a range of vocabulary and tenses in use, with some good collocations in the final section.

Mark: Good pass

Listening 2: Multiple choice

Page 36

1
Sami northern Norway, Finland, Sweden and part of Russia
Breton Brittany, north-west France
Ladin South Tyrol, northern Italy
Provençal Provence, south of France
Frisian coastal area – northern Netherlands, north-west Germany, west of Denmark
Galego Galicia, north-west Spain

2
1 D **2** A **3** B **4** C **5** D **6** B

Language focus 2: Present and future conditionals Page 37

1
Zero conditional: c Second conditional: a First conditional: b

3
1 broken **2** happen **3** would **4** if **5** have **6** to

If + will/would/going to

1
1 Insistence (stress 'will' very strongly when saying this)
2 Refusal **3** Result **4** Intention **5** Willingness

Reading and Use of English: Gapped text Page 38

How to go about it
Smell is part of the body's reaction system to danger. (paragraph after gap 2)
If we have no sense of smell we may not be able fully to appreciate food. (paragraph after gap 3)
Smells are often the trigger that give us 'flashbacks' of memory. These things can be very powerful and make our lives richer. (paragraph after gap 4)

2
1 E **2** A **3** G **4** B **5** F **6** C
D not used

Vocabulary: Smell Page 39

Adjective + noun collocations

1a
1 bodies **2** rubber, fumes **3** coffee, bread **4** milk
5 spices, fruit

b
Possible answers
2 an airport runway or a car racing track **3** a kitchen or a café **4** a fridge in an abandoned house **5** a market

2

Positive	Negative	Neutral
mouth-watering	stale acrid rancid	pungent (often negative)

3

fresh sweet	musty overpowering sickly	faint strong (often negative) unmistakable

4
Possible answers

your classroom	an unmistakable odour
a rose garden	a pungent aroma
disinfectant	an overpowering smell
old books	a musty smell
warm pizza	a mouth-watering aroma
your favourite cheese	a strong smell
decaying rubbish	a sickly odour

Review 3 Pages 40 and 41

Reading and Use of English: Word formation
1 FACTUAL **2** EDITORIAL/EDITING
3 OBJECTIVE **4** RELIABLE
5 INACCURACY/INACCURACIES **6** CONTROVERSIAL
7 EXPERTISE **8** TRUSTWORTHY

Reading and Use of English: Open cloze
1 BY **2** WHICH **3** MORE/LONGER
4 IN/WITH **5** HAD **6** WAY/MANNER **7** OFF
8 AS

Reading and Use of English: Key word transformation
1 WE HAD NEVER GONE
2 YOU HAD KEPT MY NEWS SECRET
3 WOULD PREFER TO HAVE GIVEN/WOULD HAVE PREFERRED TO GIVE
4 NOT FOR HIS STRANGE SENSE OF
5 SHOULD/IF YOU HAPPEN TO COME/IF YOU SHOULD HAPPEN TO COME
6 WOULD PROBABLY NOT HAVE/PROBABLY WOULD NOT HAVE COME/JUMPED

Ready for Use of English

Part 1: Multiple-choice cloze Page 42

1b
The text says that city birds' songs are becoming shorter, louder and with longer pauses. They sing more at night and leave out lower-pitch notes.

2
1 C **2** A **3** D **4** D **5** A **6** C **7** B **8** D

3
3 **b** 4 **a/b** 5 **a** 6 **b** 7 **c** 8 **b**

4
1 C **2** A **3** D **4** A **5** B **6** C **7** B **8** A

Part 3: Word formation Page 44

1
1 DEFINITION **2** EMOTIONAL **3** VARIETY
4 PSYCHOLOGICAL **5** BELIEFS **6** THEORETICALLY
7 TOLERANCE **8** UNBEARABLE

2

1 *definition* is a noun.
2 *emotional* is an adjective.
3 *variety* is a noun. There is a spelling change: *-y* at the end of *vary* becomes an *i*.
4 *psychological* is an adjective.
5 *beliefs* is a noun in the plural form.
6 *theoretically* is an adverb.
7 *tolerance* is a noun.
8 *unbearable* is an adjective. The prefix *un-* makes it negative.

4

1 ENTITLED/TITLED **2** HALVED **3** ENTHUSIASTS **4** EXPERTISE **5** THREATENS **6** PERCEPTION **7** DIVERSITY **8** UNAVOIDABLE

Part 4: Key word transformation

Page 45

1 SPEAKING/TALKING ABOUT HERSELF IN
2 LOSING (SOME/A LITTLE) WEIGHT WOULD/WILL DO
3 HAVE TAKEN MORE CARE IN/WHILE/WHEN
4 A SPEECH ON BEHALF OF
5 UNTIL IT STOPS/HAS STOPPED MAKING
6 I HAD PAID MORE/GREATER ATTENTION TO

Help questions

1 speak / gerund / in
2 gerund / do
3 past / take
4 speech / on – of
5 stop + *-ing* / make
6 wish + *had* + past participle / pay / to

Unit 4 Work time

Language focus 1: Punctuation

Page 46

2

1 avoided.' **2** chance?' **3** People who **4** me. I **5** don't **6** It's **7** offers

Listening 1: Multiple matching

Page 47

2

1 D **2** F **3** H **4** A **5** G **6** B **7** D **8** F **9** C **10** G

Language focus 2: Gerunds and infinitives Page 48

A Review

2 Modal verbs (*can, should, must*, etc) are followed by the infinitive without 'to'.
3 Here, the verb 'to be' + infinitive is used to give a kind of order.
4 If the verb is the subject of the sentence, the gerund is usually used.
5 The infinitive of purpose (to = in order to), giving the reason why he put on his best suit.
6 'manage' is followed by the infinitive of the verb.
7 'to be' + adjective + infinitive
8 'recommend' is followed by the gerund (or object + infinitive – see 7 in section B Common problems).

B Common problems

1 b *let me leave/allow me to leave* 'let' is followed by an object and the infinitive without 'to'. 'allow' is also followed by an object, but is used with the full infinitive.
2 b *get used to sharing* 'to' is a preposition in both sentences and is therefore followed by the gerund.
3 a *It's not worth making* 'It's not worth' and 'There's no point' (and 'It's no use') are all followed by the gerund.
4 b *would like you to be* 'would like' (+ object) + infinitive. The use of the possessive adjective 'your' before a gerund [appreciate your agreeing] is typical of more formal English. The object pronoun 'you' would also be possible.
5 b *stop ringing* 'stop + gerund'; 'stop' can be used with the infinitive of purpose, meaning 'you stop doing one thing in order to do another', e.g. 'He stopped eating (in order) to answer his phone'. This is not the case here in sentence b). ['start' can be used with the infinitive or the gerund, with no difference in meaning]
6 a *mind going* 'mind' + gerund
7 b *recommended him to have/recommended having/recommended (that) he (should) have* the infinitive is only used with 'recommend' if 'recommend' is followed by an object.
8 b *breaking/having broken* 'Admit to doing something'. In this case, 'breaking' would be a more elegant answer, avoiding the repetition of 'have' and 'having'.

C Nouns followed by the infinitive

1 determination, effort **2** tendency, attempts
3 opportunity, refusal **4** capacity, decision
5 willingness, ability

Writing: Essay Page 49

1

a your tutor (at university/college, etc)
b two methods
c Say which method is more important and provide reasons.
d The opinions are those of the people talking on the documentary.
e The opinions give an example of what you might say or include about each method.
f No – but if you want to, you can.
g that the method you've chosen is the most important and/or most appropriate

2

e-learning

3

C

4a

It is clear that ...
It is therefore essential that ...
We need to begin by asking ...
A major factor is ...

... ing ... would therefore enable ...
It might be a more practical solution to ...
If ..., ... could ...

4b
could, would, might, should

5

Sample answer

Today's world forever is changing. Pupils in school need to learn how to keep up with these changes. They should be encouraged to follow their passion, but also they need to see their future in a practical and realist manner. The question is what can schools do to help pupils in their journey into the world of work.

Schools need to be more concentrated in work-related subjects. If a pupil studies economics there should be a strong practical element and not too much theorical materials. They could learn to work in a team and set up their own business. In addition they could be taught about computer programmes to gain knowledges of money management. There should also be specific classes to help them search a job, for example they could fill up application forms, look at ways of writing a CV and do some role-plays of job interviews.

Another problem pupils have is knowing which type of job to apply for. It would be a good idea to invite employers into the school to give talks about the type of work they do in their company. The pupils should be encouraged to ask questions. It would be perfect if also the pupils could visit different companies or pass some time doing work experience.

In conclusion, pupils have to be conscious that their career is like a long journey and they need to take profit from each stage and should learn from their experience. If schools provide them with some basic tools then the journey will be an exciting and enjoyable one.

262 words

Examiner's comments

Content: The writer addresses the main points successfully. Good realization of task.

Communicative achievement: Register is consistently formal. The target reader would be well informed.

Organization: Paragraphing and simple linking devices have been used effectively. Clear introduction and conclusion.

Language: There are some grammatical errors, e.g. with word order – *forever is changing*, misuse of prepositions – *concentrated in*, uncountable nouns – *knowledges*. However, the writer has a good command of the tenses – *should be encouraged, have is knowing*.

Vocabulary is sometimes used incorrectly – *fill up, pass, take profit*, and there are word formation errors – *realist manner, theorical*. However, the writer has used a good range of expressions and vocabulary related to the theme – *follow their passion, a strong practical element, job to apply for, their career is like a long journey, basic tools*.

Mark: Good pass

Reading and Use of English: Cross-text multiple matching Page 52

How to go about it

- The central theme of the four texts
  resolving issues concerning office politics
- Relevant words to underline in the questions

2 *the definition of office politics*

3 *the extent to which office politics exists*

4 *the attitudes of some managers towards office politics*

- References to the role of managers

B *... on no account should a department head or other person in authority approach the individuals concerned ...*

C *If senior managers step in before proper procedures have been followed, they risk being accused of favouritism.*

D *... swift and direct intervention by immediate superiors is the most effective way to stop minor issues amongst juniors from getting out of hand and escalating into major crises.*

- Answer to question 1

D is the only text which recommends *'swift and direct intervention'* by managers.

2

1 D
See above key.

2 C
B *We are not talking here about minor concerns such as arguments over the timekeeping of workmates ...*
C *This may not matter so much when it comes to petty gossip about the social lives of colleagues outside of work, for example, and besides, this sort of problem does not really fit within the category of office politics.*

3 B
A *Yet all these situations may have a profound impact on the workplace dynamics of any business or industry.*
B *By no means is this kind of behaviour common to all workplaces ...*
C *Despite the fact that office politics occurs in all kinds of business ...*
D *Over the last decade, my research team and I have studied a range of workplaces with office politics issues, from small family-run enterprises to vast corporations.*

4 A
A *Unfortunately, office politics is an area that a number of department heads admit to ignoring, in the vain hope that problems will resolve themselves.*
C *Research suggests that in many cases, they will just turn a blind eye to such situations.*

Vocabulary 1: Body idioms Page 54

1a
1 shoulder
2 ear
3 eye
4 finger
5 hand
6 backs

2 Suggested answers
1 being treated in an unfriendly way (by someone you know)
2 pay attention to what people are doing or saying
3 pretend not to notice something bad that is happening (so that they do not have to do anything about it)
4 accuse somebody else of doing something wrong or bad
5 going out of control
6 criticizing or saying bad things about someone without them knowing

Listening 2: Sentence completion

Page 55

2
1 (forward) planning
2 realistic
3 tiredness
4 (our) health
5 perfection
6 self-discipline
7 (most) fulfilling
8 television

Vocabulary 2: Time Page 55

1
1 in **2** off **3** against, for **4** for, up **5** aside

2
a half: *football*
b record-breaking: *athletics*
c flying: *aeroplanes*
d prime: *television*
e sale: *shops*
f harvest: *farming*

Review 4 Pages 56 and 57

Word combinations
1 hand **2** point **3** pressed **4** viewing **5** set **6** available **7** way **8** hate **9** great **10** every

Gerunds and infinitives
1 going, trying, to get, to go
2 smoking, eating/to eat
3 noticing, asking
4 not to keep, to think
5 giving, to come, talk
6 agreeing, to help, to set, to do
7 to enter, cutting
8 to claim, seeking

Reading and Use of English: Key word transformation
1 TAKE MOST CREDIT FOR THE SUCCESS
2 RISK BEING ACCUSED OF
3 HAS HAD SUCH AN IMPACT ON
4 WHEN IT COMES TO
5 TURNING/HAVING TURNED A BLIND EYE TO
6 THIS MATTER TO BE DEALT WITH

Unit 5 Getting on

Listening 1: Multiple choice

Page 59

1
1 A **2** B **3** B **4** C **5** C **6** D

Reading and Use of English: Gapped text Page 60

2
1 F **2** A **3** D **4** G **5** B **6** E
C not used

Vocabulary 1: Verb + noun collocations Page 61

1
express their feelings
take pains (to do something)
show physical affection
show their emotions

2
drift off: gradually fall asleep
break away: to leave a person, place or situation
see through the mask: understand the truth behind the appearance
backed up by research: to show that an explanation or belief is probably true
stumbled on motherhood's best-kept secret: to find something by accident
let down their defences: lower their (emotional) defences and open up

Language focus 1: Reference and ellipsis Page 62

A Reference

1
a in my own student years
b sons leaving home at 18 to move into jobs for life
c ways of putting up new defences
d encouraging boys to show their emotions
e the fact that a confidential mood would come over him and air what was on his mind
f confide in their mothers

2
1 so **2** not **3** do **4** ones **5** those, one **6** This

B Ellipsis

1

a midnight **b** stumbled on motherhood's best-kept secret
c he, prevail

2

1 A Do you think you'll be home before midnight?
B I should be ~~home before midnight~~.
2 I asked him to play a tune on the piano and he said he didn't want to ~~play a tune on the piano~~.
3 She always comes to class on Tuesdays but ~~she~~ hardly ever ~~comes to class~~ on Thursdays.
4 He left without saying goodbye. I have no idea why ~~he left without saying goodbye~~.
5 A I have a feeling he was sacked from his last job.
B Yes, he might well have been ~~sacked from his last job~~.
6 He told me to apologize to her, but ~~I'd already apologized to her~~ I already had (*or* I'd already done so).

3

Possible answer

For most of **her** working life my mother taught chemistry in a secondary school. She always said the reason she had entered the teaching profession was because her father had virtually forced her **to (do so.) Her parents were both teachers**, though she herself had no intention of becoming **one**. However, whereas my grandmother felt that my mother should only follow in their footsteps **if she wanted to (do so)**, my grandfather was determined that she should teach for a living – **so she did**.

She'd actually like to have become a pharmacist and run her own business, but she wasn't sufficiently qualified **(to do so)**. Apart from **this**, she might well have had problems raising the necessary capital, and if she'd asked her father to lend **it to her**, he probably wouldn't have **(done so)**. I think my mother resented my grandfather for the pressure **he** had put on her, and **she** always encouraged me to make my own decisions. **I did (so)** – and now I work as a teacher, and my son **does**, **too**!

Vocabulary 2: Relationships Page 63

1

1 a/b get **2 a/b** put **3 a/b** had **4 a** turned **4 b** turn
5 a/b took **6 a/b** look **7 a** kept **7 b** keep

2

1 a positive	**b** negative
2 a negative	**b** negative
3 a negative	**b** negative
4 a negative	**b** negative
5 a positive	**b** negative
6 a positive	**b** negative
7 a usually negative	**b** positive

Listening 2: Multiple choice Page 65

1 B **2** C **3** A **4** A **5** A **6** B

Language focus 2: Relative clauses

Page 66

1

1 a Scott
b an occasion
c All that precedes it, i.e. the fact that you don't just learn the part, you live it.
d actors she worked with
e the new play

2 c, **d** and **e** contain non-defining relative clauses, but **a** and **b** contain defining clauses.
3 *who* and *which* in **a** and **b** respectively
4 *which* or *that* – In a defining relative clause such as this, if the relative pronoun (here: *which* or *that*) refers to the object (*ideas*) of the verb in the relative clause (*I hadn't … thought of*), the pronoun can be omitted.

2

1 I went walking with my husband at the weekend, **which** is something **which/that**/*omit* we haven't done for a long time.
2 The novel is set in Kaunas, **which** at that time was the capital of Lithuania. The initial chapters focus on Vitas's father, **whose** fiery temperament had a lasting effect on the boy.
3 **What** I'd like to know is what happened to that boxer **who/that**/*omit* she was seeing. Are they still going out together?
4 He left all his money to a woman **who/that** had never shown him any affection. The reason **why/that**/*omit* he did this has never been fully understood.
5 Her mother, **who** hated city life, longed to return to the village **which/that**/*omit* she grew up in and **where** she still owned a small plot of land.
6 Is there anyone **who's/that's** got a car or **whose** mum or dad could give us a lift?

Writing: Proposal Page 66

1

Yes

2

B

3

Activities/verbs	People	Other
transfer (to/from a branch/ place) (not) do their job properly carry out (an interview) lead/organize (a session) have good rapport with leave work early take time off make up (hours) work from home extend their hours discriminate against resolve (a problem) fulfil (the terms of a contract)	members of staff company (long-term) employee colleague new staff staff members	productivity training day training sessi a policy family commitments staff relations workmates

4

a

I suggest that we have …
I recommend this be led by …

I propose that we create ...
We should indicate ...

b
This has had a negative effect on ...
... ill feeling has resulted from this.
This sometimes means that ...
In this way, ...

5
b

Sample answer

Introduction

As a tutor representative of the students in Saint Martin's College, I have recived information from students, in which they explains their experiences and problems in adjusting to college life.

I'm gonna outline the reasons for the problems and suggest to improve college life for our students.

Problems and solutions

One of the most repeated complaints from our students is that they have not chance to communicate with native people, time in college is limited and they say that they do not have time enough to practice oral expression. I suggest to organize with the people of the area different open days, international days, and any kind of cultural events that make native and international students know each other and allow them to exchange opinions and experiences.

Another problem that students complaint about was the leak of appropriate food provided in the restaurant in the college. I suggest a more international menu should be offered so they feel more homely. Also students complaint saying that they don't have time to eat lunch or relax during breaks because they are only 30 minutes long. This means they sometime arrive to class late. I insist the tutors look at timetables to make sure students have at less one hour for lunch. I am certain the atmosphere in class will be better if students get more relaxed in theirs breaks.

Conclusion

As far as I'm concerned you should take my recommendations and then I am sure this problems will resolv and international students will be feeling much more relax in our college.

260 words

Examiner's comment

Content: Reasonable realization of task. Proposal covers the problems and makes suggestions.

Communicative achievement: The information asked for has been provided, but the tone is inconsistent at times and could be considered rude – *I'm gonna, I insist, As far as I'm concerned you should take*. The overall effect on the target reader would be negative.

Organization: The introductory paragraph describes the purpose of the proposal adequately and subsequent paragraphs are reasonably well organized. Effective use of simple linking devices.

Language: The number of basic errors would distract the reader and create a negative effect, e.g. incorrect verb agreement – *they explains*, wrong choice of word – *leak, homely, at less*, word order – *have time enough*, misuse of the infinitive – *suggest to*, misspelt words – *recived, resolv*. The range of language is limited and there is evidence of translation from the candidate's first language.

Mark: Borderline

Review 5 Pages 68 and 69

Vocabulary
1 down **2** on **3** on **4** to **5** on **6** in for **7** to **8** down on **9** up **10** to

Reference and ellipsis
1 old one keeps **2** I hope not **3** and neither/nor is **4** but I do. **5** If so **6** It should be **7** I have already! *or* I already have! *or* I've already done so! **8** love to. **9** should have been. **10** he hasn't

Reading and Use of English: Multiple-choice cloze
1 A **2** D **3** B **4** C **5** A **6** D **7** C **8** B

Reading and Use of English: Open cloze
1 WERE **2** WOULD **3** THEM **4** SINCE **5** TO **6** DESPITE **7** WHICH **8** WITHOUT

Unit 6 All in the mind?

Speaking and reading Page 70

2
Gardner would rank them all the same.

Listening 1: Multiple matching

Page 71

1 D **2** C **3** H **4** A **5** G **6** G **7** H **8** D **9** E **10** B

Language focus 1: Passives 1 Page 72

1
a J. K. Rowling **b** Claude Monet **c** Marie Curie **d** Charles Darwin **e** Meryl Streep

2
a She is, of course, famous for writing/having written a series of books about
The stories, which have been translated into
b These masterpieces of Impressionism were all painted at the end of the 19th century by the man who is/was generally regarded as the leader of the movement.
c He was introduced to her by a Polish acquaintance
the study she had been commissioned to do by the Society for the Encouragement of National Industry.
d He arrived at the Port of Salvador, Brazil, aboard the *HMS Beagle* ['arrive' here is an intransitive verb. Only transitive verbs can be used in the passive.]
and he was plagued/he was to be plagued by fatigue and intestinal sickness

e less of the film should have been devoted
the former British Prime Minister being played by this talented and versatile American.

3

1 c (teachers) **2** d **3** b **4** a

4b

b These masterpieces of Impressionism: passive
c He: passive
d During his travels there he: active (*contracted*) then passive (*was plagued*)
e Perhaps less of the film: passive (after *should*)
[also: it was fascinating to see the former British Prime Minister: passive]

5b

b the man who is generally regarded as the leader of the movement
c Polish acquaintance ... Encouragement of National Industry.
d fatigue and intestinal sickness
e this talented and versatile American

Practice

1 Change to passive; agent required.
The item was written by Steven Ward, former Olympic® athlete and manager of the Hythe sports centre, which sponsored the event.
2 No change. The second sentence begins with given information: 'This development'.
3 Change to passive; no agent required.
The event could be held in the 2000-seater Mulberry Hall Function Room in Scarcroft Road.
4 Change to passive; agent required.
The survey was carried out during the busy pre-Christmas shopping period by first-year students at Holmbush Business College, who designed their own questionnaire as part of their coursework.
5 Change to passive; no agent required.
I have recently been promoted to the post of Chief Accounts Clerk, in charge of a staff of five.

Vocabulary 1: Intelligence and ability

Page 73

1

a a whizzkid **b** brainy **c** I'm a dab hand at painting.
d I'm (an) ace at tennis. **e** I'm hopeless at cooking.

4

a practically **b** largely **c** absolutely

Writing: Review Page 74

3

Paragraph 1: Basic information on content of two films, including overall opinion and comment on acting performances.
Paragraph 2: Similarities between two films, including further comment on plot and opinion on Russell Crowe's appearance.
Paragraph 3: Differences between two films, including further opinion on Kate Winslet's acting and use of flashback technique.
Paragraph 4: Overall strengths of films with personal recommendation.

All paragraphs include the writer's opinion.

4

Adjectives in text
entertaining afternoon's viewing
moving portrayal
remarkably convincing
very credible (Kate Winslet)
to good effect (adverbial phrase)
powerful acting
visually appealing
plausible
a definite must-see (noun)

5

Both focus on
common to both films is the fact that
'Iris' differs from 'A Beautiful Mind' in this respect,
relying instead on
unlike the more linear American film
more visually appealing, but no less plausible

6

1 resemblance **2** terms **3** lines **4** similarities **5** difference **6** genre

7

Sample answer

The exciting world of spies is beautifully reppresented by James Bond films. In Sean Connery's 'Dr No', James Bond fights against a scientist who utilizes atomic energy to divert rockets and missiles. In Pierce Brosnan's 'Die Another Day', the enemy holds a powerfull weapon, a satellite with a diamond crown that functionates as an enormous laser.

Common to both films is the way James Bond saves the world. Another similarity is the exotic and atractive settings. 'Dr No' takes place in appealling crystal water beaches of Jamaica and 'Die Another Day' moves from picturesque 'La Habana' to the very impresive views of Iceland. But the more great similarity of all is that in both films there is a comparable scene of Ursula Andress in the first one and Halle Berry in the second one, which coming out of the water dressed in exactly the same bikini.

What sets one film apart from the other is the gap of time. Old James Bond was sciovinist and even a bit racist instead Pierce Brosnan's Bond treats Halle Berry as an equal and as well behaves it could be said as a perfect gentleman. It is also noticeable in respect of the gadgets they use, there is no comparison between the Giger Counter (to measure radioactivity) used by Sean Connery and the invisible car of Pierce Brosnan.

Both films are action-packed and compelling, which makes the perfect choice for a diverting evening's viewing, however, if you prefer a visually appealling experience, but I have to say maybe less plausible also, then 'Die Another Day' is the film for you.

266 words

Examiner's comment

Content: The writer successfully addresses the different parts of the question. The task is well fulfilled and certainly analytical rather than merely descriptive.

Communicative achievement: The register is appropriately semi-formal, as befits an arts review in a newspaper. It correctly addresses the reader directly and gives the personal opinions of the reviewer. The target reader would be informed and would consider using the piece in the magazine.

Organization: The writing is well organized and introduces similarities and differences in an appropriate and logical manner. There is clever use of paragraphing, each paragraph being clearly about something different.

Language: There are a number of mistakes which suggest a lack of control, e.g. grammatical errors – *which coming, more great*, and misspelt words – *reppresented, powerfull, atractive, appealling, impresive, sciovinist* (chauvinist).There is a range of tense and vocabulary usage, including some impressive language – *Common to both films is ...* . However, this ambition is not always successful – *a diamond crown that functionates as an enormous laser.*

Mark: Pass

Reading and Use of English: Multiple choice Page 75

1

Painting C is an example of Impressionist art (*The Path* by Wilhelm Morgner, 1912).

Painting B can be described as 'abstract' (*Flight of an Aeroplane* by Olga Vladimirovna Rozanova, 1916).

Painting A was painted by a chimpanzee.

2

a It means that different people have different opinions about what is beautiful.
b the brain and/or nervous system

Aesthetics is the study of the nature of beauty.

3 A

4

1 B **2** C **3** A **4** B **5** A **6** D

Listening 2: Sentence completion Page 78

4

1 diagnosis
2 hormone
3 emotion(s)/surges of emotion
4 hallucinations
5 social life
6 interview
7 machinery/machines
8 personality

Vocabulary 2: Sleep Page 78

1

a snooze
b doze off, fall asleep, nod off

2

A
1 good **2** soundly **3** deep **4** fast
B
1 rough **2** wide **3** sleepless **4** light

Language focus 2: Passives 2 Page 79

A Reporting verbs

2

a The Prime Minister is expected to announce his resignation later today.
b The 22-year-old striker is understood to be considering a move to a Spanish club.
c The band are rumoured to have sacked their (*or* is rumoured to have sacked its) lead guitarist.
d He was alleged to have been selling stolen goods.
e She is reported to have been paid over £2 million for her part in the film.

B *Have/Get something done*

1

a We're painting the house at the weekend.
We're doing it ourselves.
b We're having the house painted at the weekend.
We're paying someone to do it for us.
c We're getting the house painted at the weekend.
We're paying someone to do it for us. (slightly more informal than b)

2

a I had my watch repaired last week.
Someone repaired my watch because I asked/paid them to.
b I had my watch stolen last week.
Someone stole my watch. I did not ask them to! This use of the structure is for unpleasant events (usually) over which the subject has no control.

Practice

1

Possible answers

c have had/got this dress/suit
d to get lost/to have got lost
e would have/get your eyes
f of having/getting my nose
g got caught
h to get/have the car
i had/got our house/flat
j should/ought to/'d better get/have your hair

Review 6 Pages 80 and 81

Reading and Use of English: Word formation
1 INFECTIONS **2** PARTICIPANTS **3** ANALYSIS
4 SPATIAL **5** VISUALIZING **6** COMPARISON
7 FICTIONAL **8** SYSTEMATICALLY

Vocabulary
1 poor **2** strong **3** gift **4** bright **5** promising **6** get **7** badly **8** fast **9** sets **10** choose

Reading and Use of English: Key word transformation
1 HAS BEEN PUT OFF
2 THOUGHT TO HAVE MADE
3 HOUSE DONE UP
4 BEING TAKEN FOR GRANTED
5 FEWER/LESS THAN SIX PEOPLE ARE REQUIRED
6 BELIEVED TO BE WEAK AT SPEAKING

Ready for Reading

Part 5: Multiple choice Page 82

3
1 B **2** A **3** C **4** B **5** D **6** C

4
Useful language
2 lend
3 casts
4 question
5 points
6 mocks
7 undermine
8 refutes

Part 6: Cross-text multiple matching Page 84

3
1D
A *What has to be recognized above all else is the Vikings' technological ability in boatbuilding and navigation, to which seafaring nations owe a debt of gratitude whether they realize it or not.*
B *The Vikings were one of the world's greatest seafaring peoples ... who must be singled out because of their enormous influence on boatbuilding and navigation skills, even down to the present day.*
C *... master boatbuilders whose technological know-how was a turning point for ship design and construction in Europe.*
D *While the Vikings' seafaring techniques cannot be underestimated, it is their contribution to language and artistry that has, to my mind, made the greater and more enduring impression on our European culture.*

2C
A *Ask people to think of a Viking and the image they would most likely conjure up is one of a huge, flame-haired Norseman in a horned helmet and brandishing a battleaxe. In fact, such ideas stem from romanticized tales ... which have evolved into the two-dimensional caricatures we are familiar with today. They may be captivating, but dismiss them we must.*
C *... that our clichéd images of the Vikings as mere marauders can be dispelled. This is vital if we are to admire these peoples for what they truly were ...*

3A
A *These myths have acquired such power that certain modern historians appear to have been unable to resist turning assertion into fact, attributing purposes to relics for which there is no support, and imposing their interpretations of ritual when there is no truly reliable record*
D *... on unbiased investigation of original artefacts and objective interpretation of excavation sites. I choose such adjectives because the process of Viking research has not always been conducted in these ways.*

4B
A *On our own journey of discovery, we must stick with the facts, in particular when it comes to the limits of Viking territory. Reaching North America was a triumph of sailing know-how, courage and ambition. To imagine that they went further is, at best, wishful thinking.*
B *... they went beyond North America and Asia and reached the Australian continent long before other European explorers. Despite the refusal of many scholars to even consider this proposition, the proof is there ...*
C *They were able not only to sail around the coastlines of Europe and North Africa but to reach distant Asia and North America. Some researchers have claimed evidence of Viking migration further afield, but this remains contentious speculation*
D *Even now, the current contention that the Vikings beat the Europeans to Australia shows how keen some Viking 'experts' are to promote their own theories regardless of the truth.*

Part 7: Gapped text Page 86

5
1E **2**G **3**C **4**F **5**A **6**D **B** not used

Part 8: Multiple matching Page 88

2
At the beginning, the writer says that the genre of biography is in 'a terrible state'. She implies that modern biographies are only concerned with facts and are not well written. By the end of the article, she has changed her mind and says that 'more and more interesting books are being published which deal with the lives of others'. She suggests that they are not always marketed as 'biographies' but they are still biographical. As a result, she says that 'The genre is alive and well.'

3
1 C **2** A **3** D **4** F **5** E **6** B **7** D **8** E **9** C **10** A

4
Useful language
1 disillusioned
2 remorseful
3 resigned
4 resentful
5 sceptical
6 reluctant
7 appreciative
8 cautious

Unit 7 Feeling good

Reading and Use of English 1: Multiple choice Page 90

2
1 D **2** C **3** A **4** E **5** B

3
1 A **2** C **3** D **4** A **5** D **6** B

Vocabulary: Risk and health Page 92

A Taking risks

1
1 misfortune **2** limb **3** edge **4** death **5** thrills

B Complaints and injuries

2a
1 tooth, bone
2 ankle, wrist
3 nose
4 shoulder, hip, jaw
5 ribs, thigh
6 glands, lips, feet
7 stomach

Speaking: Collaborative task Page 92

Useful language

1
a lowly
b detrimental
c straightforward

2
a significant, on
b reasonably, in
c attractive, for

3
a to
b without
c to

Reading and Use of English 2: Multiple-choice cloze Page 93

2
1 A **2** C **3** C **4** A **5** D **6** D **7** A **8** A

Writing: Essay Page 94

2
No. Although the student has clearly discussed two of the listed methods and organized the essay well, he has not indicated which method is more important. This is something that you **must** do in Part 1: Essay.

3
1 Not only
2 therefore
3 with regards to
4 neither
5 In this way
6 that reason

4
1 issue (problem/concern)
2 action (attention)
3 laws (rules/legislation)
4 choice (decision)
5 consequences (implications)
6 steps (measures)

Sample answer

The days when bullying just occurred in the playground or on the way home from school are terminated. Now, with cyberbullying victims can suffer everywhere and at every time and it has become absolutely difficult to know if a child is being subjected to this or perhaps is actually a cyberbully themselves.

The government needs to set clear guidelines on how to prevent cyberbullying in schools and what to do if pupils suffer of this problem. One idea is for part of the school syllabus to be dedicated to matters as cyberbullying. This would include group discussions which lead on to pupils drawing up their own lists of dos and don'ts. Kids could also design posters and leaflets giving advice on how to protect themselves against cyberbullies.

Punishment is another matter the government needs to work on. Cyberbullies will often be under the age of 18 so a suitable set of penalties needs to be established. Schools could start with informing parents of any unacceptable online behaviour and the police could be informed in extreme cases.

In conclusion, the government needs to do everything it can to avoid cyberbullying. Parents and teachers need to know what steps to take if it occurs. The possibility of being punished can work like a deterrent, but it is always better to educate kids to respect themselves. In this way they will get a comprehension of what is acceptable behaviour and will seek for help if they are exposed to any kind of cyberbullying.

258 words

Examiner's comment

Content: The writer covers the main points successfully. Good realization of task.

Communicative achievement: Register is consistently formal. The target reader would be well informed.

Organization: Paragraphing and simple linking devices have been used effectively. Clear introduction and conclusion.

Language: There are a number of non-impeding grammatical errors – *at every time, absolutely difficult, like a deterrent, respect themselves*. However, the writer also demonstrates a command of some more complex structures, e.g. various forms of the passive – *is being subjected to, to be dedicated to*.

The choice of vocabulary is sometimes incorrect – *terminated, matters*, but the writer also uses a good range of vocabulary related to the theme – *playground, syllabus, dos and don'ts, leaflets, deterrent*.

Mark: Good pass

Reading and Use of English 3: Cross-text multiple matching Page 96

2

1 D
C *McPherson has also rather limited his readership by focusing on the middle-class and employed, a misjudgement, to my mind.*
D *For my part, if the case studies presented had reflected a wider section of society, McPherson's work might indeed merit a public service award.*

2 B
A ... *one wonders how much McPherson has relied on the work of others in the field in order to lend his book more substance.*
B ... *McPherson offers some genuinely refreshing insights into what creates a balanced 'whole' person ...*
C ... *not a particularly pioneering work ...*
D ... *the book offers little that is new in terms of theory and concept ...*

3 B
A ... *there are occasions when extreme claims are left unsubstantiated ...* and ... *although the rationale for this line of thought is hard to pin down.*
B *Why this should be the case – when the opposite is not – is a point that McPherson does not back up with hard evidence.*

4 C
A ... *offering practical steps for confidence-building ...*
B ... *a set of sensible key strategies for 'appreciating your own worth' that can readily be put into practice.*
C *Less convincing are some of the strategies McPherson puts forward for dealing with self-confidence issues within the family hierarchy.*
D *Life skills will be enhanced by following his simple recommendations ...*

Listening: Multiple choice Page 97

2
1 C **2** A **3** A **4** D **5** B **6** D

Language focus: Reported speech
Page 98

A Direct and reported speech

1
Tense changes: present perfect in direct speech changes to past perfect in reported speech.

Other changes: use of 'if' when reporting yes/no question; changes to pronouns and possessive adjectives (*my* to *her*); changes to time adverbials (*now* disappears in the reported speech version).

2
1 admitted, had sold, pointed out, had given
2 predicted, would be, warned, might be
3 concluded, had to, reminded, didn't/did not, would go
4 announced, intends, stressed, has not/had not

Note
This 'back tense' effect is standard and common, but native speakers sometimes mix past reporting verbs with present following verbs.
In 1 *has sold* and *has given* are also possible – present perfect would suggest this is either recent or new information.
In 2 *will be* is also possible if the protest has not yet taken place.
In 3 *must/have to, don't, will go* are also possible if the speaker is thinking of the future.

B Alternative verb patterns

2
1 C **2** B **3** A **4** D

3
threaten: B recommend: A, C, D persuade: A
ask: A, B, D encourage: A demand: B, D offer: B

C Verbs and dependent prepositions
1 for **2** on **3** of **4** against **5** to

Word formation: Verbs Page 99

1
1 classify exemplify simplify identify <u>generalize/ise</u>
2 differentiate <u>qualify</u> captivate evaluate assassinate
3 characterize stabilize familiarize <u>dominate</u> computerize
4 strengthen sadden <u>enrich</u> deafen heighten
5 enlarge <u>widen</u> ensure endanger encourage

2
reappear, disappear
reread, misread
renumber, outnumber
reload, overload, unload
rehear, overhear, mishear
reuse, overuse, misuse (disused and unused – both adjectives)

3
1 evaluated **2** deafening **3** disqualified **4** outnumbering
5 familiarizing/ising **6** outlived **7** validated **8** ensures

Review 7 Pages 100 and 101

Reading and Use of English: Word formation
1 TIREDNESS **2** COMBINATIONS **3** NOTICEABLY
4 UNWANTED **5** PURIFIES **6** SHARPENS
7 IMMUNITY **8** MEMORIZE/MEMORISE

Vocabulary: Health crossword
Across: 2 complaint **6** foot **7** ankle **9** headache **11** rash **12** thigh **13** nose
Down: 1 stomach **3** pain **4** tooth **5** ill **6** fever **8** muscle **10** drug

Reported speech

1
1 having **2** about **3** need **4** them **5** of

2
Possible answers
1 She insisted we go and visit them sometime and assured us we would love it there.
2 He apologised/apologized for not phoning earlier and explained that he had been very busy.
3 He warned her that it was a very dangerous part of town and urged her not to go there on her own.
4 She recommended he wear gloves on the run the next day, and reminded him to do some warm-up exercises beforehand.
5 He/She predicted it might rain at the weekend, but promised to take them all to the funfair if it didn't.

Unit 8 This is the modern world

Listening 1: Sentence completion
Page 102

2
1 marriage
2 mainstream culture
3 (classic) cinema
4 lighting
5 exploration
6 media
7 career opportunities
8 logic

Language focus 1: Determiners and pronouns Page 103

1
1 one
2 another
3 Many
4 one
5 every
6 both

2
1 determiner **2** pronoun **3** determiner **4** pronoun **5** determiner **6** determiner

3
a
1 All **2** every **3** Several

4
a
1 every many **2** another one month **3** no many

Practice

1
1 Every other year *or* Every two years, each other *or* one another
2 most of them play, none are very welcoming
3 there's every likelihood, no intention
4 on the other hand, as much/many as 20 hours

2
1 lot, little
2 none
3 every
4 Either
5 All, any
6 few, most
7 one
8 each

Vocabulary 1: Amount Page 104

1
1 no limit **2** full refund **3** great deal **4** small discount **5** high cost **6** large/high number

2
Possible answers
1 The details of a competition.
2 A mail order company explaining the rights of customers who are not satisfied with a product they have ordered.
3 A newspaper article about a forthcoming event such as a concert or sporting contest.
4 A shop offering discount to customers who pay in cash rather than by credit card.
5 A company explaining to retailers the reasons for a recent price increase.
6 A warning letter to an employee whose work or behaviour has been the subject of complaint.

Reading and Use of English 1: Open cloze Page 105

3
1 WITHOUT
2 TO
3 HOW
4 WHILE/WHILST/WHEREAS/ALTHOUGH/THOUGH
5 IN
6 WHICH
7 THERE
8 DESPITE

Reading and Use of English 2: Gapped text Page 106

2
He states that he is an 'Internot', someone who has no interest in the Internet.
He suggests that computers often lose information, and that they are unattractive and bulky. He believes they are overpriced, but speculates that one day they may be cheaper, the size of an answering machine, and 'idiot-proof', meaning that they will be very easy to use.

3
1 C **2** G **3** D **4** F **5** E **6** A **B** not used

Vocabulary 2: Verbs formed with *up, down, over* and *under* Page 108

1 *overthrown* This is the only use of the word – a government/dictator, etc being overthrown. The meaning is something like 'remove from power'.
2 *downsizing* Again, this is the only use of the word – when a company reduces the size of its operation, in the interests of cost and efficiency.
3 *overrule* This means something like 'use your superior authority to change a decision' – could be anyone in a position of higher authority, e.g. a police inspector, a Head Teacher, etc.
upheld When a decision that has been questioned is confirmed as correct.
4 *undertook* In this context could mean 'promise', but also has the sense of 'made themselves responsible for'.
5 *undergone* In this context could mean 'had' but generally means something like 'go through an unpleasant process'.
downplaying Could also be 'playing down', meaning something like 'make it appear less important than it is'.
6 *uprooted* This means 'leave a place where you have settled down'.

Language focus 2: Modal verbs 2: *will, shall* and *would* Page 108

2
1 Refusal You could say 'It refuses to start' or 'he refused to move it'. Here *wouldn't* is simply the past of *won't*, so we have present and past refusal.
2 Willingness An unusual use of *will* which may surprise students – in this case you can use *will* with 'if'.
3 Habit This use of *would*, meaning 'used to', is well known, but *will* can be used in the same way.
4 Assumption This is assumption, because the phone rings and the speaker assumes the caller is Mike.
5 Annoying behaviour *Would* is used when there is a sense of frustration from the speaker and a feeling of 'How typical!'.
6 Request for advice/instructions Note that *will* is not normally used in this case.

3
1 car **2** television **3** portable computer game/game app on a smartphone or tablet
4 telephone (receiver) **5** oven **6** fridge/freezer

Writing: Report Page 110

2
Suggested answers
1 the room
2 stories/books/audio books/films/DVDs, etc
3 information about exams/tests
4 computers/laptops
5 audio books, audio files
6 magazines, DVDs, graded readers, etc
7 computers
8 the noise level in the room
9 no staff to help

3
who your target reader is
the school director

what the tone of your report should be
informative and persuasive

what the general content would be for each paragraph of your report
Paragraph 1: The aim of the report and how and from whom information was collected
Paragraph 2: The things in the multimedia centre that should be improved according to the students who responded to the survey
Paragraph 3: Suggestions for how spending could be reduced in the multimedia centre, e.g. no need to buy newspapers because we can read them online
Paragraph 4: The concluding paragraph: the writer's final recommendation and positive comment for the future

what headings you would choose
A clear title, e.g. Report on potential improvements for the Multimedia Centre
Paragraph 1: Introduction
Paragraph 2: Specific areas for improvement
Paragraph 3: Possible ways to reduce spending
Paragraph 4: Conclusion: Future developments

4
1 point
2 mention
3 increased
4 describe
5 carried out an investigation

5

Sample answer

Introduction

This report looks at the actual resources and facilities available in Highford Academy multimedia centre. The opinions of students using the centre have been considered in order to do suggestions for improvments. Possible cost cut measures are also being discussed.

One of the main problems which students mentioned was the lacking of space. It is often hard for students to complete their works effectively because there is not enough space. I suggest letting students to use the classroom next-door. This would not cost the school anything and would be appreciated by students.

Secondly, there are insufficient computers and students abuse of the facilities by spending too much time at social networks. It might be an idea to install a filter and only let access to educatitive websites. Also if more sockets were installed in the classroom next-door students could bring their own laptops.

A large amount of students have complained about the headphones being broken, so some new sets should be brought. PC City has some good discounts now so we can buy new ones for a cheap price. Also a system of checking the headphones in and out would encourage students to take more care of the equipments. Finally, many students enjoy reading about the news and one requested thing is that the centre pays an online subscription for some newspapers and magazines.

Conclusion

In conclusion, without spending a lot of money, the multimedia centre library could be improved a lot by letting students to use the classroom next-door, buying a few online subscriptions and controlling the use of computers and other equipments.

266 words

Examiner's comment

Content: The writer addresses the main points successfully. Good realization of task.

Communicative achievement: Register is consistently formal. The target reader would be well informed.

Organization: Features of a proposal are included. Paragraphing and simple linking devices have been used effectively.

Language: There are some errors, e.g. in the choice of words – *actual resources, do suggestions, works, amount, cheap price*, misspelt words – *improvments, educatitive*, verb tenses – *being discussed*, prepositions – *at social networks*, uncountable nouns – *equipments*, and some grammar is rather awkward – *one requested thing*. However, the writer demonstrates a good range of vocabulary – *facilities, resources, filter, sockets, headphones*, and a variety of grammar structures – *have been considered, appreciated by students, take more care of*.

Mark: Pass

Listening 2: Multiple matching

Page 111

2

1 D **2** A **3** H **4** C **5** B **6** D **7** C **8** F **9** G **10** B

Language focus 3: Talking about the future Page 111

1

a I'll probably be enjoying
b I'll have left

2

1 D *I hope she passes* means 'I want her to pass'.
I expect she'll pass means 'I think she'll pass'.
2 S No difference
3 D *Will you come* is a request or invitation.
Will you be coming is a polite way of asking about someone's plans. The speaker is suggesting that the other person, the 'you', will already have decided whether to come or not.
4 D *The parcel should arrive* means it is expected to arrive.
The parcel might arrive is simply suggesting a possibility.
5 S No difference, although whereas *due to* refers to only one train, the present simple can be used to refer to the regular daily/weekly service.
6 S No difference. Note that these two structures are more common in the past: *I was about to/on the point of.*
7 D *She's bound to get the job* means 'she's certain to get the job'.
She's likely to get the job means 'she'll probably get the job'.
8 D *He's confident of success* means 'He thinks he will succeed', i.e. it is his opinion.
He's assured of success means 'He is certain to succeed', i.e. it is the speaker's/other people's opinion.
9 D *They're planning on getting married* suggests they are more decided than in the other sentence.
10 D *The government is to spend* means 'The government will spend'.
The government is expected to spend is less certain.

Review 8 Pages 112 and 113

Determiners and pronouns

1 another **2** other **3** others **4** few **5** little **6** every **7** each **8** all **9** much **10** either

Reading and Use of English: Key word transformation

1 MADE THE MOST OF
2 ARE SECOND TO NONE
3 OF EVERY SINGLE ONE OF/MADE BY EVERY SINGLE ONE OF
4 WOULD NOT/WOULDN'T KEEP CHANGING
5 PROBABLY HAVE BEEN/GOT HELD/CAUGHT
6 HAS NO INTENTION OF MAKING/HAS NO WISH/ DESIRE TO MAKE

Reading and Use of English: Multiple-choice cloze

1 B **2** C **3** B **4** B **5** D **6** B **7** C **8** D

Unit 9 Going places

Reading and Use of English: Multiple matching Page 114

3

1 B **2** E **3** D **4** B **5** C **6** A **7** E **8** C **9** A **10** D

Vocabulary 1: Describing an adventure Page 116

1

a jungle **b** scenery **c** companion **d** stroll **e** sun **f** earthquakes

2a

run into: to meet someone by accident/unexpectedly

kick in: to start to have an effect
set off: to begin a journey
ring out: to produce a loud, clear sound
turn out: to develop in a particular way or to have a particular result
win through: to succeed after great difficulty

2b

1 kick in
2 rang out
3 set out
4 turned out
5 won through
6 set off/set out
7 ran into

Listening 1: Sentence completion

Page 116

2

1 seasonal tourism
2 uniform
3 nationality
4 (hotel) department
5 (foreign) currency
6 adventure activities
7 (local) restaurants
8 customer loyalty

Language focus: Creating emphasis

Page 117

1

a how he managed to inform every department in the hotel about those changes
b dealing with foreign currency transactions
c wasn't until I began working there

2

b He said he had problems dealing with foreign currency transactions.
c I didn't realize how huge its hospitality industry is until I began working there.

3

a an action or series of actions; a noun
b 'the only thing that'
c a prepositional phrase; a moment in time

4

1 I'd like to know is how old she is
2 did was (to) start up his own business
3 was the music (that) I enjoyed most about the film
4 was in June (that) they got married, not July
5 when he took his hat off that I recognized him
6 until I spoke to Jerry that I found out she'd moved
7 I did was (to) switch it on
8 he (ever) thinks about is his precious car

Writing: Essay **Page 118**

3

1 unregulated
2 Mass
3 endangered
4 employment
5 urban
6 environmental
7 Living
8 community
9 Waste
10 cultural

5

developers: *These are people or a company who buy land in order to construct new buildings. A developer might be connected to the tourism industry because they want to build a hotel, a resort or other facilities for tourists.*
researchers: *They might be connected to the tourism industry if they are analysing trends in tourism or looking at the effect of tourism on local habits, economies or cultures*
conservation groups: *They might be concerned about the impact of tourism on local wildlife or the environment (the oceans, coasts, forests, etc).*
residents: *These are the people that live in a particular area: they might be affected positively by tourism if jobs are created for them. They might be affected negatively if their environment is destroyed, if local prices go up, or if jobs are only given to foreigners.*
contractors: *These are people or companies who are given a contract and paid a fixed price to perform a service or job, especially in the construction industry. A contractor might be paid to build a swimming pool or to install air conditioning, etc.*
activists: *These are people who fight, campaign or protest to achieve social or political change. They might be connected to the tourism industry if they believe local people or the environment are being harmed or exploited.*
policy-makers: *They could be involved in tourism when they decide when and where hotels or tourist facilities are allowed to be built, who can be employed there, what their working conditions should be, etc.*

6

Sample answer

We all know how important can be tourism for any region. Sometimes it's the only source of money, the real motor of the economy. Anyway, it does not always have only a positive impact.

Very often the first victim is the environment. Big hotels, commercial centres and others attractions do not always respect what there was around before. Very often the money is more important that the nature that never complains. Consequently it's time to make us a question: Is it possible to make tourism sustainable? What shall we do to avoid destruction of the environment? I think that there are some solucions for this problem: First of all the local government must be very sensitive to all kind of abuse that might bring a development of such tourist resorts. It must control all kind of permissions related to construction, because if buildings are attractive a good type of tourists will visit the country.

Moreover, the local government should try to achieve employment for local people, It should be one of the most important points of any agreement with any company. If a hotel needs a guide they should have one from the local people. They should also enthuse local people to work in traditional restaurants where the tourists can eat typical food.

I think that sustainable tourism is possible. The question is if we have people good enough to provide it. I hope so, because if not, we might be very sorrow and it could be too late to turn things round.

253 words

Examiner's comment

Content: The writer addresses the main points successfully. Good realization of task.

Communicative achievement: Register is consistently semi-formal. The use of direct questions would engage the reader, and the reader would have a clear idea of the writer's opinion.

Organization: Paragraphing and linking devices have been used effectively. Clear introduction and conclusion.

Language: The number of errors shows a lack of control, e.g. incorrect word order – *important can be tourism*, use of pronoun instead of adjective – *others attractions*, awkward constructions – *the nature that never complains*, and word formation – *enthuse*, *very sorrow*. However, none of the errors obscure communication. The writer also uses vocabulary related to the theme – *source of money*, *real motor of the economy*, *victim*, *abuse*, *resorts*, *guide*.

Mark: Pass

Listening 2: Multiple choice

Page 120

2

1 A **2** B **3** D **4** A **5** C **6** C

Vocabulary 2: Anger Page 121

1

more informal: blow a fuse, get worked up

2

1 heated **2** irate **3** cross **4** seething **5** berserk

3

1 top (note that this is particularly informal) **2** rage **3** outburst **4** steam **5** tantrum

Speaking: Long turn Page 122

Useful language

2

1 might have **2** may well **3** looks as **4** fair chance **5** very likely **6** looks like

Word formation: Alternatives from the same prompt word Page 123

1

composition, composer

2

1. a timeless (an untimely death/end)
2. adopted (adoptive is not common in English – it is mainly used in 'adoptive parents')
3. deceptive (deceitful is used when talking about people wilfully deceiving others, e.g. deceitful person, his deceitful attempt to persuade her … deceptive seems to be used with 'things' or rather abstract concepts, e.g. deceptive appearance, deceptive pace)
4. supporting (a supportive friend/colleague/boss)
5. appreciable (an appreciative audience)
6. identity (identity is about 'who you are' and identification is about papers. You show identification to prove your identity)
7. consulting (a consultative committee/role)
8. entries (entrance = a door or the act of coming in – make a spectacular entrance)
9. hardship (hardness is a neutral word – the hardness of a metal)
10. advisory (It is advisable to = a good idea to)
11. imaginable (an imaginary game/situation) (an imaginative child)
12. respective (a respectable person is considered by society to be good and proper, a respectful person is one who feels or shows respect)

Review 9 Pages 124 and 125

Reading and Use of English: Word formation

1 DESTRUCTIVE **2** REGARDLESS **3** RESIDENTIAL **4** COMPOSURE **5** RESPECTFUL **6** INCONVENIENCE **7** RELATING **8** IRRITABLE

Vocabulary

1

A Sustainable tourism

2 d **3** e **4** b **5** a **6** c

B Anger

2 e fly into a rage **3** a let off steam **4** b throw a tantrum **5** f blow a fuse **6** d go berserk

2

1. let off steam
2. went, berserk
3. industry, regulated
4. sustainable tourism, achieved
5. throws a tantrum
6. provide, employment opportunities

Reading and Use of English: Key word transformation

1. WAS NOT/WASN'T UNTIL PAUL LOST
2. BETTER THAT WE RAN INTO
3. TURNED OUT TO
4. WE DID WAS (TO) SIT
5. NOT LIKELY TO SET
6. AS IF/THOUGH HE SET

Reading and Use of English: Open cloze

1 FROM
2 BEING
3 WHAT
4 WITHOUT
5 LITTLE
6 WHICH
7 UP
8 ENOUGH

Ready for Listening

Part 1: Multiple choice Page 126

2

1 A **2** A **3** C **4** B **5** B **6** A

3

Listening scripts 2.4–2.6

Extract One

W = Woman M = Man

W: Did you see that programme on global warming the other day? I thought it was kind of irresponsible to present the views of a minority of scientists who think that man-made global warming doesn't exist.

M: Yes, but remember that one of the first things we were taught on the course is that you must have a balanced approach to reporting. That means allowing the public to hear both sides of the argument. <u>At the same time, you and I know perfectly well that a real balance doesn't exist. You wouldn't, for example, give as many column inches to the enemy opinion in a war, would you?</u> And the same goes for the global warming debate. I'd say that, realistically, far more attention is given to the scientific view that climate change *is* happening – and not to the few voices that deny it.

W: I guess so. After the programme I read a lot of comments posted on the channel's website. There was quite a bit of mixed reaction. Some people were making the point 'if global warming isn't man-made, why bother taking steps to save the environment?' That's why I thought the programme had been rather reckless. But I suppose that if the media *really* had a lot of influence, people would have changed their behaviour already, like stop using their cars so much. You know what people are like – <u>only government regulations will stop them from polluting and messing up the natural world</u> – that's what it'll take in the end.

Extract Two

I = Interviewer A = Andy

I: Andy, your company, Kiss Chocolates was established a good 20 years before you took over. What made you suddenly decide to take a leap into chocolate-making?

A: Actually a combination of random events. I was made redundant in 2002, and although I absolutely loved advertising, it was a relief to leave because it meant that all the uncertainty about whether the job would last was gone. At the same time, my wife had just happened to come across the chocolate shop and was buying a gift box, when she overheard the owner mention her desire to retire. We both thought the product was excellent – <u>and we both knew there would always be a demand for chocolate.</u>

I: Yes, indeed! And there are probably a lot of people listening who are very envious of you. What's the best part of the job for you, Andy?

A: Well, the product is certainly hard to resist! But because people come in to buy the chocolate as a gift, as a token of love or of appreciation for another person, <u>you never have to face anyone in a bad mood. That's what makes it all so rewarding for me</u> – even more than the prospect of long-term financial security.

Extract Three

J = Jennifer A = Andrew

J: I have to say that I found *The Children of Hurin* completely absorbing, far more so than I expected. <u>But it's hardly uplifting, is it?</u>

A: No. Even from the early pages, <u>one has a great sense that all is not going to end well for the central character, Turin</u>. He *is* a hero in the sense that he is a brave, honourable man on a mission, but <u>fate delivers him one cruel blow after another. As events unfold, you can see how tragedy is inescapable.</u>

J: Now the book is based on various manuscripts that JRR Tolkien never completed before he died. And it's taken his son Christopher 30 years to put them together as a single cohesive story.

A: That's right – and overall, he really has produced a thing of beauty. <u>Readers will notice, however, that one passage may be written in some kind of ancient English and then the next in a more contemporary manner</u> – as you'd expect in a book pieced together from manuscripts written over a 50-year period, <u>and that can be a little distracting</u>. Tolkien's characterization is sometimes underdeveloped but not so this time, as Christopher has given us a hero we can identify ...

Part 2: Sentence completion

Page 127

2

1 basement **2** Fine Arts **3** measurements
4 newsreader **5** metal **6** position **7** five months
8 oil paint

3

2 d **3** b **4** e/g **5** f **6** c/f **7** a **8** h

Part 3: Multiple choice Page 128

3

0 C Sandra: *I reckoned I'd probably be the first to have to leave.*

4

Suggested answers

A *We are only told by Sandra that the company 'weren't making enough money'; she does not comment on her salary.*

B *Sandra says 'they were a young, dynamic group' but she does not say she was too old.*

D *She says 'I'd never felt so comfortable working in a team as I did with that group of people'; she does* not *say 'I never felt comfortable working in a team'.*

5

1 B **2** D **3** B **4** A **5** B **6** C

Listening script 2.8

I = **Interviewer** **S** = **Sandra** **D** = **David**

I: On this week's *In Partnership* programme we talk to Sandra Peyton and David Sadler, who together run the successful media company, Advert Eyes, specializing in the making of TV commercials. Sandra, if I could start with you. What were you doing before you set up in partnership with David and what made you change?

S: Well, I was directing – er, drama mostly – for a small satellite TV company. It was an interesting, experimental time for me – they were a young, dynamic group and seemed to be going places. But these were troubled times for the business in general and they just weren't making enough money. Anyway, things weren't looking too good for me; as I'd been the last to arrive, I reckoned I'd probably be the first to have to leave.

I: So you jumped before you were pushed, so to speak.

S: That's right, and that was a great shame, because I'd never felt so comfortable working in a team as I did with that group of people.

I: David, you had a similar background, didn't you?

D: Yes, I'd also made a name for myself directing TV drama, but with the much larger Trenton TV. I left them because they were moving in a different direction to where I wanted to go. But the experience proved invaluable for the future – I can see that now.

I: In what way?

D: Working in close collaboration with others is an integral part of this business – that's always been clear to me – but I came to realize that you can't rely on other people to make things work. It's a tough old world and ultimately it's down to you – it's a question of attitude. Things only happen if you let them – and if you only see grey skies and gloomy days ahead, that's what you'll get.

I: So the whole thing focused you for your future with Advert Eyes.

D: That's right, I did a lot of growing up with Trenton.

I: Well, tell us how you met each other, Sandra.

S: We were introduced at a party by a mutual friend. I remember I was very wary of David at first. He already had quite a reputation in the business – his past work spoke for itself. And he looked so serious, so apparently indifferent to everything. He mentioned some vague idea he had for setting up a business, something to do with advertising – but that wasn't what struck me most. I just couldn't get over how animated, how passionate he became when he talked about – well, everything really. It was difficult not to be carried along by his words.

I: So when he asked you to join him, you had no hesitation in accepting?

D: Well, it was actually Sandra who asked me. And I was the one who had no hesitation. My colleagues at Trenton had warned me against going into business with a complete unknown – they said it was too much of a gamble. But when I met Sandra, it was like looking into a mirror. Here at last was someone on my wavelength, someone who looked at life through the same camera lens. And, anyway, I felt it was time to do something different, to live a little dangerously.

I: And has it been? Dangerous, I mean.

D: Anything but. Funnily enough, though, it's turned out that we do have quite a lot of differences, but these have all been to our advantage. Sandra, for example, has much more of a business brain than I do.

I: Is that right, Sandra?

S: Well, yes, it seems to be a hidden talent of mine. But I've had to learn the hard way. Raising money, for example, was an absolute nightmare – we just couldn't seem to get the finance.

I: That must have been quite disheartening.

S: Well, no, you can't afford to let things like that get you down. It was no good getting upset about it; throwing a tantrum in a bank manager's office is never a good idea – you might need to go back there one day. No, I just couldn't work out what the problem was, given our experience and the way the advertising market was shaping up at the time. We were just a small concern, asking for a small amount of money.

I: But you obviously got the money.

S: Yes, I met an investor who understood what we were about – and then, once we'd made a couple of ads, money was easier to come by.

I: David, how does, er, advertising work compare with TV drama? Is it very different.

D: Well, for a start there's more money around than for normal TV work, and that can be very liberating. But the market's understanding of quality may not be the same as yours and you find your creativity stifled. Yes, it's our own company, and it may seem a creative business to an outsider. But an advert is not your own baby in the same way that a TV drama might be. There are too many people who have a say in what you do and what goes into the advert.

S: Yes, I'd go along with that, although for me, running a business can be incredibly creative.

I: So what does the future hold for Advert Eyes. What are your plans for the company?

S: Well, we can't really say too much at the moment. It's not that we're not willing to, it's just that we're not entirely certain how things will work out ourselves.

D: That's right. The normal thing might be to look at some type of long-term growth for the business, but at the moment we're concentrating on consolidating our position, rather than branching out. Who knows what the future will bring?

I: Sandra, David, the very best of luck for the future. There we must leave it. Thank you.

S and D: Thank you.

6

1

A *This idea comes up but is denied in 'but I came to realize that you can't rely on other people to make things work'.*

C *This is a misinterpretation of 'It's a tough old world'. This is not the point being made.*

D *The opposite is true – 'Working in close collaboration with others …'.*

2

A *David's 'reputation in the business' was undoubted, but it was not that which impressed her.*

B *Definitely not – he looked serious and indifferent.*

C *No, these were vague and didn't strike her.*

3

A *His colleagues warned him that it would be a risk, but there's no reference to him enjoying risks.*

C *We don't know this; we are only told she was a complete unknown.*

D *Again, we don't know this; we are only told she has a good business brain.*

4

B *The idea of being depressed is there, but what Sandra is saying is that there's no point in getting depressed.*

C *She then goes on to make the same point about being angry.*

D *Sandra says 'We were just a small concern …'. Concern here is nothing to do with worrying; it's a noun meaning 'enterprise' or 'business'.*

5

A *This is a likely idea given the context, but is not present in the text.*

C *The opposite is true. He finds the large amounts of money available a positive point.*

D *The point made about the clients is that they get too involved and stifle his creativity, not that they have unrealistic expectations.*

6

A *This idea is suggested but then contradicted by 'It's not that we're not willing to …'.*

B & D *For both of these, the opposite is true – 'The normal thing might be to look at some type of long-term growth for the business, but at the moment we're concentrating on consolidating our position, rather than branching out.'*

Part 4: Multiple matching Page 129

2

1 C **2** D **3** A **4** G **5** F **6** E **7** H **8** B **9** D **10** G

3

Listening script 2.9–2.13

Speaker 1

I could barely string two sentences together when I first arrived, and now I'm reasonably fluent. In that sense, then, I've achieved what I set out to do – just by being here and mixing with the locals. I've met some great people since I got here, especially the family I'm living with. But there's a big downside to all this. I decided to come here on my year out because it's so different to all the other places I could have gone to. Plus it seemed so exciting when I came here two years ago. However, that was on holiday and I realize now that living here is actually rather dull. I really wish I'd gone somewhere on the mainland now – my girlfriend's having a great time there.

Speaker 2

My father studied here as a young man, so I knew quite a lot about the country before I came. And when the head of my company's overseas operations told me our branch here wasn't doing too well, and would I please go and sort things out, I was very happy to accept. My husband came out shortly after I did and like me, immediately fell in love with the place. The pace of life suits us to a tee and the food is just out of this world.

Ultimately, though, we're home birds and when this posting's over we'll want to go back to be nearer our grandchildren – if we ever have any, that is!

Speaker 3

I was working in the dullest job you can imagine – nine to five every day on the computer, answering customers' email queries. But it was thanks to that job that I got to know Patti, who was over on a work exchange programme in another department. She only stayed for three months, though, so after that nearly all our contact was by email. Of course, you can't keep something going like that indefinitely, so I took the plunge and moved out here. Life is fine – despite the overcast skies and regular downpours! I have to admit, though, it does get me down sometimes. I'd like to get back home more often, but it's just too far.

Speaker 4

I only wish I'd made the break earlier. It's so vibrant in this part of the world – there's so much more going on. I think if I was still back home, I'd be so depressed, what with the current climate there and so on. The fact is I was in a bit of a rut. I was sick of the same old thing, day in, day out and I thought, 'There's got to be more to life than this'. So I looked into the price of property in different parts of southern Europe, and this area was one of the cheapest. It didn't take me long to settle in – the language isn't much of a problem and I've even got myself a little part-time job. Keeps me out of trouble!

Speaker 5

A few years ago I set up in business with a friend of mine. Then I decided to go it alone and bought out my partner's share. Unfortunately, before long, things started to go wrong and I was up to my eyes in debt. Call it cowardice, but I just couldn't deal with it and I moved out here. It got me out of a mess, but I can't say I'm having the time of my life. I know a lot of different people here, but I just don't seem to fit in with them. We share the same language – more or less – but we're worlds apart in most other respects. One thing's for sure – if ever I do go back to face the music, it'll be for good.

4

- **7** Speaker 2: *we'll want to go back to be nearer our grandchildren*
- **8** Speaker 3: *I'd like to get back home more often*
- **9** Speaker 4: *I'd be so depressed, what with the current climate there*
- **10** Speaker 5: *if ever I do go back to face the music, it'll be for good*

Unit 10 House and home

Vocabulary 1: Describing rooms and houses Page 130

1

1 c cheerful **2** e airy **3** a tidy **4** b dingy **5** d cosy **6** f cluttered

2

a lit **b** furnished **c** decorated **d** built **e** situated

Reading and Use of English: 1: Open Cloze Page 131

2

Housework is strenuous, boring, repetitive and never-ending. It is also unpaid and women, who still do most of it, often go out to work, which means they cannot do it as thoroughly as they might like.

3

- **1** TO (The verb 'suggest' would need to be in the third person singular form for a relative pronoun to be possible.)
- **2** ARE
- **3** IS
- **4** WITHOUT
- **5** HOW
- **6** FOR
- **7** NO
- **8** OUT
- **9** FROM
- **10** SOME (Only a determiner is possible here as there is no definite or indefinite article.)
- **11** LOT
- **12** TOO
- **13** MAY/MIGHT/COULD/CAN
- **14** WE
- **15** UNDER

Reading and Use of English 2: Multiple choice Page 132

3

1 C **2** D **3** C **4** D **5** B **6** D

Language focus: Participle clauses Page 134

1

So this man, (who was) living on a labourer's wage, clearly believed he was just locked out of the lifestyle.

2

- **a** Having become rather frail and vulnerable in the last few years, he and his wife were heavily reliant on the good nature of one neighbour ... (lines 29–31)
- **b** Fleeing from Estonia in 1946, he came to Britain ... (lines 41–42)
- **c** Shocked beyond belief by what they saw when they visited the house, these people began to put pressure on the council ... (lines 60–62)
- **d** 'That's the good thing about the country,' he says, looking out over the familiar prospect. (lines 74–75)

3

As the Grammar reference explains, the subject of a participle clause is usually the same as the subject of the main clause in a sentence. Sentence 2 (a) shows that a participle clause can be given its own subject to avoid ambiguity.

1. Sentence (a) suggests that the police were driving home from the pub when they stopped him.
   Sentence (b) means that the police stopped him as he was driving home from the pub.
   Sentence (b) is more likely.
2. Sentence (a) means that Elisa took over all the manager's responsibilities because the manager was ill.
   Sentence (b) suggests that because she was ill, Elisa took over all the manager's responsibilities.
   Sentence (a) is more likely.

Practice
Possible answers

1

1. *After* he won the silver medal in the 100 metres, he went on to take gold in the 200 metres and long jump.
2. Don't look now, but the woman *who* is sitting next to you is wearing shoes *which* are made of crocodile skin.
3. *If* it is drunk in moderation, red wine is thought to protect against coronary disease.
4. Mr Brown, *who* was wrapped in a blanket and looked tired after his ordeal, was full of praise for the rescue services.
5. *When* he reached for the sugar, he knocked over his glass *and* spilt orange juice over her new dress.
6. *Because* he had never been abroad before, Brian was feeling a little on edge.

2–3

1 Living within walking distance of the centre, I rarely use the car. *City*
2 Cycling in to work the other day, I saw a deer. *Rural area*
3 Having never had so much peace and quiet before, we found living here a little strange at first. *Rural area*
4 Situated at the back of the building, our bedroom has some superb views over the rooftops towards the docks. *City*
5 Played at full volume, it really annoys the neighbours. *Either*
6 Being a little off the beaten track, the house is not that easy to find. *Rural area*
7 The children having all left home, we decided to move away from the hustle and bustle. *Rural area*
8 Although not known for its tourist attractions, our neighbourhood does have one or two treasures waiting to be discovered. *City*

Listening: Multiple matching Page 135

1

1 F **2** H **3** A **4** B **5** D **6** F **7** G **8** H **9** A **10** D

Vocabulary 2: Noise and sound

Page 135

1

a loud unpleasant noise that lasts for a long time

2

1 *hushed*: very quiet; the other two describe a loud voice.
2 *unmistakable*: very easy to recognize; the others describe a sound which is/appears quiet.
3 *excessive*: too loud; the others describe noise which continues for a long time.

3

1 *goes off* (a gun, bomb or alarm *goes off*)
2 *rustle open* (leaves or paper *rustle*)
3 *hoot* (car horns *hoot*)
4 *engine* (*rowdy* describes people and their behaviour)
5 *groan* (*piercing* describes high-pitched sounds)
6 *ear* (ears can be *deafened* but not *deafening*: *deafening silence* is used when it is very noticeable that nothing was said or done)

4

1 hushed voice **2** distant sound/constant noise **3** noise dies down **4** rowdy fans **5** deafening silence **6** door slammed shut

6

Possible answer

Detectives enter a building where a gang of counterfeiters are making money. The criminals argue amongst themselves, one shoots another, the detectives rush in, fight, and leader of gang warns detectives to get back.

Reading and Use of English 3: Multiple-choice cloze Page 136

Don't forget!

What has caused the decline in communication between neighbours in Britain?
longer hours spent working at the office, together with the Internet and satellite television
What has been one of the effects of this decline?
a rise in burglaries and vandalism

2

1 A **2** D **3** A **4** D **5** C **6** A **7** B **8** B

Writing: Informal email Page 137

2

	Sample A	**Sample B**
vocabulary	There are several phrasal verbs, (hand over, run out, head down) and informal expressions (keep an eye, help yourself, keep things sweet)	There are a number of formal expressions, e.g. on arrival, highly recommended your personal use
register and tone	The writer sounds very friendly, e.g. so would you mind + ing ...? Get in touch if you need any more info	The language used is more suitable for an official notice, e.g. bottles and tins <u>must be placed</u> ... please <u>refrain from</u> ...
grammatical structure	The writer mainly uses the active voice: First, you need to know how to ... If you feel like + ing	The writer often uses the passive voice: You <u>will be let</u> into the building ... windows <u>can be left</u> open ... these <u>can be</u> access<u>ed</u> ...
organization	The writer has used different paragraphs to introduce new subjects, which makes it easier for the reader to follow.	The writer has used subheadings and bullet points; although this format presents all the information in a clear way, it doesn't give a very welcoming or friendly impression.

In the *Advanced* exam, it would be better to write an email or letter like sample A. This will allow you to use a range of informal expressions, words and phrases and use a variety of informal structures.

3
How he makes his friend feel welcome:
It's good to know that you'll be in the apartment while I'm away in Berlin / ... it's <u>reassuring</u> to have you keeping an eye on things.

What he adds to make his friend feel positive about his upcoming stay:
There's a load of stuff in the fridge and food cupboard so help yourself.
Lake Constance is a brilliant place to visit ... and you can borrow my bike, too.
I'll leave some tourist information leaflets and train timetable in the kitchen.

4

Sample answer

Hi Angela

Thanks a lot for offering to help at the boutique on Saturday. You can't imagine what an alleviation it is to know you'll be there. You are making me a big favour! Jim will post the keys through your postbox on Friday afternoon. Firstly can you arrive to there at 8.45 on Saturday. The lock on the back door is a bit annoying, you need to pull the door against you and then turn the key if not it doesn't open.

Then when you go in you'll need to turn on the lights. The box for the electricity is in the office at the back next to the cuboard. Push down the two black switches. After this could you check all the clothes on the shelfes are folded neatly and the window exhibition is okay. Open the shop door at 9.00.

Now there are a few things I need to advise you about the staff. You probably remember Julia, well she's a nice girl. I mean she's really good at maintaining the boutique tidy, but she's very shy and if there is a problem with a customer she's not very good at solving it out. So if you see her having any problems please help her. Also could you tell me what time Dave does arrive as he has been coming in late recently.

At 5.30 you can shut the shop. Remember to turn off the electricity and turn on the alarm. I'll come to your house to gather the keys on Sunday and bring you a nice present.

If you have any other problems, call to me on my mobile.

Thank you again.

Sarah

275 words

Examiner's comments

Content: The writer provides all the necessary information. Good realization of task.

Communicative achievement: Register is consistently informal, friendly and appreciative. The target reader would be well informed and clear about what is expected.

Organization: Paragraphing and simple sequencing has been used effectively.

Language: The number of mistakes suggests a lack of control. There are some cases of inappropriate word choice – *alleviation, exhibition, advise, maintaining, gather*, misspelt words – *cuboard, shelfes*, and the grammar is sometimes inaccurate – *making me a big favour, arrive to, against, solving it out, what time Dave does arrive, call to*. However, the errors do not obscure communication.

Mark: Pass

Reading and Use of English 4: Cross-text multiple matching Page 138

2
1 D
A *to 'develop' Bayview in ways that no local desires. ... the problems we are faced with – the escalation of <u>high-rise housing in single-storey areas</u>, ... these issues have to be addressed before our beautiful environment <u>is damaged beyond repair</u>.*
B *The housing issue is another matter altogether and council plans for introducing <u>out-of-character multi-storey buildings</u> to the suburb have been ill thought out.*
C *It has been estimated that <u>by building apartment blocks of four to five storeys</u>, the council will facilitate an exponential and undesirable growth in population:*
D *It is <u>expert design in conjunction with durable materials and craftsmanship</u> that <u>deserves our attention</u>. The particular <u>number of storeys</u> in a new building is <u>hardly the point</u>.*

2 C
A *Our council members, ... are now busily working on plans for the rest of Bayview, <u>again behind closed doors</u>. Only when these people finish will the public be 'invited' to submit comments, ...*
C *Many of us have asked the council for details concerning the anticipated population figures, should their high-density housing projected be enacted, <u>but they appear reluctant to disclose them</u>.*

3 A
A *And now we have to prepare <u>for further wastage</u> as the council use taxpayers' money to 'develop' Bayview in ways that no local desires.*
B *The council has announced its intention to spend a figure approaching $20 million over the next few years improving facilities and transport in Bayview. <u>This is not before time.</u>*

C ... *Bayview deserves the considerable investment that the council has proposed.*
D *But before proposals to increase housing and retail development are even considered, and the required investment made, the council needs to concede that ...*

4 B
B ... *as roads are widened and car parks are extended in downtown Bayview, but this is something we must tolerate if we aim to attract the tourist dollar and encourage residents to use local services and retail facilities.*
D *A 'park and ride' shuttle service ... would also be of great benefit ...: commuters would be able to get to their place of employment without the considerable inconvenience and cost of finding a long-term parking space ... this would free up spaces for visitors and tourists, who we must recognize bring in much needed revenue.*

Review 10 Pages 140 and 141

Vocabulary
2 f **3** b **4** g **5** d **6** a **7** h **8** e

Participle clauses
Looking through a newspaper one day, he saw a cottage for sale in a picturesque rural area. Situated in a small village near the church, it had a conservatory and a large garden containing fruit trees; it seemed perfect. Not known for his decisiveness, Charlie surprised everyone by putting down a deposit on it the very next day. Having seen it once, he immediately made up his mind to buy it.

Having moved into the cottage, he soon realized it was not the peaceful rural idyll he had expected. Chiming every hour on the hour, the church bells kept him awake at night. Also, the village being in an area of outstanding beauty, coachloads of tourists arrived every weekend disturbing the peace and quiet. Worst of all, objecting to the presence of outsiders in the village, the locals were very unfriendly towards him. Having lived there for six months, Charlie decided to move back to the city.

Reading and Use of English: Word formation
1 DISAGREEABLE **2** PRIVACY **3** ENSURE
4 LENGTH **5** CURIOSITY **6** PROCEDURE(S)
7 SETTING(S) **8** INEFFECTIVE/INEFFECTUAL

Unit 11 A cultural education

Listening 1: Multiple choice Page 142

2
1 B **2** C **3** C **4** A **5** A **6** B

Vocabulary 1: Sight Page 143

1
a look **b** view **c** sight **d** look **e** view

2
1 sight **2** eye **3** view **4** look **5** vision

Reading and Use of English: Gapped text Page 144

2
1 E **2** G **3** A **4** F **5** C **6** B **D** not used

Language focus: Inversion Page 146

1
The order of subject and auxiliary verb is reversed. Where there is no auxiliary verb, as in **a** and **d**, *do*, *does* or *did* is inserted before the subject.
The writer is adding emphasis to these words by placing them at the beginning of the sentence.

2
b We have no sooner settled .../As soon as we have settled ...
c You should on no account kiss .../You should not kiss your children on any account ...
d I do not whistle along to the music at weddings either.

Practice

1
1 do we go to the cinema these days
2 have I seen such a terrible performance of *Hamlet*
3 must bags be left unattended
4 the very last page is the identity of the murderer revealed
5 someone complained at reception did they realize the painting had been hung upside down

2
1 Never again would he play in front of a live audience.
2 Hardly had she sat down to watch her favourite programme when the phone rang.
3 Under no circumstances will you be allowed to enter the auditorium once the play has started.
4 Not only did we go to the National Gallery, but we also saw a West End musical.
5 Not since Amy went to the circus as a child had she enjoyed herself so much.

Word formation: Nouns formed with *in, out, up, down* and *back* Page 146

1
a drawbacks **b** background **c** outburst

2
1 downpour **2** upturn **3** income(s) **4** outbreak **5** insight
6 outcome **7** setback/upset **8** output **9** upbringing
10 breakdown

Listening 2: Sentence completion Page 147

1
1 (university) libraries **2** concentration **3** bad luck
4 arrogant **5** language **6** family life **7** envy **8** (bank) loans

Vocabulary 2: *Read* and *write* Page 148

1
A 'prolific writer' is one who writes a lot.
To 'read voraciously' is to read a lot of material eagerly.

2
1 aloud **2** avid **3** good **4** widely **5** well **6** rough, neatly **7** plain

Writing: Proposal Page 150

5
Structures and expressions for making suggestions:
I recommend including ...
... could report on ...
We could ... review ...
... it would be interesting to feature ...
... it might be useful for our current students to hear about ...
A further idea would be to provide ...
This could feature ...
I propose that we promote ...
I ... think ... should ...

Linking words and other cohesive devices:
Firstly,
In these
especially when, also, if they (were offering), In addition, who, In particular, their (job), (A) further (idea), as well as, This (could feature), as this (will be), also, so

6

Sample answer

I would like to suggest a weekend programe which would inform to The Far Horizons Club members about some traditional crafts of my country Sweden.

Dala Horse workshop

I would be disposed to give a workshop on how to carve a traditional Swedish Dala horse and then participants could paint the seat and straps onto some other wooden horse models that we could impart. While we do the workshop I can tell participants about the origin of the Dala horse and put a short video of how families used to make them in the long winter time in Sweden. This will be fun and help participants understand how this craft created a snug atmosphere for families.

Making Fattigman cookies

Another Swedish club member could give a demonstration on how to make delicious Fattigman cookies. They are not difficult to prepare so we can also let participants as well make some more cookies. Later in the day we can offer participants a cookie each. I never have tasted cookies as these in another country, so I think this will give a good impression of our cuisine.

Traditional Hambo dance

We could have a lesson on how to do the Hambo dance. The teacher could wear traditional clothes and show the participants the basic footsteps. This will be very lively and make all the members laugh a lot.

With my suggestions I am sure the events will be a great success and the club members will go home knowing a lot more about my country and traditions.

255 words

Examiner's comment

Content: The writer puts forward good suggestions. Effective realization of task.

Communicative achievement: Register is consistently semi-formal. The target reader would be well informed and would consider putting on the proposed event.

Organization: Proposal features are included and the writing is appropriately paragraphed using clear headings. The introduction and conclusion are concise and effective.

Language: There are a number of non-impeding grammatical errors, e.g. redundant preposition – *inform to*, word order – *as well, never have tasted*, confusion of 'like' and 'as' – *as these*, and some awkward use of language – *long winter time*. Word choice is sometimes incorrect – *disposed, seat, impart, footsteps*. However, there is also evidence of more complex vocabulary – *snug, carve, cuisine*.

Mark: Good pass

Review 11 Pages 152 and 153

Reading and Use of English: Word formation
1 FRESHNESS **2** LITERARY **3** CONSIDERABLE **4** INSPIRATION **5** SOCIALLY **6** MINORITIES **7** OUTPUT **8** UNEQUALLED

Vocabulary
1 read **2** taking **3** write **4** Look **5** suffered **6** catch **7** came **8** kept **9** turned/came **10** broke

Reading and Use of English: Open cloze
1 BEHIND **2** BE **3** BOTH **4** THAT **5** LIKE **6** WHICH **7** WOULD **8** UNTIL

Unit 12 The world about us

Listening 1: Sentence completion
Page 154

2
1 business sense
2 (local) authorities
3 behaviour
4 medicine
5 real event
6 camera/lens
7 permission
8 conservation/environmental

Vocabulary 1: Expressions and phrases with *work* Page 155

1

a to be successful
b work that you do in order to prepare for something
c It's something that you expect or is normal for this kind of work

2

1 clock
2 dog
3 order
4 knowledge
5 vigorous
6 dirty
7 skills
8 donkey

Reading and Use of English 1: Multiple choice Page 156

2

1 B **2** C **3** D **4** B **5** D **6** A

Language focus 1: Conjunctions and linking adverbials Page 158

1

A a otherwise **b** so that **c** in case
B a even though **b** whereas **c** However

2

A a On the contrary **b** By contrast **c** Despite this
B a In the meantime **b** By that time **c** From that time on
C a As **b** On, of **c** For
D a In, to **b** As, as **c** from

3

Possible answers

1 a many areas suffered heavy flooding
b high winds caused severe damage in some regions
2 a it would not be disrupted by bad weather
b last year a stage was set up in one of the city's parks
3 a he'd had time to write emails to eight of his friends
b she'd had to stay at work until 9.30 so as to get everything finished
4 a you particularly enjoy sharing a beach with 3000 other bathers
b it's certainly worth spending a day there

Reading and Use of English 2: Multiple-choice cloze Page 159

2

Andy Johnson set up the farm to commercialize crocodile meat. His idea was to sell the meat more cheaply than illegal meat and so protect crocodiles from poaching.

3

1 A **2** A **3** D **4** C **5** D **6** B **7** C **8** B

Listening 2: Multiple matching

Page 160

1

Possible answers

climate change: The build-up of carbon dioxide in the atmosphere, caused for example by high energy consumption, leads to a rise in the Earth's temperature. This in turn can lead to a melting of glaciers and the polar ice caps, and a consequent rise in sea levels, flooding and destruction to coastal areas.

whale hunting: This is still authorized by a small number of countries, despite an international moratorium and protests from environmentalists. It is justified either on scientific grounds or for commercial purposes and to prevent the whale population from growing too large and consuming huge stocks of fish.

women's rights: According to the Universal Declaration of Human Rights, women are entitled to the enjoyment of all human rights and to be treated equally to men in both economic and social life.

child labour: In many developing countries, children are forced to work in poorly paid jobs, sometimes in subhuman conditions. This is usually as a result of poverty, and in some cases because they have been orphaned by Aids. Some work in sweatshops, producing goods for Western markets. This leads to children missing out on an education and the perpetuation of poverty in the country.
The World Day Against Child Labour is celebrated every year on June 12th.

human rights: On December 10, 1948 the United Nations proclaimed the Universal Declaration of Human Rights. It included the following:

- All human beings are born free and equal in dignity and rights.
- No one shall be held in slavery or servitude.
- No one shall be subjected to torture or degrading treatment.

Violations of human rights occur throughout the World.

GM foods: Genetically modified foods, or GM foods, are grown from crops which have been altered through biotechnology to make them more resistant to insects and disease. The most common GM crops are soybeans, corn, cotton and sugar beet and are mainly used in processed foods or in animal feed.
Supporters of genetic modification say that it makes crops more productive and can also increase their nutritional value. Opponents point to the dangers of cross-pollination, whereby GM crops can spread their genes to other plants growing nearby. While producers say there are no health concerns associated with GM foods, opponents maintain that insufficient tests have been carried out and the long-term effects on health are unknown.
Since April 2004 strict regulations have been in force in the European Union concerning the labelling of foods which contain genetically modified produce.

2
1 B **2** E **3** G **4** H **5** A **6** H **7** A **8** B **9** F **10** C

Language focus 2: Modal verbs 3: *Must, need, should* and *ought to*

Page 161

1
A Speaker 5 (women's rights)
B Speaker 2 (voluntary work abroad)

2
A
1 past obligation: we were obliged to
2 speculation about the past: there were probably
3 past regret: it would have been better if we'd done

B
1 I worried, but it wasn't necessary
2 It wasn't necessary to have any special skills and I didn't have any.

3
had to and *didn't need to* are not modal verbs.
Modal verbs go with a main verb (*I can go*; can = modal, go = main)
Modal verbs express the mood or attitude of the speaker and are followed by the infinitive without *to* (with the exception of *ought to*). In addition, an auxiliary verb is not used to form the negative of a modal verb (*I must not, I shouldn't*, etc).
'*We should have done it years before*' could also be written as '*We ought to have done it years before*'.

4
a must – internal obligation: I think it is necessary to go
should – expectation: my son is expected to be home
have to – external obligation: I am required to take him

b shouldn't – recommendation: it is not good/advisable to tell lies
don't have to – no obligation: it is not necessary to tell him the whole truth
mustn't – prohibition: I don't want you to let him know

5
The modal form of *need* is not used in positive sentences, so the non-modal form is required in both cases.
You need to do it now – we're in a hurry.
You need to be tall to be a good basketball player.

Practice

1
1 needn't/shouldn't **2** must/should **3** have/need **4** should **5** needn't/don't need to/don't have to **6** ought to/must/should **7** needed to study/ought to have studied **8** should

Vocabulary 2: Attitude adverbials

Page 161

1 rightly **2** Strangely **3** Disappointingly **4** predictably **5** understandably

Reading and Use of English 3: Key word transformation Page 162

1 HAVE PAID/GIVEN CAREFUL ATTENTION TO
2 CASE YOU HAPPEN TO COME
3 IN THE MEANTIME TRY/I ADVISE YOU/I RECOMMEND YOU/YOU OUGHT
4 ON ACCOUNT OF THE FACT (THAT)
5 HAVE BEEN TOUGH/DIFFICULT/HARD TO TURN DOWN
6 HAVE TAKEN PART IN

Writing: Essay Page 163

Sample answer

I believe that technology plays a more important role than testing when wishing to improve standards of literacy in schools. Using technology can give the child a more positive learning experience, whilst testing just points up the mistakes the child is making.

Using technology children can have fun learning to read and write and as long the programmes they are using are well designed children will progress without realizing they are learning. The teacher can monitor the child's progress and deal about any problems at a later date without interrupting the flow of concentration.

Using the Internet to access books is quick and easy so if a child wishes to read a certain book they can download it rather than search the library or bookshop by what time they may have lost interest. Today's generation of children find reading from a tablet more 'cool' and teenagers who are poor readers can read at their own level without worrying about being made fun of.

I feel that testing has a very limited place in improving literacy standards. In a test situation many children experience anxiousness and will not give their best performance. Although testing can show some of the child's problems these can also be seen by the teacher in individual or group reading or writing sessions.

In conclusion, schools have to decide whether test results which may improve the school's image or using technology in an imaginative way to develop a lifelong love of literacy in their pupils is more important.

251 words

Examiner's comment

Content: All points covered. Good realization of task.

Communicative achievement: Register is consistently appropriate. The overall effect on the target reader would be very positive.

Organization: Paragraphing has been used effectively.

Language: Controlled and natural use of language. Minor errors include incorrect use of particles – *points up, deal about*, incorrect word form – *anxiousness*, omission of 'as' – *as long* and misuse of relative pronouns – *by what time*. However, these do not distract the reader.

Mark: Very good pass

Review 12 Pages 164 and 165

Reading and Use of English: Open cloze

1 THIS/THAT
2 IN
3 TOWARDS/*TOWARD
4 TO
5 NEARLY
6 OVER
7 FOR
8 NOT
*more common in American English

Modal verbs

1 could **2** would **3** might **4** needn't **5** shouldn't **6** shall **7** won't **8** must

Collocation revision: Units 1–12

1 challenge **2** changes **3** smell **4** time **5** relationship **6** sleep **7** ankle/wrist **8** decision/verdict **9** views **10** voice **11** sight **12** work

Ready for Speaking

Introduction Page 166

1 ideas **2** silences **3** vocabulary **4** attention **5** repetition **6** pictures **7** element **8** discussion **9** opportunity **10** opinion

Part 1: Social interaction Page 166

2

Comments

Ana's contributions are of reasonable length, though they could certainly be developed more. She is clearly hindered by the level of her language: she uses a limited range of vocabulary and her responses are rather inaccurate.

Jan is clearly a stronger student. He develops his responses well, uses a much wider range of language, and in this part of the test at least, there are no inaccuracies. (He corrects himself at one point.)

Part 2: Long turn Page 167

Task One

2

Comments

a No attempt is made to compare the pictures. The contribution is limited to a description of the two pictures with a single, short comment on why they might be checking the time. This candidate will probably find it difficult to continue talking for one minute, as he/she is likely to run out of things to say. Linking of ideas is limited to the use of *'because'*.

b Candidates often waste time identifying the pictures they are going to talk about. Many also use prepositional phrases (*on the right, at the top*, etc), though often incorrectly (e.g. *in the left picture down*), causing candidates to become confused as they struggle with the language. Candidates should also avoid merely repeating information given in the instructions (*'all three pictures show women checking the time'*) or stating the obvious (*'This woman is an athlete'*).

c This candidate begins comparing the pictures immediately, rather than merely describing them. Ideas are linked well (*'both convey', 'the athlete, on the other hand'*, and *'suggesting something unexpected has happened'*) and there is an attempt to use a range of grammar and vocabulary, some of which is presented in this book (e.g. *'let them know'* in Unit 12; *'her car won't start'* in Unit 8; *'fallen ill'* in Unit 7). Note too the use of the modal verb *might* rather than *perhaps* or *maybe* as in the first example.

Task Two

2

Comments

Jan's language is very varied, particularly when speculating. He uses a range of modal verbs and other structures for this purpose:
She might have realized, she may be phoning, she could also be phoning, it's very likely she's done the run before, this is probably her best time, the little boy looks as if he's watching.
However, he fails to address the part of the task which asks him to say 'how much influence time might have in their daily lives'. He seems to have forgotten this and the fact that the questions are printed on the visuals page, and he struggles to find more things to say.
Ana, on the other hand, completes her task satisfactorily, though once more her language is not very varied. She opens with *in this picture* each time and her language of speculation is limited to the use of *I think* and *maybe/perhaps* with present simple or present continuous, or else *seem(s) to be*. She searches for words, repeats *or something like that* and uses language inaccurately (e.g. *it's probable this is the mother, she is enjoying with the moment, the woman is very concentrated, she is putting the new washing machine*).

Part 3: Collaborative task Page 168

3

Comments

Interaction in this part of the test is very good. They respond to what each other says, sometimes inviting their partner to comment with a question: *Don't you agree? What do you think?* Ana asks for clarification when she isn't sure what Jan means: *'You mean they are not honest, er, corrupt?'* which is a sensible and natural strategy to take. There are no over-long moments of hesitation. When it comes to making a decision in the second task, it's clear that both students have been listening carefully to what the other person has said, and this allows them to negotiate and reach a decision. Both refer back to the discussion in the first task with phrases such as *As I said before* and *you made the point before*.
Ana seems to have gained in confidence and contributes well to the discussion, although she lacks the range of vocabulary and structure that Jan has.

They decide that a pop/rock singer probably has the most status amongst young people.

Part 4: Further discussion Page 169

2

In contrast to Part 3, in this part Jan and Ana have not understood that they can and should interact with each other. The interlocutor continually has to prompt them to respond to each other's comments, sometimes leaving a pause, which they fail to pick up on. At one point, Ana tentatively asks, *Can I say something more?*, showing that she is unaware that this is a discussion rather than a simple question and answer session. In her last turn, she does respond to a point made by Jan (*I agree with you*) but then limits herself to repeating the same ideas that he has just expressed.

Unit 13 Food for thought

Vocabulary 1: Eating and drinking

Page 170

1

1 thirst **2** hunger **3** food **4** drink **5** appetite **6** eater **7** stomach **8** meal

Reading and Use of English 1: Word formation Page 172

1 SETTING **2** DINERS **3** RESIDENTIAL
4 REVELATIONS **5** UNWELCOME **6** FINDINGS
7 OVERRATED **8** APPEARANCE

Writing 1: Informal letter Page 172

2

No. The writer has not made any attempt to reassure her friend. On the contrary, comments such as *'I'm not surprised you're a bit daunted by it all'*, *'my own bitter experience'* and *'even if it leaves you utterly exhausted'* will only serve to make him more nervous.

3

The following expressions introduce advice:
don't make the same mistake as I did and lay on
there's no point preparing
You'd be better off filling
That's not to say you shouldn't put out
it's not worth going
I wouldn't spend hours making one if I were you
whatever you do, make sure you don't let
... is not to be recommended
Other evidence of a wide range of language includes:
you're a bit daunted by it all
pass on some tips
my own bitter experience
lay on a huge spread

4

Showing interest in the event
It's hard to believe that Luke's about to celebrate his fifth birthday.
I'm sure Luke and his friends will have a great time
Let me know how it all goes, won't you?

Referring to her own experience
some tips that I learnt from my own bitter experience in September
don't make the same mistake as I did
they were the first things to disappear at Lara's party
Lara's friends hardly touched hers

5

Sample answer

Hi Berti

Yes I can certainly give you some advises about preparing a barbecue for your football club's dinner. I've gone to lots of these parties for end of season.

The first thing to think is when you want to serve the food. Obviously is the barbecue difficult to take to the venue, and it takes time to set up all the tables, etc and take all the food from your car. If you serve the food too early some people may not arrive yet. If too late and the children may get so hungry, they start getting tired and silly. So I would recommend to tell people you will serve the food at, for example, 8 o'clock.

Of course, for a barbecue, even in summer, you'll need a plan for if it rains. When I prepared it we hired a small tent. In the end we needn't have it, but better safe than sorry.

Third thing, you need to know how many people are coming and if there are vegetarians. You can get 'veggie burgers' for them. But don't go crazy with the salads – it always seems the salad that gets thrown away. It's so difficult to eat lettuce from a paper plate with a plastic fork – most people don't bother.

Anyway, that's all I can think of now, but give me a ring if you need anything. Just relax yourself and prepare it in detail – then you'll be absolutely fine and it will, too!

Dietmar

246 words

Examiner's comment

Content: The writing is slightly under length and although the letter adequately covers the first two points (detailing your previous experience and giving advice), more attention to the reassurance section would enhance the completion of the task. Simply to say *relax yourself and prepare it in detail ...* is not very reassuring.

Communicative achievement: The target reader would be partially informed, if not very reassured. The register is appropriate for an informal letter.

Organization: The organization is appropriate and logical for an informal letter. The paragraphing nicely reflects three different points the writer considers important (timing of food, a bad weather plan, preparing salad). However, a number of sentences are confusing or difficult to follow – *If you serve the food too early some people may not arrive yet, In the end we needn't have it ...* .

Language: The writing is mostly accurate despite some confusing sentences. The use of language is sometimes rather vague – *When I prepared it …, … and it will, too!*, and the use of the word *advises* in the first sentence. The range of language is sufficient yet unambitious – *you'll need a plan for if it rains, Third thing, you need to know …* .

Mark: Pass

Reading and Use of English 2: Multiple matching Page 174

2
1B **2**C **3**D **4**B **5**A **6**E **7**B **8**A **9**D **10**C

Language focus 1: Comparisons

Page 176

A Comparisons
a much, as **b** The, the **c** worst **d** later **e** fewer
f now, before

B Qualifying comparisons
a a great deal **b** far **c** just **d** slightly **e** much

C *Like* and *as*
a like **b** As **c** like

D *So* and *such*
1 **a** such **b** so **c** so
2 *so* is followed by adjectives and *such* is followed by an indefinite article in the examples given in the Coursebook.

E Further expressions
1 better **2** like, near **3** as **4** much **5** long **6** close

Listening: Multiple choice Page 177

2
1 B **2** A **3** C **4** B **5** B **6** B

Vocabulary 2: Deception Page 178

1

Noun	Verb	Adjective	Adverb
deception	deceive	deceptive	deceptively
fraud	defraud	fraudulent	fraudulently
———	mislead	misleading	misleadingly

2
1 **a** misleadingly **b** misleading
2 **a** deceptively **b** deceiving
3 **a** fraud **b** fraudulently

3
1 out **2** in **3** into **4** for **5** through **6** for

4
a bogus financial adviser
the smooth-talking confidence trickster
the conman's trickery
his false promises
I feel a bit of a mug (informal)

Language focus 2: Adverbs of degree

Page 179

1
Absolutely is used with non-gradable adjectives such as *delighted, fascinating* or *freezing*. *Fairly, a bit* and *very* are used with gradable adjectives such as those in **b**, **c** and **d**. We do not normally say *very delighted, fairly fascinating* or *a bit freezing*. Nor so we say *absolutely large* or *absolutely interesting*.

Examples of other modifiers which can be used with gradable adjectives are:
a little, slightly, rather, quite, somewhat, relatively, moderately, reasonably, pretty, extremely, really

2
Gradable: *frightened, pleased, dirty, tired*
Non-gradable: *furious, ridiculous, huge, incredible*

3
a fairly **b** absolutely

4
1 clever **2** worried **3** informed **4** old **5** qualified
6 intelligent

Review 13 Pages 180 and 181

Vocabulary
1 A **2** D **3** B **4** C **5** C **6** B **7** A **8** C **9** D **10** A **11** B **12** A

Comparisons
1 near as **2** much a **3** same as **4** the more **5** far the
6 such a **7** much the **8** did his

Reading and Use of English: Key word transformation
1 IS DECEPTIVELY SIMPLE IN (ITS)
2 INTEREST IN EATING/MY APPETITE AS SOON AS
3 FAR THE MOST IMAGINATIVE (RECIPE/ONE)
4 FROM MORE STRESS/STRESS MORE THAN EVER (BEFORE), *OR* MORE THAN EVER (BEFORE) FROM STRESS
5 NEAR AS BAD AS
6 CLOSE SECOND TO THE

Unit 14 Money matters

Vocabulary 1: Money Page 182

1
1 **b** 4, **c** 1, **d** 2
2 **a** 3, **b** 4, **c** 2, **d** 1

Verb + adverb collocations

1
a generously **b** freely **c** hard **d** heavily

Listening 1: Sentence completion
Page 183

2
1 Student Loans Company **2** term **3** budget planner
4 overdraft **5** two evenings **6** (course) tutor
7 (faculty) noticeboard **8** (student) travel

Writing: Formal letter Page 184

Useful language
1 offer the opportunity
2 supervise the training
3 assist staff members
4 enquire about the possibility
5 adapt to new situations
6 attend an interview

Reading and Use of English 1: Word formation Page 185

2
1 HANDFUL
2 ENTHUSIASTICALLY
3 DISAGREEMENT
4 ACCUSATIONS
5 MERCILESSLY
6 BANKRUPTCY
7 EDUCATIONAL
8 RELIANCE

Reading and Use of English 2: Gapped text Page 186

2
1 B **2** F **3** A **4** E **5** D **6** G **C** not used

Vocabulary 2: Quantifying nouns
Page 188

1
a series of discs (lines 52–53)
a group of words/money-related words (lines 55–56)
a set of market norms (paragraph E)
a pile of money (paragraph F)

2
a salt **b** water **c** flames **d** homework **e** soft drinks
f youths **g** furniture **h** biscuits

3
1 children **2** news **3** words **4** bees **5** progress
6 furniture **7** holiday **8** coffee **9** wool **10** sleep

Listening 2: Multiple choice Page 190

1
1 B **2** A **3** D **4** B **5** C **6** D

Language focus: Noun phrases Page 191

1
noun + noun: production methods, the January sales, shopping malls
noun 's/s'+ noun: next week's Buy Nothing Day, workers' rights, people's reactions
noun + preposition + noun: a wealth of choice, a threat to business, the ethics of shopping, at the expense of the environment

2
1 b jar of jam
2 a chicken soup
3 b the roof of our house
4 b a Sunday newspaper
5 b a three-day course
6 a that shop window/the window of that shop
7 b the top of the page
8 a the dismissal of a member of staff from the catering department
9 b a man of average height
10 b new children's clothes

3
1 'Noun of noun' (*bottle of lemonade*) is used to refer to the drink.
'Noun + preposition + noun' (*jar of jam*) is used to refer to the container.
2 'Noun + noun' (*chicken soup*) is used for products from dead animals.
The 's genitive (*lamb's wool*) is used for products from living animals.
3 *door handle* is an accepted compound noun: *house roof* is not, so an *of* structure is required. The 's genitive (*house's roof*) is not likely since house is an inanimate object.
4 The 's genitive (*last Sunday's newspaper*) with a time expression is used to refer to specific moments or events.
'Noun + noun' (*a Sunday newspaper*) is used to refer to things that occur or appear regularly.
5 The 's genitive is used with time expressions to refer to duration (*four weeks' holiday*).
When the head noun (*course*) is countable, the modifying noun (*three-day*) is normally in the singular and hyphenated. Since the modifying noun functions as an adjective, no plural s is added.
6 *Shop window* is a recognized compound noun and normally found in that form. Note the position of the demonstrative in the *of* structure.
Whilst the *source of his inspiration* is also correct, *source of inspiration* is a collocation and generally found in that form.
7 Nouns such as *top, bottom, middle, side, edge, back, front, beginning* and *end*, which refer to a part of something, are normally used in an *of* structure. *Mountain top, roadside, seaside* are exceptions.
8 When the head noun (*dismissal*) is modified by a long and/or complex phrase (a member of staff from the catering department) the *of* structure is preferred.
Note that the 's genitive can be used for an action done by or to a person,
e.g. *Mr Smith's resignation, the President's murder.*

9 'Noun + noun' (*brick construction*) can be used when talking about what something is made of. In other cases, when describing the characteristics of a person or thing, the 'Noun of noun' structure is used.

10 a (*children's new clothes*) is a 'specifying genitive' here: it refers to specific clothes worn by specific children. In this case the adjective describing the clothes can be placed between the two nouns.

b (*new children's clothes*) is a 'classifying genitive' here: it refers to clothes worn by children in general. In this case the two nouns cannot be separated.

4

2 e **3** a **4** c **5** g **6** b **7** h **8** f

Review 14 Pages 192 and 193

Noun phrases

1 state of shock, the announcement of his resignation/his resignation announcement
2 car keys/keys to the car, back of the drawer
3 mug of cocoa, cow's milk, caravan site
4 seven-hour delay/delay of seven hours, airport departure lounge/departure lounge of the airport
5 youth of average build, yesterday's robbery
6 gold neck chain/gold chain around his neck, diamond nose stud/diamond stud in his nose, matter of personal taste, idea of fashion
7 two months' work, day's rest
8 series of talks, number of topics, protection of the environment

Vocabulary

1 C **2** B **3** D **4** B **5** A **6** B **7** D **8** C **9** C **10** D

Reading and Use of English: Open cloze

1 UNTIL
2 NEVER/NOT
3 BEYOND
4 ON
5 WHAT
6 TO
7 FOR
8 WITH

Ready for Writing

Marking Page 194

2 Content **3** Organization and cohesion **4** Target reader **5** Accuracy

Planning and checking Page 195

2 d **3** g **4** h **5** e **6** f **7** a **8** b **9** i

Register Page 195

1

1 success **2** obtaining/achieving/attaining
3 expressed/showed/[*or in present tense* express/show]
4 position/post **5** employment **6** owing/due **7** unable
8 improvement **9** contact **10** meantime

2

Suggested answers

Informal letter	Formal letter
• the use of *get* in informal register	
get a grade	*obtain/achieve a grade*
try to get a job	*apply for position/post*
get better	*an improvement*
• use of phrasal verbs in informal register	
take you on	*offer you employment*
• greater use of nouns in formal register	
passing your exams	*your recent success in your examinations*
you said you'd be interested	*you expressed an interest*
the way the economy's been recently	*the current economic climate*
• use of abbreviations in informal register	
exams	*examinations*
• linking words	
But	*However*
• informal punctuation	
dashes and exclamation marks	
• other differences	
Believe me	*I assure you*
we'll be in touch	*we shall contact you*
as soon as they do	*When this occurs*
Dear Jilly/All the best	*Dear Ms Holden/ Yours sincerely*

Macmillan Education
4 Crinan Street
London N1 9XW
A division of Macmillan Publishers Limited

Companies and representatives throughout the world
ISBN 978-0-230-46357-8 (+key edition)
ISBN 978-0-230-46370-7 (-key edition)

This edition published 2014
First edition published 2004

Original design by Andrew Jones
Page make-up by xen, www.xen.co.uk
Illustrated by: Ed McLachlan pp81, 96, 99, 105, 121, 155, 172;
Oxford Designers & Illustrators pp43, 52, 94;
Gary Wing pp19, 64, 118, 119, 182, 193.
Cover photograph by Getty Images/John Cumming
Picture research by Victoria Gaunt

Authors' acknowledgements
Amanda French would like to thank Liam, Georgia and Joe Keane for their support, patience and bad jokes. Roy Norris would like to thank his wife, Azucena, for all her support, and his daughters, Elisa and Lara, for understanding that their dad often had to spend more time with his computer than with them. A big thank you from both of us to all of the Macmillan team, past and present.

The publishers would like to thank all those who have participated in the development of the project, with special thanks to the freelance editors.

The authors and publishers would like to thank the following for permission to reproduce their photographs:
The Advertising Achives/Alcoa Aluminium p21(br);
Alamy/allesalltag p204(l), Alamy/YAY Media AS p147, Alamy/Batchelder p138(bl), Alamy/Cultura Creative (RF) pp31(r), 38(br), 90(tmr), Alamy/Pedro Luz Cunha p106(tr), Alamy/Art Directors & TRIP p171(tl), Alamy/Tim Gainey p42, Alamy/GoPlaces p116(tr), Alamy/imagebroker pp171(tr), 174(tl), Alamy/Dunstone Images p138(bmr), Alamy/Israel Images p32(c), Alamy/Blue Jean Images p54(bm), Alamy/Juice Images p6(c), Alamy/OJO Images Ltd pp6(tc), 32(t), Alamy/UpperCut Images p169(tml), Alamy/Thomas Imo p177(t), Alamy/INTERFOTO p106(tml), Alamy/Juice Images p189(cl), Alamy/Andrey Kekyalyaynen p174(tr), Alamy/Martin Lehmann p138(bml), Alamy/Angela Hampton Picture Library p30(tl), Alamy/Dave Marsden p44, Alamy/MBI p162(bm), Alamy/Moodboard pp65(r), 189(cl), Alamy/Ivan Montero p106(tmr), Alamy/Pablo Paul p177(b), Alamy/Jonathan Rabinovitz p75(tl), Alamy/Rtimages p38(bl), Alamy/Peter Phill/Travel Shots.com p189(tl), Alamy/stockbroker pp100, 184, Alamy/Art Directors & TRIP p109(bl), Alamy/David Young-Wolff p185(l);
Bananastock pp32(b), 52;
The Bridgeman Art Library p21(tl), The Bridgeman Art Library/Morgner, Wilhelm (1891-1917)/Kunstsammlung Bochum, Bochum, Germany p75(tr),The Bridgeman Art Library/Art Museum, Samara, Russia p75(tm);
Buy Nothing Day p190;
Corbis pp51, 70(bm), 159(tr), 167(bl), 189(tr), Corbis/Fernando Bengoechea/Beateworks p130(l), Corbis/Bettmann p70(tl), Corbis pp18(l), 34(br), 58(br,tm,bl), Corbis/Hulton-Deutsch Collection 21(bl),
Corbis/Peter Guttman p36(r), Corbis/Dave G. Houser p169(tl), Corbis/Jose Luis Pelaez Inc/Blend Images p58(tl), Corbis/Ian Lishman/Juice Images p38(t), Corbis/Radius Images p55, Corbis/ Duane Osborn/Somos Images p174(tm), Corbis/Barry Lewis p34(plane), Corbis/Tim Pannell p189(bm), Corbis/Kate Mitchell p78, Corbis/Roy Morsch p149(bl), Corbis/Robert Niedring p54(br), Corbis/Neil Rabinowitz p149(tr), Corbis/MIGUEL VIDAL/X01219/Reuters p84, Corbis/BAZUKI MUHAMMAD/Reuters p149(tm), Corbis/Anders Ryman p142(b), Corbis/Aril Skelley p197, Corbis/Klaus Tiedge pp109(tr, br), 207(b), Corbis/Bo Zaunders p43;
FLPA/David Hosking p154(tl), FLPA/Frans Lanting p154(b);
Getty Images pp18(m,r), 21(tr), 70(bl, tmr,tr,br), 74(bl), p127(t), 156(tl), 160(tl, tm), Getty Images/AFP p65(l), p74(br), 149(tl), 169(tr), Getty Images/Ursula Alter p159(cl), Getty Images/Bloomberg p177(c), Getty Images/Kenneth Cheung p106(tl), Getty Images/Gene Chutka p30(tr), Getty Images/FenykepezGetty p156(b), Getty Images/fstop123 p110, Getty Images/Yasuhide Fumoto p187(l), Getty Images/Michael Hevesy p162(br), Getty Images/Glow Images Inc p31(l), Getty Images/Kidstock p167(br), Getty Images/David Leahy p71, Getty Images/Giorgio Magini p30(br), Getty Images/Fiona McIntosh p7, Getty Images/Graham Monro/gm photographics p6(t), Getty Images/CountryStyle Photography p132, Getty Images/FilmMagic p127(b), Getty Images/David Milne p138(br), Getty Images/moodboard p204(m), Getty Images/Gary John Norman p86, Getty Images/Compassionate Eye Foundation/David Oxberry p102, Getty Images/Per Magnus Persson p130(r), Getty Images/Apostrophe Productions p204(r), Getty Images/Redferns p169(tmr), Getty Images/kristian sekulic p207(tr), Getty Images/Image Source pp54(tr,bl), Getty Images/Jorn Georg Tomter p36(l), Getty Images/David Wall p116(tmr), Getty Images/Noah Webb p171(br), Getty Images/WireImage p74(tl);
Glow Images/J. De Meester p6(bc);
Imagesource pp12(b,c), 53(b,c), 187(r);
Reprinted with kind permission of Pan Macmillan p88(l,m,r);
Mary Evans/Grenville Collins Postcard Collection p142(t), Mary Evans/Illustrated London News Ltd p70(tml);
Photodisc/Getty Images/Robert Glus p165;
Photoshot/Woodfall Wild Images p114;
Rex Features p116(tml), Rex/c.New Line/Everett p25(r), Rex/Richard Gardner p74(tr), Rex/Neale Haynes p116(tl), Rex/Brian J. Ritchie/Hotsauce p156(tr), Rex/Tony Kyriacou p185(c), Rex/Moviestore p24(m), Rex/Design Pics Inc p160(tr), Rex Snap p68, Rex/Snap Stills pp24(l,r), 25(l), 90(tr);
Superstock/Belinda Images pp90(tm), 109(tl), 143, 207(tl), Superstock/Corbis pp59, 149(br), Superstock/Tetra Images pp82, 83, Superstock/Photononstop p162(bl), Superstock/Pixtal p90(tl), Superstock/Stockbroker 171(cl);
Thinkstock/Goodshoot p167(tr), Thinkstock/Hemera p171(bl), Thinkstoock/iStockphoto pp6(b), 8, 12(t), 53(t), 54(tl), 58(tr), 90(tml), 141, 153, Thinkstock/Jupiterimages p61, Thinkstock/Digital Vision p169(tm).

The authors and publishers are grateful for permission to reprint the following copyright material:

p36 Fictional interview with Helena Drysdale using extracts from 'Mother Tongue', reprinted by permission of A P Watt *at* United Agents on behalf of Helena Drysdale;
p41 Material from article 'Listening to Vegetables' first published in Fortean Times September 2002, reprinted by permission of Dennis Publishing; p38 Material from article 'Scents and sensitivity' by Lucy Mangan, copyright © Lucy Mangan 2004, first published in The Guardian 20.07.04, reprinted by permission of the author; p60 Material from article 'Motherhood's best kept secret' by Maureen Freely, first published in Woman and Home Magazine, reprinted by permission of the author; p70 Material from article 'What does David Beckham have in common with Albert Einstein' by Anjana Ahuja, copyright © Anjana Ahuja 1999, first published in The Times 23.11.99, reprinted by permission of the News International Syndication Ltd; p69 Material from article 'The new generation' by Lesley Garner, first published in Saga Magazine December 2002, reprinted by permission of Acromas Holdings Ltd; p136 Material from article 'Working Britons don't even know their neighbours' by Senay Boztas, copyright © Senay Boztas 2000, first published in The Sunday Times 05.03.00, reprinted by permission of the author; p113 Material from article 'Designer's gadgets for the future' by Chris Millar, copyright © Chris Millar 2002, first published in The Evening Standard 21.06.02, reprinted by permission of the publisher; p82 Material from article 'First contact: will we ever hear from aliens' by Robin McKie, copyright © Robin McKie 2010, first published in The Observer 07.02.10, reprinted by permission of the publisher; p89 Material from article 'The art of biography is alive and well' by Kathryn Hughes, copyright © Kathryn Hughes 2013, first published in The Guardian 15.02.13, reprinted by permission of the publisher; p174 Material from article 'A nice cup of tea beats bottled water every time' by Andrew Martin, copyright © Andrew Martin 2012, first published in The Independent 10.06.12, reprinted by permission of the publisher; p87 Material from article 'Better people make better students': Best-selling book reveals building character is best way to nurture educational success' by Hilary Wilce, copyright © Hilary Wilce 2013, first published in The Independent 06.03.13, reprinted by permission of the publisher; p8 Material from article 'One cool dude: How Parker Liautaud aims to save the world, one polar expedition at a time' by Guy Adams, copyrigh © Guy Adams 2012, first published in The Independent 11.08.12 reprinted by permission of the publisher; p205 Material from article 'Britain's maligned moths suffer drastic decline' by Terri Judd, copyright © Terri Judd 2007, first published in The Independent 20.07.07, reprinted by permission of the publisher; p105 Material from article 'The main problem for a manned Mars mission? Sleep deprivation' by Steve Connor, copyright © Steve Connor 2013, first published in The Independent 08.01.13, reprinted by permission of the publisher; p144 Material from article 'Modern audiences do anything but listen' by Stephen Pollard, copyright © Stephen Pollard 2002, first published in The Independent 04.12.02, reprinted by permission of the publisher; p159 Material from article 'Crocodile farms: is it cruel to keep these wild creatures captive?' by Sanjida O'Connell, copyright ©Sanjida O'Connell 2006, first published in The Independent 05.10.06, reprinted by permission of the publisher; p172 Material from article 'Taste test reveals unpalatable truth' by Roger Dobson, copyright © Roger Dobson 2003, first published in The Independent 20.04.03, reprinted by permission of the publisher; p132 Material from article 'The joy of plumbing' by Natasha Walter, copyright © Natasha Walter 1999, first published in The Independent 16.03.99, reprinted by permission of the publisher; p106 Material from article 'The last unwired man on earth' by Martin Newell, copyright © Marin Newell 1999, first published in The Independent 17.12.99, reprinted by permission of the publisher; p125 Material from article 'Travelling on a student budget' by Charley Utton, copyright © Charley Utton 2013, first published in The Independent 28.01.13, reprinted by permission of the publisher; p20 Material from article 'Creator of Barbie' by David Usborne, copyright © David Usborne 2002, first published in The Independent 29.04.02, reprinted by permission of the publisher; p42 Material from article 'Twitter in the city: The urban life of birds' by Roger Dobson, copyright © Roger Dobson 2011, first published in The Independent 31.01.11, reprinted by permission of the publisher; p43 Material from article 'Bergen Railway: Great Train Journeys' by Anthony Lambert, copyright © Anthony Lambert 2013, first published in The Telegraph 26.03.13, reprinted by permission of the publisher; p156 Material from article 'What comes naturally' by Giles Smith, copyright © Giles Smith 2002, first appeared in The Sunday Telegraph 26.10.02, reprinted by permission of the publisher; p78 Material from article 'My constant fight to stay awake' by Bryony Gordon, copyright © Bryony Gordon 2002, first appeared in The Telegraph 01.10.02, reprinted by permission of the publisher; p7 Adapted material from 'Get the picture? Art in the brain of the beholder' by Kat Austen taken from New Scientist Magazine 17.07.12, © _20 Reed Business Information – UK. All rights reserved. Distributed by Tribune Media Services; p80 Adapted material from 'Amnesiacs struggle to imagine future event events' by Roxanne Khamsi taken from New Scientist Magazine 15.01.07, © _20 Reed Business Information – UK. All rights reserved. Distributed by Tribune Media Services; p164 Adapted material from 'Happy as a pig…in a waterbed' by Michelle Knott taken from New Scientist Magazine 23.11.02, © _20 Reed Business Information – UK. All rights reserved. Distributed by Tribune Media Services; p186 Adapted material from 'Why money messes with your mind' by Mark Buchanan taken from New Scientist Magazine 18.03.09, © _20 Reed Business Information – UK. All rights reserved. Distributed by Tribune Media Services; p115 Material from article 'Climbing Margherita which appeared in Travel Africa Magazine.

Printed and bound in Thailand

2018 2017 2016 2015 2014
10 9 8 7 6 5 4 3 2 1